NEUROPSYCHOLOGICAL
DIFFERENTIAL DIAGNOSIS

STUDIES ON NEUROPSYCHOLOGY, DEVELOPMENT, AND COGNITION

Series Editor:

Linas A. Bieliauskas, Ph.D.
University of Michigan, Ann Arbor, MI, USA

NEUROPSYCHOLOGICAL DIFFERENTIAL DIAGNOSIS

Konstantine K. Zakzanis
University of Toronto, Toronto, ON, Canada

Larry Leach
Baycrest Centre for Geriatric Care, Toronto, ON, Canada

Edith Kaplan
Boston University School of Medicine, Boston, MA, USA

SWETS & ZEITLINGER
PUBLISHERS

| LISSE | ABINGDON | EXTON (PA) | TOKYO |

Library of Congress Cataloging-in-Publication Data

Zakzanis, Konstantine K., 1971–
Neuropsychological differential diagnosis / Konstantine K. Zakzanis, Larry
    Leach, Edith Kaplan.
        p.   cm. — (Studies on neuropsychology, development, and cognition)
    Includes bibliographical references and index.
    ISBN 9026515529 (hardback)
    1. Neuropsychological tests. 2. Diagnosis, Differential. 3. Neurobehavioral
        disorders—Diagnosis. I. Kaplan, Edith, 1924– . II. Title. III. Series.
        [DNLM: 1. Neuropsychological Tests. 2. Brain Diseases—diagnosis. 3. Cognition. 4.
        Diagnosis, Differential. 5. Mental Disorders—diagnosis. WL 141 Z21n 1999]
    RC386.6.N48Z35 1999
    616.8'0475—dc21
    DNLM/DLC
    for Library of Congress   99–16397
                                                                                                                            CIP

Cover design: Bert Haagsman, Magenta Grafische Produkties
Typesetting: Red Barn Publishing, Skeagh, Skibbereen, Co. Cork, Ireland
Printed in The Netherlands by Krips b.v., Meppel

© 1999 Swets & Zeitlinger b.v., Lisse

ISBN 90 265 1552 9 (hardback)

Contents

Acknowledgements

In August of 1997, at the annual meeting of the American Psychological Association, one of us (KKZ) approached the Swets & Zeitlinger exhibit to peruse the latest issues of the *Clinical Neuropsychologist* and the *Journal of Clinical and Experimental Neuropsychology*. Taking place just beside the display table was a conversation between Martha L. Chorney, the senior editor at Swets & Zeitlinger and the editors from these all significant journals. Before moving on, however, Martha had excused herself from her conversation and asked whether I was enjoying my visit to the convention and the city of Chicago and whether there was something she could help me with. This was Martha's manner: Polite, considerate, unconditional, unassuming, curious, and welcoming. Our conversation quickly turned academic, and in an ever-telling manner, I began to recount the presentation I was about to give that morning on meta-analysis and the frontal-executive hypothesis in schizophrenia. Rather than disengage herself she listened with interest and before long we exchanged ideas regarding the possibility of turning the basis of the presentation into a book. Since then, Martha and Dr. Linas Bieliauskas (Series Editor) have appreciated the need for a book such as this. Needless to say, without them this book would not exist.

As neuropsychologists, we are trained to appreciate antecedents. In other words, it is not just behaviour we are interested in but brain as well. As such, it is important to recognize the many contributions of Dr. R. Walter Heinrichs, Associate Professor in the Department of Psychology at York University in Toronto, Canada. Walter was the person that introduced us to meta-analytic methodology and its application to brain and behavior- particularly within the area of schizophrenia research. His creative thinking inspired many of the ideas expressed in our work. In particular, his ideas and thoughts on schizophrenia have been incorporated into our chapter on this most puzzling disease. Our expression of gratitude can serve only a fraction of what he has given us.

We are indebted also to Dr. Guy B. Proulx, Chief Psychologist of the Department of Psychology at Baycrest Centre for Geriatric Care in Toronto, Canada. He has always believed that a psychology department should foster the academic work of its faculty. His leadership and his willingness to take upon himself the administrative burden of the department enabled us to pursue our academic interests. We continue to benefit from his support and friendship.

We are also grateful to Dr. Morris Freedman, Director of the Behavioral Neurology Program at Baycrest Centre for Geriatric Care in Toronto, Canada, for his help with the progressive supranuclear palsy and Parkinson's disease chapters. Moreover, his endless energy and dedication to his work and patients served on many occasions as inspiration to complete our project.

Appreciation is also expressed to Dr. Josée Rivest, assistant professor in the Department of Psychology at Glendon College (York University) in Toronto, Canada, for her most helpful comments and meticulous editing of our work.

We wish to acknowledge the library staff at Baycrest Centre for Geriatric Care for their courteous and prompt assistance in obtaining the obscure literature. Moreover, our colleagues and friends in the Department of Psychology at Baycrest Centre for Geriatric Care and the Departments of Cognitive Neurology and Neuropsychology at Sunnybrook Health Science Centre, including Ruby Nishioka, Dr. Morris Moscovitch, Dr. Sandra E. Black, Dr. Dmytro Rewilak, Brian Richards, Dr. Norman Park, Dr. Katherine Stokes, and Dr. David Kurzman are to be recognized for their many comments that served to better our project. Moreover, although they remain anonymous, we want to personally thank the two Swets & Zeitlinger reviewers for their helpful comments and Elja Dekker for her editorial efforts.

Finally, we wish to thank our families and those who are dear to us. They also make a significant contribution each and every day to our work and lives.

From the series editor

Dear Reader,

Neuropsychological Differential Diagnosis represents a worthy addition to our *Series on Neuropsychology, Development, and Cognition.* As with our other authors, Drs. Zakzanis, Leach, and Kaplan have summarized appropriate experimental literature in specific areas of neuropsychological interest and explicated it in an open way that presents its clinical relevance. As Dr. Zakzanis describes in his introduction, this book aims to "place diagnostic inference in the neuropsychology of dementia and neuropsychiatry on firmer scientific grounds." Differential diagnosis in clinical neuropsychology is often based on combinations of performance on different neuropsychological tests in the light of relevant moderating variables. The authors have surveyed appropriate literature in commonly presenting neuropsychological syndromes, subjected it to meta-analytic techniques, and calculated effect sizes to provide summary tables on which tests tend to be affected most in which disorders. Importantly, mediating factors are taken into account and the methodology of the analysis and literature search are clearly explained. Each clinical chapter is organized along domains of interest so that the reader can readily follow the path of the relevant analyses and their implications for patient diagnosis. Finally, each clinical chapter presents an appropriate summary as is also presented in the last chapter for the entire text. Clinicians will find the conclusions produced by this pattern analysis often confirmatory, but occasionally controversial and challenging to their traditional beliefs.

This text achieves its aim of providing a state-of-the-art summary of a vast clinical experimental literature. Dr. Zakzanis and his colleagues have thus provided a pivotal critical review of the contemporary literature in clinical neuropsychology, and a welcome reference, both to the clinicians in established practice as well as to those setting up newer laboratory and clinical services in various settings.

Linas Bieliauskas

Ann Arbor, September, 1999

To all the primary authors we have cited, without whose work this meta-analytic book would not have been possible

Chapter 1

INTRODUCTION

Introduction

Neurologic and neuropsychiatric disorder is construed here not as a disease but as a generic term embracing a number of neuropsychological syndromes. That is, degenerative diseases that cause dementia and conditions such as schizophrenia have unique and characteristic distributions of pathology and do not affect all brain systems uniformly (Black, 1996; Snowden, Neary & Mann, 1996). Important psychological processes like language, memory, and spatial skills are regionally organized rather than equipotentially distributed. It follows that preservation of some cognitive functions and deterioration of others should exist across the spectrum of dementia and neuropsychiatric syndromes. From a clinical perspective, neuropsychological assessment has come to play a critical role in identifying the presence of dementia and neuropsychiatric disorder and in the differential diagnosis of its myriad causes (Bondi, Salmon, & Kaszniak, 1996). Research efforts in the neuropsychology of dementia and neuropsychiatry have focused on identifying the pattern, progression and neuropathological correlates of the cognitive deficits associated with various disorders. Clinicians and researchers have succeeded in showing that different patterns of relatively preserved and impaired cognitive abilities can be identified among dementing and neuropsychiatric diseases. Accordingly, the neuropsychologist has available a variety of standardized tests that have known reliability and validity for the detection of cognitive deficits associated with either focal or diffuse cerebral damage (Lezak, 1995; Spreen & Strauss, 1998). These tests have been designed to assess specific aspects of a wide range of cognitive domains, including attention and concentration, verbal and performance skill (including spatial cognition and perceptual functions), delayed recall, memory acquisition, manual dexterity, and cognitive flexibility and abstraction. Because neuropsychological tests generally meet psychometric criteria of acceptable reliability and validity, they provide accurate procedures for describing the cognitive strengths and weaknesses of an individual (Bondi, Salmon, & Kaszniak, 1996). Such accuracy is also of importance in detecting the presence of dementia and neuropsychiatric disorder, and in determining whether the observed pattern of impaired and preserved cognitive functions is consistent with patterns predicted by theory and pathophysiology.

Diagnostic practice in neuropsychology recognizes the need to look at multiple domains of function with the "battery" approach. Briefly, approaches to the assessment process can be characterized as falling somewhere on a continuum between what has been referred to as the "fixed battery approach" (e.g., Reitan & Davison, 1974) and a flexible hypothesis-testing approach (Lezak, 1995). In the former, a large comprehensive battery is routinely administered to all patients. This approach is exemplified by the Halstead-Reitan battery, which consists of a large number of specific neuropsychological measures, (e.g. tests of tactual performance, sensory extinction, finger tapping, categorization, language functioning) which are often supplemented with a full length WAIS III and personality inventories. In the second approach, measures are selected to test hypotheses derived from the neuropsychological literature in relation to a patient's known or suspected disorder. The process is a dynamic one; the results of preliminary testing are used to test or modify existing hypotheses and generate new ones. As a simple example, screening measures may detect problems with the organization of visual material which are consistent with spatial and/or planning deficits; follow-up measures can then be administered to evaluate these competing possibilities.

Both the fixed and flexible approaches, however, are not without limitation. Proponents of the flexible approach acknowledge that there is a potential danger of failing to detect a patient's difficulties in some cognitive domains if the clinician focused too rapidly on testing preliminary hypotheses. They argue, however, that the fixed battery approach may represent an inefficient use of resources and is simply not an option in some hard pressed services. More importantly, both approaches are limited by subjective test inclusion decision criteria. That is, the decision to administer and include specific test measures in clinical and research batteries has often been based on clinical lore, theoretical speculation, and perhaps most commonly, on the basis of subjective appraisal of the published literature (e.g. Peyser, Rao, LaRocca, & Kaplan, 1990; Derix, 1994; Lezak, 1995; Nixon, 1996).

Eminent researchers and clinicians construct and recommend neuropsychological test batteries without providing evidence of test sensitivity and reliability. Take for example Lezak's (1995) multiple sclerosis test battery protocol (p. 124). The author recommends the inclusion of several tests encapsulating the cognitive domains of attention, visuoperception and visual reasoning, memory and learning, verbal functions and academic skills, concept formation, and emotional status. Lezak notes that "the battery was designed to assess the areas of functioning known to be vulnerable to multiple sclerosis" (p. 124) and qualifies this rationale based on her clinical experience and theoretical knowledge of this patient population. But how do we know that the neuropsychological tests included in her protocol meet psychometric criteria of acceptable reliability and sensitivity to patients with multiple sclerosis? What ensures that the recommended tests provide the best procedures for describing the cognitive strengths and weaknesses of patients with MS? For instance, do we know empirically that the Rey Auditory Verbal Learning Test is more sensitive than the California Verbal Learning Test to multiple sclerosis? Similarly, was the Category Test included into Lezak's test protocol because it differentiates patients with multiple sclerosis from healthy controls more efficiently than the Wisconsin Card Sorting Test does?

To illustrate further the subjective basis in which tests are selected into clinical and research batteries, take for example Peyser et al., (1990) who propose a very different multiple sclerosis test battery guideline based on a "a review of key issues of clinical need and experimental interest." Of the 17 tests included in their recommended core battery of neuropsychological tests for use in this population, only four of these are to be found in Lezak's (1995) recommended test battery.

Other examples exist that underscore the subjective inclusion criteria of neuropsychological tests into research and diagnostic batteries. For example, Nixon (1996) describes a test battery employed at the University of Oklahoma Neuropsychology Laboratory for use with patients with Alzheimer's disease. To test memory function, both immediate and 30-minute delayed testing using the logical memory and visual reproduction subtests from the Wechsler Memory Scale-Revised are recommended. Again, do we know empirically that these specific WMS-R measures are the most efficient way to detect the presence of Alzheimer's disease?

More recently, Neary et al., (1998) published a consensus on clinical diagnostic criteria for fronto-temporal lobar degeneration (FTD). They note that "supporting clinical features of FTD include significant impairment on frontal lobe tests, in the absence of severe amnesia, aphasia, or perceptuospatial disorder. Impairment on frontal lobe tests is defined operationally as failures (scores below the fifth percentile) on conventional tests of frontal lobe function (e.g., Wisconsin Card Sorting Test, Stroop, Trail Making) in which a qualitative pattern of performance typically associated with frontal lobe dysfunction is demonstrated" (p.1550). But on what basis did this group select "frontal lobe tests" (namely the Wisconsin Card Sorting Test, Stroop, and Trail Making) as being most sensitive and most likely to support a diagnosis of FTD? Theoretical speculation? Clinical experience? Clinical lore? Subjective appraisal of the published literature? Perhaps all or none of these considerations were involved.

To improve the design of research and the selection of clinical instruments it is important to create an empirical basis that can inform the decision making process. Hence, this book aims to place diagnostic inference in the neuropsychology of dementia and neuropsychiatry on firmer scientific grounds. This will be done by:

(1) quantitatively assessing individual test sensitivities to different dementia and neuropsychiatric syndromes, and
(2) generating preserved and impaired ability profiles from different dementia and neuropsychiatric syndromes to guide diagnostic practice.

This book will provide clinicians and researchers involved in the evaluation, diagnosis, and treatment of patients with dementia and neuropsychiatric disorder with a recommended test battery with empirically derived test inclusion sensitivities and an accompanying discussion regarding the differentiation of dementia and neuropsychiatric syndromes. This will be done through analysis of test sensitivity to specific dementia and neuropsychiatric syndromes and through review of the accumulated neuropsychological literature.

Quantitative evidential review is an essential ingredient of instrument selection and diagnostic decision-making. Given a rapidly increasing prevalence and the requirement of adequate care of the burgeoning population of patients with dementia and neuropsychiatric disorder, there has been a growth of interest in the neuropsychological aspects of these disorders that has generated a literature that is both impressive and bewildering. Accordingly, the dissemination of information of relevance to clinicians and researchers is often made possible from substantive reviews of topics spanning the scope of neuropsychology. A literature review can help the interested reader keep up-to-date on relevant issues outside of their immediate areas of expertise by quantifying the data in the literature into a single review. Moreover, a review identifies relations, gaps, and inconsistencies in the literature and includes ideas regarding the next steps for a solution to a problem (see American Psychological Association, 1994, p. 5; Bem, 1995). One methodological approach to literature review is termed "meta-analysis," and this is the method we employed to systematically integrate the existing neuropsychological literature on dementia and neuropsychiatric disease.

More specifically, we wanted to review the literature that encapsulates the performance of patients with dementing and neuropsychiatric disease on commonly used cognitive measures. By systematically reviewing the literature for each of the disorders presented in this book, we felt it was possible to construct statistical profiles that would draw attention to specific test variable sensitivity to a given dementing or neuropsychiatric disease which would aid in the diagnosis and differentiation of these disorders. Thus, what the reader will find here, is a compendium of profiles. Profiles that reflect the performance of patients on measures of cognitive function based on the synthesis of our knowledge base – the neuropsychological literature. These profiles include "effect sizes" that can indicate both the magnitude of impairment on a cognitive measure and the sensitivity of a cognitive measure to diagnose a specific disorder. What the reader will not find here, however, is a discussion regarding the gathering of additional data beyond that gained with neuropsychological test measures that will further aid in making a differential diagnosis. That is, we don't mean to under-mine the importance of neurologic, neurophysiologic, neuroradiologic, or neu-rosurgical data which often provide the most important context for understanding and/or planning the neuropsychological examination. The absence of such discussion should not be taken to imply that one can do neu-ropsychological assessment and differential diagnosis with little more than test tools – a seriously erroneous notion that must be discredited. Similarly, we don't want the reader to mistake this text as though it was written in a medical vac-uum, as any practicing clinician well knows, that a carefully documented histo-ry from a patient and their family or friends, can often provide the best diagnostic clues in the absence of meaningful neuropsychological test data. Hence, as our work as neuropsychologists is very much tied in and integrated with all of the above named medical and research specialties, the reader is urged to seek discussions of these important aspects of the neuropsychological exam-ination in the excellent texts of Lezak (1995), Spreen and Strauss (1998), Snyder and Nussbaum (1998), Strub and Black (1993), Damasio and Damasio (1989), Patten (1995), Adams, Victor, and Ropper (1997), Heilman and Valenstein (1993), and Cummings and Benson (1992).

Before presenting the cognitive profiles it is important to further delineate the purpose of our review and how it might be of some value to the clinician and researcher interested in brain-behavior relationships. After doing so, in Chapter 2 the reader can find a theoretical discussion regarding methodology and how meta-analysis and effect sizes can be used to validly review the neuropsychologi-cal literature. The chapter also serves as a primer on meta-analysis and in the interpretation of effect sizes within the context of brain-behavior relations. Chapter 3 describes in detail how our review was conducted. This chapter was included in hope that such a description could enable the reader to evaluate the appropriateness of our methods and the validity of our profiles. In chapters 4 through 14 the reader can find our reviews and the corresponding profiles for the following dementia and neuropsychiatric syndromes: Dementia of the Alzheimer's type, fronto-temporal dementia, primary progressive aphasia, progressive supranuclear palsy, Parkinson's disease, Huntington's disease, multiple sclerosis, schizophrenia, major depressive disorder, obsessive compulsive disorder, and finally, mild traumatic brain injury. It should be noted that we chose to review these specific syndromes in keeping with the available literature. That is, a meta-analysis must adhere to some very specific methodological criteria (see Chapter 3 for a list of such criteria). Of these criteria, the presence of a control group is essential if effect sizes are to be calculated and used to articulate the magnitude of cognitive deficit. Hence, although there may indeed exist a great literature on alcohol and substance abuse, multi-infarct or vascular dementia, bipolar disor-ders, or encephalitic/anoxic events, which all entail neuropsychological sequelae, there was an inadequate number of studies that used a control group design that would meet criteria for meta-analytic inclusion. Finally, the chapters are followed by a more quantitative summary and overview including a recommended test bat-tery derived from our profiles to aid in differential diagnosis in Chapter 15.

Purpose of our review

The purpose of our review is two-fold. First, cognitive profiles grounded in statistically valid quantitative methodology coupled with qualitative description can provide the clinician with a basis to make informed neuropsychological differential diagnoses. That is, in an individualized neuropsychological examination, the examiner rarely knows exactly which tests will be given before the examination has begun. The examiner usually starts with a basic battery that touches upon the major dimensions of cognition and then makes many choices as the examination proceeds (Lezak, 1995). As the examiner raises and tests hypotheses regarding possible diagnoses, it often becomes necessary to go beyond the basic battery and use techniques relevant to the patient at that time (Lezak, 1995). To assist clinicians in testing their hypotheses regarding possible diagnosis, cognitive profiles that rank order specific test variable sensitivity to a particular disease would aid in the further selection of cognitive tasks that could confirm (or refute) the diagnosis. Indeed, information obtained from the addition of tasks that are "known" to be most and least sensitive to a specific disorder will reflect further the gross outlines of mental impairment patterns. This should lead to enough clarity to permit the examiner to form a diagnostic impression.

If diagnostic ambiguity persists, the compendium of profiles will allow clinicians to further test hypotheses regarding differential diagnosis. The inclusion of rank-order effect sizes in the tables satisfies the need for objective, readily replicable data cast in a form that permits valid interpretation and meaningful comparisons. Indeed, effect sizes provide the means for reducing a vast array of different behaviors to a single numerical system. This standardization enables the examiner to quantitatively compare the pattern of performance across profiles while keeping with qualitative observations of patient performance. The examiner can work between profiles by using the effect size tables to select tests that can help rule out a particular disease process from others not included in the differential. Indeed, the best diagnostic discriminations should be obtained by selecting a combination of tests from the tables, including some that are sensitive to specific impairment, some to general impairment, and others that tend to draw out diagnostic markers for a specific disorder (i.e., with the use of heuristic benchmark criteria – see below; also see Lezak, 1995).

In essence, the diagnostic process involves the successive elimination of alternative possibilities. The examiner formulates the first set of hypotheses on the basis of the referral question, the information obtained from the history or informants, and the initial impression of the patient (Lezak, 1995; Spreen & Strauss, 1998). As the examination proceeds, the examiner can progressively refine general hypotheses (e.g., by selecting tests from the effect size profiles that are "known" to be most and least sensitive to a specific disease) into increasingly specific hypotheses (e.g., by selecting tests from the profiles that are "known" to be most and least sensitive to the specific disease(s) to be differentiated). Each diagnostic hypothesis is tested by comparing what is known from the patient's pattern of performance on neuropsychological evaluation (including history, appearance, interview behavior, test performance) with what neuropsychological test results are expected for that particular diagnostic classification according to the profiles.

This procedure illustrates the method of double dissociation as it identifies which components of complex cognitive activities are impaired and which are preserved in a specific neurologic or psychiatric disease (Teuber, 1955). For example, given two tests and their associated effect sizes, if patients with dementia X do poorly on Test 1 but succeed on the second, while patients with dementia Y do poorly on Test 2 but not on the first, then Test 1 can be considered specific for dementia X while Test 2 is specific for dementia Y. Thus, by providing an index of specific test effect sizes and associated sensitivity to various neurologic and psychiatric syndromes, the clinician is able to differentiate these syndromes by the method of multiple dissociation.

Such an approach to neuropsychological evaluation can provide diagnostically useful information as well as greater efficacy than can be gained from simple screening techniques to identify neuropsychological syndromes. Thus, this book will aid clinicians in their decisions as to which diagnostic test data best differentiate between syndromes. As such, we think our approach to neuropsychological differential diagnosis will assist in making an accurate diagnosis, support the application of a specific and possibly efficacious treatment, and ultimately lead to a better clinical outcome for the patient and family.

When a diagnosis is known, our profiles might assist the clinician in a slightly different manner. That is, the clinician can select tests and examination techniques from the tables for their appropriateness for the patient and for their relevancy to those diagnostic or compensatory planning questions that prompted the examination as well as those that may arise during its course. For instance, if patient X has been diagnosed previously with dementia Y, and has been referred for re-evaluation or follow-up, the tables can be used to aid in the selection of tests to be administered to patient X. The clinician can select tests from the dementia Y profile that are most sensitive (those tests with the largest effect sizes), to document the progression and severity of the disease process (assuming a ceiling effect has not yet been achieved), and those tests that are least sensitive (those tests with the smallest effect sizes), to index those cognitive abilities that remain relatively spared in keeping with the profile and the expected disease characteristics. Indeed, the tables can be used to evaluate the patient efficiently by knowing beforehand that the selected tests will likely yield a profile of maximal and minimal deficits that will both help confirm (or refute) the original diagnosis and aid in establishing a rehabilitative strategy. Moreover, the limitations of the tests must be known and the information elicited by the selected tests interpreted accordingly. Ultimately, however, the content and direction of any neuropsychological examination that is adapted to the patients needs and capacities must be decided by the examiner (Kaplan, 1988, 1990; Milberg, Hebben, & Kaplan, 1996). Thus, these tables can help the clinician pick the one or the few tests that will best meet the clinical requirements (Lezak, 1995).

The second purpose for our review relates to the usefulness of the tables for prospective neuropsychological research. That is, as the profiles constitute a "compendium" of neuropsychological research, the research investigator can conveniently peruse the tables to gather a sense of existing neuropsychological findings. Indeed, researchers can utilize the tables quickly in such a way that might generate new testable hypotheses concerning the investigation of specific neurologic and psychiatric disorders and their behavioral disabilities. Furthermore, if from the tables, there is no (or little) documented evidence of performance on a task in the existing literature, a "compendium" can be used to justify the need for further experimentation with a specific test in a particular neuropsychological syndrome.

Moreover, the cognitive tables can provide the researcher with a rationale for test selection in his or her research design. Usually, when following a research protocol, the examiner is not free to exercise the flexibility and inventiveness that characterize the selection and presentation of test materials in the clinical setting. For research purposes, the prime consideration in selecting examination techniques is whether they will effectively test the hypotheses. Other important issues when putting together a research design include practicality, time, and the appropriateness of the instruments for the population under consideration (Lezak, 1995; Spreen & Strauss, 1998). Moreover, since the research investigator cannot change instruments or procedures in midstream without losing or confounding data, selection of a research test battery will be better served if the sensitivity of a given task to a given syndrome is known. Thus, our compendium of profiles of cognitive test sensitivity to various neurologic and psychiatric syndromes provide a point of reference to aid in the selection and development of test batteries for research purposes.

Finally, these tables might also prove useful in the development of strategies of rehabilitation and/or compensation. Indeed, neuropsychological assessment is also concerned with the documentation and description of preserved functions – the patient's behavioral competencies and strengths (Lezak, 1995; see Sohlberg & Mateer, 1989). Thus, as the profiles provide an index of measures that are least altered due to neuropathological degeneration and alteration, the relatively preserved ability on these measures can perhaps influence the development of strategies that might in turn, reduce disability caused by the neuropathological process.

With these considerations in mind, we have put together a compendium of cognitive profiles for some of the more common neurologic and neuropsychiatric syndromes in hope of meeting our purpose(s) for this review.

Chapter 2

LITERATURE REVIEWS AND THE NATURE OF EVIDENCE

We include this chapter because it serves as a theoretical basis for our review. We hope the reader finds the argument put forth here useful in understanding the rationale behind our work. Moreover, the chapter also serves as a primer on meta-analysis and on the interpretation of effect sizes in the context of brain-behavior relations.

On methodology

Neuropsychology is defined by its knowledge base, which is typically meant to represent the accumulation of scientific study of the relationship between brain and behavior. Indeed, the first attempts to localize mental processes to the brain may be traced back to antiquity when Hippocrates of Croton claimed that the brain was the organ of intellect and the heart the organ of the senses (see Heilman & Valenstein, 1993). It was not until Gall laid the foundation of modern neuropsychology, however, that scientists like Bouillard (1825), Broca (1865), Wernicke (1874), Lichtheim (1885), Liepmann, (1920), and later, Geschwind (1965), further advanced our science by way of careful observation followed by analysis and then hypothesis-testing based on the observation of single case studies (Heilman & Valenstein, 1993). This rich methodological tradition has been elegantly employed over the past few decades to further define the relationship between brain and behavior (e.g., Benson, 1994; Cummings, 1993; Damasio, 1994; Heilman, 1973; Heilman & Valenstein, 1972, 1979; Kaplan, 1988; Kertesz, 1994; Luria, 1973; Mesulam,

1982; Ogden, 1996; Scoville & Milner, 1957; Shallice, 1988; Snowden, Neary, & Mann, 1996).

A vast number of investigations that pass for research in the field of neuropsychology today, however, entail the use of experimental research designs and statistical tests of significance. "Most characteristically, when a psychologist finds a problem he wishes to investigate, he converts his intuitions and hypotheses into procedures which will yield a test of significance, and will characteristically allow the result of the test of significance to bear the essential responsibility for the conclusions he will draw" (Bakan, 1966, p. 1). As such, the experimental approach to neuropsychological research has enabled researchers to test a hypothesis based on a far greater number of patients compared to the n of 1 in single case studies. By allowing the level of significance (i.e., $p < .05$), however, to bear the essential responsibility for the conclusions that we draw in our experimentation, we fail to give due consideration to the magnitude of effect, which in essence, is the principal measure used in the single case study approach (e.g., brain ablation paradigms).

Perhaps a major attraction of significance testing among modern researchers and consumers of research findings is the apparent simplicity and meaningfulness in dichotomizing all statistical results (involving associations) as "significant" ($p < .05$) or "nonsignificant" ($p > .05$). In fact, this common practice has no scientific meaning and was introduced by statisticians in the early part of the century to confront common decision-making problems (e.g., which of two fertilizers should be used?) not causal inference in science (see Cowles, 1989). Thus, not only does dichotomizing p values at an arbitrary level degrade the available statistical evidence, but it readily leads to misinterpretations of findings.

The purpose of this chapter is to demonstrate that sole reliance on tests of statistical significance in the review of neuropsychological findings can systematically confound the conclusions drawn from our neuropsychological research regarding brain-behavior relations. Some have argued (e.g., Bakan, 1966; Cohen, 1994; Hunter & Schmidt, 1990; Schmidt, 1992, 1996) that null hypothesis statistical significance testing has not only failed to support the advancement of psychology as a science but also has seriously impeded it (see Frick [1996] for a debate of this point). The argument herein is that effect sizes and their associated statistics, rather than statistical significance, can better serve the clinician and researcher in the interpretation and review of neuropsychological findings. Before providing a rationale for such a conclusion, it should first be noted that the argument to be put forth here is not new and has been voiced in the field of general psychology. It has been articulated in different ways by Rozeboom (1960), Bakan (1966), Meehl (1967), Carver (1978), Guttman (1985), Oakes (1986), Loftus (1991, 1994), Cohen (1994), and most recently by Schmidt (1996). Accordingly, it shall be argued here that the most valid way in which we could review the field of neuropsychology and formulate a model of neuropsychological differential diagnosis, was with more appropriate statistics, namely point estimate effect sizes and meta-analysis for the analysis and review of data from multiple studies. Justification for this deduction will be demonstrated from the reanalysis of published neuropsychological test findings rather than reiterating the illogical statistical intricacies of null hypothesis statistical significance testing which have been eloquently articulated in the works of Schmidt (1996), Cohen (1994), and others (Bakan, 1966; Carver, 1978; Guttman, 1985; Rozeboom, 1960).

The test of significance in neuropsychological research

All too often we find competing hypotheses in neuropsychology, or even "empirical" findings that do not correspond to our clinical experience with patients who suffer from neurologic or psychiatric disease. Take for example our understanding of schizophrenia. It has long been debated that schizophrenia is a disease of the frontal lobes – the so-called frontal executive hypothesis (Zakzanis & Heinrichs, 1997, 1999). Proponents of this hypothesis (e.g., Morice & Delhunty, 1996; Weinberger, 1988) have "consistently demonstrated" that patients with schizophrenia perform poorly on neuropsychological tasks that are sensitive to frontal executive functioning (e.g., Wisconsin Card Sorting Test [WCST]; Heaton, Chelune, Talley, Kay, & Curtiss, 1993) by providing data that achieves statistical significance. Despite illustrating that two groups (typically patients with schizophrenia and normal healthy controls) are statistically different from one another, the question that fails to be addressed when support for a hypothesis is based solely on the interpretation of a dichotomized p value is *how much of a difference* is there between the two groups being compared, or more accurately, *what is the magnitude of deficit* (or effect) in the patient sample and how confident can we be in our obtained results? Further, it is all too often that a significant p value is taken to imply the presence of a "significant" deficit. This is a fatal error in data interpretation (Soper, Cicchetti, Satz, Light, & Orsini, 1988). To illustrate, a re-analysis of Wisconsin Card Sorting Test (WCST) results in patients with schizophrenia from published studies with "competing" conclusions will serve the point being made. Although the issues raised in this chapter are illustrated with a specific example of a cross-sectional comparison of a continuous outcome (i.e., WCST performance) between two groups (i.e., patients with schizophrenia and healthy normal controls), the reader is reminded that the point being made applies to all types of experimental, quasi-experimental, and observational designs involving the estimation of effects in populations.

In the first study of frontal-executive functioning, WCST results for 117 patients with schizophrenia and 68 healthy normal controls are presented. A statistically significant two-tailed independent sample t test with a level of significance at $p < .05$ is reported for the perseverative error score on the WCST. This is interpreted to support frontal-executive impairment in patients with schizophrenia. In a second study, a nonsignificant ($p > .05$) two-tailed independent sample t test is reported for the perseverative error score on the WCST for 10 patients with schizophrenia and 10 healthy normal control comparisons. This result is interpreted as failing to support frontal-executive impairment in schizophrenia, but is also qualified with "if there were more patients and controls in the respective groups, the trend toward a significant difference would surely have achieved statistical significance". What have these two studies told us? The first study supports the frontal-executive hypothesis in schizophrenia whereas the other does not. Neither study has reported the magnitude of frontal-executive impairment in patients with schizophrenia. Is it little or none? Is it a defining characteristic of schizophrenia? Are the normals more impaired than the patients? The studies have only demonstrated a statistically significant difference between two group means on the WCST perseverative error variable. Granted, a quick glimpse at the mean performance from each group will reveal which group obtained a greater number of perseverative errors, but that glimpse, and the reported statistical significance and its corresponding p value will not provide a quantifiable index of frontal-executive impairment. This index would make clear to what extent the frontal-executive system is impaired in schizophrenia and, therefore, settle any competing hypotheses. Thus, the question that lingers is how could one review such a literature without bias? Moreover, the second study demonstrates the type of convoluted logic that has indeed served neuropsychology wrongly. That is, if all that is needed to give truth to our hypotheses is "to increase the sample size", then what is the purpose in testing any hypothesis? Being theoretically possible (see Meehl, 1967), then all our hypotheses regarding brain-behavior relations automatically can be given truth in keeping with a large enough sample size and the test of significance. One has to wonder, if Gall had had available the test of significance, would we still be practicing Craniology?

What then is our alternative, if the test of significance is really of such limited appropriateness? As Bakan (1966) notes, "at the very least it would appear that we would be much better off if we were to attempt to estimate the magnitude of the parameters in the populations, and recognize that we then need to make other inferences concerning the psychological phenomenon which may be manifesting themselves in these magnitudes" (pp. 27). The effect size estimate d measures magnitude. It is a measure of the degree to which the phenomenon is present in the population or the degree to which the null hypothesis is false (Cohen, 1988). In mathematical terms, d is simply the difference in patient and control means calibrated in pooled standard deviation units (i.e., *patient mean − control mean / pooled standard deviation*). The effect size d is not dependent on nor influenced by sample size. Moreover, effect sizes can demonstrate test score overlap dispersion between two groups by utilizing and inverting Cohen's (1988) idealized population distributions. That is, a hypothetical percent overlap is associated with the varying degrees of effect size (see Table 2.1). For example, an effect size of 0.0 corresponds to complete overlap. The two groups are completely indistinguishable from one another on the variable measure. If $d = 1.0$, the corresponding overlap is 45 % – about half of the patient group can be discriminated from the control group on the basis of the variable measure. If $d = 3.0$, the corresponding overlap is less than 5%. The two groups are approximately completely distinguishable from one another with respect to the variable

Table 2.1.   Overlap Percent (OL%) Corresponding to Effect Size d.

Overlap Percent	Effect Size d
100.0	0.0
92.3	0.1
85.3	0.2
78.7	0.3
72.6	0.4
66.6	0.5
61.8	0.6
57.0	0.7
52.6	0.8
48.4	0.9
44.6	1.0
41.1	1.1
37.8	1.2
34.7	1.3
31.9	1.4
29.3	1.5
26.9	1.6
24.6	1.7
22.6	1.8
20.6	1.9
18.9	2.0
1⌂.⏉	?.?
13.0	2.4
10.7	2.6
8.8	2.8
7.2	3.0
5.8	3.2
4.7	3.4
3.7	3.6
3.0	3.8
2.3	4.0

measure. Thus, if d does equal about 3.0 for the variable measure, the effect size may serve as a heuristic marker on account of approximate complete discriminability between experimental (i.e., patient) and control groups (see Zakzanis, 1998a, e). Briefly, a diagnostic marker should be capable of discriminating approximately all patients from all normal healthy controls on the dependent variable of interest. Such discriminability would have to have an associated effect size greater than 3.0 as this size of effect corresponds to test score dispersion overlap of less than 5% between patients and normal healthy controls. For example, Zakzanis (1998e) showed that delayed recall and hippocampal atrophy in patients with dementia of the Alzheimer's type correspond to effect sizes greater than 3.0 and percentage overlap (OL%) values of less than 5%. This finding was taken to support the notion that delayed recall and hippocampal atrophy are markers for dementia of the Alzheimer's type (Zakzanis, 1998e). In doing so, heuristic benchmark criteria were proposed (i.e., $d > 3.0$ OL% < 5) that could help articulate further the strength of neuroanatomic and neuro-psychological evidence in other disorders with prominent brain pathology. Although such a standard is not entirely justifiable, it can serve as an heuristic benchmark in which the magnitude of an effect size can be articulated when interpreting brain-behavior relations from experimental studies.

When an effect size d is calculated for the two examples given above, a very different interpretation regarding perseverative error in schizophrenia is met based on the author's original data. In the first study the calculated effect size is 0.5 corresponding to approximately 67% overlap between patient and control test score distributions. In the second study, the calculated effect size is 1.1 which corresponds to 41% overlap. On the basis of these results (and remember, study one had a statistically significant result, whereas study two did not), study two would be in a better position to argue for frontal-executive impairment in schizophrenia than study one which uses its statistically significant finding to argue in favor of the hypothesis. The "true" significance of the study findings, how-ever, masquerade behind convoluted statistical tests of significance (also see Bieliauskas, Fastenau, Lacey, & Roper, 1997). The reinterpretation of the data using effect size analyses provides a much more valid index of frontal-executive impairment in patients with schizophrenia which is not directly determined by sample size.

Returning to our previous example, the calculated effect sizes coupled with Cohen's (1988) corresponding inverted overlap percentages from these two par-ticular studies indicate that most patients with schizophrenia obtain an average number of perseverative errors on the WCST which makes them indistinguish-able from healthy normal controls, whereas a minority of patients obtain scores that clearly discriminates them from healthy normal controls. Further, because the mean effect size cannot completely discriminate all patients with schizo-phrenia from healthy controls (i.e., $d > 3.0$), it would be hard to argue in favor of frontal-executive impairment as being an integral characteristic of the illness, assuming of course, that perseverative error was sensitive and specific to frontal-executive function in schizophrenia.

In keeping with the conclusion from the re-analysis of the published data, it would be safe to say that such a conclusion is free of convoluted logic. That is, the conclusion has not been based on the "significance" of the finding that is directly determined by sample size alone. Most importantly, it is based on the magnitude of deficit, rather than a statistically significant difference between two means. Unfortunately, the effect size statistic does not allow one to generalize from patient samples to the population because it is not an inferential statistic but a statistic of distribution description in a most simplistic sense. It is the accu-mulation and synthesis of effect sizes across independent studies that can reveal the reliability of a finding and allow generalizations to be made. This can be accomplished with meta-analysis.

Meta-analysis for the analysis of data from multiple studies

"While the test of significance has been carrying too much of the burden of scientific inference in psychology" (Bakan, 1966, p. 1), it has resulted in the impediment of our knowledge base as well as created the difficult and onerous task of trying to compare and synthesize the myriad of neuropsychological findings into systematic and objective profiles of cognitive function in patient samples. That is, systematic knowledge about neuropsychological phenomenon are commonly dependent on research conducted within the experimental framework. In keeping with the WCST example, such research can often yield an ambiguous mix of results – decidedly significant, suggestive, convincingly null, and sometimes hopelessly inconclusive (Lipsey & Wilson, 1993). Researchers are then left with the meticulous task of trying to weigh the evidence that is reported with each conclusion, while clinicians pick through the results with hopes of finding a preponderance of evidence supporting a consistent neuropsychological profile. Moreover, although our science purports to serve the acquisition of knowledge and the pursuit of truth, it is all too easy to fall into the trap of interpreting data selectively in the service of an a priori position (Jacobson & Hollon, 1996). When comparing and/or synthesizing more than one "statistically significant" finding, there is no numeric unit which allows for valid comparison or synthesis of "statistically significant" results. What is lacking from the literature that will aid in the valid comparison and synthesis of neuropsychological findings across studies is magnitude or evidential strength calibrated in numerical bits of data – information that the test of significance does not provide.

An empirically valid index by which we can weigh and compare the evidential strength of neuropsychological findings across studies is the effect size statistic. One methodological approach that utilizes this statistic is meta-analysis. Meta-analysis has become a statistically sophisticated tool for objective research integration (Cooper & Hedges, 1994; Glass, McGaw, & Smith, 1981; Hedges & Olkin, 1985; Hunter, Schmidt, & Jackson, 1982; Rosenthal, 1991; Schimdt, 1996). In addition to solving problems with traditional literature reviews (such as the selective inclusion of studies often based on the reviewer's own impressionistic view of the quality of the study; differential subjective weighting of studies in the interpretation of a set of findings; misleading interpretations of study findings; failure to examine characteristics of the studies as potential explanations for disparate or consistent results across studies; and failure to examine moderating variables in the relationship under examination [Wolf, 1986], meta-analysis provides tools for the analysis of magnitude (i.e., the effect size d). Eligible research studies comprising a common dependent variable and statistics that can be transformed into effect sizes are viewed as a population to be systematically sampled and surveyed. Individual study results (typically means and standard deviations from each group) and moderator variables (e.g., education, duration of disease, gender, age) are then abstracted, quantified and coded, and assembled into a database that is statistically analyzed (Lipsey & Wilson, 1993). The main statistic presented in a meta-analysis is the mean effect size when there is little or no heterogeneity of effect observed across studies. This statistic is meant to reflect the average individual effect size across the sample of studies included in the synthesis. In the vast majority of meta-analyses in which there is appreciable heterogeneity of effect observed across studies, however, the primary goal should be to document and explain such heterogeneity in terms of various characteristics of the study populations or methods along with the mean effect across studies. That is, moderator variables are correlated to the effect size in order to parse relationships of subject characteristics that may influence the magnitude of the size of effect between the groups being compared. Moreover, as indicated above, the effect size can then be transformed into an overlap percentage by inverting Cohen's (1988) nonoverlap idealized distributions which can then be used as a measure of sensitivity that can indicate neuroanatomic or neuropsychological markers for a disease (Zakzanis, 1998e).

As might be anticipated with any empirical approach such as meta-analysis, this method of research synthesis has not been free from criticism, nor is it a panacea for resolving all the problems associated with building reliable and valid scientific knowledge and theory (Wolf, 1986). While we will not address these criticisms in depth, it is important for informed clinicians and researchers to be alerted to these potential problems and issues. Glass et al. (1981) have grouped these criticisms into four categories:

(1)   Logical conclusions cannot be drawn by comparing and aggregating studies that include different measuring techniques, definitions of variables, and subjects because they are too dissimilar.

(2)   Results of meta-analyses are uninterpretable because results from "poorly" designed studies are included along with results from "good" studies.

(3)   Published research is biased in favor of significant findings because nonsignificant findings are rarely published; this in turn leads to biased meta-analytic results.

(4)   Multiple results from the same study are often used which may bias or invalidate the meta-analysis and make the results appear more reliable than they really are, because these results are not independent.

The first criticism has been referred to as the "apples and oranges problem", in that it is argued that diversity makes comparisons inappropriate (Wolf, 1986). More specifically, a critic of our approach would likely argue, for example, that one cannot combine two entirely different measures of memory and take a mean effect size. We could not agree more. Hence, in our defense we present specific effect sizes for each cognitive task and test variable found in the literature. We only later combine measures to organize the myriad of findings (see Chapter 3). Moreover, we have only included in our review those primary studies that incorporate research diagnostic criteria specific to a neurological or neuropsychiatric syndrome. Thus making patient samples homogeneous in terms of diagnosis.

The second criticism was also handled by ensuring that cognitive assessments were always administered under the supervision of a trained psychologist. If the primary study did not use qualified test administrators, the study was not included in our review. Fortunately, this was never the case.

The third criticism relates to the implausibility that a literature review will uncover every study of a hypothesis that has been conducted. Rosenthal (1979) has called this the "file drawer problem" because of the tendency for studies supporting the null hypothesis of no significant results to be more likely to be buried away in file drawers. Kraemer and Andrews (1982; in Wolf, 1986) note: Published research studies tend to be biased toward positive findings. A study is often abandoned if it is apparent that statistically significant findings will not be forthcoming. Reports of nonsignificant findings are generally unpublishable even when they are replications of earlier studies reporting significant results (p. 405).

Hence, this may enhance the likelihood of a type I publication bias error in finding more positive results than is really the case were all studies to be located and included in our review of the neuropsychological literature. Fortunately, this criticism relating to the nontypicality and bias in favor of significant results in published research studies, can be addressed in several ways (see Wolf, 1986). One such approach was suggested by Rosenthal (1979), who noted that we calculate the number of studies confirming the null hypothesis that would be needed to reverse a conclusion that a significant relationship exists. Cooper (1979) called this the Fail Safe N (Nfs) for the number of additional studies in a meta-analysis that would be necessary to reverse the overall probability obtained from our combined test to a value higher than our critical value for statistical significance, which we set at .01. We have incorporated this statistic into our profiles.

The fourth criticism concerns the number of results from the same experimental study that should be used. Because we reviewed the results of specific cognitive tasks and not, let's say, the combined results from three tests of memory in one study, this criticism does not apply to our review.

With these considerations in mind, if we return to our example of WCST deficit in schizophrenia and the frontal-executive hypothesis, it has been shown that the meta-analytic mean effect size across studies ($N = 28$) for WCST perseverative errors is 0.87 (Zakzanis & Heinrichs, 1997). This corresponds to approximately 48% overlap between patients with schizophrenia and healthy normal controls. Thus, the meta-analytic effect size supports the conclusion that frontal-executive impairment is not a core deficit of schizophrenia. That is, schizophrenia is not a necessary nor sufficient cause of frontal-executive impairment so that all cases of such deficit are not caused by schizophrenia and that all patients with schizophrenia will not display such a neuropsychological deficit. Indeed it is true that to negate the necessary-cause hypothesis, we could simply identify some confirmed cases of frontal-executive impairment among nonschizophrenics. Similarly to negate the sufficient-cause hypothesis, we could simply identify some chronic patients with schizophrenia who never develop frontal-executive impairment. Why then must we do a meta-analysis to reach a similar conclusion regarding schizophrenia as that indicated above? Besides being a much simpler and direct way of reaching such a conclusion, meta-analysis allows the clinician and researcher to test how robust the evidence is over the accumulation of studies. That is, we can never be sure that the conclusions drawn from a single study are not attributable to chance or error, even with a test of significance (see Schmidt, 1996). If the results from all studies are considered together (as in meta-analysis), however, the clinician and researcher are in a better position to evaluate and articulate the nature and pattern of brain-behavior relations knowing that a given finding is a reliable, or unreliable, finding.

For example, the conclusion of insufficient frontal-executive deficit in schizophrenia can be taken with considerable evidence of reliability. That is, Zakzanis (1998f) demonstrated that the mean meta-analytic effect size from four independent reviewers of WCST performance in patients with schizophrenia correspond to an intraclass reliability correlation for d of 0.98. This is excellent reliability. The four independent reviewers reached the same conclusion based on their meta-analytic results. The unity in the interpretation of their results is unlike the conflicting hypotheses and interpretations regarding frontal-executive impairment in schizophrenia that can be found in single experimental studies or in typical narrative reviews where the strength of a hypothesis is often based on a count of significant and non-significant findings (e.g., Taylor, 1995; Weinberger, 1988). Indeed, meta-analysis has been employed by several investigators to review and resolve controversies regarding brain-behavior relationships (e.g., Binder, Rohling, & Larrabee, 1997; Christensen, Griffiths, Mackinnon, & Jacomb, 1997; Heinrichs & Zakzanis, 1998; Kinderman & Brown, 1997; Meiran & Jelicic, 1995; Thornton & Raz, 1997; Zakzanis, 1998 b, c, g; Zakzanis & Heinrichs, 1998; Zakzanis, Leach, & Freedman, 1998; Zakzanis, Leach, & Kaplan, 1998). Thus, in the analysis of cognitive data from multiple studies, meta-analysis is a valid methodological approach to research integration.

Summary

It has been shown that the reader of neuropsychological reviews will be better served if due consideration is given to the magnitude of effect in the synthesis of experimental studies of brain and behavior. It should be evident in keeping with the example that point estimate effect sizes and meta-analysis for the analysis of data from multiple studies is a requirement for valid and reliable literature review. Accordingly, we systematically reviewed the literature and converted all relevant experimental statistical findings into effect sizes. We employed meta-analytic methodology to synthesize these effects. Our methodology is spelled out in more detail in the following chapter.

Chapter 3

METHOD

This chapter describes in detail how our review was conducted. We hope that such a description enables the reader to evaluate the appropriateness of our methods and the reliability and validity of our results. It also permits the investigator to replicate our review should they so desire.

More specifically, in this chapter we describe the specific means by which we selected primary studies and delineate their inclusion criteria. We also describe the literature search conducted and the variables recorded from each primary study. Our rationale for the inclusion of independent effects and the organization of the cognitive tasks and test variables into the supraordinate neuropsychological domains is also outlined.

Criteria for primary study inclusion

To be included in the review, primary studies must have incorporated a control group experimental research design. Specifically, a control group comprising healthy participants was a prerequisite in the derivation of the effect sizes. Primary studies must have also included statistics convertible to effect size d. That is, Cohen's d can be obtained from several formulas. The most accurate estimate of d can be obtained by subtracting patient and control group means and dividing the total by the pooled standard deviation (Cohen, 1988). Most effects were based on this standard transformation. However, several studies did not report basic descriptive statistics such as means and standard deviations. In such instances, the effect size d was estimated by converting test statistics such as F or t to d (see Johnson, 1989; Wolf, 1986). Studies reporting only significance levels with no descriptive or inferential statistics had to be excluded.

If a primary study met the methodological and statistical criteria for inclusion, it was then examined for diagnostic patient criteria. For each neurologic and psychiatric syndrome, an attempt was made to include diagnostically homogeneous patient samples to avoid biasing effects. Specific diagnostic criteria for each of the syndromes is detailed in each of the chapters.

Literature search

According to Green and Hall (1984), meta-analysts doing a literature search should page through the volumes of pertinent journals for a topic year by year. This was done with every issue for the journals listed in Table 3.1. The search span included all journal issues published between the years 1980 to 1997. This proved to be an effective way to search for usable articles in keeping with the small and focused set of key words in any particular abstract or title that a computer data base uses to search for key words. Despite its apparent cost in time, the reasoning behind using the individual journal technique was to avoid missing a useful paper that lies outside a computerized database's regular purview. This serves to reduce the likelihood that bias was involved in the search outcome (White, 1994).

To avoid missing a primary study that was not published in our choice of pertinent journals, the *PsychInfo* and *Medline* computerized databases were also utilized to locate additional studies that met inclusion criteria for the review. The key words used were specific to the neurologic and psychiatric syndromes reviewed, and are presented in Table 3.2. For each "hit" the study abstract was perused. If any indication was made that cognitive tests were employed, the actual study was obtained and included in the review if its content met inclusion criteria.

Variables recorded

For each primary study, we recorded the full study reference (i.e., author[s], journal, volume, pages, title, year of publication). Basic demographic and clinical variable data from primary studies were also recorded. Specifically, we extrapolated study sample sizes, along with clinical and demographic variables specific to each syndrome. Common variables reported across syndromes included patient age, education, and gender of patient and control groups. Less commonly reported variables included duration of disease, age at disease onset, number of hospitalizations, and medication status. Clinical variables specific to a neurologic or psychiatric syndrome were also gathered and reported. These demographic and clinical variables were compiled and are presented for each of the syndromes in their respective chapters.

Table 3.1.   Journals Perused by Hand to Locate Potential Studies Meeting Inclusion
              Criteria.

Journal name

American Journal of Psychiatry
Annals of Neurology
Archives of Clinical Neuropsychology
Archives of General Psychiatry
Archives of Neurology
Biological Psychiatry
Brain
Brain and Cognition
British Journal of Psychiatry
Dementia
Journal of Abnormal Psychology
Journal of Affective Disorders
Journal of Clinical and Experimental Neuropsychology
Journal of Clinical Neuropsychology
Journal of Nervous and Mental Disease
Journal of Neurology, Neurosurgery, and Psychiatry
Journal of the International Neuropsychological Society
Neurology
Neuropsychiatry, Neuropsychology, and Behavioral Neurology
Neuropsychologia
Neuropsychology
Neuropsychopharmacology
Schizophrenia Bulletin
Schizophrenia Research
The Clinical Neuropsychologist

Table 3.2.   Key Word[s] Used in *PsychInfo* and *MedLine* Searches.

Neurologic or Psychiatric Syndrome	Key Word[s]
Alzheimer's disease	"Alzheimer's disease"
	"dementia of the Alzheimer's type"
	"Alzheimer's"
	"Alzheimer's dementia"
Fronto-temporal dementia	"Fronto-temporal dementia"
	"Frontal lobe dementia"
	"dementia of the non-Alzheimer type"
	"Frontal lobar degeneration"
	"Pick's complex"
Primary progressive aphasia	"Primary progressive aphasia"
	"Progressive aphasia"
	"Nonfluent aphasia"
	"Progressive nonfluent aphasia"
	"Mesulam" + "Aphasia"
	"Progressive aphemia"

Table continues

Table 3.2. (continued)

Neurologic or Psychiatric Syndrome	Key Word[s]
Progressive supranuclear palsy	"Progressive supranuclear palsy" "Steele-Richardson-Olszewski syndrome" "Parkinson plus syndrome"
Parkinson's disease	"Parkinson's disease" "Paralysis agitans" "Idiopathic Parkinson's disease"
Huntington's disease	"Huntington's disease" "Huntington's chorea"
Multiple sclerosis	"Multiple sclerosis" "White matter dementia" "Subcortical dementia"
Depression	"Depression" "Unipolar depression" "Major depression" "Unipolar major depression" "Major depressive disorder"
Schizophrenia	"Schizophrenia" "Dementia praecox"
Obsessive Compulsive Disorder	"Obsessive compulsive disorder"
Mild traumatic brain injury	"Traumatic brain injury" "Head injury" "Brain injury"

Moderator variable analysis is an essential part of meta-analytic investigation. It assesses the contribution of study differences in sample attributes, design and instrument features to effect size heterogeneity and replication. Moderator analysis, however, is dependent on the individual reporting practices of different investigators and, presumably, on the expectations of journal editors and reviewers. In terms of moderator variables the published literature on neurocognition in neurologic and psychiatric syndromes is surprisingly limited and often inadequate. We found that even basic subject attributes like age, education and gender composition were not reported by all studies. Clinical variables of special relevance to these conditions, like neuroleptic medication dose, age of illness onset, and duration of illness were so seldomly reported that we were able to conduct only a limited correlational study of potential moderators, with many correlations missing statistical significance because of inadequate power. More consistent reporting of these sample attributes by researchers in their individual studies will increase statistical power for meta-analytic purposes and facilitate future efforts at understanding how cognitive and clinical variables are related in the published literature. Nonetheless, it was possible to report significant relations between moderator variables (both clinical and demographic) and the cognitive effect sizes for each of the neurologic and psychiatric syndromes (see their respective chapters).

Variables recorded also included the cognitive tasks and test variables from primary studies. In keeping with Lezak's (1995) rationale,

> selection favored tests that are in relatively common use, represent a subclass of similar tests, illustrate a particularly interesting assessment method, or uniquely demonstrate some significant aspect of behavior. The selection criteria of availability and ease of administration eliminated those tests that require bulky, complicated, expensive equipment or material that cannot be easily obtained or reproduced by the individual clinician or researcher. These criteria eliminated all tests that have to have a fixed laboratory installation, as well as all those demanding special technical knowledge of the examiner (p. 334).

Accordingly, if the primary study met inclusion criteria, its cognitive task and test variable(s) were included in a cognitive profile. Some of the variables listed in the cognitive profiles are based on one study and thus do not meet the definition of meta-analysis. The rationale for the inclusion of the variable and the construction of the profile was as follows: First, the reported reliability is that of the original published primary study, only it is now transformed and presented to reflect magnitude (i.e., the effect size) rather than statistical significance. Second, knowing that a task or test variable has only been reported once for a patient sample can be used to justify future research. This is especially meaningful if certain tasks or test variables are found to be particularly sensitive to specific disease-control discrimination but have never been replicated. Thirdly, by estimating the number of additional studies with nonsignificant results that would be necessary to reverse a conclusion drawn from the meta-analysis (the Fail-Safe N), it became apparent that even single effect sizes with reasonable magnitude were robust and provide some estimate of validity. Finally, it can be justified on the basis of factor analytic work and published meta-analyses (e.g., Zakzanis, 1998b, c, g) that some scores can be combined to reflect a more general cognitive domain (e.g., combining the recall of trial 1 of the CVLT list A with that of trial 5 represents a domain of "memory acquisition") which will eliminate the uncertainty of an $n = 1$. However, any derived composite effect size based on a combination of scores from two or more measures of different tasks or same test variables results in loss of data points that otherwise, could be used to differentiate disorders. That is, a meta-analytic approach that minimizes the inclusion of specific test variables by subsuming a number of test variables under a single supraordinate neuropsychological domain can result in serious distortions in the interpretations and recommendations drawn from its conclusions. To be neuropsychologically meaningful, a meta-analysis should represent as few kinds of behaviors or dimensions of cognitive function as possible. Further, should the levels of performance for combined measures differ, the composite effect size which make up the meta-analysis – being somewhere between the highest and the lowest of the combined effects – will be misleading. Indeed, effect sizes calculated by summing or averaging a set of tasks or even same test variables can be quite removed from the behavior they represent. It is for this reason that independent effect sizes *are* included in the profiles.

Nevertheless, the cognitive effects are also pooled and presented by functional domain to help organize the myriad of test variables that make up the profiles. Each chapter is organized by neuropsychological domain according to the order in which the domain is most to least impaired for a specific syndrome. The reader can find a more concise quantitative summary in table format of the rank-order of neuropsychological domains for each of the specific syndromes in a summary chapter (see Chapter 15).

An effort has been made to classify the tests according to the major functional activities they elicit. This was possible for many of them. Many others, however, call upon several functions so that their assignment to a particular neuropsychological domain was somewhat arbitrary. Indeed, organizing the myriad of cognitive test variables reported in the literature into a coherent classification was a major challenge. Several strategies exist in the literature for organizing diverse tests into domains of cognitive function and each of these strategies has both advantages and disadvantages. First, there are a priori approaches such as Lezak's (1995) classification. These are influenced by theoretical and practice-related considerations about the test measures and their putative underlying processes. For example, Lezak (1995) includes motor and executive ability tasks in the same chapter, presumably on the basis of a common substrate in the frontal lobes, or some other assumed links. Such classifications have no quantitative statistical underpinning and even advocates of this approach admit to an element of arbitrariness in this test organization (see Lezak, 1995, pp. 333–334). A second approach is based on factor-analytic studies of neuropsychological test batteries (see Goldstein, 1984, pp. 184–210; Larrabee & Curtis, 1992; 1995; Larrabee, Kane, Schuck, & Francis, 1985; Leonberger, Nicks, Larrabee, & Goldfader, 1992). Factor analysis provides a quantitative description that relates different tests to a smaller number of underlying abilities. It is the validity of this approach, however, as a general strategy for organizing tests in a meta-analysis depends in part on the availability of factor analyses that include all of the tests in the literature that were reviewed. In practice, it is the standard test batteries like the Halstead-Reitan (e.g., Ernst, Warner, Hochberg & Townes, 1988) and Luria-Nebraska (e.g., Mckay & Golden, 1981) that tend to be studied factor-analytically. In the present case, we were unable to find factor-analytic studies that included all, or even most, of the cognitive test variables reported in the selected literature. A further consideration is that regardless of classification method, many cognitive tests are probably influenced by several component processes (see Kaplan, 1988). For example, scores on the Trail Making Test may reflect visual scanning and perception, but also motor speed, hand-eye coordination and attention (Lezak, 1995, pp. 382–384). Hence, categorizing tests on the basis of a faulty assumption that test performance is determined by only one process is misleading (Kaplan, 1988).

Accordingly, we tried to avoid aggregating different tests and their effect sizes into hypothetical categories, and adopted a strategy, presented in Table 3.3, whereby assignment of test measures to domain was guided by factor analytic

Table 3.3.   Classification of Cognitive Tasks and Test Variables by Neuropsychological
              Domain.

Attention/concentration
Backward Masking (David & Cutting, 1994)
Continuous Performance Tasks (Mirsky, 1989)
Dichotic Listening (Kimura, 1967)
Letter Cancellation (Diller, Ben-Yishay, & Gerstman, 1974)
Dementia Rating Scale Attention subscale (DRS; Mattis, 1988)
Paced Auditory Serial Addition Test (PASAT; Gronwall, 1977)
Seashore Rhythm Test (Reitan & Wolfson, 1989)
Stroop word and color reading (Stroop, 1935)
Trail Making Test Part A (Reitan, 1958)
Wechsler Memory Scale-Revised Mental Control (WMS-R; Wechsler, 1987)

Memory acquisition
Benton Visual Retention Test (number or errors) (Benton, 1974)
Buschke Selective Reminding Test total recall (BSRT; Buschke & Fuld, 1974)
Consonant Trigrams (Peterson & Peterson, 1959)
Corsi block tapping test (Milner, 1971)
California Verbal Learning Test list A trial 1 (CVLT; Delis, Kramer, Kaplan, & Ober, 1987)
CVLT list A trial 5 (Delis, Kramer, Kaplan, & Ober, 1987)
CVLT list A trials 1-5 (Delis, Kramer, Kaplan, & Ober, 1987)
CVLT list B (Delis, Kramer, Kaplan, & Ober, 1987)
CVLT short delay free recall (Delis, Kramer, Kaplan, & Ober, 1987)
CVLT short delay cued recall (Delis, Kramer, Kaplan, & Ober, 1987)
DRS Memory subscale (Mattis, 1988)
Rey Auditory Verbal Learning Test trial 1 (RAVLT; Rey, 1964)
Rey-Osterrieth Complex Figure immediate recall (ROCF; Rey, 1941; Osterrieth, 1944)
Tactual Performance Test (Halstead, 1947)
Wechsler Adult Intelligence Scale-Revised Digit Span forward (WAIS-R; Wechsler, 1981)
WAIS-R Digit Span backward (Wechsler, 1981)
WMS-R Logical Memory immediate recall (Wechsler, 1987)
WMS-R Paired Associates immediate recall (Wechsler, 1987)
WMS-R Visual Reproduction immediate recall (Wechsler, 1987)

Delayed recall
BSRT delayed recall (Buschke & Fuld, 1974)
BSRT recognition (Buschke & Fuld, 1974)
CVLT long delay free recall (Delis, Kramer, Kaplan, & Ober, 1987)
CVLT long delay cued recall (Delis, Kramer, Kaplan, & Ober, 1987)
CVLT recognition discriminability (Delis, Kramer, Kaplan, & Ober, 1987)
Famous People Test (Albert, Butters, & Levin, 1979)
Presidents Test (Hamsher & Roberts, 1985)
RAVLT delayed recall (Rey, 1964)
RAVLT recognition (Rey, 1964)
ROCF delay recall (Rey, 1941; Osterrieth, 1944)
WAIS-R Information (Wechsler, 1981)
Warrington Facial Recognition (Warrington, 1984)
Warrington Word Recognition (Warrington, 1984)
WMS-R Logical Memory delayed recall (Wechsler, 1987)

Table continues

Table 3.3. (continued)

WMS-R Paired Associates delayed recall (Wechsler, 1987)
WMS-R Visual Reproduction delayed recall (Wechsler, 1987)
Cognitive Flexibility and Abstraction
Category Test (Halstead, 1947)
Controlled Oral Word Association Test (COWAT; Benton & Hamsher, 1989)
Design Fluency (Jones-Gotman & Milner, 1977)
Go-No-Go Tasks (Luria, 1973)
Mattis DRS Initiation/Perseveration subscale (Mattis, 1988)
Porteus Mazes (Porteus, 1959, 1965)
Raven's Progressive Matrices (Raven, 1982)
Stroop interference (Stroop, 1935)
Tinker Toy Test (Lezak, 1995)
Tower of Hanoi, London, Toronto (Shallice, 1982)
Trail Making Test Part B (Reitan, 1958)
Trail Making Test B-A (Lezak, 1995)
WAIS-R Arithmetic (Wechsler, 1981)
WAIS-R Similarities (Wechsler, 1981)
Wisconsin Card Sorting Test perseverative errors (WCST; Heaton, 1981; Heaton, Chelune, Talley, Kay, & Curtiss, 1993)
WCST perseverative responses (Heaton, 1981; Heaton, Chelune, Talley, Kay, & Curtiss, 1993)
WCST categories achieved (Heaton, 1981; Heaton, Chelune, Talley, Kay, & Curtiss, 1993)
WCST errors (Heaton, 1981; Heaton, Chelune, Talley, Kay, & Curtiss, 1993)

Verbal skill
Boston Diagnostic Aphasia Examination (Goodglass & Kaplan, 1983a)
Boston Naming Test (Kaplan, Goodglass, & Weintraub, 1983)
Mill Hill Vocabulary Scale (Raven, 1960, 1982)
Multilingual Aphasia Examination (Benton & Hamsher, 1989)
National Adult Reading Test (NART; Nelson, 1982)
Peabody Picture Vocabulary Test-Revised (Dunn & Dunn, 1981)
Pyramids and Palm Trees (Howard & Patterson, 1992)
Semantic Fluency (Perret, 1974)
Token Test (De Renzi & Vignolo, 1962)
Western Aphasia Battery (Kertesz, 1979, 1982)
WAIS-R Comprehension (Wechsler, 1981)
WAIS-R Verbal IQ (Wechsler, 1981)
WAIS-R Vocabulary (Wechsler, 1981)
Wide Range Achievement Test-Revised Reading (WRAT-R; Jastak & Wilkinson, 1984)

Performance skill
Affect Recognition (Bowers, Bauer, & Heilman, 1993)
Bender Gestalt (Bender, 1938)
Benton Facial Recognition (Benton, Sivan, Hamsher, Varney, & Spreen, 1994)
BVRT copy (Benton, 1974)
Clock Drawing Test (Freedman, Leach, Kaplan, Winocur, Shulman, & Delis, 1994)
Finger Localization (Benton, Sivan, Hamsher, Varney, & Spreen, 1994)
Hooper Visual Organization Test (HVOT, Hooper, 1983)
Judgment of Line Orientation (Benton, Sivan, Hamsher, Varney, & Spreen, 1994)
Mattis DRS Construction subscale (Mattis, 1988)

Table continues

Table 3.3. (continued)

ROCF copy (Rey, 1941; Osterrieth, 1944)
Symbol digit modalities test (Smith, 1968)
WAIS-R Block Design (Wechsler, 1981)
WAIS-R Digit Symbol (Wechsler, 1981)
WAIS-R Object Assembly (Wechsler, 1981)
WAIS-R Performance IQ (Wechsler, 1981)
WAIS-R Picture Arrangement (Wechsler, 1981)
WAIS-R Picture Completion (Wechsler, 1981)

Manual dexterity
Purdue Pegboard (Purdue Research Foundation, no date)
Grooved Pegboard (Klove, 1963)
Finger Tapping Test (Reitan & Wolfson, 1993)
Grip Strength Test (Reitan & Wolfson, 1993)

research (Larrabee & Curtis, 1992; 1995; Larrabee, Kane, Schuck, & Francis, 1985; Leonberger, Nicks, Larrabee, & Goldfader, 1992), recently published neu ropsychological meta-analyses (e.g., Binder, Rohling, & Larrabee, 1997; Zakzanis, 1998b, c, g), and Lezak's (1995) theoretical and practice-related a pri ori classification. Thus, cognitive measures were assigned to one of seven domains. These included attention/concentration, memory acquisition, delayed recall, cognitive flexibility and abstraction, verbal skill, performance skill, and manual dexterity. The more general screening measures, such as the Mattis Dementia Rating Scale total score and the Mini Mental State Exam, were not included in the composite neuropsychological domains by virtue of their non-specific properties. Table 3.3 provides an index to the classification of the cog-nitive task and test variables reviewed parceled by neuropsychological domain. What follows is a brief description of the cognitive tasks and test variables that together, defined a particular neuropsychological domain.

Attention and concentration
Attention and concentration are basic cognitive functions involved to some degree in all test performances. Nonetheless, several tests make relatively mod-est demands on higher-level cognition and are regarded primarily as measures of attention, selection, concentration and vigilance. They include the Continuous Performance Tasks, which is a class of attentional tasks that all involve a requirement to respond to target and ignore non-target stimuli over a period of time (see Mirsky, 1989). Scores like target "hits", errors, and sensi-tivity measures based on signal detection theory are available for the test. In their analysis of the Continuous Performance Tasks, Van den Bosch, Rombouts, and Van Asma (1996) concluded that motor speed along with attentional mech-

anisms contribute to successful performance. The same almost certainly applies to the Trail Making Test Part A which Lezak (1995, pp. 382–384) considers an attentional task with perceptual and motor components. Completion time or errors were coded for Trail Making Test (Part A). In contrast, the Stroop Color and Word test does not require a manual response. Stroop word reading and color naming, but not the interference trial were included in the attention/concentration domain. Error, or reaction time in the congruent color-word conditions were collected from primary studies. Backward masking and dichotic listening, two experimental tasks of attention were also considered. Total score performance (i.e., number of correct responses and errors) was used to generate the effect sizes. Letter cancellation which requires visual selectivity at fast speed on a repetitive motor response task was also included in the attention/concentration domain. The basic format for these tests follows the vigilance test pattern (Lezak, 1995, p. 354). Scores collected included errors and time to completion. The Paced Auditory Serial Addition Test was also included in the attention/concentration domain. This test simply requires that the patient add 60 pairs of randomized digits so that each is added to the digit immediately preceding it (Lezak, 1995, p. 372). Effect sizes were derived in terms of the percentage of correct responses or the mean score (see Spreen & Strauss, 1998). The Seashore Rhythm Test, although used most widely for nonverbal auditory perception, is most useful as a measure of attention and concentration (Lezak, 1995, p. 422). Accordingly, the number of errors on the task was used to generate effect sizes. The Mental Control subtest from the Wechsler Memory Scale-Revised was also included in this domain. This three-item test of mental tracking has consistently been shown by two factor analytic studies (Bornstein & Chelune, 1988, 1989) to belong to the domain of attention. Total score on the subtest was used to calculate effect sizes. Finally, effect sizes derived from total scores from the Attention subscale of the Mattis Dementia Rating Scale was also included in the attention/concentration domain.

Memory acquisition
The neuropsychological domain of memory acquisition included those measures of span of immediate retention, short term retention with interference, learning in terms of extent of recent memory, how well newly learned material is retained after a short delay, and learning capacity. Both verbal and visual (or nonverbal) measures were included. Accordingly, appropriate test variables from the California Verbal Learning Test, Rey-Auditory Verbal Learning Test, Wechsler Memory Scale-Revised Logical Memory, Visual Reproduction, and Paired Associates subtests, Buschke's Selective Reminding Test, Consonant Trigrams, Mattis Dementia Rating Scale memory subscale, Wechsler Adult Intelligence Scale-Revised forward and backward Digit Span subtests, Corsi Block Tapping Test, Benton's Visual Retention Test, Tactual Performance Test, and Rey-Osterrieth Complex Figure task were gathered (see Table 3.3). Total scores for each variable measure always were used to derive the effect sizes.

Delayed recall

The neuropsychological domain of delayed recall included both verbal and non-verbal measures of retrieval and recognition of both recently learned and long stored information (i.e., remote memory). Appropriate test variables were gathered from Buschke's Selective Reminding Test, the California Verbal Learning Test, Rey Auditory Verbal Learning Test, Wechsler Memory Scale-Revised Logical Memory, Visual Reproduction, and Paired Associates subtests, the Rey-Osterrieth Complex Figure, Warrington's Word and Facial Recognition Tasks, the Presidents test, Famous Persons Test, and the Wechsler Adult Intelligence Scale-Revised Information subtest (see Table 3.3). Again, total scores (e.g., total number of words recalled on the California Verbal Learning Test long delay free recall) for each variable measure always produced the effect sizes.

Cognitive flexibility and abstraction

The cognitive flexibility and abstraction domain comprised several measures that were grouped based on their sensitivity to frontal lobe damage. Although most of these measures have been found to be sensitive to damage beyond the frontal cortex, their inclusion in the cognitive flexibility and abstraction domain seemed most fitting in keeping with previous definitions of frontal-executive function (see Lezak, 1995, Spreen & Strauss, 1998) and detailed neuroimaging-neuropsychological correlations (e.g., Stuss et al., 1998). According to Lezak (1995), frontal-executive functions can be conceptualized as having four components: (1) volition; (2) planning; (3) purposive action; and (4) effective performance. Accordingly, we included planning measures such as the Porteus Maze Test, the Tower of Hanoi, London, and Toronto, and Part B of the Trail Making Test. Purposive action measures included the constructional Tinkertoy test, phonemic fluency or the Controlled Oral Word Association Task, design fluency, the Mattis Dementia Rating Scale Initiation/Perseveration subscale, and go-no-go tasks. Moreover, the fourth component, effective performance, was thought to include those specific measures of abstraction (which might better be considered measures of concept formation and reasoning), and cognitive flexibility. Thus, we also included in the cognitive flexibility and abstraction domain all variables from the Wisconsin Card Sorting Test, the interference trial effect from the Stroop where subjects have to name the ink color that the dissonant color word is printed in, the Category test, total score on Raven's Progressive Matrices, and the Similarities and Arithmetic subtests from the Wechsler Adult Intelligence Scale-Revised.

Verbal skill

In the domain of verbal skill, measures of comprehension (which could have easily been classified as measures of cognitive flexibility and abstraction), naming, vocabulary, semantic fluency, and reading ability were combined. General aphasia screening measures were also included in the verbal skill domain. These included the Boston Diagnostic Aphasia Examination, the Multilingual Aphasia Examination, and the Western Aphasia Battery. Their product always included a wide range of tasks so that the nature and severity of the language problem and associated deficits in a patient sample may be determined. Both specific scores (e.g., Boston Naming Test performance) and index scores (e.g., Western Aphasia Battery Aphasia Quotient) were gathered. Similarly, we included here the Wechsler Adult Intelligence Scale-Revised Verbal Intelligence Quotient (IQ). It should be noted that the Verbal IQ (as well as the Performance IQ) are based on averages of some quite dissimilar functions that have relatively low inter-correlations and bear no regular neuroanatomical or neuropsychological rela-tionship to one another (Lezak, 1995, p. 690). As such, subtest components of the Verbal IQ, like the Similarities subtest, reach far beyond the domain of ver-bal skill. This highlights the need to present effect sizes related to independent task and test variables. Accordingly, specific measures of verbal skill included comprehension tasks such as the Token Test and the Comprehension subtest from the Wechsler Adult Intelligence Scale-Revised. Total scores were used to derive effect sizes. Naming measures were always indexed with the Boston Naming Test. Total scores were again used to produce effect sizes. Vocabulary measures varied considerably. We computed effect sizes based on total scores from the Mill Hill Vocabulary Scale, the nonverbal Peabody Picture Vocabulary Test, and the Vocabulary subtest from the Wechsler Adult Intelligence Scale-Revised. Semantic fluency was also included in the domain of verbal skill. This task simply asks the patient to generate as many words belonging to a specific semantic category (e.g., animals) over the period of one minute. Effect sizes were based on the total number of words generated. Finally, reading ability effect sizes were computed from total scores on the National Adult Reading Test and the Wide Range Adult Achievement Test-Revised.

Performance skill
The broad rubric "performance skill" was used to represent visuospatial, visuoperceptual, and constructional ability measures. These included four tests from Benton's laboratory: Facial Recognition, Judgment of Line Orientation, Finger Localization, and the ability to copy Visual Retention Test figures (see Benton, Sivan, Hamsher, Varney, & Spreen, 1994). Total performance scores from each of the measures were used to generate effect sizes. All Wechsler Adult Intelligence Scale-Revised performance subtests were included in this domain. These included the Block Design, Digit Symbol, Object Assembly, Picture Arrangement, and Picture Completion subtests. The composite Wechsler Adult Intelligence Scale-Revised Performance IQ was also included. Total scores on these subtests were also used to generate effect sizes. It should be noted that the Wechsler Adult Intelligence Scale-Revised performance subtests are largely time-dependent. That is, poor performance scores on these measures may arise from slowed performance and not from a higher order cognitive impairment. Thus, the domain of performance skill was titled as such to reflect the possibility of defective performance arising from non-visuospatial, visuoperceptual, or visuo-constructional abilities but from slowed cognitive or motoric processing as well. Where appropriate, we have interpreted the performance skill measure effect

sizes qualitatively to distinguish a higher order impairment from poor performance due to slowed reaction time. Also included in the performance skill domain was the Symbol Digit Modalities Test which preserves the substitution format of Wechsler's Digit Symbol test, but reverses the presentation of the material so that the symbols are printed and the numbers are written in (Smith, 1968; see also Lezak, 1995, p. 379). This format not only enables the patient to respond with the more familiar act of number writing but also allows a spoken response trial. In keeping with the visuomotor component, only "written" performance scores were used to generate effect sizes and included in the domain of performance skill. Moreover, the ability to copy the Rey-Osterrieth Complex Figure, a clock, and the Bender Gestalt figures were also used to index visuospatial, visuoperceptual, and visuoconstructional integrity. Total scores were again used to generate effect sizes. Finally, effect sizes based on total performance scores for the visuoperceptual Hooper Visual Organization Test was also included in the domain of performance skill.

Manual dexterity

Finally, the manual dexterity domain was made up of effect sizes from both Purdue and Grooved pegboard scores (total time to completion), Finger Tapping Test total scores, and Grip Strength Test scores. These tests were combined as they all measure manipulative agility, and/or are all timed speeded tests that may aid in the detection of a lateralized disability (see Lezak, 1995).

Taken together, these seven neuropsychological domains were used to organize the discussion of the cognitive deficits in each disorder reviewed. Again, each chapter is organized by neuropsychological domain according to the order in which the domain is most to least impaired for a specific syndrome. The reader can find a more concise quantitative summary in table format of the rank-order of neuropsychological domains for each of the specific syndromes in a summary chapter (see Chapter 15).

Chapter 4

DEMENTIA OF THE ALZHEIMER'S TYPE

In 1907 Alois Alzheimer published a case report describing the cerebral cortex of a 55-year-old woman with a progressive dementia (Alzheimer, 1977). The patient that Alzheimer described manifested persecutory delusions, had impaired memory, and could not find her way about her own apartment. Her language abnormalities included a naming disturbance, paraphasic substitutions, and impaired comprehension. In contrast, she did not display an abnormal gait, incoordination, and her reflexes were unaffected. She gradually deteriorated and died after 4.5 years of hospitalization. At autopsy, the brain appeared grossly atrophic. Microscopic study revealed cortical cell loss, neurofibrillary degenerative changes involving many of the neurons, and numerous miliary foci (neuritic plaques) throughout the cortex. Although the progressive clinical and pathological features then described by Alzheimer are now considered classic characteristics of the disease (Cummings & Benson, 1992; Cummings & Kaufer, 1996; Parks, Zec, & Wilson, 1993), it has more recently been conceptualized as an aetiologically heterogeneous disorder (Cummings & Khachaturian, 1996; Friedland, 1993). This heterogeneity, however, may indeed resolve as finer diagnostic markers based on clinical features are identified that can aid in the differential diagnosis of Alzheimer's disease from other disorders of dementia (e.g., fronto-temporal dementia; see Snowden, Neary, & Mann, 1996; Zakzanis, 1998c).

Today, dementia of the Alzheimer's type (DAT) is the most well known of all dementing disorders and probably accounts for 35 to 60% of progressive dementias evaluated in hospital based settings (Cummings & Benson, 1992). It is well recognized that patients with DAT undergo steadily progressive intellectual deterioration. Indeed, the sequence in which higher cognitive functions are lost and the temporal order in which behavioral and neurologic disabilities occur are important clues for establishing the clinical diagnosis (see Bondi, Salmon, & Kaszniak, 1996; Corey-Bloom et al., 1995; Drachman, O'Donnell, Lew, & Swearer, 1990; Rasmusson, Carson, Brookmeyer, Kawas, & Brandt, 1996). The principle cognitive alterations in early stages of the disease include memory disturbance, visuospatial impairment, and language difficulties. More specifically, the initial memory disturbance in DAT is characterized by impaired ability to learn new material and mild difficulty recalling remote information and is nearly always the first intellectual deficit noted by the patient's family or co-workers (Lishman, 1987; Sjogren, 1950; Stengel, 1943). Like memory, visuospatial skills are often impaired (Adams & Victor, 1977; Sim & Sussman, 1962) as patients commonly get lost in familiar environments, lose their way while driving, and may eventually become disoriented in their own homes (Cummings & Benson, 1992). Finally, language changes are sensitive indicators of cortical dysfunction, and the specific pattern of linguistic disturbance aids in the diagnosis of DAT. The first abnormalities to become apparent in spontaneous speech are impaired word finding and circumlocution imparting an empty quality to the verbalizations (Benson, 1979; Goodman, 1953; Rothschild, 1934; Whitworth & Larson, 1989).

The diagnosis of Alzheimer's disease and study inclusion criteria

There are three widely used criteria-based approaches to the diagnosis of DAT: the International Classification of Diseases, 10th Edition (ICD–10; World Health Organization, 1992), the Diagnostic and Statistical Manual of Mental Disorders, 4th Edition (DSM-IV; American Psychiatric Association, 1994), and the National Institute of Neurological and Communicative Disorders and Stroke-Alzheimer's Disease and Related Disorders Association Work Group criteria (NINCDS-ADRDA; McKhann, Drachman, Folstein, Katzman, Price, & Stadlan, 1984). Not surprisingly, the three definitions share many common features (see Cummings & Khachaturian, 1996 for a summary).

For an article to be considered in the present review, the diagnosis of DAT must have been based on the NINCDS-ADRDA Work Group criteria for the clinical diagnosis of "probable" Alzheimer's disease (McKhann, Drachman, Folstein, Katzman, Price, & Stadlan, 1984). According to the criteria, probable Alzheimer's disease is characterized by the presence of dementia established by a questionnaire and confirmed by neuropsychological testing, deficits in two or more areas of cognition, including progressive worsening of memory and other cognitive functions, no disturbance of consciousness, onset between 40 and 90 years of age, and absence of systemic disorders or brain diseases that could account for the memory and cognitive deficits. Dementia is defined in these criteria by decline in memory and other cognitive functions, in comparison with premorbid level of function. NINCDS-ADRDA Work Group study inclusion criteria was preferred in accord with its demonstrated reliability (Farrer et al., 1994; Kukull, Larson, Reifler, Lampe, Yerby, & Hughes, 1990; Lopez et al., 1990; however see Baldereschi et al., 1994 who suggest that the NINCDS-ADRDA "probable" and "possible" categories be merged) and validity (Blacker, Albert, Bassett, Go, Harrell, & Folstein, 1994; Tierney et al., 1988). Accordingly, the literature was searched for primary articles back to 1984 as it corresponded to the introduction of the NINCDS-ADRDA criteria.

The review

One hundred ninety-nine studies published between 1984 and 1997 met criteria for inclusion in the present analysis. In total, cognitive test results from 7,156 patients with DAT and 8,772 normal healthy controls were recorded across primary studies.

Descriptive demographic and clinical variable data available from primary studies from the published literature are presented in Table 4.1 for patients with DAT. The table indicates a slightly increased occurrence of DAT among females in patient samples (54.4%). It is generally accepted, however, that gender has little influence on the prevalence or incidence of DAT as the increased prevalence among women reported in early studies probably reflected the relative longevity of women and a disproportionate number of females surviving into the period of greater risk for the disease (Cummings & Benson, 1992; Sulkava et al., 1985). Moreover, at the time of most primary studies, the modal patient with DAT was approximately 72 years of age with a 12 grade education. The average age at disease onset was estimated at approximately 64 years. The mean duration of illness was approximately 4 years. Patients with DAT were typically non medicated, although the rising popularity of cognitive enhancers (e.g.,

Table 4.1.   Descriptive Statistics for Alzheimer's Disease Cognitive Studies.

Variables	M	SD	Range	N
Sample size				
DAT samples	36	41	6–354	199
Control samples	44	91	5–990	199
Patients' age	71.6	4.4	61.7–86.9	192
Onset age	63.6	10.8	23.0–72.4	18
Duration of illness (yrs.)	3.8	1.4	0.6–7.0	44
Percentage of males	45.6	16.8	0.0–100	134
Patients' education (yrs.)	12.5	2.3	5.1–18.0	162
Percentage on medication	2.2	4.9	0–11	5

Note. M = mean; SD = standard deviation of the mean; N = number of studies in which the variable was reported.

Aricept) will perhaps change the composition of pharmacotherapy usage in patients with DAT in future studies.

A number of demographic and clinical variables correlated significantly to the cognitive task effect sizes. Table 4.2 includes each of these significant product moment correlations. A positive correlation can be interpreted to reflect greater deficit on the cognitive task as related to increases of the demographic or clinical variable. A negative correlation reflects greater impairment on the cognitive task as related to decreases of the demographic or clinical variable. For example, as Alzheimer's disease progresses, greater effect sizes (or, greater impairment) on the Boston Naming Test and on forward and backward WAIS-R digit span are apparent (see Table 4.2). From the table it can also be seen that poorer performance on several WAIS-R indices including the Information, Vocabulary, and Similarities subtests, and Verbal and Performance IQ, are related to the age of the patient with DAT. That is, the older the patient gets, the worse the patient does on these cognitive tasks. Further, education is inversely tied to WAIS-R Full Scale, Performance and Verbal IQ, as the number of years of formal education is related to larger effects on the composite WAIS-R variables (also see Filley & Cullum, 1997). A limited education is also related significantly to the patient's ability to copy the Rey-Osterrieth Complex Figure and to quickly connect an array of numbers scattered across a page [(i.e., Trail Making Test (Part A)]. Finally, as the number of males included in patient sample increases, greater effect sizes on the Boston Naming Test are obtained. Taken together, these relationships underscore the fact that DAT is a progressive disease, with a pattern of deficits that may change in an individual patient over

Table 4.2.   Significant Clinical and Demographic Moderators of Effect in Patients with Alzheimer's Disease.

Clinical or demographic variable	Cognitive task	Pearson Correlation (sample size)
Age	WAIS-R Verbal IQ	$r = .69$ ($n = 12$)
Age	WAIS-R Performance IQ	$r = .61$ ($n = 12$)
Age	WAIS-R Information	$r = .70$ ($n = 13$)
Age	WAIS-R Vocabulary	$r = .57$ ($n = 18$)
Age	WAIS-R Similarities	$r = .53$ ($n = 16$)
Duration of illness	Boston Naming Test	$r = .68$ ($n = 10$)
Duration of illness	WAIS-R Forward digit span	$r = .81$ ($n = 10$)
Duration of illness	WAIS-R Backward digit span	$r = .86$ ($n = 11$)
Education	WAIS-R Full scale IQ	$r = -.56$ ($n = 17$)
Education	WAIS-R Verbal IQ	$r = -.62$ ($n = 11$)
Education	WAIS-R Performance IQ	$r = -.74$ ($n = 11$)
Education	Rey-Osterrieth Complex Figure Copy	$r = -.71$ ($n = 10$)
Education	Trail Making Test Part A	$r = .62$ ($n = 16$)
Percent male	Boston Naming Test	$r = .34$ ($n = 38$)

Note. All Pearson correlations correspond to $p < .05$.

time. For research purposes, it is therefore important to control for disease stage as indicated by its duration.

Cognitive deficits in dementia of the Alzheimer's type

Effect size summaries are presented for specific cognitive tasks and test variables in Table 4.3. Mean *d*'s presented in the column are the raw effect sizes. Test variables are presented according to the rank order of the effect size. Effect sizes are included along with the corresponding standard deviation and the number of effect sizes used to calculate the mean *d*. To help describe the dispersion of effect sizes, a minimum and maximum *d* value are also presented. The table also includes the Fail Safe N (Nfs) for the number of additional studies that would be necessary to reverse the overall probability obtained from our obtained effect size to a value higher than our critical value for statistical significance, which was set at .01 (see Wolf, 1986 for an elaboration). Chapter 15 [Table 15.1] includes similar statistics for the composite neuropsychological domains. The following description of cognitive task and test variable effect sizes are grouped by domain and presented in the order of most to least impaired in DAT.

Table 4.3   Effect Size Results in Rank Order for Patients with Dementia of the Alzheimer's Type.

Neuropsychological Test/ Test Variable	N *d*	M *d*	SD *d*	Min. *d*	Max. *d*	Nfs	OL % (approx.)
WMS-R Memory Quotient	7	−4.64	1.26	−3.16	−6.16	3241	
Buschke SRT delayed recall	4	−4.63	2.39	−1.99	−7.41	1848	
CVLT long delay free recall	4	−4.47	1.59	−3.02	−6.72	1784	
CVLT long delay cued recall	3	−4.02	0.42	−3.54	−4.30	1203	< 2.0
CVLT short delay free recall	4	−3.90	0.43	−3.35	−4.38	1556	
Mattis DRS memory scale	10	−3.77	0.89	−2.58	−5.05	3760	
Rey-Osterrieth Complex Figure delayed recall	7	−3.74	0.93	−2.95	−5.70	2611	
CVLT short delay cued recall	4	−3.47	0.99	−2.67	−4.92	1384	
CVLT total recall trials 1–5	4	−3.40	1.08	−1.93	−4.49	1356	
WMS-R Logical Memory II delayed recall	26	−3.36	1.32	−0.85	−7.72	8375	
RAVLT delayed recall	3	−3.31	2.36	−1.79	−6.03	990	
Buschke SRT total recall	10	−3.11	0.80	−1.90	−4.39	3100	
Mattis DRS Total Score	64	−3.11	1.40	−2.09	−8.67	19840	
WMS-R Visual Reproduction II delayed recall	14	−3.01	1.18	−1.00	−5.31	4200	
CVLT recognition	3	−3.00	0.92	−2.32	−4.05	897	< 5.0
CVLT list A trial 5	2	−2.94	0.54	−2.56	−3.32	586	
CVLT false recognition	1	2.74	–	2.74	2.74	273	
Mini Mental State Exam	105	−2.73	2.60	−2.10	−6.92	28560	
CVLT list B	1	−2.66	–	−2.66	−2.66	265	

Table continues

Table 4.3. (continued)

Neuropsychological Test/ Test Variable	N d	M d	SD d	Min. d	Max. d	Nfs	OL % (approx.)
Rey-Osterrieth Complex Figure immediate reproduction	9	−2.64	1.13	−0.69	−4.14	2367	
RAVLT trial 1	5	−2.60	1.54	−1.27	−5.16	1295	
WMS-R Logical Memory I immediate recall	37	−2.59	0.93	−0.47	−4.93	9546	
Semantic fluency	28	−2.49	0.81	−1.24	−3.92	6944	15.0
WAIS-R Arithmetic	5	−2.39	1.41	−1.06	−4.19	1190	
WMS-R Visual Reproduction I immediate recall	16	−2.35	0.97	−0.38	−4.23	3744	
Stroop color word reading	1	−2.30	−	−2.30	−2.30	229	
Trail Making Test Part B	15	2.25	1.86	0.256	6.32	3360	
WAIS-R Full scale IQ	23	−2.16	1.09	−0.29	−5.11	4945	
WAIS-R Performance IQ	12	−2.14	1.51	−0.18	−5.59	2556	
WAIS-R Picture Arrangement	5	−2.09	1.08	−1.16	−3.64	1040	
Tinker Toy Test	1	−2.08	−	−2.08	−2.08	207	
CVLT list A trial 1	1	−2.05	−	−2.05	−2.05	204	20.0
Buschke SRT recognition	1	−1.95	−	−1.95	−1.95	194	
WAIS-R Block Design	26	−1.94	1.26	−0.19	−6.29	5018	
WMS-R Paired Associates I & II	14	−1.87	1.01	−0.12	−3.60	2604	
Raven's Progressive Matrices	11	−1.78	0.54	−0.86	−2.89	1947	
WAIS-R Digit Symbol	14	−1.78	0.69	−0.63	−3.26	2478	
Stroop interference	8	−1.77	1.24	−0.17	−3.12	1408	
RAVLT trial 5	2	−1.75	0.24	−1.58	−1.92	348	
Corsi spatial span	6	−1.72	0.21	−1.44	−2.10	1026	
WCST categories achieved	5	−1.72	0.90	−0.84	−2.98	855	
Boston Naming Test	55	−1.64	0.75	−0.20	−4.66	8965	
Hooper Visual Organization Test	2	−1.63	0.23	−1.46	−1.79	324	
Symbol digit modalities test	1	−1.60	−	−1.60	−1.60	159	
Mattis DRS Initiation/ Perseveration scale	9	−1.56	0.58	−0.67	−2.41	1395	
Judgment of Line Orientation	3	−1.55	1.60	−0.12	−3.29	462	
CVLT cued recall intrusions	2	1.53	0.05	1.51	1.54	304	
WAIS-R Verbal IQ	12	−1.53	1.00	0.02	−3.13	1824	
Benton Visual Retention Test number of errors	7	1.50	1.22	1.00	3.33	1043	30.0
COWAT	59	−1.50	0.82	−1.41	−3.19	8791	
Rey-Osterrieth Complex Figure copy	11	−1.44	0.51	−0.81	−2.54	1573	
WAIS-R Information	13	−1.44	0.66	−0.34	−2.39	1859	
Token Test	7	1.40	0.95	1.10	1.90	973	
WAIS-R Similarities	17	−1.40	0.56	−0.30	−2.16	2363	
Peabody Picture Vocabulary Test	1	−1.39	−	−1.39	−1.39	138	
Benton Facial Recognition	8	−1.39	0.78	−0.46	−2.78	1104	
Clock Drawing Testto command	8	−1.39	0.52	−0.40	−2.07	1104	
Blessed Dementia Rating Scale	9	1.38	0.49	1.11	1.88	1233	
CVLT semantic clustering	2	−1.38	0.32	−1.15	−1.6	274	
WAIS-R comprehension	8	−1.29	0.67	−0.26	−2.13	1024	
Mattis DRS conceptualization	9	−1.28	0.70	−0.09	−2.75	1143	
Letter Cancellation	3	1.23	0.11	1.12	1.33	366	
WMS-R Mental Control	4	−1.16	1.04	−0.15	−2.57	460	
WAIS-R Digit Span backward	33	−1.15	0.56	−0.36	−2.25	3762	
Trail Making Test Part A	22	1.13	0.86	−1.65	2.70	2464	

Table continues

Table 4.3. (continued)

Neuropsychological Test/ Test Variable	N d	M d	SD d	Min. d	Max. d	Nfs	OL % (approx.)
WAIS-R Vocabulary	18	−1.12	0.45	−0.60	−2.25	1998	
Buschke SRT intrusions	2	1.09	0.43	0.78	1.39	216	
WCST perseverative errors	3	1.07	0.45	0.64	1.54	318	
WCST perseverative responses	4	1.07	0.38	0.63	1.52	424	
WAIS-R Picture Completion	5	−1.03	0.26	−0.74	−1.36	510	
Mattis DRS Attention scale	10	−1.02	0.40	−0.53	−1.67	1010	
Continuous Performance Task response inhibition	4	−1.01	0.49	−0.55	−1.40	400	
Finger Tapping Test left hand	3	1.01	0.35	0.69	1.38	300	
Design fluency	1	−1.00	–	−1.00	−1.00	99	45.0
WCST nonperseverative errors	2	0.99	0.68	0.50	1.47	196	
WAIS-R Object Assembly	3	−0.98	0.23	−0.72	−1.14	291	
WCST errors	2	0.93	0.60	0.50	1.35	184	
RAVLT recognition	3	−0.91	0.67	−0.42	−1.68	273	
RAVLT intrusions	1	0.88	–	0.88	0.88	87	
WRAT-R reading	4	−0.87	0.35	−0.40	−1.19	344	
Porteus Mazes	8	−0.86	2.17	−0.11	−3.11	680	
Finger Tapping Test right hand	3	0.85	0.46	0.53	1.38	252	
Clock Drawing copy	2	−0.84	0.20	−0.70	−0.98	166	
WAIS-R Digit Span forward	36	−0.82	0.49	0.33	−1.96	2916	
Go-No-Go	1	0.79	–	0.79	0.79	78	
CVLT free recall intrusions	4	0.76	0.50	0.37	1.19	300	
Geriatric Depression Scale	6	0.64	1.14	−0.36	2.75	378	
Grooved Pegboard right hand	1	0.61		0.61	0.61	56	
Grooved Pegboard left hand	1	0.57	–	0.57	0.57	56	
Mattis DRS Construction scale	9	−0.51	0.44	0.00	−1.06	450	65.0
Benton Visual Retention Test copy	4	0.48	0.86	−0.63	1.43	188	
WCST failure to maintain set	2	0.44	0.13	0.35	0.53	86	
CVLT perseverations	1	0.42	–	0.42	0.42	41	
National Adult Reading Test	17	−0.39	0.62	0.67	−1.59	646	
Stroop word reading	3	0.38	1.96	−1.81	1.97	111	
Hamilton Depression Rating Scale	6	−0.30	1.10	1.69	−2.52	174	
Beck Depression Inventory	7	0.27	0.48	−0.59	0.76	182	
Continuous Performance Task simple condition	4	−0.20	0.16	−0.01	−0.32	76	
Tower of Hanoi	1	0.07	–	0.07	0.07	6	> 95.0

Note. Nd = number of effect sizes; Md = mean effect size; SDd = standard deviation around the effect size; Min.d = smallest effect size obtained; Max.d = largest effect size obtained; Nfs = fail safe N; SRT = Selective Reminding Test; DRS = Dementia Rating Scale; CVLT = California Verbal Learning Test; RAVLT = Rey Auditory Verbal Learning Test; WAIS-R = Wechsler Adult Intelligence Scale-Revised; WMS-R = Wechsler Memory Scale-Revised; COWAT = Controlled Oral Word Association Task; WCST = Wisconsin Card Sorting Test.

Delayed recall

The cardinal neuropsychological feature of DAT is a profound, global amnesia (Zec, 1993). Correspondingly, a disproportionate decline in memory function relative to other cognitive domains is among the most salient features that distinguish DAT from other dementia or neuropsychiatric states (Moss & Albert, 1992). Indeed, performance on measures of delayed recall correspond to the largest effect sizes in Table 4.3 and the most impaired neuropsychological domain in DAT (see Chapter 15, Table 15.1).

In keeping with the early stages of DAT, there is an anterograde amnesia, which impairs the encoding and storage of new information resulting in severe and progressive difficulty in learning and retaining new episodic information. As such, delayed recall on measures such as the Buschke Selective Reminding Test (BSRT), California Verbal Learning Test (CVLT), Rey-Osterrieth Complex Figure (ROCF), Logical Memory and Visual Reproduction subtests of the Wechsler Memory Scale-Revised (WMS-R), and the Rey Auditory Verbal Learning Test (RAVLT), all correspond to effect sizes greater than 3.0 (OL%, 5). This suggests that, for the above mentioned measures, approximately all patients with DAT can be discriminated from healthy normal controls based on long delay recall test score dispersion. Indeed, Welsh, Butters, Hughes, Mohs, and Heyman (1992) have noted that delayed recall is the most sensitive measure to early or mild DAT, as it reflects both a failure to learn over multiple practice trials and a failure to retain over time. Further, Zakzanis (1998b, e) has shown that delayed recall measures are more sensitive to the integrity of temporal-hippocampal function in DAT than structural and functional neuroimaging measures (also see O'Brien, 1995). Thus, each of the above mentioned measures of delayed recall meets heuristic benchmark criteria ($d = -3.0$ OL% = 5) that can signify, or mark, the presence of Alzheimer's disease (see Zakzanis, 1998b, e). Because even mildly demented patients often have severe memory deficits that result in near floor performance on tests of delayed recall, consequently, measures of recognition memory, verbal fluency, confrontation naming, and praxis may be better suited for staging dementia severity or tracking its progression once a diagnosis of probable DAT has been made (Bondi, Salmon, & Kaszniak, 1996).

A smaller mean effect size across recognition measures was obtained ($d = -1.95$ OL% = 19). There is considerable variability, however, in keeping with the sensitivity of recognition measures. For example, recognition on the RAVLT corresponds to an effect of $-.91$ (OL% = 48), whereas recognition on Buschke's SRT corresponds to a considerably larger effect size ($d = -1.95$ OL% = 19), but not as large as that obtained on the CVLT ($d = -3.00$ OL%, 5). This discrepancy may reflect the inability of patients with DAT to benefit from semantically related list learning items during encoding and free recall (i.e., CVLT semantic clustering $d = -1.38$ OL% = 33). This interpretation is supported by the finding that greater effects are obtained on CVLT measures that aid in the encoding process, compared to RAVLT measures that do not (see Table 4.3). Moreover, the presence of semantically and phonemically related items on the CVLT recognition trial might further impair performance in patients with DAT as the mean obtained effect for false recognition on the CVLT corresponds to a large effect of 2.74 (also see Moss, Albert, Butters & Payne, 1986, for a discussion of recognition memory for different classes of stimuli).

With respect to verbal and nonverbal delayed recall measures, a significant discrepancy between effect sizes is not apparent from Table 4.3. This is in contrast to a previous narrative review of this literature that suggests nonverbal measures to be decreased to a greater extent than are verbal measures in DAT (e.g., Nixon, 1996). As Zec (1993) noted, because memory systems in both cerebral hemispheres are typically damaged in DAT, both verbal and nonverbal memories are impaired. If there is a large discrepancy between these memories, and thus, possibly a lateralized cerebral involvement, Zec suggests that a diagnosis other than DAT should be considered (such as stroke).

Finally, semantic memory as indexed with the Information subtest from the WAIS-R corresponds to a much smaller effect size of -1.44 (OL% = 31) suggesting relatively less impaired retrieval of overlearned information compared to episodic memory. Retrieving overlearned information is part of one's general fund of knowledge and does not depend on temporal and spatial contextual cues for retrieval (Martin, 1992). As performance on the Information subtest is significantly related to the age of the patient with DAT, and therefore to the duration of disease, however, progressive impairment in semantic memory is expected to occur as the patient ages and the disease evolves. Thus, the WAIS-R Information subtest may be suited for staging dementia severity and/or tracking its progression. Moreover, other tasks that can be considered measures of semantic memory, such as vocabulary and verbal fluency, are discussed below under verbal skill and cognitive flexibility and abstraction.

Memory acquisition
The second most defective neuropsychological domain in DAT is memory acquisition (see Chapter 15, Table 15.1). Indeed, poor learning appears regularly in the initial stages of the disease and is nearly always the first intellectual deficit noted by the patient's family or workmates (Cummings & Benson, 1992; Lishman, 1978). Neuropsychological investigations indicate that these patients have difficulty encoding information as it is rapidly lost from short-term memory and storage for eventual recall is compromised (Miller, 1971, 1972). As such, performance on measures of memory acquisition is compromised. For example, an effect size of -3.40 (OL%, 5) was obtained for total recall across list A trials 1–5 on the CVLT. This effect size corresponds to heuristic benchmark criteria which reflects absolute discriminability in test scores between patients with DAT and healthy normal controls. Total recall across list A trials 1–5 on the CVLT may then, mark the presence of DAT. Further, total recall on list A trial 5 also approached benchmark criteria ($d = -2.94$ OL% = 8), which might also aid in the recognition of DAT. Again, it is believed that a discrepancy between effects on CVLT and RAVLT list A trial 5 recall ($d = -2.94$ CVLT vs. $d = -1.75$ RAVLT) reflects the inability of patients with DAT to benefit from semantically related list learning items during encoding and free recall (see Zakzanis, Leach, & Kaplan, 1998).

More qualitatively, patients with DAT have been reported to display a reduced primacy effect and an exaggerated recency effect for recall of list learning items on the CVLT (see Morris & Baddeley, 1988). The presence of a reduced primacy effect and an exaggerated recency effect, however, are not helpful in the differential diagnosis of the dementias because all memory disorders tend to show this pattern (Zec, 1993).

Large effect sizes were also obtained on visual memory acquisition tasks (see Table 4.3). For example, test scores for immediate reproduction of the Rey-Osterrieth Complex Figure correspond to 90% nonoverlap between patients and healthy normal controls ($d = -2.64$). Test performance on immediate visual reproduction of the WMS-R figures was also quite sensitive to the presence of DAT, as the obtained effect size of -2.35 was able to discriminate 85% of patients from healthy normal controls. Finally, on measures of span, patients with DAT performed more poorly on the more visual-spatial demanding Corsi-block tapping task ($d = -1.72$ OL% = 25) compared to verbal digit-span on the WAIS-R ($d = -1.15$ OL% = 40 backward & $d = -0.82$ OL% = 53 forward).

Verbal skill

Measures of verbal and or language skill are the next most sensitive indices to DAT (see Chapter 15, Table 15.1). Verbal and language deficits occasionally precede general cognitive decline, and more often become evident 1 to 3 years after onset of DAT, and thereafter are clearly progressive (Sjogren, Sjogren, & Lindren, 1952). An anomic aphasia typically is evident early in the course of the disease (Kertesz, 1979). Anomic aphasia involves naming difficulty in the context of relatively intact speech fluency, auditory comprehension, articulation, prosody, and repetition (Cummings & Benson, 1992; Zec, 1993). Although many studies have demonstrated impaired confrontational naming ability in patients with DAT, mild patients are sometimes not significantly impaired (Zec, 1993). As such, even if a large, mean effect size was obtained for the Boston Naming Test ($d = -1.64$ OL% = 26), depending on the sample of patients, it was unreliable across studies. The range of effects ($d = -0.20/-4.66$) clearly supports the notion that word-finding difficulty is not always pathognomic of DAT as the mean effect size across accumulated studies does not meet heuristic benchmark criteria. In other words, the Boston Naming Test does not discriminate reliably patients with DAT from healthy normal controls based on test score dispersion. Qualitatively, patients differ. The presence of semantic paraphasias (e.g., "plane" for "helicopter") and circumlocutions (e.g., "horse with a horn" for "unicorn"), however, appear relatively often during early stage evaluation of naming ability, whereas phonemic paraphasias (e.g., "harmotica" for "harmonica") and phonemic transpositions only appear in the later stages of the disease (Appell, Kertesz, & Fishman, 1982). Such dissociation in the qualitative aspects of confrontational naming errors can aid in the differentiation of DAT from other disorders with prominent features of language dysfunction (e.g., primary progressive aphasia – see chapter 6).

Measures of comprehension correspond to much smaller effect sizes (e.g., d = 1.40 OL% = 32 Token Test) relative to confrontational naming effect sizes. Thus, measures of comprehension such as the Token Test are not likely to aid in the early differentiation of DAT. Comprehension deficits become more severe as the dementia progresses however, and, consequently, the patient with Alzheimer's disease increasingly resembles a transcortical sensory aphasic (Cummings & Benson, 1992). As the disease evolves further, repetition declines in the late stages of the disease and then the language disorder more closely resembles a Wernicke's aphasia (Cummings, Benson, Hill, & Read, 1985). During the final stages of the disease, the patient with DAT may display a more global aphasia (Appell, Kertesz, & Fishman, 1982). Thus, the sensitivity of comprehension measures will increase in keeping with disease duration.

Generative naming or word fluency tasks, along with episodic memory tasks, are among the most sensitive measures for differentiating patients with mild DAT from healthy normal controls (Storandt, Botwinick, Danziger, Berg, & Hughes, 1984). Word fluency is typically measured by the quantity of words produced, usually within a restricted category or in response to a stimulus, and usually within a time limit (Lezak, 1995). These tests are commonly used in the evaluation of suspected dementia because they have proven useful in the early detection of DAT and because they are very brief and easy to administer. Two commonly used variants of generative naming, each sensitive to differing anatomic loci, are phonemic and semantic word fluency. The latter task requires the patient to generate examples of a particular semantic category (i.e., animal names), whereas the former task requires the patient to generate words that begin with a given letter (i.e., F. A. S.). It has been shown that semantic fluency is sensitive to temporal lobe function whereas phonemic fluency is sensitive to frontal lobe function (see Martin, Loring, Meador, & Lee, 1990; Micheli, Caltagirone, Gainotti, Masullo, & Silveri, 1981). In keeping with the distribution of pathophysiological alterations in Alzheimer's disease, a larger mean effect size was obtained for semantic fluency (d = –2.49 OL% = 12) compared to that obtained for phonemic fluency (d = –1.50 OL% = 29). Thus, semantic word fluency may be considerably more useful than phonemic word fluency in the differential diagnosis of patients with DAT. When the differential diagnosis includes other disorders with prominent features of language disorder, however, such as primary progressive aphasia, double dissociation of phonemic and semantic word fluency effect sizes can aid in establishing the probable diagnosis of DAT (i.e., phonemic effects > semantic effects in primary progressive aphasia; semantic effects > phonemic effect in DAT). Moreover, phonemic word fluency may also be useful for eliciting intrusion errors to help confirm the diagnosis of DAT because patients with Alzheimer's disease tend to lose set (derailment) on this task (e.g., to the letter "p", saying pears, then apples). Patients also tend to make more repetitions and make more semantic errors (e.g., giving cities for the category "states") than healthy normal controls on generative naming tasks (Zec, 1993).

Finally, WAIS-R Vocabulary subtest effect sizes correspond to considerable overlap between patients and healthy normal controls ($d = -1.12$ OL% $= 41$). As performance on the WAIS-R Vocabulary subtest is significantly related to the age of the patient with DAT, and therefore to the duration of disease, however, progressive impairment in test performance is expected to occur as the patient ages and the disease evolves. Thus, the WAIS-R Vocabulary subtest is yet another measure suited for staging dementia severity and/or tracking its progression.

Performance skill

Performance skill measures including those of visuospatial, visuoperceptual, and constructional ability are often employed in the evaluation of dementia and Alzheimer's disease because neuropathological studies (Brun & Gustafson, 1976) and brain imaging studies (Jernigan, Salmon, Butters, & Hesselink, 1991; Kidron et al., 1997; Parks, Haxby, & Grady, 1993; Tikofsky, Hellman, & Parks, 1993) demonstrate that by about the middle stages of the disease, disproportionate structural and functional alterations in posterior cortical areas (including the parietal lobe) gives rise to such deficits (Adams, Victor, & Ropper, 1997; Cummings & Benson, 1992). As such, neuropsychological measures of performance skill are the next most sensitive indices to Alzheimer's dementia (see Chapter 15, Table 15.1).

The most sensitive performance skill measure to DAT is the composite WAIS-R Performance IQ ($d = -2.14$ OL% $= 18$). Because Performance IQ scores are based on averages of some quite dissimilar functions that have relatively low intercorrelations and bear no regular neuroanatomical or neuropsychological relationship to one another (Cohen, 1957; Lezak, 1995; Parsons, Vega, & Burn, 1969), however, caution should be exercised in drawing inferences about neuropsychological status (Lezak, 1988). Note that the obtained mean effect size for Performance IQ is larger than that obtained for the composite WAIS-R Verbal IQ ($d = -1.53$ OL% $= 28$). This implies that overall patients with DAT will perform poorer on subtests that make-up the WAIS-R Performance IQ compared to those that make-up the WAIS-R Verbal IQ. As the opposite dissociation is true for more subcortical degenerative diseases, such as progressive supranuclear palsy (see chapter), the pattern of effect sizes for these composite measures may indeed aid in the differentiation of dementia syndromes (also see Derix, 1994; Zakzanis & Freedman, 1999; Zakzanis, Leach, & Freedman, 1998).

A more specific measure of performance skill such as the Block Design subtest from the WAIS-R corresponds to a mean effect size of -1.94 (OL% $= 20$) indicating that not all patients with DAT can be discriminated from healthy normal controls based on these test scores. The range of effects ($d = -0.19/-6.29$), however, does underscore that visuospatial deficits can sometimes be the initial presenting cognitive deficit in DAT (Martin, 1987), or can only manifest itself later as the disease evolves. The mean effect size also implies that visuospatial impairment as measured by the Block Design subtest is more severe in DAT, than in most subcortical dementias (also see Cummings, 1990; Zakzanis,

1998g). This dissociation may then aid in the differentiation of DAT from other subcortical degenerative diseases.

Other specific measures of performance skill without absolute reliable sensitivity included the Digit Symbol subtest from the WAIS-R (d = -1.78 OL% = 23), the Hooper Visual Organization Test (d = -1.63 OL% = 26), Judgment of Line Orientation (d = -1.55 OL% = 28), copy of the Rey-Osterrieth Complex Figure (d = -1.44 OL% = 30), and Benton's Facial Recognition (d = -1.39 OL% = 32). Although these mean effect sizes do not reliably discriminate patients with DAT from healthy normal controls, the range of effect sizes again imply that depending on the duration of the disease, the sensitivity of these measures will vary. Specifically, heuristic benchmark criteria (i.e., $d > 3.0$ OL% < 5) will be approached as the disease evolves, or is met in the striking exception of early onset visuospatially impaired cases (e.g., Albert, Duffy, & McAnulty, 1990).

Finally, the mean and range of obtained effect sizes for WAIS-R Picture Completion (d = -1.03 OL% = 44) and Object Assembly (d = -0.98 OL% = 45), copy of a Clock Drawing (d = -.84 OL% = 50), Mattis Dementia Rating Scale Construction subtest (d = -0.51 OL% = 66), and copy of Benton's Visual Retention Test figures (d = 0.48 OL% = 67), all correspond to effect sizes that do not reliably discriminate patients with DAT from healthy normal controls. Indeed, on the basis of the mean and range of effect sizes, and according to heuristic benchmark criteria, performance on these measures are not expected to be maximally impaired either early nor later in the course of Alzheimer's disease.

Cognitive flexibility and abstraction
The next most impaired neuropsychological domain in patients with DAT was that domain that included those tests sensitive to frontal-executive function (see Chapter 15, Table 15.1). The range of effects for specific measures was quite variable. For example, a mean effect size of 2.25 (OL% = 15) was obtained for Trail Making Test (Part B) whereas an effect size of 0.07 (OL%. 95) was obtained on the Tower of Hanoi. Such disparate performance has sometimes been interpreted as evidence of frontal lobe involvement in Alzheimer's disease. Yet in many instances, it is likely to be secondary to other cognitive deficits and disease duration (Snowden, Neary, & Mann, 1996).

For example, the WCST demands skills of comprehension, immediate memory span, visual perception and spatial localization, which may all be impaired in DAT (Snowden, Neary, & Mann, 1996). As such, a mean effect size of -1.72 (OL% = 24) was obtained for the number of categories achieved on the WCST. Because the number of categories achieved score on the WCST has limited sensitivity and is vulnerable to both diffuse and focal deficits beyond the prefrontal cortex (Anderson, Damasio, Jones, & Tranel, 1991; Heaton et al., 1993; Lezak, 1995; Milner, 1963, 1964; Van der Does, & Van den Bosch, 1992), it is the measures of perseveration on the test that are often regarded as the best index of focal prefrontal pathology (Stuss, 1996). Thus, because the effect sizes obtained for the perseveration measures on the WCST were considerably smaller in magnitude

(d = 1.07 OL% = 43 for both perseverative errors and responses), it is likely that the larger effect obtained for the number of categories achieved is indeed inflated when not determined by the integrity of neuroanatomic structures other than the prefrontal cortex. Moreover, a mean effect size of –1.50 (OL% = 29) was obtained for the Controlled Oral Word Association Test. Because patients with DAT may have difficulty keeping track of responses or in keeping with the test instructions over the course of a minute, this effect size might also be inflated when not determined by pathological alterations beyond the frontal-executive system. Taken together, these effects may, or may not, support the view that other cognitive deficits are frequently sufficient to account for impaired scores on measures of cognitive flexibility and abstraction (such as the WCST and phonemic fluency task).

On other measures of cognitive flexibility and abstraction, patients with DAT could not be validly discriminated from normal healthy controls. For example, Tinkertoy Test (see Lezak, 1982) performance corresponds to an effect size of –2.08 (OL% = 18). This test allows the patient to initiate, plan, and structure and carry out a potentially complex activity (Lezak, 1995). Thus, the Tinkertoy Test is quite sensitive to frontal-executive function. An effect size of –1.40 (OL% = 32) was obtained on the Similarities subtest of the WAIS-R which requires the patient to formulate a supraordinate verbal concept similarities for the word pairs. An even smaller effect size was obtained for Design Fluency (d = –1.00 OL% = 45).Considered a nonverbal counterpart to word fluency, it requires the patient to "invent as many different drawings" as they can in five minutes after being shown examples of acceptable and unacceptable drawings (see Lezak, 1995). A similar effect (d = –.86 OL% = 49) was obtained for the Porteus Maze Test which has been shown to be correlated to frontal dysfunction using a physiological measure (Porteus, 1959, 1965; Smith, 1960).

Impairment of calculation skills (i.e., acalculia) has been noted to appear early in DAT (Cummings & Benson, 1992). It is however, difficult to classify this test since it is unclear whether these deficits are primarily due to impaired cognitive flexibility and abstraction skills or due to impairments in other cognitive functions (e.g., attention, semantic memory, visuospatial skill). Nevertheless, a significantly greater effect size of –2.39 (OL% = 13) was obtained for the Arithmetic subtest of the WAIS-R relative to other tasks of cognitive flexibility and abstraction.

In keeping with the above interpretation of effect sizes, it should be emphasized that an impairment in cognitive flexibility and abstraction is not sufficient to make the differential diagnosis of DAT. In DAT other deficits are frequently sufficient to account for impaired scores, whereas in those disorders with prominent frontal lobe degeneration such as fronto-temporal dementia, they are not (Snowden, Neary, & Mann, 1996; Zakzanis, 1998c). In addition, patients with a low educational level and, often those with learning disability, will have difficulty on selected tasks of cognitive flexibility and abstraction. Therefore, performance on these tasks should be considered within the context of other cognitive tasks, age, education, and premorbid abilities.

Attention/concentration

Measures of attention and concentration correspond to the next most impaired neuropsychological domain in DAT (see Chapter 15, Table 15.1). Although attentional deficits may play a role in most other neuropsychological domains, pure cognitive measures of attention are few and rarely referred to in primary studies of DAT. This is unfortunate given a longitudinal study of a small group of patients that suggested that the first nonamnestic neuropsychological consequence of DAT is a loss of attentional capacity (Grady et al., 1988). Nevertheless, the obtained effect sizes on Continuous Performance, Stroop, letter cancellation, and Trail Making tasks can help articulate the nature of attentional function in DAT.

Focused attention in DAT where selection can be made on the basis of a clear physical dimension and where there are no conflicting response tendencies attached to the distractors is relatively unimpaired (e.g., Continuous Performance Task simple condition $d = -0.20$ OL% = 85 vs. Continuous Performance Task response inhibition condition $d = -1.01$ OL% = 44). When such conflicting response tendencies are present [as in the interference condition of the Stroop test ($d = -1.77$ OL% = 23)], selectivity suffers. The magnitude of this effect, however, is relatively small compared to the slow reading ($d = 0.38$ OL% = 74) and color naming ($d = -2.30$ OL% = 15) seen in those respective subtasks (also see van Zomeren & Brouwer, 1994). Moreover, on letter cancellation tasks, an effect size of 1.23 (OL% = 37) was obtained. These tasks require the patient to cross out a specified digit or letter each time it appears in an array on a printed page (Lezak, 1995). Zec (1993) noted that mildly demented patients with DAT do not show a significant impairment on this type of task, whereas those moderately demented usually do exhibit impaired performance.

Divided attention performance is determined by the availability of processing mechanisms, their capacities and the strategies for utilizing those capacities (van Zomeren & Brouwer, 1994). Although this aspect of attention was not readily tested in the clinical setting by way of dichotic listening and or dual-task techniques, Nebes and Brady (1992) performed a meta-analysis of all reaction time studies carried out with patients with DAT. They conclude that Alzheimer's disease produces a generalized slowing of cognitive processing, rather than a slowing of specific stages, that increases with dementia severity (Nebes & Brady, 1992). This general slowness in information processing would indeed result in deficits of divided attention (van Zomeren & Brouwer, 1994).

Sustained attention as documented by the simple condition of the Continuous Performance Task is the second least sensitive task to DAT ($d = -0.20$ OL% = 85). Patients with DAT cannot be reliably discriminated from healthy controls based on CPT simple condition test scores.

Finally, at a more theoretical level, it has been suggested that patients with DAT exhibit a supervisory attentional system deficit (van Zomeren & Brouwer, 1994). For example, if performance on Trail Making Test (Part B) can be interpreted as an index of supervisory attentional control, the obtained effect size (d

= 2.25 OL% = 15) would support the notion that this aspect of attention is most impaired in patients with DAT.

Taken together, although studies of attentional impairments in DAT are not abundant, the available evidence allows for the conclusion that attention is globally impaired. The most conspicuous effects are in the areas of divided attention and supervisory attentional control. Relatively speaking, focused and sustained attention are less impaired (also see van Zomeren & Brouwer, 1994).

Manual dexterity

Measures of manual dexterity correspond to the least affected neuropsychological domain in DAT (see Chapter 15, Table 15.1). Indeed, obtained effect sizes on the Finger Tapping Test and Grooved Pegboard could discriminate no more than 55% and 39% of patients from healthy normal controls respectively. More specifically, Finger Tapping Test effect sizes were slightly larger in comparison to Grooved Pegboard effect sizes (left and right hand mean $d = 0.91$ for Finger Tapping Test vs. left and right hand mean $d = .59$ for Grooved Pegboard). No significant lateralizing differences were apparent (see Table 4.3).

Despite the absence of large effects on measures of manual dexterity, it should be noted that ideomotor (an inability to execute a motor activity in response to a verbal command that is easily performed spontaneously) and conceptual (an inability to carry out a serial act even though each separate activity could be successfully performed) apraxia occurs in the later stages of Alzheimer's disease, after memory and language impairments have usually become severe (Cummings & Benson, 1992). As such, performance on measures of manual dexterity may indeed be defective secondary to a disorder of skilled movement not caused by more elementary sensory or motor deficits, nor caused by intellectual deterioration, poor comprehension, or uncooperativeness (see Rothi & Heilman, 1997; Heilman & Rothi, 1993; Roy, 1996; Roy, Brown, Winchester, Square, Hall, & Black, 1993). As noted, because even mildly demented patients often have severe memory deficits that result in near floor performance on tests of delayed recall, measures of praxis may be better suited for staging dementia severity and/or tracking its progression once a diagnosis of probable DAT has been made (Bondi, Salmon, & Kaszniak, 1996).

Summary

Our review of the neuropsychological literature of Alzheimer's disease provides a basis for which the remaining neurologic and psychiatric diseases can be differentiated. That is, given the exceedingly recognizable sequence in which higher cognitive functions are lost and the temporal order in which behavioral and neurologic disabilities occur in patients with DAT (see Bondi, Salmon, & Kaszniak, 1996; Stern et al., 1998), and, in keeping with one of the most researched and established hypotheses regarding etiology in all of neuroscience that posits involvement of the temporal-hippocampal formation as a core deficit in DAT (see Hyman, Van Hoesen, Damasio, & Barnes, 1984; O'Brien, 1995), it follows that our meta-analytic review of cognitive deficits in DAT, based on approximately 200 studies, might provide the most reliable and conceptually valid profile. As Table 15.1 (Chapter 15) illustrates, the two neuropsychological domains of memory function (i.e., delayed recall followed by memory acquisition) were impaired most in DAT, followed by impairment in verbal skill and performance skill (visuospatial ability). This is indeed the exact order in which cognitive deficits in Alzheimer's disease have been noted to most commonly evolve (see Cummings & Benson, 1992). Moreover, although caution must be exercised in extrapolating from behavioral tests to neuroanatomy (Freedman, 1994), the magnitude of impairment on many measures of delayed recall (see Table 4.3) indicate markers in keeping with heuristic benchmark criteria (i.e., $d > 3.0$ OL% < 5). Coupled with the magnitude of degeneration of the temporal-hippocampal formation which is the area of the greatest and probably the earliest pathological change in patients with DAT (see Boller & Ducyckaerts, 1997; Johnson et al., 1998; Hyman, Arriagada, Van Hoesen, & Damasio, 1993; Moss & Albert, 1988; Zakzanis, 1998e), it would seem justified to utilize such benchmark criteria in establishing cognitive markers that can aid in leading to a differential diagnosis.

Chapter 5

FRONTO-TEMPORAL DEMENTIA

Fronto-temporal dementia (FTD) refers to a clinicopathological syndrome characterized behaviorally by features indicative of frontal lobe dysfunction and pathologically by "simple" neuronal degeneration (Gustafson, 1987; Neary, Snowden, Northem, & Goulding, 1988; Snowden, Neary, & Mann, 1996). The pathological alterations in FTD are most concentrated in the frontal and anterior temporal lobes of the brain (Englund & Brun, 1987; Knopman, Mastri, Frey, Sung, & Rustan, 1990; Miller et al., 1991; Risberg, 1987; Risberg, Passant, Warkentin, & Gustafson, 1993), where three distinct types of histological alterations which underlie the atrophy often share an identical anatomical distribution (Brun, 1987, 1993; Mann & South, 1993; Mann, South, Snowden, & Neary, 1993). The most common pathology is that of nerve cell loss and spongiform change (microvacuolation), together with a mild or moderately severe astrocytic gliosis in the outer cortical layers, and is designated frontal lobe degeneration (The Lund and Manchester Groups, 1994). This is to distinguish it from the typical Pick-type histology characterized by intense astrocytic gliosis in the presence of intraneuronal inclusion bodies and inflated neurons in all cortical layers (The Lund and Manchester Groups, 1994). Finally, in the third type the above histological changes are combined with spinal motor neuron degeneration (Snowden, Neary, & Mann, 1996).

Indeed, the microvacuolar versus gliotic-type histology, and the presence versus absence of neuronal inclusions cannot be predicted on the basis of the clinical syndrome, which reflects the topographical distribution of the pathology rather than the specific histological change (Neary & Snowden, 1996).

Nevertheless, in keeping with the progressive lobar atrophy that characterizes the entity of FTD, cognitive deficits have been described to include reduced executive skill in the absence of severe memory, visuospatial, motor, and language deficits in the context of profound behavioral and personality changes (Elfgren, Passant, & Risberg, 1993; Miller, Chang, Oropilla, & Ismael, 1994; Miller et al., 1991; Neary, Snowden Northem, & Goulding, 1988; Pachana, Boone, Miller, Cummings, & Berman, 1996; Pasquier, Lebert, Grymonprez, & Petit, 1995; Snowden, Neary & Mann, 1996; Zakzanis, 1998c).

The diagnosis of fronto-temporal dementia and study inclusion criteria

The diagnosis of FTD varied considerably across studies, perhaps reflecting the considerable controversy regarding the heterogeneity of the disease (a recent consensus of clinical diagnostic criteria has, however, been published; See Neary et al., 1998). Some consistencies were noted however. These included, patients meeting Diagnostic and Statistical Manual-III-Revised criteria for dementia; no computed tomography or magnetic resonance imaging evidence of focal brain lesions; a score of less than 5 on the Hachinski Ischemic Scale; normal results on routine lab tests; no history of alcohol or closed head injury; and, evidence of focal single photon emission computed tomography hypoperfusion and/or positron emission tomography hypometabolism or hypoperfusion.

The review

Eight studies published between 1985 and 1997 yielding 68 effect sizes met criteria for inclusion in the present analysis. In total, cognitive test results from 88 patients with FTD and 100 normal healthy controls were recorded across primary studies.

Descriptive demographic and clinical variable data available from primary studies from the published literature are presented in Table 5.1. The modal patient with FTD was approximately 64 years of age, has had 12 years of education, and was first diagnosed with FTD at the age of 61. The patient with FTD was just as likely to be male or female. Moreover, because of an inadequate number of studies none of the clinical or demographic variables correlated significantly to any of the cognitive measures. Qualitative longitudinal studies of patients with FTD, however, have provided a careful description of related cognitive impairments with basic clinical and demographic variables (see Snowden, Neary, & Mann, 1996).

Cognitive deficits in fronto-temporal dementia

Effect size summaries are presented for specific cognitive tasks and test variables in Table 5.2. Mean *d*'s presented in the column are raw effect sizes. Test

Table 5.1. Descriptive Statistics for Fronto-Temporal Dementia Cognitive Studies.

Variables	Mdn	M	SD	Range	N
Sample size					
FTD samples	10.0	11.0	3.5	7–16	8
Control samples	10.0	12.5	8.1	6–31	8
Patients' age	64.0	64.3	1.8	63–68	8
Onset age	61.2	61.2	1.1	60–62	2
Duration of illness (in years)	3.2	3.3	1.1	1.8–4.8	6
Percentage of males	51.8	48.5	12.8	37–71	6
Patients' education (in years)	12.6	11.9	3.9	6.6–17	8

Note. Mdn. = median; M = mean; SD = standard deviation of the mean; N = number of studies in which the variable was reported.

Table 5.2. Effect Size Results in Rank-Order for Patients with Fronto-Temporal Dementia.

Neuropsychological Test/ Test Variable	N d	M d	SD d	Min. d	Max. d	Nfs	OL % (approx.)
Semantic fluency	1	–4.14	–	–4.14	–4.14	413	<2.0
WCST-categories achieved	3	–3.28	2.58	–1.14	–6.14	981	
Mini Mental State Exam	6	–3.14	1.33	–2.34	–5.78	1878	<5.0
WAIS-R Performance IQ	1	–2.52	–	–2.52	–2.52	251	15.0
WAIS-R Block Design	1	–2.45	–	–2.45	–2.45	244	
WCST-perseverations	3	2.30	0.82	1.26	2.74	687	
COWAT	5	–2.29	0.94	–1.16	–3.57	1140	
Benton Visual Retention Test number of errors	1	2.28	–	2.28	2.28	227	
Mattis DRS Total Score	1	–1.99	–	–1.99	–1.99	198	20.0
Consonant trigrams	1	–1.72	–	–1.72	–1.72	171	
WMS-R Logical Memory II delayed recall	3	–1.71	1.08	–0.98	–2.95	510	
WAIS-R Digit Span forward	4	–1.56	0.89	–0.45	–2.50	620	
Trail Making Test Part B	2	1.54	0.37	1.28	1.81	308	
Stroop interference	2	1.49	0.38	1.22	1.75	296	30.0
WAIS-R Full Scale IQ	2	–1.49	0.88	–0.87	–2.11	296	
WAIS-R Verbal IQ	1	–1.44	–	–1.44	–1.44	143	
WAIS-R Digit Span backward	4	–1.27	1.16	–0.13	–2.50	504	
Rey Osterrieth Complex Figure delayed reproduction	4	–1.26	0.44	–0.96	–1.91	500	
WMS-R Logical Memory I immediate recall	2	–1.19	0.22	–1.14	–1.24	236	
WMS-R Visual Reproduction II delayed recall	2	–1.00	0.28	–0.80	–1.19	198	45.0
Rey Osterrieth Complex Figure copy	4	–0.88	0.50	–0.36	–1.54	348	
Trail Making Test Part A	2	0.85	0.58	0.44	1.26	168	
Corsi block tapping span	1	–0.84	–	–0.84	–0.84	83	
Boston Naming Test	3	–0.78	0.36	–0.42	–0.78	231	
RAVLT trial 5 free recall	1	–0.76	–	–0.76	–0.76	75	

Table continues

Table 5.2. (continued)

Neuropsychological Test/ Test Variable	N d	M d	SD d	Min. d	Max. d	Nfs	OL % (approx.)
RAVLT recognition	1	−0.68	−	−0.68	−0.68	67	
Raven's Progressive Matrices	1	−0.64	−	−0.64	−0.64	63	
RAVLT delayed recall	1	−0.63	−	−0.63	−0.63	62	
Token Test	2	−0.55	0.12	−0.55	−0.56	108	65.0
Buschke's SRT short term memory index	1	−0.45	−	−0.45	−0.45	44	
Buschke's SRT long term memory index	2	−0.34	0.22	−0.18	−0.50	66	

Note. N*d* = number of effect sizes; M*d* = mean effect size; SD*d* = standard deviation around the effect size; Min.*d* = smallest effect size obtained; Max.*d* = largest effect size obtained; Nfs = Fail Safe N; SRT = Selective Reminding Test; DRS = Dementia Rating Scale; CVLT = California Verbal Learning Test; RAVLT = Rey Auditory Verbal Learning Test; WAIS-R = Wechsler Adult Intelligence Scale-Revised; WMS-R = Wechsler Memory Scale-Revised; COWAT = Controlled Oral Word Association Task; WCST = Wisconsin Card Sorting Test.

variables are presented according to the rank order of the effect size. Effect sizes are included along with the corresponding standard deviation and the number of effect sizes the mean *d* was based on. To help describe the dispersion of effect sizes, a minimum and maximum *d* value are also presented. The table also includes the Fail Safe N (Nfs) for the number of additional studies that would be necessary to reverse the overall probability obtained from our obtained effect size to a value higher than our critical value for statistical significance, which was set at .01 (see Wolf, 1986 for an elaboration). Chapter 15 (Table 15.2) includes similar statistics for the composite neuropsychological domains. The following description of cognitive task and test variable effect sizes are grouped by domain and presented in the order of most to least impaired in FTD.

Cognitive flexibility and abstraction
Performance on measures of cognitive flexibility and abstraction such as the Wisconsin Card Sorting Test (WCST) and semantic fluency task, correspond to effect sizes that yield test score dispersion of less than 5% overlap between patients with FTD and normal controls based on Cohen's (1988) inferential idealized distributions. Therefore, the discriminability of FTD from normal healthy controls is reliable in keeping with patient performance on these tasks as the corresponding overlap suggests that the obtained magnitude of effect is consistent with that of a neuropsychological marker (Zakzanis, 1998a, e). For example, if hippocampal atrophy is a core marker found in all patients with probable Alzheimer's disease, an effect size capable of completely discriminating patients from healthy controls is a defensible expectation. Such an effect size would have to be about 3.0 or greater, as the corresponding overlap associated with the effect is less than 5%. With an effect size considerably smaller (i.e., corresponding overlap of say, > 15%), it would be hard to argue in favor of hippo-

campal atrophy as being a core feature of probable Alzheimer's disease. Indeed, it has been demonstrated (see Zakzanis, 1998e) that such an effect is achievable using meta-analytic procedures to index the integrity of temporal-hippocampal function in dementia of the Alzheimer's type with heuristic benchmark criteria for neuroanatomic and neuropsychological markers (i.e., $d > 3.0$ OL% < 5). Although such a standard may not be entirely justifiable, it can nonetheless serve as a benchmark against which the present findings can be articulated. Thus, performance on tasks of semantic fluency and the number of categories achieved on the WCST correspond to effect sizes > 3.0 (OL% < 5). Therefore, performance on these measures may serve as clinical markers for FTD that can aid in the proper recognition and differentiation of FTD from other disorders with prominent features of dementia.

Moreover, when grouped as a neuropsychological domain, measures of cognitive flexibility and abstraction were most impaired in FTD (see Chapter 15, Table 15.2).

Performance skill

Performance skill measures reviewed included the performance IQ and the block design subtest from the Wechsler Adult Intelligence Scale-Revised (WAIS-R), and copy of the Rey-Osterrieth Complex Figure (ROCF). Although impairment on the WAIS-R measures were evident, they do not meet benchmark criteria despite considerable nonoverlap in the distribution of test scores (e.g., WAIS-R performance IQ $d = -2.32$ OL% $= 12$, WAIS-R block design $d = -2.43$ OL% $= 13$). Moreover, because the WAIS-R performance IQ provides an average of some quite dissimilar functions that have relatively low intercorrelations and bear no regular neuroanatomical or neuropsychological relationship to one another (Lezak, 1995, p. 690), scores on the specific subtests that make up the WAIS-R performance IQ must be considered independently both between and within tasks if they are to aid in the recognition of FTD. For example, impaired performance on the block design subtest of the WAIS-R may not be attributed to a primary spatial deficit, but to exceeding prescribed time limits that can likely stem from poor organizational and monitoring of skill, and perhaps, poor initiation and general slow processing speed (see Snowden, Neary, & Mann, 1996). In agreement, a smaller effect size for the untimed copy of the ROCF is obtained ($d = -0.88$ OL% $= 50$). It is indeed likely that impaired performances arise for reasons which are not primarily spatial. As a neuropsychological domain, however, performance skill measures were second most sensitive to cognitive alterations in FTD (see Chapter 15, Table 15.2).

Memory acquisition

Tasks of memory acquisition including the short term memory index from Buschke's Selective Reminding Test (SRT), trial 5 from the Rey Auditory Verbal Learning Test (RAVLT), immediate recall on the logical memory subtest from the Wechsler Memory Scale-R (WMS-R), forward and backward digit span from the WAIS-R, Corsi Block Tapping span, and the Brown-Peterson

Consonant Trigram test correspond to an overall effect size of 1.29 (see Chapter 15, Table 15.2). More specifically, the effect sizes on memory acquisition tasks obtained between patients with FTD and normal control subjects are considerably below those reported by Christensen, Hadzi-Pavlovic and Jacomb (1991) between individuals with probable Alzheimer's disease and normal controls. For example, Christensen et al. found that the Buschke selective reminding procedure yielded an effect size of 3.28 (OL% < 5) in patients with probable Alzheimer's disease, whereas the current results produced a considerably smaller effect ($d = -0.45$ OL% = 70) for performance on this same measure in patients with FTD. Thus, providing that these same measures are found to be highly sensitive (i.e., meeting benchmark criteria – e.g., $d > 3.0$ OL% < 5) to other disorders with prominent features of cortical and subcortical dementia, even the cognitive tasks and test variables that are least sensitive to FTD (i.e., those below the median of ± 1.35 in Table 5.2) can also aid in the proper recognition and differentiation of FTD.

Attention/Concentration
Purely attentional defects appear as distractibility or impaired ability for focused behavior, regardless of the patient's intention (Lezak, 1995). Indeed, patients with FTD are commonly described as inattentive (Gustafson, 1987, 1993). Thus, as most of the cognitive tasks and test variables are dependent either primarily or peripherally on attentional mechanisms, the influence of deficient attentional processes on test performance is profound and best illustrated in qualitative case studies of FTD (see Snowden, Neary, & Mann, 1996). The Trail Making Test (Parts A and B), however, is considered a test of complex visual scanning with a motor component, with attention and concentration contributing greatly to success on the task (Lezak, 1995). The obtained effect size on part A could discriminate 50% of patients with FTD from normal controls ($d = 0.85$), whereas performance on the more difficult part B, could discriminate 70% of patients with FTD from normal controls ($d = -1.56$). The larger obtained effect size on part B may indeed reflect the integrity of frontal association cortex on successful performance and therefore, a deficit in supervisory attentional systems. Indeed, part B requires establishing and sustaining the set to serially alternate between two automatized series of numbers and letters (Benson & Miller, 1997; Stuss & Benson, 1986). This interpretation is consistent with the large obtained effect size for cognitive flexibility and abstraction which similarly relies on the integrity of supramodal and heteromodal frontal association cortices (Benson, 1994; Benson & Miller, 1997).

Delayed recall
Neuropsychological measures of delayed recall including the long term memory index from Buschke's SRT, delayed recall and recognition scores from the RAVLT, delayed visual reproduction on the WMS-R, and delayed recall of the ROCF correspond to an overall effect of 1.08 as a neuropsychological domain (see Chapter 15, Table 15.2).

The more qualitative cognitive profile suggests some patterns in function. Specifically, impairment on tasks of delayed non-verbal recall (e.g., mean d across delayed non-verbal recall tasks of 1.13) is greater than the equivalent performance on tasks of verbal recall (e.g., mean d of 0.89). Moreover, performance on delayed recall of the logical memory subtest of the WMS-R was more impaired (e.g., $d = -1.71$ OL% = 24) than that of the more "cue" structured Buschke's SRT ($d = -0.34$ OL% = 78). This difference suggests that patients have access to information that they do not (or are unable to) generate spontaneously. Further, since recognition after a delay corresponds to a minimal effect size of -0.68 (OL% = 58; RAVLT recognition), it appears that patients with FTD have difficulty in spontaneous information generation and in organized search retrieval. They do not have an inability to acquire and retain new information (see Snowden, Neary, & Mann, 1996). This is qualified with the small obtained effect size on tasks of memory acquisition (e.g., free recall on trial 5 of the RAVLT; immediate recall on the logical memory subtest of the WMS-R) that do not validly discriminate patients with FTD from normal controls. Finally, considering the magnitude of impairment and non-absolute discriminability (i.e., $d < 3.0$ OL% > 5) of these delayed recall tasks in patients with FTD from normal controls, performance on these less sensitive measures to FTD can be used to aid in the differentiation of FTD from probable Alzheimer's disease where the pattern of impairment on these measures meets benchmark criteria (i.e., $d > 3.0$ OL% < 5).

Verbal skill

Verbal skill tasks including the Token Test, the Boston Naming Test, and the composite WAIS-R Verbal IQ correspond to the least impaired neuropsychological domain in FTD (see Chapter 15, Table 15.2). Thus, performance on formal tests of comprehension (e.g., Token Test) and naming to confrontation (e.g., Boston Naming Test) are typically not entirely normal, but may appear to be governed by the mental demands of the task (Snowden, Neary, & Mann, 1996). Indeed, effortful verbal skill tasks, requiring mental manipulation or abstraction of information that rely on fronto-temporal structures, such as phonemic and semantic fluency tasks, are disproportionately impaired (see Table 5.2). Moreover, given the small obtained effect size for the Boston Naming Test ($d = -0.78$ OL% = 55), this measure might also aid in the proper recognition and differentiation of FTD from highly focal cognitive degenerative diseases such as primary progressive aphasia, where an anomic aphasia typically is evident early in the course, and prominent as the disease progresses (Mesulam, 1982, 1987; also, see Snowden, Neary, & Mann, 1996 for a discussion on "semantic dementia" and its differentiation from FTD). Although patients with fronto-temporal degeneration can present with an aphasic syndrome, the initial diagnosis of primary progressive aphasia is made when other mental faculties such as memory, visuospatial skills, reasoning, and comportment are relatively free of primary deficits, and when language impairment is the only factor that compromises daily living activities for at least the first 2 years of the disease (Mesulam &

Weintraub, 1992). Thus, a severe and selective impairment on confrontational naming in the absence of poor performance on tasks that top the FTD profile would support a diagnosis of primary progressive aphasia in keeping with the diagnostic criteria proposed by Mesulam and Weintraub (1992) and the specific history and examination of the presenting patient.

Summary

The results indicate that patients with FTD are most deficient on tests of cognitive flexibility and abstraction, followed by performance on measures of performance skill, memory acquisition, attention/concentration, delayed recall, and, finally, verbal skill. More specifically, it was also revealed that the magnitude of effect on semantic fluency tasks and the number of categories achieved on the WCST are consistent with heuristic benchmark criteria for neuropsychological markers (i.e., $d > 3.0$ OL% < 5). Conversely, the discriminability of patients with FTD from normal controls was minimal when taking into account the obtained magnitude of effect on Buschke's SRT as the corresponding overlap could discriminate no more than 25% of patients with FTD from normal controls. Because the Alzheimer's profile (see Chapter 4) includes effect sizes that correspond to benchmark criteria for Buschke's SRT in patients with probable Alzheimer's disease, the magnitude of impairment and non-absolute discriminability of this task and the presence of valid WCST and semantic fluency markers in patients with FTD can aid in the differentiation of FTD from probable Alzheimer's disease (also see Zec, 1993). Some qualification is necessary, however.

Most patients late in their dementing illness may have different cognitive profiles and may obtain very different scores on the WCST, semantic fluency task, and Buschke's SRT. For example, as Alzheimer's disease is a progressive disorder and in more advanced phases patients will fail the WCST and have severe difficulties on verbal fluency tasks, they could be mistaken for FTD if other aspects of the examination and history were not taken into account. Further, it is presently unknown whether the histological patterns in FTD represent a spectrum of nonspecific changes or have distinct etiological significance (see Hachinski, 1997; Kertesz, 1997; Neary, 1997). Consequently, an empirical approach to the formulation of a cognitive profile would be more helpful if the topographical distribution of the pathology rather than the specific histological change determined the nature and pattern of this profile. As such, Neary (1997) has emphasized the conceptual need to distinguish between clinical syndrome, its topography of brain pathologic features, and underlying histological appearances, since each may ultimately contribute to the elucidation of disease origin and pattern of cognitive function. Until this need is fulfilled, the nature and pattern of cognitive deficit in FTD can only be articulated by way of anatomy and not specified by the type of histological characteristics involved (i.e., microvacuolar versus gliotic-type histology, and the presence versus absence of neuronal inclusions). This has led some (e.g., Kertesz, 1997) to propose an umbrella label – "Pick complex" – as it is premature to regard overlapping histologic variations and morphological features as distinct entities when they are not specific to any clinical phenotype. With these considerations in mind, the present findings should be cautiously applied in the clinical setting when a definite diagnosis is sought.

Chapter 6

PRIMARY PROGRESSIVE APHASIA

The sudden onset of aphasia is common after acute lesions in the left hemisphere (Benson, 1993; Benson & Ardila, 1996; Kaplan, Gallagher, & Glosser, in press). Aphasia may also emerge gradually in such chronic degenerative conditions as fronto-temporal dementia and Alzheimer's disease (Cummings & Benson, 1992; Snowden, Neary, & Mann, 1996; Zec, 1993). In the latter instances, however, the aphasia is merely one component of a progressive dementia and parallels additional and more salient disturbances of memory, intellect, and comportment (Mesulam, 1982, 1987).

In 1982, Mesulam (1982) described a "slowly progressive aphasia without generalized dementia" in six patients whose clinical course could be differentiated from that usually encountered in Alzheimer's dementia. In particular, five of Mesulam's patients who experienced an insidious onset and gradual worsening of aphasic symptoms over a period of 5 to 11 years presented with nonfluent agrammatic speech, severe anomia, and relative preservation of auditory comprehension (the sixth case had pure word deafness). Since his original description, the term "primary progressive aphasia" (PPA) has become a clinical designation given to individuals who present with progressive and restricted loss of language function, when no expanding space-occupying lesion, infarction, or other identifiable structural disorder is present to explain the deficit (Lippa, Cohen, Smith, & Drachman, 1991). Subsequently, a number of patients presenting with selective disorders of language have been described (e.g., Craenhals, Raison-van Ruymbeke, Rectum, Seron, & Laterre, 1990; Green, Morris, Sandson, McKeel & Miller, 1990; Karbe, Kertesz, & Polk, 1993; Snowden,

Neary, Mann, Goulding, & Testa, 1992; Watt, Jokel, & Behrmann, 1997; Weintraub, Rubin, & Mesulam, 1990). These reports do not describe a unitary clinical syndrome. Several patterns of deficit have been encompassed by the broad rubric of "progressive aphasia," reflecting a breakdown in distinct functional systems. For example, a very different form of PPA characterized by fluent empty speech, impoverished expressive and receptive vocabulary, and impaired single-word comprehension has also been described (e.g., Hodeges, Patterson, Oxbury, & Funnell, 1992; Poeck & Luzzatti, 1988; Snowden et al., 1992; Tyrrell, Warrington, Frackowiak, & Rosser, 1990). This syndrome of focal language disturbance has been conceptualized as a progressive "semantic dementia" (see Black, 1996; Kertesz, Davidson, & McCabe, 1998).

Our review of the literature focuses on patients with a primary progressive non-fluent aphasia. A pattern of language breakdown similar to that described by Mesulam (1982) and others (e.g., Craenhals et al., 1990; Delecluse, Andersen, & Waldemar, 1990; Snowden, Neary & Mann, 1996). Hence, PPA presents as an insidious and progressive decline in linguistic fluency, culminating in mutism (Mesulam, 1982). It also presents with word finding difficulties, qualified by hesitant and attenuated utterances containing phonemic paraphasic errors and impaired repetition. This is in contrast to preserved insight and comprehension (Weintraub, Rubin, & Mesulam, 1990). Reading and writing are comparably impaired. Despite their impoverished ability to communicate, memory and visuospatial skills remain preserved late into the disorder so that patients are able to carry out a range of executive skills and succeed at activities of daily living for many years (Snowden, Neary, & Mann, 1996).

The diagnosis of primary progressive aphasia and study inclusion criteria

The initial diagnosis of PPA is made when other mental faculties such as memory, visuospatial skills, reasoning, and comportment are relatively free of primary deficits, and when language impairment is the only factor that compromises daily living activities for at least the first 2 years of the disease (Mesulam & Weintraub, 1992). Hence, patients must have met diagnostic criteria for PPA as proposed by Mesulam and Weintraub (1992) in primary studies to have been included in our review.

The review

Twenty-two studies published between 1982 and 1997 met criteria for inclusion in the present analysis. In total, neuropsychological test results from 55 patients with PPA and 162 normal healthy control subjects were recorded across primary studies.

Descriptive demographic and clinical variable data available from primary studies from the published literature are presented in Table 6.1. Onset age is

Table 6.1.   Descriptive Statistics for Primary Progressive Aphasia Cognitive Studies.

Variables	*M*	*SD*	Range	*N*
Sample size				
PPA samples	3.0	2.5	1–10	22
Control samples	40	42	10–99	4
Patients' age	62	5.6	51–73	22
Onset age	56	4.6	45–70	7
Duration of illness (years)	8.1	2.9	4–12	13
Percentage of males	75	33	0–100	22
Patients' education (years)	12.2	5.8	6–20	4

Note. M = mean; *SD* = standard deviation of the mean; *N* = number of studies in which the variable was reported.

typically presenile – usually between 50 and 65 years, although onset age in reported cases of PPA has ranged from 45–70 years (see Table 6.1). Moreover, there is no clear relationship between age at onset of initial aphasic symptomatology and the likelihood of progression of cognitive impairment (Duffy & Petersen, 1992). PPA occurs in both men and women. An equal sex incidence is not evident however (Weintraub & Caserta, 1998). Table 6.1 reveals that approximately 75% of patients with the diagnosis of PPA have been men, although, the relative sex incidence is difficult to determine precisely since the condition is relatively rare. That is, the incidence of PPA in relation to presenile Alzheimer's disease has been approximated at 1:40 (Snowden, Neary, & Mann, 1996). Table 6.1 also reveals a duration of illness of approximately 8 years, although a considerable range (4–12) has been reported. Additionally, PPA is sometimes familial yet often appears sporadically. Finally, there is an absence of neurological signs as general health is characteristically well preserved in PPA.

Cognitive deficits in primary progressive aphasia

Effect size summaries are presented for specific cognitive tasks and test variables in Table 6.2. Mean *d*'s presented in the column are raw effect sizes. Test variables are presented according to the rank order of the effect size. Effect sizes are included along with the corresponding standard deviation and the number of effect sizes the mean *d* was based on. To help describe the dispersion of effect sizes, a minimum and maximum *d* value are also presented. The table also includes the Fail Safe N (Nfs) for the number of additional studies that would be necessary to reverse the overall probability obtained from our obtained effect size to a value higher than our critical value for statistical significance, which was set at .01 (see Wolf, 1986 for an elaboration). Chapter 15 (Table 15.3) includes similar statistics for the composite neuropsychological domains. The

Table 6.2.   Effect Size Results in Rank Order for Patients with Primary Progressive
Aphasia.

Neuropsychological Test/ Test Variable	N d	M d	SD d	Min. d	Max. d	Nfs	OL % (approx.)
Boston Naming Test	8	−6.06	2.87	−1.30	−10.7	4840	
RAVLT delayed recall	3	−4.42	1.00	−3.27	−5.00	1323	<2.0
Mattis DRS Total Score	1	−3.74	–	−3.74	−3.74	373	
Mini Mental State Exam	2	−3.25	1.06	−2.50	−4.00	650	
Mattis DRS Initiation/ Perseveration scale	1	−3.13	–	−3.13	−3.1	3312	
RAVLT trial 5	2	−3.09	1.07	−2.33	−3.85	616	< 3.0
WMS-R Paired Associates	1	−2.12	–	−2.12	−2.12	211	
Western Aphasia Battery Aphasia Quotient	1	−2.05	–	−2.05	−2.05	204	
BDAE Oral Reading sentences	2	−2.00	2.82	0.00	−4.00	398	20.0
RAVLT trial 1	1	−2.00	–	−2.00	−2.00	199	
COWAT	7	−1.99	0.58	−1.25	−2.84	1386	
BDAE Repetition sentences	2	−1.98	0.11	−1.78	−2.05	394	
BDAE Repetition words	2	−1.95	2.90	0.10	−4.00	388	
WAIS-R Digit Span backward	6	−1.92	0.83	−1.00	−3.00	1152	
Trail Making Test Part B	1	1.89	–	1.89	1.89	188	
RAVLT recognition	3	−1.75	1.08	−0.50	−2.50	522	
WAIS-R Vocabulary	3	−1.72	1.55	−0.67	−3.50	516	
Semantic fluency	3	−1.45	0.61	−0.80	−2.02	432	30.0
WAIS-R Digit Span forward	7	−1.45	0.95	−0.15	−3.00	1008	
WAIS-R Verbal IQ	7	−1.14	1.02	−0.13	−2.33	791	
WAIS-R Similarities	3	−1.00	0.88	−0.33	−2.00	297	45.0
Rey-Osterrieth Complex Figure immediate recall	1	−0.95	–	−0.95	−0.95	94	
Western Aphasia Battery comprehension	1	−0.90	–	−0.90	−0.90	89	
WAIS-R Full Scale IQ	3	−0.87	0.90	0.06	−1.73	258	
WAIS-R Information	4	−0.82	1.25	0.33	−2.50	324	
WMS-R Memory Quotient	3	−0.78	0.83	−0.27	−1.73	231	
Raven's Progressive Matrices	7	−0.76	1.29	1.40	−2.41	525	
Mattis DRS Memory scale	1	−0.65	–	−0.65	−0.65	64	
WAIS-R Arithmetic	3	−0.56	1.26	0.33	−2.00	168	
Mattis DRS Construction scale	1	−0.50	–	−0.50	−0.50	49	65.0
WAIS-R Block Design	8	−0.23	1.10	1.00	−1.57	184	
WAIS-R Object Assembly	3	−0.22	1.83	1.00	−2.33	63	
WAIS-R Performance IQ	12	−0.15	0.89	1.07	−1.53	168	
Benton Facial Recognition	2	−0.10	1.49	1.00	−1.10	18	
WAIS-R Picture Arrangement	3	−0.03	0.58	0.33	−0.67	6	
BDAE Oral Reading words	1	0.00	–	0.00	0.00	–	100.0
Orientation	1	0.00	–	0.00	0.00	–	
Pyramids and Palm Trees	1	0.00	–	0.00	0.00	–	

Table continues

Table 6.2. (continued)

Neuropsychological Test/ Test Variable	N d	M d	SD d	Min. d	Max. d	Nfs	OL % (approx.)
—— patient's with PPA performed better than controls ——							
Benton Visual Retention Test							
number of errors	5	−0.04	1.05	−1.50	1.42	15	
Rey-Osterrieth Complex Figure							
copy	5	0.05	0.80	−1.06	1.00	20	
BDAE comprehension	4	0.08	0.22	−0.12	0.34	28	
WCST categories achieved	2	0.10	0.70	−0.40	0.60	18	
WAIS-R Digit Symbol	2	0.13	1.60	−1.00	1.26	24	
Token Test	2	0.14	0.00	0.14	0.14	26	
Bender Gestalt	3	0.17	0.29	0.00	0.50	48	
Judgment of Line Orientation	3	0.37	0.64	0.00	1.10	108	
WMS-R Logical Memory							
immediate recall	2	0.38	3.05	−1.78	2.53	74	
Hooper Visual Organization Test	1	0.60	–	0.60	0.60	59	
WAIS-R Comprehension	1	0.67	–	0.67	0.67	66	
Rey-Osterrieth Complex Figure							
delayed recall	4	0.81	1.83	−0.91	2.92	320	
WAIS-R Picture Completion	2	1.33	1.41	0.33	2.33	264	
WMS-R Visual Reproduction I							
immediate recall	1	1.36	–	1.36	1.36	135	

Note. Nd = number of effect sizes; Md = mean effect size; SDd = standard deviation around the effect size; Min.d = smallest effect size obtained; Max.d = largest effect size obtained; Nfs = Fail Safe N; DRS = Dementia Rating Scale; CVLT = California Verbal Learning Test; RAVLT = Rey Auditory Verbal Learning Test; WAIS-R = Wechsler Adult Intelligence Scale-Revised; WMS-R = Wechsler Memory Scale-Revised; COWAT = Controlled Oral Word Association Task; WCST = Wisconsin Card Sorting Test; BDAE = Boston Diagnostic Aphasia Exam.

following description of cognitive task and test variable effect sizes are grouped by domain and presented in the order of most to least impaired in PPA.

Verbal skill

Considering the primarily focal language deficits in PPA, it is not surprising that tests of verbal skill correspond to the poorest scores on neuropsychological evaluation, and thus, are associated with the largest composite effect sizes (see Chapter 15, Table 15.3). Therefore, a more detailed description of language deficit in PPA is presented.

Conversational speech. Spontaneous speech in patients with PPA is typically slow, hesitant, and sometimes agrammatic (Karbe, Kertesz, & Polk, 1993). Speech is nonfluent and encompasses a stuttering quality resembling that of Broca's or transcortical (perisylvian) motor aphasia. As patients search for words that remain within their vocabulary, phonemic paraphasias and transpositional errors (e.g., 'animal' pronounced as 'aminal'; 'car park' pronounced as 'par cark') are common (Snowden, Neary, & Mann, 1996). With disease progression, patients demonstrate increasing effort in word search, a loss of speech prosody and output becomes hypophonic (Scholten, Kneebone, Denson, Field, & Blumbergs, 1995). When tested serially on verbal fluency measures such as the Controlled Oral Word Association Test (COWAT; Benton & Hamsher, 1989) and semantic fluency task (Perret, 1974), patient performance is considerably impaired (Belano & Ska, 1992; Lippa, Cohen, Smith, & Drachman, 1991). More specifically, on tasks of word generation, performance is typically superior for semantic category ($d = -1.45$ OL% = 30) than for initial letter trials ($d = -1.99$ OL% = 19), illustrating greater benefit from a semantic than a phonological cue. This is in contrast to patients with Alzheimer's disease who typically perform slightly better on phonemic compared to semantic fluency tasks (Zec, 1993).

   Repetition. The ability to repeat words, sentences, and digits is severely compromised in PPA (Chiacchio, Grossi, Stanlone, & Trojano, 1993; Graff-Radford, Damasio, Hyman, Hart, Tranel, Damasio, Van Hoesen, & Rezai, 1990). Indeed, patient performances on tasks such as the Wechsler Adult Intelligence Scale Digit Span subtest (WAIS-R; Wechsler, 1981), and word repetition of the Boston Diagnostic Aphasia Exam (BDAE; Goodglass & Kaplan, 1982), are significantly below normal limits (e.g., $d = -1.45$ OL% = 30 WAIS-R digit span backward; $d = -1.95$ OL% = 20 BDAE word repetition). For example, Benson and Zaias (1991) describe a patient with a clinical diagnosis of PPA who obtained a scaled score of 3 on the Digit Span subtest of the WAIS-R. This corresponds to a score that is approximately two standard deviations below the normative mean. This score would correspond to an effect size of approximately 3.0 (OL% < 5). Such inability to repeat is common in PPA (Karbe, Kertesz, & Polk, 1993).

   Comprehension. While comprehension is severely impaired in semantic dementia, or, 'progressive fluent aphasia' (see Graham, Hodges, & Patterson, 1994), it is initially relatively preserved in PPA. As Snowden, Neary, and Mann (1996) noted, "patients are able to understand the meaning of words that they themselves are unable to produce . . . providing support for the view that word-finding difficulties are not semantically based, but arise at the level of access to the correct phonological word form" (p.78). Correspondingly, the meta-analysis reveals that patients with PPA perform within normal limits on formal tests of comprehension such as the Token Test ($d < 0.0$ OL% = 100; De Renzi & Faglioni, 1978), the Comprehension subtest from the BDAE ($d = < 0.0$ OL% = 100), and the Comprehension subtest from the WAIS-R ($d < 0.0$ OL% = 100), although impairment has been noted on the Comprehension subtest of the Western Aphasia Battery ($d = -0.90$ OL% = 48;WAB; Kertesz, 1982). Patient differences in disease duration might account for this discrepancy in test results as comprehension becomes increasingly difficult with progression of disease. Moreover, the degree to which understanding of individual word meaning is retained is impossible to determine in view of the absence of communication skills on the part of the patient in the later phase of disease (Snowden, Neary, & Mann, 1996). Thus, formal assessment of comprehension in late stage PPA remains a perplexing task for the clinician.

Naming. Anomia is considered the hallmark of PPA. Indeed, the poor performance on confrontational naming tasks, such as the Boston Naming Test (Kaplan, Goodglass, & Weintraub, 1983), can be considered a core clinical marker for PPA syndrome as its associated sensitivity is excellent ($d = -6.06$ OL% < 1). This specificity is however limited because patients with Alzheimer's disease or vascular dementia also often perform poorly on this task. Nevertheless, qualitative aspects on naming tasks can differentiate the diseases. In particular the prominence of phonemic errors distinguishes patients with non-fluent forms of PPA from those with naming deficits in the context of the fluent aphasias associated with dementia of the Alzheimer's type (Weintraub, Rubin, & Mesulam, 1990).

Reading & Writing. Reading aloud and written output mirror the patient's spoken output. Reading aloud is non-fluent and effortful with phonemic paralexias while written output is produced slowly and contains numerous spelling errors and letter omissions (Snowden, Neary, & Mann, 1996; Snowden et al., 1992). The quality of oral reading performance, however, is subject to patient variability and dependent on phrase length. Single word reading performance of four patients with PPA on the BDAE is indistinguishable from normal healthy controls with respect to test scores in Weintraub, Rubin, and Mesulam's (1990) ($d = 0.0$ OL% = 100) study. In contrast, reading sentences on the BDAE was significantly impaired in these same patients ($d = -4.00$ OL% < 3; see Weintraub, Rubin, & Mesulam, 1990), but within normal limits in Graff-Radford et al.'s (1990) patient ($d = 0.0$ OL% = 100).

Delayed recall

Measures of delayed recall made up the second most impaired cognitive domain (see Chapter 15, Table 15.3). Patients with PPA, however, are typically well oriented in time and place (Mesulam, 1982). Moreover, performance on tasks of delayed recall yield poor scores in comparison to normal controls (e.g., RAVLT delayed recall) which is surprising considering that patients demonstrate functional memory skills in their daily living activities. This disparity suggests that impaired test performance may arise as a secondary consequence of patients' language disorder, or may represent a material-specific memory deficit (Snowden, Neary, & Mann, 1996). Indeed, the meta-analysis indicates delayed recall performance on the Rey Auditory Verbal Learning Test (RAVLT; Rey, 1964) to be impaired in PPA ($d = -4.42$ OL% < 2), whereas delayed recall of the Rey-Osterrieth Complex Figure (ROCF; Lezak, 1995) is within normal limits ($d < 0.0$ OL% = 100). This finding is consistent with the above interpretation, as performance is impaired principally for tests of delayed verbal recall, but not for tasks of delayed visual memory.

Cognitive flexibility and abstraction

The next most impaired cognitive domain was that which included measures of cognitive flexibility and abstraction (see Chapter 15, Table 15.3). On those related tasks such as the Wisconsin Card Sorting Test (WCST; Heaton, 1981), patients with PPA are indistinguishable from normal controls ($d < 0.0$ OL% = 100 WCST categories achieved). For example, Cohen, Benoit, Van Eackhout, Ducarne, and Brunet (1993) describe a patient who achieved 5 categories on the WCST. This is within normal limits in keeping with the patients' age and education. When the tasks of cognitive flexibility and abstraction are verbal in nature, patients with PPA are indeed impaired compared to normal controls. As mentioned, patients with PPA display a poor ability to generate words on phonemic fluency tasks which is so severe, that most of them can be differentiated from normal controls solely on the basis of test scores ($d = -1.99$ OL% = 19). Moreover, poor abstraction of commonalities between word pairs on the Similarities subtest of the WAIS-R is also apparent ($d = -1.00$ OL% = 44.6). Poor performance on these tasks, however, can be explained in terms of language production deficits. Further, patients typically do not exhibit the qualitative features associated with frontal-executive dysfunction such as perseveration, concreteness, and inflexibility of responses (Snowden, Neary, & Mann, 1996).

Memory acquisition

Performance on measures of memory acquisition were next most impaired (see Chapter 15, Table 15.3). The pattern of performance on tasks of memory acquisition – as with delayed recall, suggests that the impairment may arise as a secondary consequence of patients' language disorder, or may represent a material-specific memory deficit. For example, poor recall on trials 1 ($d = -2.00$ OL% = 19) and 5 ($d = -3.09$ OL% < 5) of the RAVLT, poor performance on the Paired Associates subtest of the WMS-R ($d = -2.12$ OL% = 17), and poor scores on both forward and backward digit span on the WAIS-R ($d = -1.92$ OL% = 20 backward; $d = -1.45$ OL% = 30 forward) have all been demonstrated by patients with PPA (Graff-Radford et al., 1990; Green et al., 1990; Scheltens, Hazenberg, Lindeboom, Valk, & Wolters, 1990). In contrast, nonverbal tasks of memory acquisition are performed within normal limits. For example, it has been shown that patients with PPA perform above average levels on the Benton Visual Retention Test ($d = 0.04$ OL% > 95; Chiacchio et al., 1993; Graff-Radford et al., 1990; Green et al., 1990; Kirshner, Tanridag, Thurman, & Whetsell Jr., 1987), and on immediate recall of the WMS-R visual reproduction figures ($d < 0.0$ OL% = 100; Belano & Ska, 1992). This pattern of performance is indeed consistent with the notion that memory, both acquisition and delayed recall, is impaired secondary to the consequence of patients' language disorder, and therefore, represents a material-specific memory deficit.

Attention/Concentration

Performance on measures of attention and concentration were next most impaired (see Chapter 15, Table 15.3). As noted, orientation remains intact in patients with PPA. On tasks of attention and concentration that incorporate a psychomotor component without the requirement of frontal-executive stress (i.e., Digit Symbol subtest of the WAIS-R), patients with PPA demonstrate normal motor persistence, sustained attention, response speed, and visuomotor coordination ($d < 0.0$ OL% = 100). Given a frontal-executive component to an attentional task, however, patient performance is impaired. For example, Green et al., (1990) administered the Trail Making Test Part B (Reitan, 1958) to eight patients with PPA and found performance to be significantly slow in comparison to normal controls ($d = 1.89$ OL% = 21). If the problem lies in the inability to actually sustain the set to serially alternate between letters and numbers, this may indeed indicate a frontal-executive deficit. This however, might also reflect the added burden of verbal encoding as the task requires the patient to shift between letters and numbers as well as sustained attention and response speed.

Performance skill

The performance skill domain corresponds to an overall effect size based on 43 effects of 0.01 (OL% > 99). It corresponds to the most intact cognitive domain (see Chapter 15, Table 15.3). More specifically, on subtests that make up the WAIS-R Performance IQ such as Block Design ($d = -0.23$ OL% = 85), Picture Completion ($d < 0.0$ OL% = 100), Object Assembly ($d = -0.22$ OL% = 85), and Picture Arrangement ($d = -0.03$ OL% > 97), the meta-analysis reveals that patients with PPA typically perform within normal limits (Benson & Zaias, 1991; Feher, Doody, Whitehead, & Pirozzolo, 1991; Green et al., 1990). Moreover, in Mesulam's (1982) original description of the syndrome, he clearly noted the particular discrepancy in WAIS-R Verbal versus Performance IQ, where Verbal IQ was markedly lowered in comparison to Performance IQ. This has been a consistent finding in subsequent reports (Caselli et al., 1993; Fuh, Liao, Wang & Lin, 1994; Kirshner et al., 1987; Lippa et al., 1991; McDaniel, Wagner, & Greenspan, 1991; Parkin, 1993; Yamamoto et al., 1990) and in the present quantitative review ($d = -1.14$ OL% = 40 Verbal IQ; $d = -0.15$ OL% 90 Performance IQ). Patients with PPA also demonstrate no difficulty on tasks of spatial skill such as the Hooper Visual Organization Test ($d < 0.0$ OL% =100; Lezak, 1995), and Judgment of Line Orientation ($d < 0.0$ OL% = 100; JLO; Benton, Hamsher, Varney, & Spreen, 1983; Benton, Varney, & Hamsher, 1978). Further, copy of the ROCF is also within normal limits in patients with PPA ($d < 0.0$ OL% = 100). For example, Graff-Radford et al.'s, (1990) patient with PPA obtained a perfect score of 36 in comparison to the corresponding age and education norm of 32. Indeed, most tasks of visuospatial ability are executed normally, showing preservation of perceptuo-spatial skill until very late in the disease when it is no longer possible to formally assess them. The patients' ability to orient visual attention and localize objects in the environment, however, would still suggest some preservation of spatial function in late stage PPA (Snowden, Neary, & Mann, 1996).

Manual dexterity

Patient performance on tasks of manual dexterity such as the Grooved and Purdue Pegboards (see Lezak, 1995), Finger Tapping and Grip Strength tests (Reitan & Wolfson, 1993) have not been reported in published studies. Considering the focal degeneration of the left fronto-perisylvian region, however, manual dexterity is not a function that is at risk for alteration. Indeed, patients with PPA carry out normally manipulative hand-eye coordination tasks, suggesting that manual dexterity in PPA remains well preserved. There may be, however, evidence of dyspraxia with progression of disease (Snowden, Neary, & Mann, 1996).

Summary

A minority of patients with Alzheimer's disease present initially with symptoms of language breakdown, and features of language disorder which may precede the development of other cognitive deficits by months or even years. Such patients may be incorrectly regarded as suffering from PPA (Snowden, Neary, Mann, 1996). Conversely, the language disorder of PPA may be wrongly interpreted as a focal manifestation of Alzheimer's disease (Mesulam, 1987). As such, the differential diagnosis of PPA from Alzheimer's disease is often arduous to say the least. In most cases this differentiation can be established by serial evaluation of patients where in patients with PPA, language disorder will remain the focal area of dysfunction whereas, in Alzheimer's disease, deficits will emerge in other areas of cognition – namely memory. As Snowden, Neary, and Mann (1996) note, however, this tenet does not have absolute diagnostic value as the psychological deficits in Alzheimer's disease may remain remarkably circumscribed over a prolonged period of time. Further, with disease progression, the range of symptomatology may increase in PPA as the spread of pathological change becomes more extensive. There remain, nonetheless, qualitative clinical features which can help to differentiate PPA from Alzheimer's disease.

   In general, language in nonfluent PPA is dissimilar to the fluent aphasic output that is typical in Alzheimer's disease. Indeed, the involvement of morphosyntactic and phonologic features in patients with PPA stand in sharp contrast with the selective impairment of lexical and semantic aspects of language frequently observed in patients with a clinical diagnosis of Alzheimer's disease (Weintraub, Rubin, & Mesulam, 1990). Patients with PPA can have any type of aphasia (a nonfluent variant has been described here, but keep in mind that a 'fluent' semantic dementia has also been described), whereas patients with dementia of the Alzheimer's type almost always have a fluent aphasia of the anomic, transcortical sensory, or Wernicke's type (Zec, 1993). Therefore, the one aphasic subtype that most clearly differentiates the two clinical syndromes of PPA and Alzheimer's disease is the presence of a nonfluent (Broca's or transcortical motor) type, since this is almost never reported in Alzheimer's disease but is quite frequent in PPA (Mesulam, 1982, 1987).

Further, the aphasic qualities in PPA include phonemic paraphasias, whereas in Alzheimer's disease, they are typically infrequent and sporadic (Weintruab, Rubin, & Mesulam, 1990).

Because memory impairment – a core clinical feature of Alzheimer's disease, is not always spared in PPA, additional information about memory performance needs to be evaluated. Patients with PPA perform relatively poorly on tasks of delayed recall and acquisition secondary to language disturbance (see Table 6.2). Indeed, non-verbal memory is substantially better in PPA, whereas non-verbal and verbal memory are both affected in Alzheimer's disease (see Chapter 4). This material-specific impairment may further aid in the differentiation of PPA from Alzheimer's disease.

With respect to performance skill, or in particular visuospatial skill, performance is preserved in PPA and impaired early in Alzheimer's disease. Thus, impaired performance on tasks such as Judgment of Line Orientation, Block Design, and cube, house, or clock drawing, would suggest more posterior, parietal involvement consistent with Alzheimer's pathology. Moreover, apraxia for both symbolic and nonsymbolic acts are common in Alzheimer's disease but not in PPA. In addition, unlike patients with PPA, those with Alzheimer's disease may have apperceptive agnosia. This agnosia can help differentiate the diagnosis of dementia of the Alzheimer's type from PPA which typically manifests itself without involvement of posterior cortices.

Chapter 7

PROGRESSIVE SUPRANUCLEAR PALSY
(STEELE-RICHARDSON-OLSZEWSKI SYNDROME)

Progressive supranuclear palsy (PSP), or the Steele-Richardson-Olszewski syndrome, is a progressive neurological disorder characterized by supranuclear ophthalmoplegia, axial rigidity and dystonia, pseudobulbar palsy, and cognitive impairment (Albert, Feldman, & Willis, 1974; Kristensen, 1985; Litvan & Agid, 1992; Steele, Richardson, & Olszewski, 1964). Neuropathological changes are most marked in the globus pallidus, subthalamic nucleus, red nucleus, substantia nigra, superior colliculi, nuclei cuneiformis and subcuneiformis, periaqueductal gray matter, pontine tegmentum, and dentate nucleus (Hauw et al., 1994; Litvan et al., 1997; Steele, Richardson, & Olszewski, 1964; Verny, Jellinger, Hauw, Bancher, Litvan, & Agid, 1996). In keeping with the prominent subcortical lesions in PSP, the cognitive deficits associated with PSP have been described by Albert, Feldman, & Willis (1974) as constituting the syndrome of subcortical dementia (Albert, Feldman, & Willis, 1974; Cummings, 1990; McHugh & Folstein, 1975, 1979). The pattern of deficits include memory loss, impaired abstracting and/or calculating ability (manipulation of acquired knowledge), changes in personality that include apathy, inertia, occasional irritability, and general slowness of thought processes. This pattern of deficits has been suggested to reflect dysfunction of fronto-subcortical neuronal systems (Cummings, 1993; Freedman & Albert, 1985).

The small but steadily growing literature on PSP has characterized the clinical presentation of this disorder. For example, Kristensen (1985) provides an excellent narrative summary of the literature 20 years after Steele, Richardson and Olszewki (1964) first introduced PSP as a distinct nosological entity. More recently, Grafman, Litvan, and Stark (1995), Bak and Hodges (1998), and

Zakzanis, Leach, and Freedman (1998) have reviewed the neuropsychological features of PSP and conclude that patients with PSP have dramatically slowed information processing and motor execution, rapid forgetting, problems in orienting attentional resources, and difficulty in planning and shifting conceptual sets. Indeed, PSP is considered the prototypical subcortical dementia.

The diagnosis of progressive supranuclear palsy and study inclusion criteria

The diagnosis of PSP remains primarily dependent on analysis of the clinical features: the pattern of evolution of the symptoms over time, the physical findings, and the clinical setting (see Duvoisin, 1992). In the fully developed case, the clinical picture is usually distinctive. The difficulty of establishing the diagnosis and differentiating the disease from Parkinson's disease and multiple system atrophy, however, should not be underestimated, especially during the earlier phases of the disease when pathognomonic clinical signs have not yet developed (Duvoisin, 1992). Therefore, to be included in the review patients with PSP must have been diagnosed in primary studies by a board certified neurologist and met diagnostic criteria for PSP proposed by Golbe, Davis, Schcenberg and Duvoisin (1988), Lees (1987), or Litvan et al., (1996) or presented with the following neurological signs: rigidity and bradykinesia, axial dystonia, supranuclear gaze palsy, postural instability with backward falls, and progressive cognitive impairment with frontal lobe signs.

The review

Twenty-three studies published between 1987 and 1997 met criteria for inclusion in the present analysis. In total, cognitive test results from 229 patients with PSP, and 357 normal healthy controls were recorded across primary studies.

Descriptive demographic and clinical variable data available from primary studies from the published literature reflects PSP samples that typically are even in gender composition, are approximately 66 years of average age, have completed 11 years of education, are 4 years in disease duration, and were initially hospitalized and diagnosed in their early 60s (see Table 7.1). None of the demographic or clinical variables correlated significantly with the effect sizes from any of the cognitive variables. Single case studies and narrative reviews, however, have provided a careful description of related cognitive impairments with basic clinical and demographic variables (e.g., Grafman, Litvan, & Stark, 1995; Kristensen, 1985; Litvan & Agid, 1992).

Cognitive deficits in progressive supranuclear palsy

Effect size summaries are presented for specific cognitive tasks and test variables

Table 7.1.   Descriptive Statistics for Progressive Supranuclear Palsy Cognitive Studies.

Variables	M	SD	Range	N
Sample size				
PSP samples	10.0	5.4	3–25	23
Control samples	17.0	16.7	4–82	23
Patients' age	66.4	5.4	55–85	23
Onset age	59.6	0.9	59–60	3
Duration of illness (in years)	3.8	0.9	2.1–4.9	13
Percentage of males	54.6	13.3	44–88	9
Patients' education (yrs.)	11.1	2.9	8.5–15.3	10

Note. M = mean; SD = standard deviation of the mean; N = number of studies in which the variable was reported.

in Table 7.2. Mean d's presented in the column are raw effect sizes. Test variables are presented according to the rank order of the effect size. Effect sizes are included along with the corresponding standard deviation and the number of effect sizes the mean d was based on. To help describe the dispersion of effect sizes, a minimum and maximum d value are also presented. The table also includes the Fail Safe N (Nfs) for the number of additional studies that would be necessary to reverse the overall probability obtained from our obtained effect size to a value higher than our critical value for statistical significance, which was set at .01 (see Wolf, 1986 for an elaboration). Chapter 15 (Table 15.4) includes similar statistics for the composite neuropsychological domains. The following description of cognitive task and test variable effect sizes are grouped by domain and presented in the order of most to least impaired in PSP.

Attention/Concentration
The neuropsychological domain of attention/concentration was found to be most impaired in patients with PSP (see Chapter 15, Table 15.4). More specifically, measures of attention and concentration produced effects sizes that all met heuristic benchmark criteria. For example, the most sensitive measure to the presence of PSP was the Stroop word reading task ($d = -4.46$ OL% < 5) followed closely by the Stroop color reading task ($d = -4.12$ OL% < 5). Trail Making Test (Part A) performance was also highly sensitive ($d = 3.41$ OL% < 5) to PSP. Thus, patients with PSP can validly be discriminated from healthy normal controls based on Stroop and Trail Making Test (Part A) scores.

Taken together these effects underscore the bradyphrenic quality and/or opthalomoplegia typically present in the patient with PSP. In keeping with the akinesia, depression, and frontal dysfunction of the patient, however, it is important to parse the effects of motor or affective disturbance from the genuine slowing of central processing time on measures of attention and concentration. Because performance skill and manual dexterity measures that generally follow a reaction time paradigm (i.e., WAIS-R Block Design, Digit Symbol; Finger

Table 7.2. Effect Size Results in Rank Order for Patients with Progressive Supranuclear Palsy.

Neuropsychological Test/ Test Variable	N d	M d	SD d	Min. d	Max. d	Nfs	OL % (approx.)
Stroop word reading	1	−4.46	−	−4.46	−4.46	445	
Mattis DRS Total Score	1	−4.25	−	−4.25	−4.25	424	
Stroop color reading	1	−4.12	−	−4.12	−4.12	411	< 2.0
WAIS-R Full Scale IQ	2	−3.60	0.39	−3.32	−3.87	718	
WAIS-R Performance IQ	2	−3.54	0.74	−3.02	−4.07	706	
Trail Making Test Part A	1	3.41	−	3.41	3.41	340	
Purdue Pegboard bilateral	2	−3.32	0.98	−2.63	−4.01	662	
Stroop interference	2	−3.14	0.08	−3.10	−3.18	626	< 5.0
Purdue Pegboard right hand	2	−2.89	1.15	−2.08	−3.71	576	
Trail Making Test Part B	2	2.87	0.06	2.81	2.92	572	
Semantic fluency	4	−2.80	0.93	−1.89	−3.85	1116	
CVLT list A total 1–5	1	−2.77	−	−2.77	−2.77	276	
Purdue pegboard left hand	2	−2.71	0.89	−2.08	−3.34	540	
COWAT	5	−2.57	0.75	−1.39	−3.21	1280	
WMS-R Memory Quotient	4	−2.56	0.73	−1.73	−3.21	1020	
WCST categories achieved	4	−2.54	2.15	−1.18	−5.75	1012	
WAIS-R Verbal IQ	2	−2.51	0.44	−2.20	−2.82	500	15.0
Raven's Progressive Matrices	1	−2.33	−	−2.33	−2.33	232	
WMS-R Visual Reproduction II delayed recall	1	−2.02	−	−2.02	−2.02	201	20.0
Design fluency	2	−1.80	0.49	−1.46	−2.15	358	
WMS-R Visual Reproduction I immediate recall	1	−1.73	−	−1.73	−1.73	172	
CVLT short delay free recall	1	−1.62	−	−1.62	−1.62	161	
WCST errors	1	1.51	−	1.51	1.51	150	30.0
WCST percent perseverative error	1	1.29	−	1.29	1.29	128	
Finger Tapping Test	1	−1.28	−	−1.28	−1.28	127	
Go No Go	1	−1.26	−	−1.26	−1.26	125	
Boston Naming Test	4	−1.23	0.61	−0.43	−1.84	488	
WMS-R Logical Memory II delayed recall	1	−1.16	−	−1.16	−1.16	115	
WMS-R Logical Memory I immediate recall	1	−1.16	−	−1.16	−1.16	115	
CVLT long delay free recall	1	−1.12	−	−1.12	−1.12	111	
WAIS-R Arithmetic	1	−1.09	−	−1.09	−1.09	108	45.0
Corsi Block Tapping Span	2	−0.80	−	−0.69	−0.92	158	
WAIS-R Digit Span	1	−0.09	−	−0.09	−0.09	8	> 95.0
Rey-Osterrieth Complex Figure copy	1	−0.01	−	−0.01	−0.01	0	

Note. Nd = number of effect sizes; Md = mean effect size; SDd = standard deviation around the effect size; Min.d = smallest effect size obtained; Max.d = largest effect size obtained; Nfs = Fail Safe N; DRS = Dementia Rating Scale; CVLT = California Verbal Learning Test; WAIS-R = Wechsler Adult Intelligence Scale-Revised; WMS-R = Wechsler Memory Scale-Revised; COWAT = Controlled Oral Word Association Task; WCST = Wisconsin Card Sorting Test.

Tapping Test) correspond to larger effect sizes than those obtained on measures of attention/concentration and cognitive flexibility and abstraction, the rank order of effects supports the notion that central processing time is indeed slowed in patients with PSP. It is likely that this is related to striatofrontal dysfunction (also see Pillon & Dubois, 1992).

Performance skill

The reason we chose the words "performance skill" to indicate a neuropsychological domain was to include the interplay of cognitive and motor speed in successful performance on measures of visuospatial, visuoperceptual, and constructional ability. This is indeed most apparent in patients with PSP as slowing of thought processes is an essential feature of their cognitive dysfunction. As such, WAIS-R Performance IQ effect sizes met heuristic benchmark criteria ($d = -3.54$ OL% < 5) indicating that patients with PSP can be validly discriminated from healthy normal controls based on test score dispersion. Specific effects for each WAIS-R performance subtest were not obtained as to date no published control-group study has elucidated such data. Copy of the Rey-Osterrieth Complex Figure is entirely normal ($d = -0.01$ OL% > 95), however, which supports the notion that poor WAIS-R performance task scores reflect slowed speed of information processing and response execution rather than a higher order impairment in visuospatial, visuoperceptual, and constructional ability.

Manual dexterity

Manual dexterity is next most impaired in patients with PSP (see Chapter 15, Table 15.4). For example, bilateral performance on the Purdue Pegboard produced effect sizes that reached benchmark criteria ($d = -3.32$ OL% < 5). Unilateral performance also produced large effects that approached benchmark criteria (e.g., $d = -2.89$ OL% = 8 for the right hand; $d = -2.71$ OL% = 9 for the left hand). In keeping with unilateral Purdue Pegboard effect sizes (i.e., right vs. left), there appears to be no evidence for an asymmetrical deficit in PSP. Finally, a significantly smaller effect size was obtained on the Finger Tapping Test ($d = -1.28$ OL% = 35) relative to Purdue Pegboard effects. This dissociation might reflect the added dimension of visual coordination that contributes to successful performance on the Purdue Pegboard. Because the Finger Tapping Test is a more pure measure of motor speed which does not require vertical voluntary gaze, the loss of volitional downgaze found in patients with PSP does not further burden them on this task, whereas this eye movement difficulty would hinder their performance on the Purdue Pegboard.

Cognitive flexibility and abstraction

Taken together measures of cognitive flexibility and abstraction constitute the next most impaired neuropsychological domain in PSP (see Chapter 15, Table 15.4). As these measures are generally sensitive to frontal-brain system integrity, and in keeping with neuropathological deafferentiation between the basal ganglia and prefrontal cortex in PSP, the close relation between subcortical structures and the prefrontal cortex underscores their complementarity in an anatomicofunctional "subcorticofrontal system" that impairs patient performance on these tasks. In some cases, however, cognitive slowing itself may account for a poor performance on tasks used to investigate cognitive flexibility and abstraction. For example, slow reaction time might have contributed to the large effect size obtained on phonemic fluency (COWAT; $d = -2.57$ OL% $= 11$), as the time allotted to generate as many words that begin with a certain letter (e.g., F, A, S) is usually limited to 60 seconds (Lezak, 1995). Moreover, the nonverbal counterpart to phonemic fluency – design fluency, corresponds to a much smaller effect size of -1.80 (OL% $= 23$). As this measure is more sensitive to right-sided prefrontal lesions (Jones-Gotman & Milner, 1977), it has yet to be shown that PSP or Parkinson's disease is characterized by asymmetrical cognitive dysfunction in verbal or nonverbal fluency (Sandson & Albert, 1987).

A spontaneous tendency to perseverate may also account for some of the observed deficits, especially on tasks involving concept formation and shifting ability (Kristensen, 1985; Pillon & Dubois, 1992). For example, performance on the interference trial of the Stroop task yielded a large effect size meeting benchmark criteria ($d = -3.14$ OL % < 5). The inability of patients to shift set was also evinced in the large obtained effect size for the Trail Making Test (Part B) ($d = 2.87$ OL% $= 11$) and the number of WCST categories achieved ($d = -2.54$ OL% $= 12$). This deficit of shifting aptitude, like the poor performance of patients with PSP on the WCST and Part B of the Trail Making Test, indicate a lack of conceptual flexibility. Oculomotor deficits, however, could certainly account for much of the poor performance on these tasks, given that the WCST percent perseverative error corresponds to a much smaller effect of -1.26 (OL% $= 37$), for example.

Finally, it has been noted elsewhere (see Pilon & Dubois) that abstract thinking tasks that require neither sorting nor problem solving (e.g., WAIS-R Similarities, Concept Formation subtest of the Mattis DRS) are also poorly performed by patients with PSP. The magnitude of these deficits, however, can not be articulated at this time as patient performance on these specific measures have not been incorporated into a control-group research design that would lend itself to effect size analysis.

Verbal skill

The concept of "subcortical dementia" implies a characteristic pattern of dementia which does not include those considered to be in the category of the "higher cortical functions" such as aphasia (see Albert, Feldman, & Willis, 1974). Speech is typically slurred or difficult to understand in PSP because of dystonic dysarthria however (Pillon & Dubois, 1992). As such, performance on aphasic measures such as the Boston Naming Test was minimally impaired ($d = -1.28$ OL% $= 37$). Only when verbal skill measures incorporate a "time-dependent" component to successful performance can patients with PSP be discriminated validly from healthy normal controls. For example, on semantic fluency tasks, an effect size of -2.80 (OL% $= 9$) was obtained. Poor semantic fluency performance is typically related to poor retrieval from semantic memory, however, in keeping with the rank order of effects, performance on measures of memory acquisition and delayed recall fell well below performance on measures of attention/concentration and performance skill which are mostly time dependent (see Table 7.2). Thus, defective semantic fluency likely reflects the patient's inability to generate as many words as possible in one minute because of poor initiation, slowed central processing (bradyphrenia), and perhaps, perseveration.

Finally, WAIS-R Verbal IQ effects ($d = -2.51$ OL% = 12) were also capable of discriminating a large number of patients with PSP from healthy normal controls as the obtained mean effect size approached benchmark criteria. Although large, the WAIS-R Verbal IQ effect size was smaller than that obtained for the Performance IQ however. This dissociation may aid in the differentiation of cortical versus subcortical dementias: Verbal IQ effects were larger in the cortical dementias, and Performance IQ effects were larger in the subcortical dementias.

Delayed recall

When considering the performance of patients with PSP on measures of delayed recall and memory acquisition, it is important to refer to the pattern of effects displayed in Table 7.2, rather than the rank order of these composite neuropsychological domains. For example, in keeping with the rank order of neuropsychological domains, it would appear that delayed recall is more impaired than memory acquisition. A closer inspection of the effect sizes would suggest otherwise however. That is, CVLT long delay free recall corresponds to an effect size of -1.12 (OL% = 41). The magnitude of this effect, can at most, differentiate approximately 50% of patients with PSP from healthy normal controls. Conversely, patients with PSP demonstrate a significantly greater impairment of free recall immediately following presentation (e.g., $d = -2.77$ OL% = 9) suggesting superior retention of information over delay intervals. Moreover, it has also been noted that recognition performance, though impaired, tends to be disproportionately better in patients with PSP (Litvan, Grafman, Gomez, & Chase, 1989). This pattern of memory failure is consistent with deficient retrieval (Butters, Delis, & Lucas, 1995; Butters, Wolfe, Granholm, & Martone, 1986; Massman, Delis, Butters, Levin, & Salmon, 1990). Moreover, it has also been shown that patients with PSP display relatively intact perceptual priming, and dramatically impaired procedural learning (Grafman, Litvan, & Stark, 1995).

Finally, the magnitude of effect obtained for delayed recall of the WMS-R Visual Reproduction figures was twice as large as that obtained for delayed recall of the WMS-R Logical Memory stories ($d = -2.02$ OL% = 18 and $d = -1.16$ OL% = 41, respectively). This dissociation likely reflects the greater complexity of the Visual Reproduction task which requires intact perceptuomotor and vertical gaze ability for successful performance. Measures of retention on the WMS-R Visual Reproduction and Logical Memory immediate and delayed recall subtests would indeed elucidate further the nature of this dissociation. Such data has yet to be reported in the primary literature. Therefore, it is difficult at this time to conclude whether a true dissociation between verbal and nonverbal delayed recall performance does indeed characterize PSP.

Memory acquisition

Measures of memory acquisition correspond to the least impaired neuropsychological domain in PSP. Again however, it is important to refer to Table 7.2 and the independent effects rather than assuming all tasks of memory acquisition are less sensitive than all tasks of delayed recall as the rank order of neuropsychological domains would suggest.

The magnitude of effects obtained for immediate recall of the WMS-R Visual Reproduction figures and the Logical Memory stories were no different ($d = -1.73$ OL% = 24 and $d = -1.16$ OL% = 41, respectively). Again, it is difficult to articulate the nature of this dissociation without retention measures. CVLT short delay free recall and total recall across trials 1–5 correspond to greater effects ($d = -1.62$ OL% = 26 and $d = -2.77$ OL% = 9, respectively) compared to CVLT long delay free recall effects ($d = 1.12$ OL% = 41). This pattern of effects is consistent with a retrieval based impairment from episodic memory, in keeping with noted superior recognition scores in single case studies of patients with PSP (see Litvan, Grafman, Gomez, & Chase, 1989).

Finally, on measures of verbal span, patients with PSP perform entirely within normal limits as there is an almost complete overlap in score distribution ($d = -0.09$ OL% > 95 WAIS-R Digit Span). Unfortunately, forward and backward digit span have not been reported separately in the literature to date (for an exception see Kaplan, Fein, Morris, & Delis, 1991). On the nonverbal block tapping spatial span, a greater effect was obtained ($d = -0.80$ OL% = 53). This dissociation might also reflect the influence of sluggish manual dexterity and perceptuo-motor and vertical gaze impairments on successful spatial span performance, making these effects seem greater than they really are in the context of memory acquisition.

Summary

The pattern of results suggest that the dementia in PSP can be distinguished as a clinical entity by the presence of a characteristic cluster of neuropsychological deficits that are related to fronto-subcortical system dysfunction together with mild memory loss occurring without associated aphasia, apraxia, and agnosia (Albert, Feldman, & Willis, 1974; Freedman & Albert, 1985; Zakzanis, Leach, & Freedman, 1998). The clinical profile that emerged from our quantitative synthesis is consistent with that proposed by Albert, Feldman, and Willis (1974), and reviewed by Freedman and Albert (1985). That is, patients with PSP show impairment of memory function which is primarily retrieval based. Their manipulation of acquired knowledge is also impaired. Their thought processes are also slowed. Taken together, the concept of subcortical dementia seems particularly appropriate to PSP as the pattern of cognitive changes seems to be specific and differs from that seen in Alzheimer's disease (see Chapter 4), fronto-temporal dementia (see Chapter 5), and primary progressive aphasia (see Chapter 6). Moreover, these changes are observed in the absence of significant lesions of the cerebral cortex as measured with Positron Emission Tomography (see Goffinet et al., 1989). The cognitive subcortical system alterations may therefore result from the severe degeneration of subcortical structures, particularly the damage of the striatopallidothalamic complex (Steele, 1972), leading to deafferentation of the prefrontal cortex (Pillon & Dubois, 1992). Unfortunately, the fourth element of subcortical dementia proposed by Albert, Feldman, and Willis (1974), personality changes marked by apathy or inertia with occasional episodes of irritability, was not systematically assessed in the literature reviewed.

Chapter 8

PARKINSON'S DISEASE

Idiopathic Parkinson's disease (PD) is a degenerative disorder of unknown etiology affecting mainly the pigmented neurons from the pars compacta of the
substantia nigra and the integrity of functional neuronal loops connecting basal
ganglia and frontal cortex (Cornford, Chang, & Miller, 1995; Corsellis, 1976;
Cummings, 1993; Freedman & Albert, 1985; Turner, 1968). Pathophysiologic
alterations ascribed primarily to dopamine deficiency of the substantia nigra and
the presence of characteristic eosinophilic cytoplasmic inclusions (or Lewy bodies) produce a complex motor system disturbance including bradykinesia, cog-
wheel rigidity, tremor, masked facies, and disturbances of gait, posture, and
equilibrium (Cummings & Benson, 1992; Freedman, 1990; Huber &
Cummings, 1992; Marsden, 1994; Parkinson, 1817).

Although there is now compelling evidence that cognitive abnormality is
associated with PD (Boller, 1980; Charcot, 1875; Huber & Bornstein, 1992), in
his original descriptive essay of the disease, James Parkinson (1817) specifically denied the presence of cognitive changes and noted that "the senses and intellect [are] uninjured". Indeed, there is still considerable controversy regarding
the frequency with which PD is accompanied by cognitive decline as well as the
exact pattern of cognitive impairment associated with PD (McPherson &
Cummings, 1996). A number of studies, however, accounting for a large number of patients with PD, indicate that even those without overt dementia manifest a reduced ability for learning and recall of information, loss of cognitive
flexibility, and psychomotor slowing (Mahurin, Feher, Nance, Levy, &
Pirozzolo, 1993; McPherson & Cummings, 1996; Soukup & Adams, 1996;

Zakzanis & Freedman, 1999). Similarly, a dementia syndrome of PD has also been described (Boller, 1980; Cummings, 1990; Freedman, 1990) to embody neuropsychological deficits associated with typical subcortical dementing processes including a slowing of cognition and motor skills, memory disturbances characterized by poor recall with preservation of recognition abilities, executive dysfunction, and alterations in mood (Albert, Feldman, & Willis, 1974; Cummings & Benson, 1984; McHugh & Folstein, 1979).

The diagnosis of Parkinson's disease and study inclusion criteria

The diagnosis of probable idiopathic PD in primary studies must have been made based on the presence of at least three of the four following neurologic signs: tremor, bradykinesia or akinesia, rigidity, and postural instability (Calne, Snow, & Lee, 1992) and the absence of clinical or laboratory evidence of systemic disease, a history of alcoholism, head injury, psychiatric disorder, or evidence of multi-infarct dementia [using a criteria score of less than 3 on the Modified Hachinski Ischemic Scale (Hachinski, Iliff, & Zilhka, 1975; Rosen, Terry, Fuld, Katzman, & Peck, 1980)].

Moreover, the classification of patients with PD as demented or nondemented was determined variously in primary studies. Patients were classified; (1) on the basis of normative data obtained from the normal control group, i.e., patients with PD with scores falling below the maximum of the range of scores attained by the normal controls (typically on a general mental status rating scale, e.g., Mini-Mental State Exam, or Mattis Dementia Rating Scale) were classified as having dementia (for an example, see Freedman & Oscar-Berman, 1997); (2) on the basis of DSM criteria for dementia; and/or (3) on the basis of specific mental status examination scores that fell below cut-off criteria for dementia. For example, a score of less than 123 on the Dementia Rating Scale (DRS; Mattis, 1988) or a score of less than 24 on the Mini-Mental State Examination (MMSE; Folstein, Folstein, & McHugh, 1975). Despite these differences in parsing patients into demented and nondemented groups, the obtained effect sizes on the MMSE and the DRS did not differ significantly when the different classification schemes were compared statistically ($F = 1.01$, $p > .05$). Freedman and Oscar-Berman's (1997) classification method, however, is designed to reliably yield an approximate effect size d of 3 or greater that corresponds to less than 5% overlap between screening test score distributions between patients with demented and nondemented PD and normal controls. This method of classification can therefore ensure the exclusion of demented patients and the inclusion of nondemented patients in normally defined PD experimental groups.

The review

Ninety-nine studies[1] published between 1980 and 1997 met criteria for inclusion in the present analysis. In total, cognitive test results from 2,730 patients with PD (2,134 nondemented, 596 demented), and 2,464 normal healthy controls were recorded across primary studies.

Descriptive demographic and clinical variable data available from primary studies from the published literature are presented in Table 8.1 for nondemented patients with PD (n = 2,120). These patients represent 78% of all patients with PD who have been studied in the published literature. Table 8.1 reflects nondemented patient samples that are about equally distributed between men and women which is consistent with recent studies that report no significant gender differences in the prevalence of PD (Soukup & Adams, 1996). Nondemented patients with PD were approximately 63 years of age, had 13.2 years of formal education, and had an average age at disease onset of 59 years. The mean duration of illness was approximately 5.9 years. When medication regimen was described in primary studies (n = 44), approximately 87% of patients in study samples were on various types of pharmacotherapies (typically a levodopa preparation, such as Sinemet). The mean score on the Modified Hoehn and Yahr scale (Hoehn & Yahr, 1967) was 2.1 which is meant to reflect a patient who presents with bilateral disease without impairment of balance.

In terms of possible moderator variables, in keeping with disease progression, the duration of illness for nondemented patients with PD was related to a more impaired score on the Modified Hoehn and Yahr scale ($r = 0.39$, $p < .05$, n =

Table 8.1.   Descriptive Statistics for Nondemented Parkinson's Disease Cognitive Studies.

Variables	M	SD	Range	N
Sample size				
nondemented				
PD samples	29	20	8–107	75
Control samples	24	14	5–90	75
Patients' age	63	5.5	44–73	74
Onset age	59	8.6	39–69	12
Duration of illness (yrs.)	5.9	2.9	0.20–13	52
Percentage of males	61	9.4	44–80	45
Patients' education (yrs.)	13.2	2.6	6.2–19	58
Percentage on medication	87	25	0–100	44
Hoehn & Yahr scale	2.1	0.7	1–3	48

Note. M = mean; SD = standard deviation of the mean; N = number of studies in which the variable was reported.

1. Studies that tested both demented and nondemented patients with PD were counted as two different studies. Thus, 83 actual studies served as the data base for the review.

40). Also, education correlated significantly with performance on the Controlled Oral Word Association Task (COWAT; Benton, Hamsher, Varney, & Spreen, 1983; Spreen & Strauss, 1991) ($r = -0.40, p < .05$, n = 28). The number of words generated on the COWAT is related to the number of years of formal education completed. The less education, the larger the effect size between non-demented patients with PD and normal controls. Finally, the number of categories achieved on the Wisconsin Card Sorting Test (WCST; Heaton, 1981; Heaton, Chelune, Talley, Kay, & Curtiss, 1993) was related to a more impaired score on the Modified Hoehn and Yahr scale ($r = -0.77, p < .05$, n = 10). Thus, considering the significant relationship between the duration of illness and physical disability as rated on the Modified Hoehn and Yahr scale in nondemented patients with PD, the number of categories achieved on the WCST might provide an indication of parallel progressive cognitive impairment over repeated test-retest assessments. This finding is in contrast to Huber, Freidenberg, Shuttleworth, Paulson, and Christy's (1989) conclusion that neuropsychological impairments do not develop in a uniform manner with progression of PD. Huber et al., (1989), however, did not include the WCST as a measure of progressive neuropsychological impairment in their study.

Table 8.2 presents descriptive demographic and clinical variable data for 588 demented patients with PD. These patients represent 22% of all patients with PD who have been studied in the published literature. This is consistent with previous frequency estimates of dementia that report a 27.7% prevalence rate (Aarsland, Tandberg, Larsen, & Cummings, 1996). These patients were typically 68 years of age, were ill for 7.3 years, and had completed approximately 12.1 years of formal education. The percentage of males was 68%. Therefore, in comparison to nondemented patients with PD, demented patients were older at the time of most studies, were younger with respect to onset of PD, were more likely to be male, and had a longer disease duration than the patients without dementia. When medication use was described in primary studies (n = 9),

Table 8.2.   Descriptive Statistics for Demented Parkinson's Disease Cognitive Studies.

Variables	M	SD	Range	N
Sample size				
demented PD samples	26	21	5–76	24
Control samples	29	20	5–90	24
Patients' age	68	11	62–76	24
Onset age	58	7.8	45–65	5
Duration of illness (yrs.)	7.3	3.4	1.1–13	15
Percentage of males	68	17	38–100	13
Patients' education (yrs.)	12.1	2.3	7–16	18
Percentage on medication	83	32	0–100	9
Hoehn & Yahr scale	2.6	0.7	2–3.5	11

Note. M = mean; SD = standard deviation of the mean; N = number of studies in which the variable was reported.

approximately 83% of patients were using levodopa preparations (e.g., Sinemet). The low frequency in which medication usage was reported in primary studies made moderator variable analysis infeasible (see Saint-Cyr, Taylor, & Lang, 1993 for a review). The average score on the Modified Hoehn and Yahr scale for the demented patients with PD was 2.6 which is meant to reflect a patient who has mild bilateral disease with "recovery on pull test".

In terms of possible moderator variables, the duration of illness for demented patients with PD was related ($r = -.87$, $p < .05$, n = 17) to larger obtained effect sizes on the Beck Depression Inventory (BDI; Beck, 1987). This is consistent with Starkstein, Preziosi, Bolduc, and Robinson's (1990) finding that the frequency and severity of depression is higher in late stages of the disease. Debate continues about whether the high frequency of depression occurs as a consequence of progressive physical impairment or whether depression is a manifestation of the functional changes in specific brain areas (see Soukup & Adams, 1996; Starkstein, Preziosi, Berthier, Bolduc, Mayberg, & Robinson, 1989). Moreover, the only other moderator variable to approach significance was the age at disease onset in demented patients with PD to MMSE performance. Previous findings have shown that dementia increases with advancing age in PD, and that cognitive changes are also found in patients with early onset of disease (e.g., Hietanen & Teravainen, 1988; Katzen, Levin, & Llabre, 1998).

Cognitive deficits in Parkinson's disease

Effect size summaries are presented for specific cognitive test variables in Tables 8.3 and 8.4. Test variables are presented according to the rank order of the effect size. Effect sizes are included along with the corresponding standard deviation and the number of effect sizes the mean d was based on. To help describe the dispersion of effect sizes, a minimum and maximum d value are also presented. The tables also include the Fail Safe N (Nfs) for the number of additional studies that would be necessary to reverse the overall probability obtained from our obtained effect size to a value higher than our critical value for statistical significance, which was set at .01 (see Wolf, 1986 for an elaboration). Chapter 15 (Table 15.5 and 15.6) includes similar statistics for the composite neuropsychological domains. Unlike previously, the following description of cognitive task and test variable effect sizes are not grouped by domain and not presented in the order of most to least impaired in PD because different orders were found for demented and nondemented patient deficits and they are both considered together. A "general intelligence" section is also first included to help articulate the differences between demented and nondemented patients in light of the inconsistent parsing of patients in primary studies.

General intelligence measures
With respect to general intelligence as measured with standardized tests such as the Wechsler Adult Intelligence Scale-Revised (WAIS-R; Wechsler, 1981) and

Table 8.3.   Effect Size Results in Rank Order for Nondemented Patients with Parkinson's Disease.

Neuropsychological Test/ Test Variable	N d	M d	SD d	Min. d	Max. d	Nfs	OL % (approx.)
Hamilton Depression Rating Scale	3	2.27	2.37	0.80	5.00	678	
CVLT list A trial 5	1	−2.25	−	−2.25	−2.25	224	
Buschke SRT delay recall	2	−2.24	3.73	0.40	−4.87	448	
CVLT long delay free recall	1	−2.04	−	−2.04	−2.04	203	20.0
CVLT list A trial 1	1	−1.98	−	−1.98	−1.98	197	
Tower of Toronto	1	1.82	−	1.82	1.82	181	
CVLT list B	1	−1.66	−	−1.66	−1.66	165	
CVLT list A trials 1–5	3	−1.57	0.51	−1.25	−2.15	468	
CVLT short delay free recall	2	−1.53	0.95	−0.86	−2.21	304	30.0
CVLT short delay cued recall	1	−1.46	−	−1.46	−1.46	145	
Rey Osterrieth Complex Figure copy	2	−1.39	0.08	−1.35	−1.42	276	
Rey Osterrieth Complex Figure delay reproduction	2	−1.29	0.50	−0.94	−1.65	256	
CVLT perseverations	1	1.26	−	1.26	1.26	125	
Stroop word reading	2	−1.14	0.35	−0.89	−1.38	226	
Warrington Facial Recognition	3	−1.09	0.69	−0.69	−1.89	324	
CVLT discriminability	2	−1.04	0.22	−0.89	−1.20	206	
Geriatric Depression Scale	4	1.01	0.21	0.78	1.26	400	45.0
Buschke SRT recognition	1	−0.99	−	−0.99	−0.99	98	
WMS-R Logical Memory II delayed recall	5	−0.97	0.61	−0.17	−1.37	480	
Purdue Pegboard bilateral	3	−0.96	0.52	−0.37	−1.35	285	
WAIS-R Picture Arrangement	2	−0.94	0.01	−0.93	−0.94	186	
CVLT long delay cued recall	1	−0.88	−	−0.88	−0.88	87	
Buschke SRT total recall	3	−0.88	0.85	0.10	−1.48	261	
Mattis DRS Initiation/ Perseveration scale	1	−0.87	−	−0.87	−0.87	86	
WAIS-R Digit Symbol	5	−0.84	0.20	−0.76	−1.00	420	
Speech Sounds Perception Test	2	0.83	0.02	0.81	0.85	164	
WMS-R Visual Reproduction I immediate recall	3	−0.85	0.00	−0.85	−0.85	252	
WRAT reading	2	−0.85	0.00	−0.85	−0.85	168	
Zung Depression Rating Scale	1	0.82	−	0.82	0.82	81	
WAIS-R Object Assembly	1	−0.80	−	−0.80	−0.80	79	
Raven's Progressive Matrices	9	−0.75	0.33	−0.23	−1.27	666	
WAIS-R Arithmetic	1	−0.75	−	−0.75	−0.75	74	
COWAT	33	−0.72	1.23	0.52	−6.90	2343	
Mattis DRS Conceptualization scale	1	−0.71	−	−0.71	−0.71	70	
Stroop color word reading	3	−0.71	0.24	−0.45	−0.92	210	
Go-No-Go	1	0.70	−	0.70	0.70	69	
WAIS-R Similarities	11	−0.70	0.35	−0.12	−1.29	759	
WMS-R Memory Quotient	6	−0.70	0.58	0.11	−1.29	414	

Table continues

Table 8.3. (continued)

Neuropsychological Test/ Test Variable	N d	M d	SD d	Min. d	Max. d	Nfs	OL % (approx.)
Beck Depression Inventory	23	0.68	0.65	−0.26	2.50	1541	
Finger Tapping Test left hand	2	−0.68	0.05	−0.66	−0.70	134	
WCST perseverative errors	4	0.68	0.11	0.64	0.77	268	
WMS-R Logical Memory I immediate recall	9	−0.67	0.57	0.20	−1.37	594	
WAIS-R Block Design	15	−0.66	0.28	−0.12	−1.24	975	
Sentence repetition	2	−0.64	0.01	−0.63	−0.64	126	
WAIS-R Performance IQ	6	−0.63	0.59	−0.08	−1.68	372	
WCST categories achieved	10	−0.63	0.34	−0.07	−1.09	620	
Benton Facial Recognition	5	0.61	0.13	0.12	1.18	300	
RAVLT delay recall	1	−0.57	–	−0.57	−0.57	56	
Block span backward	3	−0.55	0.14	−0.45	−0.67	162	
Block span forward	3	−0.54	0.14	−0.40	−0.67	159	
Judgment of Line Orientation	9	−0.53	0.44	−0.03	−1.27	468	
Mattis DRS Memory scale	1	−0.52	–	−0.52	−0.52	51	
WMS-R Paired Associates I & II	10	−0.52	0.40	0.28	−1.11	510	
WAIS-R Information	5	−0.51	0.22	−0.17	−0.70	250	65.0
WMS-R Visual Reproduction II number recall	2	0.49	0.00	0.49	0.49	96	
Finger Tapping Test right hand	2	−0.46	0.01	−0.46	−0.47	90	
Benton Visual Retention Test number of errors	7	0.46	0.81	−0.51	1.79	315	
RAVLT trials 1–5	2	−0.46	0.12	−0.38	−0.55	90	
WCST perseverations	11	0.46	0.47	−0.66	0.92	495	
Semantic fluency	16	−0.45	0.28	0.00	−0.86	704	
WAIS-R Vocabulary	16	−0.44	0.44	0.27	−1.46	688	
Design fluency	1	−0.43	–	−0.43	−0.43	42	
Hooper Visual Organization Test	1	−0.39	–	−0.39	−0.39	38	
CVLT intrusions	1	0.34	–	0.34	0.34	33	
WCST total errors	4	0.32	0.39	−0.03	0.70	124	
Boston Naming Test	14	−0.31	0.41	0.50	−0.91	420	
WAIS-R Full Scale IQ	8	−0.29	0.51	0.21	−1.36	224	
WAIS-R Digit Span backward	18	−0.25	0.32	0.40	−1.00	432	
Mattis DRS Construction scale	1	−0.23	–	−0.23	−0.23	22	
WAIS-R Picture Completion	1	−0.22	–	−0.22	−0.22	21	
Warrington word recognition	1	−0.22	–	−0.22	−0.22	21	
WAIS-R Digit Span forward	19	−0.21	0.40	0.40	−1.00	380	
Mattis DRS Attention scale	1	−0.18	–	−0.18	−0.18	17	
WAIS-R Comprehension	5	−0.18	0.33	0.34	−0.52	85	
WCST failure to maintain set	1	0.15	–	0.15	0.15	14	
Stroop interference	9	−0.13	0.70	−0.71	1.69	108	
WAIS-R Verbal IQ	12	−0.11	0.37	0.55	−0.69	120	
Token Test	1	0.09	–	0.09	0.09	8	
Trail Making Test Part A	1	0.08	–	0.08	0.08	7	
Benton Right-Left Orientation	1	−0.04	–	−0.04	−0.04	3	

Table continues

Table 8.3. (continued)

Neuropsychological Test/ Test Variable	N d	M d	SD d	Min. d	Max. d	Nfs	OL % (approx.)
National Adult Reading Test	14	−0.04	0.61	1.00	−1.44	42	
Famous Faces Test	1	0.00	−	0.00	0.00	−	100.0
Seashore Rhythm Test	1	0.00	−	0.00	0.00	−	

Note. Nd = number of effect sizes; Md = mean effect size; SDd = standard deviation around the effect size; Min.d = smallest effect size obtained; Max.d = largest effect size obtained; Nfs = Fail Safe N; SRT = Selective Reminding Test; DRS = Dementia Rating Scale; CVLT = California Verbal Learning Test; RAVLT = Rey Auditory Verbal Learning Test; WAIS-R = Wechsler Adult Intelligence Scale-Revised; WMS-R = Wechsler Memory Scale-Revised; COWAT = Controlled Oral Word Association Task; WCST = Wisconsin Card Sorting Test.

Table 8.4.   Effect Size Results in Rank Order for Demented Patients with Parkinson's Disease.

Neuropsychological Test/ Test Variable	N d	M d	SD d	Min. d	Max. d	Nfs	OL % (approx.)
WAIS-R Performance IQ	2	−3.40	2.33	−1.75	−5.05	678	
Purdue Pegboard right hand	2	−3.38	2.20	−1.82	−4.93	674	<5.0
Purdue Pegboard bilateral	2	−2.88	0.48	−2.54	−3.22	574	
Semantic fluency	4	−2.85	1.62	−1.23	−4.31	1136	
WAIS-R Digit Symbol	2	−2.16	0.10	−2.11	−2.20	430	
Finger Tapping Test right hand	2	−2.15	1.05	−1.40	−2.89	428	
COWAT	8	−2.05	0.94	−0.75	−3.24	1632	
Raven's Progressive Matrices	2	−2.03	0.93	−1.37	−2.68	404	
WAIS-R Arithmetic	1	−2.01	−	−2.01	−2.01	200	20.0
Benton Visual Retention Test number of errors	1	1.82	−	1.82	1.82	181	
WMS-R Logical Memory II delayed recall	2	−1.81	0.57	−1.41	−2.22	360	
Purdue Pegboard left hand	1	−1.79	−	−1.79	−1.79	178	
WMS-R Memory Quotient	2	−1.78	1.36	−0.82	−2.74	354	
WAIS-R Block Design	6	−1.68	0.91	−0.17	−2.72	1002	
WAIS-R Similarities	4	−1.68	0.45	−1.33	−2.33	668	
WMS-R Paired Associates I & II	4	−1.63	0.75	−0.84	−2.64	648	
WAIS-R Verbal IQ	3	−1.58	1.73	−0.35	−3.56	471	
WCST categories achieved	4	−1.55	0.52	−1.04	−6.19	616	
WCST perseverative errors	1	1.50	−	1.50	1.50	149	30.0
Hamilton Depression Rating Scale	2	1.40	0.18	1.27	1.53	278	
Finger Tapping Test left hand	1	−1.33	−	−1.33	−1.33	132	
Beck Depression Inventory	11	1.28	0.75	0.20	2.69	1397	
WMS-R Logical Memory I immediate recall	3	−1.28	0.61	−0.63	−1.83	381	
WAIS-R Information	1	−1.19	−	−1.19	−1.19	118	

Table continues

Table 8.4. (continued)

Neuropsychological Test/ Test Variable	N d	M d	SD d	Min. d	Max. d	Nfs	OL % (approx.)
WAIS-R Full Scale IQ	4	−1.14	1.34	−0.05	−2.85	452	
Benton Facial Recognition	1	−1.04	–	−1.04	−1.04	103	
Boston Naming Test	7	−1.04	0.30	−0.66	−1.43	721	
National Adult Reading Test	3	−1.03	0.84	−0.22	−1.89	306	
Stroop word reading	1	−1.02	–	1.02	1.02	101	45.0
WCST perseverations	5	0.99	0.68	−0.12	1.56	490	
Hooper Visual Organization Test	1	−0.95	–	−0.95	−0.95	94	
Famous Faces Test	1	−0.94	–	−0.94	−0.94	93	
Stroop color reading	1	0.91	–	0.91	0.91	90	
WAIS-R Comprehension	2	−0.81	1.14	0.00	−1.61	160	
Trail Making Test Part A	1	0.80	–	0.80	0.80	79	
Trail Making Test Part B	1	0.80	–	0.80	0.80	79	
Judgment of Line Orientation	1	−0.76	–	−0.76	−0.76	75	
WCST errors	1	0.75	–	0.75	0.75	74	
Stroop interference	1	−0.72	–	0.72	0.72	71	
WAIS-R Vocabulary	3	−0.46	0.31	−0.24	−0.82	135	65.0
WAIS-R Digit Span backward	4	−0.27	0.41	0.18	−0.77	104	
WAIS-R Digit Span forward	4	−0.26	0.38	0.20	−0.72	100	
WCST failure to maintain set	2	0.14	0.08	0.09	0.18	26	> 95.0

Note. Nd = number of effect sizes; Md = mean effect size; SDd = standard deviation around the effect size; Min.d = smallest effect size obtained; Max.d = largest effect size obtained; Nfs = Fail Safe N; SRT = Selective Reminding Test; DRS = Dementia Rating Scale; CVLT = California Verbal Learning Test; RAVLT = Rey Auditory Verbal Learning Test; WAIS-R = Wechsler Adult Intelligence Scale-Revised; WMS-R = Wechsler Memory Scale-Revised; COWAT = Controlled Oral Word Association Task; WCST = Wisconsin Card Sorting Test.

National Adult Reading Test (NART; Nelson, 1982), there is a similar pattern, but significant differences in magnitude of effect between nondemented and demented patients with PD relative to controls. More specifically, for the non-demented patients with PD the obtained effect size for WAIS-R Performance IQ ($d = -0.63$ OL% = 61) is considerably larger than that obtained for the Verbal IQ effect size ($d = -0.11$ OL %= 93). Previous findings have indeed revealed that 85% of patients with PD show Verbal IQ being greater by about 10 points as compared to Performance IQ; this discrepancy exists in only about 15% of the normal population (Loranger, Goodell, McDowell, Lee, & Sweet, 1972). Because response speed and the integrity of sensory and motor functions contribute more to the performance IQ than to the verbal IQ, however, it is not possible to determine whether visuospatial functions are more vulnerable to loss than are verbal abilities using composite IQ indexes. Moreover, the obtained effect size ($d = -0.04$) for the NART confirms that the residual vocabulary of patients with nondemented PD may be the best indicator of their premorbid mental ability, as the corresponding overlap of NART scores between nondemented patients with PD and controls is greater than 97%.

Although demented patients with PD tend to show modest deficits in WAIS-R Verbal IQ as compared to controls ($d = -1.58$ OL% = 27), they are larger than those obtained by nondemented patients with PD. Similarly, their Performance IQ is less than their Verbal IQ; a large WAIS-R performance IQ effect size ($d = -3.40$) corresponding to less than 5% overlap and a much smaller verbal IQ effect size ($d = -1.58$) corresponding to 27% overlap in test score dispersion between normal and demented patients with PD were obtained. Moreover, the discriminability of demented patients with PD from normal controls is maximal with respect to the WAIS-R Performance IQ index as the corresponding overlap suggests that the obtained magnitude of effect is consistent with that of a neuropsychological marker. The Performance IQ index that corresponds to an effect size > 3.0 may serve as a clinical marker that can aid in the proper recognition of demented PD and its differentiation from other dementing disorders.

Verbal skill

Although speech production is often impaired to include dysprosody, hypophonia, and dysarthria, verbal skill abilities are relatively spared and show only gradual decline with disease progression (Mahurin et al., 1993). Indeed, on tests of verbal skill including sentence repetition (Benton & Hamsher, 1989), and the Boston Naming Test (Kaplan, Goodglass, & Weintraub, 1983), nondemented patients with PD cannot be validly discriminated from normal controls ($d = -0.64$ OL% = 60 sentence repetition; $d = -0.31$ OL% = 78 Boston Naming Test). Moreover, even smaller effects were obtained on tests of verbal comprehension such as the Token Test (De Renzi & Vignolo, 1962) and WAIS-R comprehension subtest (see Table 8.3). Overall, verbal skills were the least impaired neuropsychological domain in nondemented patients with PD (see Chapter 15, Table 15.5).

Demented patients with PD showed a similar pattern of mild deficit on confrontational naming tasks such as the Boston Naming Test ($d = -1.04$ OL% = 44), with smaller effects obtained on tests of comprehension such as the WAIS-R subtest ($d = -0.81$ OL% = 52). In keeping with disease progression, it is evident that verbal skill abilities, although relatively spared throughout the course of the disease, do indeed decline as the demented patients with PD have an overall greater impairment on tasks of verbal skill compared to the nondemented patients with PD. Given the generalized breakdown of semantic language that characterizes Alzheimer's dementia, these specific tasks of verbal skill that do not provide absolute discriminability (i.e., $d > 3.0 < 5\%$ overlap) of demented patients with PD from normal controls can also aid in the differentiation of PD from Alzheimer's dementia. Indeed, in Alzheimer's disease performance on such verbal skill tasks is maximally impaired (see Chapter 4; also see Christensen, Hadzi-Pavlovic, & Jacomb, 1991; Zec, 1993).

Attention/Concentration
Performance on simple tests of attention and concentration including the Mattis Dementia Rating Scale (DRS; Mattis, 1988) attention subtest, the Trail Making Test (Reitan, 1958), and the Seashore Rhythm Test (Reitan & Wolfson, 1993) are generally intact in nondemented patients with PD. More specifically, nondemented patients were completely indistinguishable on the Seashore Rhythm Test ($d = 0.00$ OL% = 100), while performance on the DRS attention subtest could discriminate no more than 12% of patients from controls ($d = -0.18$ OL% = 88). On the more complex tasks of attentional function that depend on speed of processing, however, some impairment was found in nondemented patients with PD. Specifically, on the Stroop word reading task (Stroop, 1935), a substantially larger effect size of -1.14 (OL% = 40) was obtained. Rather than attribute this effect to some failure of selective attention, it might be attributed to slow reading speed. The slowed reading performance on the Stroop word reading task may underscore the bradyphrenic quality found in most patients with PD. Indeed, generally intact performance on the DRS attention subtest that is not dependent on processing speed, and generally impaired performance on the Trail Making Test (Part A) that is a nonverbal, but time dependent, task of attention supports the primary feature of cognitive slowing in PD.

Although demented patients with PD exhibit a similar pattern of generally intact performance on tasks of attention and concentration relative to other neuropsychological domains, the effect sizes are somewhat larger in comparison to those obtained for the nondemented patients with PD on attention tasks that incorporate a motor component (e.g., Trail Making Test). More specifically, performance on Stroop word reading could discriminate a similar number of demented patients as nondemented patients from controls ($d = -1.02$ OL% = 45 demented patients and $d = -1.14$ OL% = 40 nondemented patients). The less sensitive Trail Making Test (Parts A and B), however, both correspond to an effect of 0.80 (OL% = 52) in demented patients which is significantly larger to that obtained for nondemented patients with PD ($d = 0.08$). Interestingly, performance on the more difficult part B, that requires serially alternating between numbers and letters and is time limited, did not correspond to a larger effect. This was unexpected given that successful performance on the task may depend on the integrity of functional neuronal loops connecting basal ganglia and frontal cortex (Cummings, 1993; Freedman & Albert, 1985; Marsden, 1982, 1990; Taylor & Saint-Cyr, 1992).

Memory acquisition
A number of studies have demonstrated that various aspects of memory are differentially affected in PD, with some memory processes evidencing substantial loss and others remaining wholly or partially intact (e.g., Freedman, Rivoira, Butters, Sax, & Feldman, 1984; Litvan, Mohr, Williams, Gomez, & Chase, 1991; Massman, Delis, Butters, Levin, & Salmon, 1990). More specifically, with respect to performance on tasks of memory acquisition, nondemented patients with PD demonstrate little deficit on tasks of working memory (e.g., $d = -0.21$ OL% =

85 digit span forward), greater deficits and differences on verbal (e.g., California Verbal Learning Test measures; CVLT; Delis, Kramer, Kaplan, & Ober, 1987) versus nonverbal (e.g., Wechsler Memory Scale-Revised visual reproduction immediate recall; WMS-R; Wechsler, 1987) measures, and an even larger difference on memory acquisition tasks that aid in organizational retrieval strategies (e.g., CVLT) versus tasks that do not aid in the encoding strategy (e.g., Rey Auditory Verbal Learning Test; RAVLT; Lezak, 1995, pp. 454–455). Specifically, on the CVLT, words are categorized into four semantic categories which can aid encoding strategies, whereas on the RAVLT, the task consists of 16 non-related words; it does not support encoding strategies and any encoding strategies utilized during the test are idiosyncratic subject dependent. The magnitude and differences in obtained effect sizes on the RAVLT versus the CVLT suggest that nondemented PD patients are slower than normal controls in acquiring new material and in organizing retrieval strategies. Indeed the larger obtained effect sizes on the CVLT suggest a selective effect on encoding processes in episodic memory. The largest cognitive test effect size obtained in nondemented patients with PD was the number of words out of 16 recalled after 5 trials on the CVLT ($d = -2.25$ OL% = 15). In contrast, the magnitude of effect for the number of words recalled from trials 1–5 on the RAVLT ($d = -0.46$) corresponds to 70% overlap between patient and control scores. Moreover, given the non-absolute discriminability (i.e., $d < 3.0$) of memory measures to nondemented PD-control differences, and the absolute discriminability ($d > 3.0$) of memory measures such as the WMS-R logical memory immediate recall subtest in Alzheimer's dementia, patient performance on these particular memory tasks can be used to aid in the differential diagnosis. Finally, nondemented patients with PD display a large impairment on repeated presentations of a test of rule learning (Tower of Toronto $d = 1.82$ OL% = 22) suggesting impaired procedural memory in most nondemented patients. This is in contrast to Alzheimer's disease where procedural (implicit) skill learning remains generally intact early in the course of the disease (Bondi & Kaszniak, 1991). This dissociation may also aid in the differentiation of PD from Alzheimer's dementia (Huberman, Moscovitch, & Freedman, 1994; Mahurin et al., 1993).

With respect to demented patients with PD, working memory is also grossly intact as indexed with the WAIS-R digit span forward ($d = -0.26$ OL% = 83) and backward subtests ($d = -0.27$ OL% = 82) respectively. Moreover, immediate recall of the WMS-R logical memory subtest corresponds to a two-fold effect ($d = -1.28$ OL% = 35) in demented versus nondemented patients with PD. Given the rank-order magnitude of effect, however, deficits in memory acquisition in demented patients with PD is impaired secondary to subcortical deafferentation of the frontal lobes and may be associated with slowed information processing (see Sagar, 1987; Wheeler, Stuss, & Tulving, 1995, 1997), as the neuropsychological domain(s) and majority of the cognitive tasks ranked at the higher end of the demented PD profile are dependent on frontal lobe integrity (see Table 8.4 and Chapter 15, Table 15.6). This is in contrast to the nondemented PD profile that is most characterized by impairment in delayed recall.

Delayed recall

Performance on tasks of delayed recall including Buschke's Selective Reminding Test (SRT; Buschke & Fuld, 1974) delayed recall index, long delay free recall on the CVLT, the delayed reproduction of the Rey-Osterrieth Complex Figure (ROCF; Osterrieth, 1944; Rey, 1941), and the WMS-R logical memory delayed recall subtest correspond to some of the largest effect sizes in nondemented patients with PD. Indeed, as a neuropsychological domain, performance on tasks of delayed recall correspond to the largest composite effect size in nondemented patients with PD (see Chapter 15, Table 15.5). More specifically, the obtained effect size on the SRT delayed recall index ($d = -2.24$ OL% = 15) was able to discriminate 85% of nondemented patients from controls. Consideration of the range of effect sizes obtained, however, suggests considerable heterogeneity (minimum and maximum d of 0.40 and –4.87, respectively) where nondemented patients can either be completely discriminated (OL% < 5) or non-distinguishable (OL% > 95) from normal controls. A closer inspection of these outlier effects reveals differing diagnostic for criteria for the classification of patients as being nondemented. This may indeed account for the heterogeneous findings and support the decision that uniform criteria for the diagnosis of dementia in PD research be adopted. Moreover, despite the large effects found on tests of delayed recall, measures of recognition including the CVLT discriminability index, the SRT recognition measure, and Warrington's facial and word recognition measures (Warrington, 1982), correspond to smaller differences in performance between patients and controls (e.g., $d = -0.22$ OL% = 85 Warrington word recognition). Thus, the memory deficit in nondemented patients with PD appears to be associated with inefficient retrieval strategies, rather than impaired storage and consolidation as seen in Alzheimer's dementia (Freedman, 1990; Mahurin et al., 1993; Soukup & Adams, 1996). This pattern of deficit however, has not been specifically explored in demented patients with PD as no measures of recognition were found in the literature review. Finally, remote memory as measured with the Famous Faces Test developed by Albert, Butters, and Levin (1979) corresponds to an effect size d of 0.00 (OL% = 100) in nondemented patients with PD and a small effect of –0.94 (OL% = 47) in demented patients. Moreover, Freedman et al., (1984) did not find a temporal gradient in demented patients with PD such as that seen in patients with Korsakoff's syndrome (see Freedman et al., 1984).

Cognitive flexibility and abstraction

The most sensitive tasks of cognitive flexibility and abstraction to nondemented PD-patients was the DRS initiation/perseveration scale ($d = -0.87$ OL% = 50) which is primarily a score of semantic fluency (see Mattis, 1988), and the COWAT ($d = -0.72$ OL% = 56). The obtained effect size for the COWAT in demented patients with PD also ranked as the most sensitive task of cognitive flexibility and abstraction ($d = -2.05$ OL% = 18%), next to performance on semantic fluency tasks that correspond to an effect size capable of discriminating almost all demented patients with PD from normal controls ($d = -2.85$

OL% = 8). Conversely, the least sensitive task to nondemented and demented PD-control differences was the Stroop interference variable (d = –0.13 OL% = 90 nondemented PD; d = –0.72 OL% = 56 demented PD). Moreover, the magnitude of effect for the number of perseverative errors on the WCST was also two-fold in demented (d = 1.50) versus nondemented (d = 0.68) patients with PD. When taken together, the pattern of deficits on measures of cognitive flexibility and abstraction differ greatly with respect to the overall pattern and magnitude of neuropsychological impairment in patient groups. That is, tasks of cognitive flexibility and abstraction were generally second most sensitive to cognitive alterations in demented patients with PD next to tasks of manual dexterity, whereas in nondemented patients, these tasks were less impaired than the delayed recall, manual dexterity, performance skill, and attention/concentration domains (see Chapter 15, Tables 15.5 and 15.6).

Performance skill
Although it has been reported that nondemented and demented patients with PD often exhibit deficits on tests of visuoperceptual and visuospatial processing (e.g., Levin, Tomer, & Rey, 1992; Pirozzolo, Hansch, Mortimer, Webster, & Kuskowski, 1982), when the magnitude of these deficits are taken into consideration as indexed in effect sizes, they must be considered minimal (also see Brown & Marsden, 1986; Waterfall & Crowe, 1995). For example, nondemented patient performance on the Hooper Visual Organization Test (HVOT; Hooper, 1983) corresponds to an OL% statistic of 73 (d = –0.39). Similar effect sizes of –0.53 (OL% = 66) on Judgment of Line Orientation (JLO; Benton, Varney, & Hamsher, 1978), and –0.66 (OL% = 60) on the WAIS-R block design subtest were obtained. An effect (d = –1.39 OL% = 32) was obtained for the nondemented patients on the copy trial of the ROCF. Because copy of the ROCF is a visuoconstructive test that requires planning and production of a complex motor sequence, however, the larger magnitude of effect does not directly implicate an isolated deficit in visuospatial abilities. Involvement of fronto-subcortical control functions may contribute to the results by affecting the organization and execution of visuospatial and visuomotor strategies during copy of the ROCF (Mahurin et al., 1993).

In demented patients with PD, the magnitude of effect for WAIS-R block design was large (d = –1.68 OL% = 25), but may be an artifact of timing constraints and slowed performance rather than a higher level disturbance in visuoperceptual and visuospatial processes (see Benton & Tranel, 1993). When indices of visuospatial ability without a time dependent score are considered for Judgment of Line Orientation (d = –0.76 OL% = 54) and the Hooper Visual Organization Test (d = –0.95 OL% = 46), smaller effect sizes are obtained. It is likely that poor performance on the WAIS-R block design does indeed arise from simple defects in manual dexterity. Qualitative observation does indeed support this hypothesis (Lezak, 1995).

Manual dexterity

Fine manual motor speed and dexterity are considered core deficits in PD (White, Au, Durso, & Moss, 1992). As such, the discriminability of demented patients with PD from normal controls is maximal ($d > 3.0$ OL% < 5) in keeping with Purdue pegboard (Lezak, 1995) right hand performance as the corresponding test score overlap meets heuristic benchmark criteria for a neuropsychological marker. Moreover, overall performance on tasks of manual dexterity including the finger tapping test (Reitan & Wolfson, 1993; Spreen & Strauss, 1991) correspond to the largest impaired neuropsychological domain in demented patients with PD (see Chapter 15, Table 15.6). Despite being a core deficit in demented patients with PD, however, performance on neuropsychological tasks of manual dexterity in nondemented patients does not conform to the largest impaired neuropsychological domain (see Chapter 15, Table 15.5). More specifically, the largest obtained effect size ($d = -0.96$) on a task of manual dexterity (Purdue pegboard bilateral condition) was considerably below most corresponding effect sizes for tasks of delayed recall and memory acquisition that aid in the encoding process such as the CVLT (see Table 8.3). Further, finger tapping test performance could discriminate even fewer nondemented patients from controls ($d = -0.68$ OL% $= 60$ left hand; $d = -0.46$ OL% $= 70$ right hand).

Moreover, manual dexterity is more impaired than motor speed in both demented and nondemented patients with PD, as effect sizes were larger for Purdue pegboard performance compared to finger tapping test effects (see Tables 8.3, 8.4). This may indicate that motor dysfunction in PD is primarily a deficit in the programming and integration of complex goal-directed movements as these deficits are linked to dysfunction of frontal-basal ganglia regions and associated projection areas that control the execution of motor programs (Marsden, 1982). Lateralizing indices were generally non-existent in nondemented patients, although right hand was slightly more impaired than left hand on the Purdue pegboard and the finger tapping test in demented patients. This may reflect patients with unilateral motor deficit or indicate a disproportionate impairment in motor function lateralized to one side of the body (Raskin, Borod, & Tweedy, 1990). In demented patients with PD, it was found that there was a relationship between the asymmetry of motor dysfunction and cognitive dysfunction (Direnfeld, Albert, Volicer, Langlais, Marquis, & Kaplan, 1984).

Summary

Our profiles confirm that a large proportion of nondemented patients with PD are impaired on standard cognitive tests, and that a disparate pattern of impairment is evident in comparison to demented patients with PD. Our findings also suggest that relative to healthy controls, nondemented patients were most impaired on tests of delayed recall, whereas demented patients were most impaired on tasks of manual dexterity. The disparate pattern of impairment in nondemented and demented patients may indeed reflect disease progression given the significant relationships evident between duration of disease, physical disability, and cognitive impairment in nondemented patients. Taken together, these results might indicate a cognitive continuum of degeneration from subtle neuropsychological impairment in nondemented patients to severe alterations in demented patients. In keeping with the locus of pathology in PD, memory dysfunction in nondemented patients with PD may indeed be specifically associated with fronto-subcortical system deficits. These may disturb executive control of attentional systems that in turn, hinder encoding processes that disrupts performance on measures of memory acquisition and delayed recall. As the disease progresses, the dopamine deficiency of the substantia nigra further disrupts the integrity of functional neuronal loops connecting basal ganglia and frontal cortex. Concurrently, performance on measures of manual dexterity and cognitive flexibility and abstraction become more impaired relative to the already present poor performance on measures of memory acquisition and delayed recall.

Moreover, demented patients can be validly discriminated from controls on the Purdue pegboard (right and bilateral trials), semantic fluency task, and WAIS-R Performance IQ as the corresponding effect sizes and overlap meet heuristic benchmark criteria for a neuropsychological marker (i.e., $d > 3.0$ OL% < 5). Given the maximal sensitivity of these tasks to cognitive alterations in demented patients with PD, these specific tasks and test variables can aid in the differentiation of PD from other disorders with prominent features of subcortical degeneration such as progressive supranuclear palsy (see Chapter 7). Further, the non-absolute discriminability (i.e., $d < 3.0$) of memory measures to demented PD-control differences, and the absolute discriminability ($d > 3.0$) of memory measures such as the WMS-R logical memory immediate recall subtest or Buschke's SRT in Alzheimer's dementia (see Chapter 4; also see Christensen et al., 1991; Zakzanis, 1998e), patient performance on these particular memory tasks can be used to validly differentiate dementia of the Alzheimer's type from PD.

Finally, the results also indicate that in comparison to nondemented patients with PD, demented patients were older at the time of most studies, were younger with respect to onset of PD, were more likely to be male, and had a longer disease duration than patients without dementia. Further, relations between cognitive impairment and clinical and demographic attributes of nondemented patients with PD were revealed including significant relationships between the duration of illness and the Modified Hoehn and Yahr scale score, education and COWAT effect sizes, and WCST categories achieved effect sizes and the Modified Hoehn and Yahr scale score. Thus, it was proposed that the number of categories achieved on the WCST over repeated test-retest assessment could indicate progressive cognitive impairment that may parallel the physical deterioration as indexed with the Modified Hoehn and Yahr scale. This neuropsychological measure may thus be used to predict a dementing course in patients.

Chapter 9

HUNTINGTON'S DISEASE

Huntington's disease (HD) is an autosomal dominant degenerative disorder of the nervous system with a localized genetic locus to the short arm of chromosome 4 that entails a characteristic triad of clinical features consisting of dementia, chorea, and mood change. (Cummings, 1990; Cummings & Benson, 1992; Gusella, Wexler, Conneally et al., 1983; Huntington, 1872). Neuropathological changes are most marked in the head of the caudate, and to a lesser extent in the putamen and globus pallidus with histologic changes found most prominently in the neostriatum (Corsellis, 1976; Cummings, 1990; Dom, Malfroid, & Baro, 1976; Dreese & Netsky, 1968).

The syndrome associated with this disease has been noted to include early-onset behavioral changes, such as irritability, untidiness, and loss of interest, in addition to cognitive changes such as a slowing of cognition, impairment of intellectual function, and memory disturbances (Brandt & Butters, 1986; Brandt & Bylsma, 1993; McHugh & Folstein, 1975). This profile has also been noted to constitute the syndrome of subcortical dementia (Albert, Feldman, & Willis, 1974; McHugh & Folstein, 1975) and its pattern of deficits has been suggested to reflect dysfunction of frontal-subcortical neuronal circuitry (Cummings, 1993; Freedman & Albert, 1985).

The work of several authors (e.g., White, Vasterling, Koroshetz, & Myers, 1992; Zakzanis, 1998g) has contributed to the description and understanding of the cognitive subcortical system deficits of patients with HD. They conclude that patients with HD show changes in short-term memory performance at the earliest stages, followed by deficits in motor function and a constellation of cognitive changes in the early to intermediate stages of dementia. These deficits include diminished verbal fluency, problems with attention and executive function, deficits in visuospatial processing, and impaired abstract reasoning. In the final stages of the illness, language skills become affected, resulting in a marked word retrieval deficit. Several authors (Bondi, Salmon, & Kaszniak, 1996; Brandt & Butters, 1986, 1996; Brandt & Bylsma, 1993; Gusella, MacDonald, Ambrose, & Duyao, 1993; McHugh, 1989; Shoulson, 1990) also provide excellent summaries of the clinical, genetic, neuropathological, cognitive, psychiatric, neuroimaging, and management features of HD.

The diagnosis of Huntington's disease and study inclusion criteria

The diagnosis of HD must have been made by a board-certified neurologist based on a positive family history of HD and the presence of chorea. Whenever severity of HD was assessed in the primary articles, typically with the Huntington's Disease Functional Capacity Scale (Shoulson & Fahn, 1979), the mean stage of disease severity was recorded [ranging from stage 1 (minimal disability) to 5 (complete disability)].

The review

Thirty-six studies published between 1980 and 1997 met criteria for inclusion in the present analysis. In total, neuropsychological test results from 760 patients with HD and 943 normal healthy control subjects were recorded across primary studies.

Descriptive demographic and clinical variable data available from primary studies from the published literature are presented in Table 9.1. The table reflects HD samples that are typically equivalent in gender composition, are approximately 46 years of age, have had 13 years of education, have been ill for 5 years, and had a Stage 2 or 3 severity on Shoulson and Fahn's (1979) Functional Capacity Scale. When medication regimen was described (n = 4), approximately 70% of patients in the HD samples were on various types of pharmacotherapies (typically haloperidol and tetrabenazine) to reduce choreiform movements. There were no statistically significant relationships found between neuropsychological impairment and clinical or demographic attributes of patients with HD.

Cognitive deficits in Huntington's disease

Effect size summaries are presented for specific cognitive tasks and test variables in Table 9.2. Mean d's presented in the column are raw effect sizes. Test variables are presented according to the rank order of the effect size. Effect sizes are

Table 9.1. Descriptive Statistics for Huntington's Disease Cognitive Studies.

Variables	Mdn	M	SD	Range	N
Sample size					
HD samples	13.0	21.1	21.4	6–120	36
Control samples	14.0	26.2	43.3	6–263	36
Patients' age	46.2	46.2	5.3	29–60	36
Duration of illness (yrs.)	4.8	5.4	2.5	3–10	6
Percentage of males	53.0	54.1	15.2	13–88	29
Patients' education (yrs.)	13.3	12.9	1.21	9.7–14.7	31
Percentage on medication	76.0	71.2	28.5	33–100	4
Shoulson and Fahn Scale	2.7	2.5	0.59	1.5–3.0	14

Note. Mdn. = median; M = mean; SD = standard deviation of the mean; N – number of studies in which the variable was reported.

included along with the corresponding standard deviation and the number of effect sizes the mean d was based on. To help describe the dispersion of effect sizes, a minimum and maximum d value are also presented. The table also includes the Fail Safe N (Nfs) for the number of additional studies that would be necessary to reverse the overall probability obtained from our obtained effect size to a value higher than our critical value for statistical significance, which was set at .01 (see Wolf, 1986 for an elaboration). Chapter 15 [Table 15.7] includes similar statistics for the composite neuropsychological domains. The following description of cognitive task and test variable effect sizes are grouped by domain and presented in the order of most to least impaired in HD.

Delayed recall

Tests of delayed recall correspond to the largest obtained effect sizes compared to the other neuropsychological domains. More specifically, verbal and visual delayed recall on the Logical Memory and Visual Reproduction subtests of the Wechsler Memory Scale-Revised (WMS-R; Wechsler, 1987) are the two most sensitive neuropsychological tasks for indexing cognitive dysfunction in HD. These effect sizes correspond to less than 5% overlap between HD-control score distributions. Other large effects were obtained on the California Verbal Learning Test (CVLT; Delis, Kramer, Kaplan, & Ober, 1987) Long Delay Cued Recall ($d = -2.65$, OL% = 9) and Long Delay Free Recall ($d = -2.50$, OL% = 11) indices.

The poor performance of patients with HD on measures of delayed free recall may not however reflect a truly severe memory impairment as implied by the magnitude of effect, because these patients perform relatively well when memory is tested in a recognition format. That is, the obtained effect size for CVLT discriminability is -1.49 (OL% = 29). Contrary to the poor performance of Alzheimer's disease patients on both recall and recognition measures (see Brandt & Rich, 1995; Zec, 1993), the pattern of results suggest that patients with HD have only a mild to moderate memory impairment that results from a retrieval deficit which may be due to their frontal-striatal dysfunction (see Brandt & Bylsma, 1993; Brandt & Rich, 1995). With such a locus of neuropathology, it is indeed likely that patients with HD are retrieving poorly in light of poor encoding strategies, which have been correlated to dorsolateral left frontal lobe function (Wheeler, Stuss, & Tulving, 1995; 1997) and is the main afferent point in frontal-striatal cortical-subcortical loops (Cummings, 1993).

Memory acquisition

When considered as a neuropsychological domain, memory acquisition tasks were the next most sensitive. Total words recalled on list A of the CVLT produced an effect size ($d = -3.03$) that was capable of almost complete discriminability of patients from controls (OL% = 7). Moreover, performance differences between patients with HD and controls slightly increase as a function of the number of learning trials on the CVLT ($d = -3.03$ list A total; $d = -2.91$ list A Trial 5; $d = -2.82$ list A Trial 1). Again, however, the magnitude of effect on these particular memory acquisition tasks does not reflect severe memory impairment when the qualitative nature of the disease is taken into account. Quantitatively speaking, because performance on the CVLT discriminability ($d = -1.49$ OL% = 29) and the WMS-R Paired Associate subtest ($d = -1.53$ OL% = 29) measures were considerably better than recall performance, the pattern of results are indeed consistent with a retrieval deficit. Moreover, performance on the Wechsler Adult Intelligence Scale-Revised (WAIS-R; Wechsler, 1981) Digit Span subtest suggests intact working memory. This was true for digit span backward test, as the associated overlap with respect to the obtained effect ($d = -0.57$ OL% = 64) could discriminate only 36% of patients from controls.

Cognitive flexibility and abstraction

Performance on the Wisconsin Card Sorting Test (WCST; Heaton, 1981; Heaton et al., 1993) was able to discriminate approximately 82% of patients with HD from healthy controls ($d = -2.12$ for categories achieved). As noted, the categories achieved variable, however, is vulnerable to diffuse as well as focal deficits beyond the dorsolateral prefrontal cortex (Anderson, Damasio, Jones, & Tranel, 1991; Lezak, 1995). The percent perseverative error on the test provides a better index of focal frontal pathology (Stuss, 1996). The obtained effect size for this WCST variable was considerably smaller for percent perseverative error ($d = 1.42$, OL% = 32). Together with the clinical and neuropathological features of HD, this pattern is consistent with the widespread cognitive alterations expected from frontal-subcortical circuit dysfunction (see Cummings, 1993) and not with the effects of an isolated dorsolateral prefrontal lesion (see Stuss & Benson, 1984, 1986). Moreover, the obtained effect size on the Tower of London (Shallice, 1982) was able to discriminate 79% of patients with HD from controls ($d = 1.90$) suggesting that some patients with HD retain consistently normal performances, while others, perhaps those in their late stage, obtain defective scores (Lezak, 1995). This task is also sensitive to predominately left anterior lesions (Shallice, 1982).

The inclusion of phonemic word fluency in the cognitive flexibility and abstraction domain was meant to reflect the similar anatomical influence (i.e., the dorsolateral prefrontal lobe) on performance (see Stuss et al., 1998). The obtained effect size on the Controlled Oral Word Association Test (COWAT; Benton & Hamsher, 1989) was –2.13 (OL% = 17). This effect size is very similar to that obtained for WCST categories achieved. This effect is also somewhat smaller than that obtained for semantic fluency (d = –2.49, OL% = 12), which presumably reflects temporal lobe function, but is substantially larger than the effect size obtained for confrontation naming (d = –0.88, OL% = 50) as measured by the Boston Naming Test (Kaplan, Goodglass, & Weintraub, 1983). Overall, the cognitive flexibility and abstraction domain is more impaired in HD compared to the other domains, including verbal skill (see Chapter 15, Table 15.7).

Manual dexterity
Given the presence of choreiform movement, and the subcortical neuropathology of HD, performance on tasks of manual dexterity were impaired as expected. Surprisingly however, the obtained effect sizes for right-hand performance on the Purdue Pegboard (Lezak, 1995), the Grooved Pegboard (Lezak, 1995), and the Finger Tapping Test (Reitan & Wolfson, 1993) were all considerably larger than those obtained on these same tasks for the left hand or bilateral conditions (see Table 9.2).

Attention/Concentration
Tests of attention such as the Trail Making Test (Parts A and B) (Reitan, 1958) are moderately impaired in HD. More specifically, performance on Part A was similarly impaired (d = 1.92, OL% = 20) compared to Part B (d = 1.82, OL% = 22), probably underscoring the generalized slowing that is a prominent feature of subcortical dementia (Freedman & Albert, 1985). Performance on the Stroop tests (Lezak, 1995; Stroop, 1935) is more sensitive than the Trail Making Test to attention/concentration cognitive alterations in HD. Color naming on the Stroop test is most sensitive (d = –2.73, OL% = 10), followed by Stroop colored word reading (d = –2.03, OL% = 18), followed by color naming with word reading inhibition (d = –1.87, OL% = 21). Again, the pattern of results is consistent with generalized cognitive slowing, rather than a core deficit of some failure of selective attention or failure of response inhibition (Lezak, 1995).

Performance skill
As noted, because the WAIS-R Performance IQ provides an average of dissimilar functions that have relatively low intercorrelations and bear no regular neuroanatomical or neuropsychological relationship to one another (Lezak, 1995), the sensitivity of specific subtests that make up the WAIS-R Performance IQ were considered. Performance on the WAIS-R Digit Symbol Substitution Test

Table 9.2.   Effect Size Results in Rank Order for Patients with Huntington's Disease.

Neuropsychological Test/ Test Variable	N d	M d	SD d	Min. d	Max. d	Nfs	OL % (approx.)
WMS-R Visual Reproduction II delayed recall	1	−4.04	–	−4.04	−4.04	403	<2.0
WMS-R Logical Memory II delayed recall	1	−3.52	–	−3.52	−3.52	351	
Purdue Pegboard right hand	1	−3.11	–	−3.11	−3.11	310	
CVLT list A total	1	−3.03	–	−3.03	−3.03	302	<5.0
CVLT short delay free recall	1	−2.94	–	−2.94	−2.94	293	
CVLT list A trial 5	1	−2.91	–	−2.91	−2.91	290	
CVLT list A trial 1	1	−2.82	–	−2.82	−2.82	281	
WMS-R Visual Reproduction I immediate recall	4	−2.76	0.73	−2.01	−3.55	1100	
Stroop color reading	2	−2.73	1.80	−1.45	−4.00	544	
CVLT long delay cued recall	1	−2.65	–	−2.65	−2.65	264	
Mattis DRS Total Score	15	−2.62	0.73	−1.50	−4.12	3915	
CVLT long delay free recall	1	−2.50	–	−2.50	−2.50	249	15.0
Semantic fluency	1	−2.49	–	−2.49	−2.49	248	
Porteus Maze Test	1	−2.41	–	−2.41	−2.41	240	
WMS-R Logical Memory I immediate recall	4	−2.38	0.51	−1.91	−2.99	948	
CVLT short delay cued recall	1	−2.34	–	−2.34	−2.34	233	
Grooved Pegboard right hand	2	2.25	0.13	2.16	2.34	448	
COWAT	5	−2.13	0.50	−1.35	−2.55	1060	
WMS-R Memory Quotient	3	−2.13	0.42	−1.79	−2.60	636	
WCST categories achieved	1	−2.12	–	−2.12	−2.12	211	
WAIS-R Full Scale IQ	4	−2.08	0.35	−1.73	−2.51	828	
Finger Tapping Test right hand	3	−2.05	0.55	−1.48	−2.57	612	
Stroop word reading	2	−2.03	0.21	−1.88	−2.17	404	
WAIS-R Digit Symbol	5	−2.03	0.49	−1.27	−2.51	1010	20.0
Grooved Pegboard left hand	1	1.99	–	1.99	1.99	198	
WAIS-R Similarities	4	−1.99	0.52	−1.25	−2.48	792	
WAIS-R Performance IQ	3	−1.94	0.40	−1.51	−2.31	579	
Trails Making Test Part A	1	1.92	–	1.92	1.92	191	
Tower of London (illegal moves)	1	1.90	–	1.90	1.90	189	
Famous Faces Test	1	1.87	–	1.87	1.87	186	
Stroop interference	3	−1.87	0.95	−1.07	−2.92	558	
Trail Making Test Part B	1	1.82	–	1.82	1.82	181	
Finger Tapping Test left hand	2	−1.79	0.43	−1.48	−2.09	356	
CVLT False Positives	1	1.70	–	1.70	1.70	169	
Rotary Pursuit	1	−1.69	–	−1.69	−1.69	168	
CVLT List B	1	−1.68	–	−1.68	−1.68	167	
Ravens Progressive Matrices	1	−1.58	–	−1.58	−1.58	157	
CVLT Semantic Clustering	1	−1.56	–	−1.56	−1.56	155	
WMS-R Paired Associates	1	−1.53	–	−1.53	−1.53	152	
WAIS-R Block Design	4	−1.52	0.75	−0.43	−2.04	604	
WAIS-R Verbal IQ	2	−1.52	0.21	−1.37	−1.67	304	
WAIS-R Picture Completion	3	−1.50	0.34	−1.18	−1.86	447	30.0

Table continues

Table 9.2. (continued)

Neuropsychological Test/ Test Variable	N d	M d	SD d	Min. d	Max. d	Nfs	OL % (approx.)
CVLT Discriminability	1	−1.49	−	−1.49	−1.49	148	
WCST % perseverative errors	1	1.42	−	1.42	1.42	141	
Benton Visual Retention Test number of errors	1	−1.39	−	−1.39	−1.39	138	
Beck Depression Inventory	2	1.35	0.13	1.24	1.35	268	
Grip Strength	1	−1.35	−	−1.35	−1.35	134	
WAIS-R Comprehension	2	−1.34	0.30	−1.13	−1.55	266	
WAIS-R Arithmetic	4	−1.33	0.65	−0.40	−1.82	528	
Purdue Pegboard bilateral	3	−1.28	1.07	−0.63	−2.51	381	
Mini-Mental State Exam	5	−1.27	0.73	0.00	−1.82	630	
Clock Drawing copy	1	−1.26	−	−1.26	−1.26	125	
WAIS-R Picture Arrangement	4	−1.24	0.55	−0.47	−1.64	496	
Clock Drawing command	1	−1.21	−	−1.21	−1.21	120	
WAIS-R Vocabulary	7	−1.16	0.81	0.04	−2.12	805	
CVLT Cued Recall Intrusions	1	1.15	−	1.15	1.15	114	
WAIS-R Object Assembly	2	−1.12	0.14	−1.02	−1.22	222	
Purdue Pegboard left hand	1	−1.11	−	−1.11	−1.11	110	
National Adult Reading Test	5	−1.01	0.53	0.48	−0.75	500	
Rey-Osterrieth Complex Figure copy	1	−1.01		−1.01	−1.01	100	45.0
Boston Naming Test	1	−0.88	−	−0.88	−0.88	87	
WAIS-R Information	2	−0.86	0.46	−0.53	−1.18	170	
Probable Classification Task	1	0.78	−	0.78	0.78	77	
Mirror Tracing	1	0.58	−	0.58	0.58	57	
WAIS-R Digit Span backward	4	−0.57	0.38	−0.23	−1.10	224	
Semantic Fluency perseverations	1	0.55	−	0.55	0.55	54	
CVLT free recall intrusions	1	0.52	−	0.52	0.52	51	65.0
WAIS-R Digit Span forward	4	−0.52	0.40	−0.15	−1.00	204	
Semantic fluency intrusions	1	0.37	−	0.37	0.37	36	
CVLT serial clustering	1	0.22	−	0.22	0.22	21	
CVLT perseverations	1	−0.21	−	−0.21	−0.21	20	
CVLT response bias	1	−0.16	−	−0.16	−0.16	15	
COWAT intrusions	1	0.00	−	0.00	0.00	−	100.0
COWAT perseverations	1	0.00	−	0.00	0.00	−	

Note. N*d* = number of effect sizes; M*d* = mean effect size; SD*d* = standard deviation around the effect size; Min.*d* = smallest effect size obtained; Max.*d* = largest effect size obtained; Nfs = Fail Safe N; DRS = Dementia Rating Scale; CVLT = California Verbal Learning Test; WAIS-R = Wechsler Adult Intelligence Scale-revised; WMS-R = Wechsler Memory Scale-revised; COWAT = Controlled Oral Word Association Task; WCST = Wisconsin Card Sorting Test.

yielded the largest effect size ($d = -2.03$, OL% = 18) followed by performance on the WAIS-R Block Design ($d = -1.52$ OL% = 29). It is likely that the poor performance on these measures is a function of slowed cognitive processing. That is, the obtained effect size for measures of pure visuospatial function that are not dependent on time, such as the copy of the Rey-Osterrieth Complex Figure (Lezak, 1995), corresponds to a smaller moderate effect of -1.01 (OL% = 44). Moreover, the remaining performance skill tasks, such as the WAIS-R Picture Completion, Picture Arrangement, and Object Assembly subtests, corresponded to effect sizes that discriminated fewer than 65% of patients from controls (see Table 9.2).

Verbal skill

Verbal skill is least impaired in HD. More specifically, the WAIS-R Verbal IQ, which also represents an average of dissimilar functions (Lezak, 1995), corresponds to an effect size of -1.52 (OL% = 29). The effect sizes of subtests that make up the Verbal IQ, however, were generally smaller and ranged from -1.99 (Similarities) to -1.16 (Vocabulary). Performance on confrontation naming, as noted previously, was generally intact (-0.88 OL% = 50), as indexed by the Boston Naming Test. Finally, the National Adult Reading Test (NART; Nelson, 1982), which provides a good index of premorbid verbal ability, corresponded to an effect size capable of discriminating 56% of patients from controls ($d = -1.01$ OL% = 44).

Subsequent analysis

A subsequent comparison of primary study findings was conducted as a means of containing homogeneity bias. That is, of the 36 primary studies found in the literature search, 17 (47%) articles that were included in the current meta-analyses were from the University of California San Diego (UCSD) group headed by the late Dr. Nelson Butters. These 17 studies were likely included the same basic patient group with analyses done on an evolving database. The multiple use of the same sample will inflate the homogeneity of the findings and may produce an unacceptable bias in the meta-analysis. Therefore, a comparison of demographic and cognitive variables between the 17 UCSD studies and the remaining 19 studies was conducted.

No differences were found using paired-sample t tests for basic demographic variables such as age, duration of illness, percentage of males, education, and examiner rating on the Shoulson and Fahn scale. Moreover, a comparison of MMSE raw scores between the UCSD and the remaining studies did not reflect substantial differences ($M = 24.4$ UCSD, $n = 1$ vs. $M = 26.23$ remaining studies, $n = 3$) between patients with HD. The total raw score on the Mattis DRS ($M = 119.99$ UCSD, $n = 13$ vs. $M = 122.25$ remaining studies, $n = 2$) also did not reflect significant impairment differences between study group samples. The limited sample size of similar cognitive test scores between study groups made statistical analyses implausible for these more general cognitive screening measures and for the remaining specific cognitive tasks and test variables.

A statistical comparison of effects, however, using paired-sample t tests for the neuropsychological domains was possible and revealed no significant differences between the 17 UCSD and the remaining 19 studies used in the current meta-analysis.

Summary

The review indicates that patients with HD are most deficient on tests of delayed recall, followed by performance on measures of memory acquisition, cognitive flexibility and abstraction, manual dexterity, attention/concentration, performance skill, and, finally, verbal skill. A qualitative breakdown of effect sizes, however, reveals a multitude of cognitive deficits on cognitive tasks and test variables in patients with HD as reported in Table 9.2. Moreover, specific patterns of neuropsychological test performance, including evidence for a retrieval-based memory deficit, are apparent in the profile. More specifically, maximal deficits for patients with HD compared to normal controls were found on the WMS-R Visual Reproduction and Logical Memory delayed recall, Purdue Pegboard (right hand), and CVLT total words recalled from list A. The effect sizes for these particular variables correspond to test score distribution overlap values of less than 5%, and therefore meet the proposed heuristic benchmark criteria for cognitive markers as the associated overlap is capable of discriminating virtually all patients from normal controls.

Chapter 10

MULTIPLE SCLEROSIS

Multiple sclerosis (MS) is a common idiopathic inflammatory disorder of unde termined etiology that involves the white matter of the cerebral hemispheres, brainstem, optic nerves, cerebellum, and spinal cord (Cummings & Benson, 1992; Kurtzke, 1988; Weinshenker, 1994). The clinical presentation in MS is highly variable owing to the nearly random distribution of demyelinating lesions scattered throughout the central nervous system white matter (Beatty, 1996; Cummings, 1990; Cummings & Benson, 1992; Rao, 1986, 1993).

The presence of cognitive impairment in MS is well recognized to include deficits in memory, speed of information processing, and a general decline of cognitive processes including language, attention/concentration, cognitive flex- ibility and abstraction, and visuoperceptual and visuospatial processing (e.g., Beatty, 1996; Beatty & Gange, 1977; Minden, Moes, Orav, Kaplan, & Reich, 1990; Rao, 1986, 1990, 1993; Rao, Leo, Bernardin, & Unverzagt, 1991; Thornton & Raz, 1997; White, 1990; White, Nyehnhuis, & Sax, 1992; Zakzanis, 1999). Indeed, although the disease is rarely diagnosed on the basis of cognitive impairment, cognitive dysfunction has been estimated to occur in approximately 40% to 60% of patients with MS (Peyser, Rao, LaRocca, & Kaplan, 1990; Rao, Leo, Bernardin, & Unverzagt, 1991). As such, most clini- cal investigators accept the general notion that MS is associated with cognitive abnormalities, but there are many unresolved questions and controversies regarding their magnitude, pattern, and whether purported deficits are indica- tive of clinical course and subtype classification.

The diagnosis of multiple sclerosis and study inclusion criteria

The year 1983 was chosen as a cut-off limit because it corresponded roughly to the introduction of more reliable diagnostic criteria for MS (i.e., Poser, Paty, Scheinberg, et. al., 1983). That is, the diagnosis of MS must have been made based on Poser et al., (1983) criteria for MS.

The review

Thirty-four studies published between 1983 and 1997 met criteria for inclusion in the present analysis. In total, cognitive test results from 1,845 patients with MS (351 chronic progressive, 636 relapse-remitting, 858 mixed or not specified), and 1,265 normal healthy controls were recorded across primary studies.

Descriptive demographic and clinical variable data available from primary studies from the published literature are presented in Table 10.1 for the entire sample of patients with MS (n = 1,845). The table reflects patient samples that are typically female which is consistent with previous prevalence reports that estimate MS as 1.5 to 1.9 times more common in females than males (Baum & Rothschild, 1981; McIntosh-Michaelis et al., 1991). Patients with MS were approximately 41 years of age, and have completed 13.9 years of education, with an average age at onset of 27 years. The mean duration of illness was approximately 11 years. When medication regimen was described in primary studies (*n* = 11), approximately 36% of patients in study samples were on various types of pharmacotherapies (typically anti-depressants to treat concurrent affective disturbances). The mean score on the Expanded Disability Status Scale (EDSS; Kurtzke, 1983) was 4.1 reflecting a patient who is fully ambulatory without aid despite relatively severe disability in one functional system (see Kurtzke, 1983). On the Ambulation Index (Hauser et al., 1983), the average score was 3.4 which reflects a patient who is independent or requires unilateral support to walk [e.g., cane or single crutch (see Hauser et al., 1983)].

In terms of possible moderator variables, a few of the demographic and clinical variables correlated significantly with the cognitive tasks. Age was significantly related to performance on the Controlled Oral Word Association Test (COWAT; Benton, Hamsher, Varney, & Spreen, 1983; Spreen & Strauss, 1998) ($r = -.81$ $p < .0005$ $n = 18$), as was duration of illness ($r = -.64$ $p < .05$ $n = 12$). Because age invariably increases as the illness progresses in duration, performance on the COWAT is expected to decrease (see Lezak, 1995, pp. 545–546). This age related decline in COWAT performance in patients with MS, however, is worse than expected based on age related decline when the obtained effect size (see Table 10.4) is taken into account. This may reflect a tendency for a more selective distribution of demyelinating lesions to plot on frontal structures as the disease progresses, as frontal lesions tend to depress fluency scores, with left frontal lesions resulting in lower word production than right frontal ones (Lezak, 1995; Michelli, Caltagirone, Cainotti, Masullo, & Silveri, 1981;

Table 10.1. Descriptive Statistics for Multiple Sclerosis [all patients] Cognitive Studies.

Variables	M	SD	Range	N
Sample size				
MS samples	54	44	11–196	34
Control samples	37	25	11–100	34
Patients' age	41	5.6	29–52	33
Onset age	27	1.7	25–29	3
Duration of illness (yrs.)	11	4.5	1.6–18.4	22
Percentage of males	32	13	9–75	26
Patients' education (yrs.)	13.9	0.9	11.4–15.5	31
Percentage on medication	36	38	0–100	11
Ambulation Index	3.4	1.1	1.8–5.0	5
Expanded Disability Status Scale	4.1	2.8	1.0–13.9	21

Note. M = mean; SD = standard deviation of the mean; N = number of studies in which the variable was reported.

Table 10.2. Descriptive Statistics for Chronic-Progressive Multiple Sclerosis Cognitive Studies.

Variables	M	SD	Range	N
Sample size				
MS samples	39	26	11–100	9
Control samples	39	27	11–100	9
Patients' age	45	4.9	37–52	9
Duration of illness (yrs.)	13	4.4	6.0–18.4	8
Percentage of males	28	13	9–43	7
Patients' education (yrs.)	14.1	0.7	13.2–15.2	9
Percentage on medication	45	18	20–60	4
Ambulation Index	5.0	–	5.0–5.0	1
Expanded Disability Status Scale	6.4	3.0	4.1–13.9	9

Note. M = mean; SD = standard deviation of the mean; N = number of studies in which the variable was reported.

Perret, 1974). Further, age was also inversely related to disability as measured on the EDSS (Kurtzke, 1983) ($r = .67$ $p < .001$ $n = 21$). This relationship may however have been influenced by patients with chronic progressive MS, as they invariably gain higher scores on the EDSS as the disease evolves. An inadequate number of studies ($n = 9$), however, did not permit a test for this hypothesis.

Table 10.2 presents descriptive demographic and clinical variable data for 351 patients with chronic-progressive MS. These patients were typically 45 years of age and had completed approximately 14 years of education. The average duration of the disease was 13 years. The percentage of females was 72%, which again, is consistent with previous prevalence estimates. When medication use was described in primary studies ($n = 4$), approximately 45% of patients were using anti-depressants. The average score on the Ambulation Index was 5.0 which is meant to reflect a patient who requires bilateral support to walk [e.g., canes, crutches or walker (see Hauser et al., 1983)]. On the EDSS, the mean rating was 6.4 which represents a patient who is able to walk 100 meters without rest with unilateral support and/or a patient who is restricted to a wheelchair, but can wheel and transfer self without assistance (see Kurtzke, 1983).

Table 10.3 includes descriptive demographic and clinical variable data on 636 patients with relapse-remitting MS. These patients were typically younger than patients with chronic-progressive MS (mean age of 36 for relapse-remitting vs. 45 for chronic-progressive). Because scores on the EDSS were negatively correlated with age, this difference in age may underscore the suggestion that relapse-remitting MS evolves into a chronic-progressive course as frequent clinical exacerbations with neurological deficit accumulate. Moreover, patients with relapse-remitting MS had an average age of disease onset at 27 years, with approximately 5 years of illness duration. Again, gender composition was 30% male. The patients with relapse-remitting MS were also less medicated (33%) than patients with a chronic-progressive course. This may reflect a difference in psychiatric disturbance although the subtypes are not equivalent in terms of the duration of their illness, age, or the severity of disability. In addition, some of the physical and cognitive sequelae of MS (e.g., fatigue and decision making deficits) may be misinterpreted as symptoms of depression. Nonetheless the mean obtained effect size from the Beck Depression Inventory (BDI; Beck, 1987) was considerably larger in patients with chronic-progressive MS (mean $d = 3.56$ OL% < 5%) than patients with relapse-remitting MS (mean $d = 1.00$ OL% = 45%). The mean Ambulation Index score was 1.8 which represents a patient

Table 10.3. Descriptive Statistics for Relapse-Remitting Multiple Sclerosis Cognitive Studies.

Variables	M	SD	Range	N
Sample size				
MS samples	71	69	12–196	9
Control samples	44	32	15–92	9
Patients' age	36	3.4	30–40	9
Onset age	27	1.7	25–29	3
Duration of illness (yrs.)	4.8	2.7	1.6–8.0	4
Percentage of males	30	3.8	27–36	6
Patients' education (yrs.)	13.8	1.0	11.4–14.8	9
Percentage on medication	33	58	0–100	3
Ambulation Index	1.8	–	1.8–1.8	1
Expanded Disability Status Scale	2.0	0.8	1.0–3.5	8

Note. M = mean; SD = standard deviation of the mean; N = number of studies in which the variable was reported.

who has abnormal gait or episodic imbalance, and reports fatigue that interferes with athletic or other demanding activities (see Hauser et al., 1983). The mean EDSS score was 2.0, which is meant to represent minimal disability in one functional system (see Kurtzke, 1983).

Cognitive deficits in multiple sclerosis

Effect size summaries are presented for specific cognitive test variables in Tables 10.4, 10.5, 10.6. Table 10.4 includes meta-analytic results from the entire sample of patients with MS. Table 10.5 presents effect sizes for cognitive test variables for patients with chronic-progressive MS, while Table 10.6 includes effect sizes for patients with relapse-remitting MS. Effect sizes are included along with their corresponding standard deviation and the number of effect sizes and their corresponding mean d. To help describe the dispersion of effect sizes, a minimum and maximum d value are also presented. The tables also include the Fail

Table 10.4. Effect Size Results in Rank Order for All Patients with Multiple Sclerosis.

Neuropsychological Test/ Test Variable	N d	M d	SD d	Min. d	Max. d	Nfs	OL % (approx.)
Beck Depression Inventory	5	1.98	2.11	0.69	5.73	985	20.0
Purdue Pegboard left hand	1	−1.76	–	−1.76	−1.76	175	
Purdue Pegboard right hand	1	−1.68	–	−1.68	−1.68	167	
Blessed Dementia Rating Scale	1	1.53	–	1.53	1.53	152	
Purdue Pegboard bilateral	2	−1.51	0.32	−1.21	−1.81	300	30.0
Buschke SRT delayed recall	3	−1.44	1.04	−0.75	−2.63	429	
Symbol Digit Modality Test	1	−1.36	–	−1.36	−1.36	135	
WMS Memory Quotient	1	−1.29	–	−1.29	−1.29	128	
WAIS-R Digit Symbol	8	−1.03	0.56	−0.37	−2.23	816	
CVLT short delay free recall	1	−1.00	–	−1.00	−1.00	99	45.0
Semantic fluency	7	−0.99	0.30	−0.53	−1.29	686	
Buschke SRT total recall	2	−0.94	0.12	−0.85	−1.02	186	
WMS Logical Memory II delayed recall	4	−0.94	0.33	−0.56	−1.36	372	
Finger Tapping Test right hand	3	−0.89	0.25	−0.64	−1.13	264	
RAVLT trial 5	3	−0.87	0.12	−0.79	−0.97	602	
CVLT list A trial 5	1	−0.84	–	−0.84	−0.84	83	
Finger Tapping Test left hand	3	−0.81	0.15	−0.67	−0.96	240	
Famous Persons Test	2	−0.79	0.12	−0.70	−0.87	156	
COWAT	18	−0.78	0.32	−0.23	−1.36	1386	
Grooved Pegboard right hand	2	−0.76	0.05	−0.74	−0.78	150	
Grooved Pegboard left hand	2	−0.74	0.06	−0.70	−0.78	146	
RAVLT delayed recall	3	−0.74	0.30	−0.46	−1.06	219	
Rey-Osterrieth Complex Figure delayed reproduction	3	−0.74	0.30	−0.46	−1.06	219	
Zung Depression Inventory	2	0.71	0.09	−0.65	−0.78	140	

Table continues

Table 10.4. (continued)

Neuropsychological Test/ Test Variable	N d	M d	SD d	Min. d	Max. d	Nfs	OL % (approx.)
WMS-R Logical Memory I							
immediate recall	5	−0.71	0.28	−0.26	−0.95	350	
CVLT total trials 1–5	1	−0.68	–	−0.68	−0.68	67	
Rey-Osterrieth Complex Figure							
immediate reproduction	2	−0.67	0.05	−0.66	−0.67	132	
Hamilton Depression Rating Scale	2	0.65	–	0.60	0.69	128	
Raven's Progressive Matrices	3	−0.63	0.21	−0.53	−0.72	189	
Stroop interference	1	0.62	–	0.62	0.62	61	
WAIS-R Object Assembly	3	−0.61	0.09	−0.58	−0.67	180	
Benton Facial Recognition	2	−0.60	0.10	−0.58	−0.68	118	
RAVLT recognition	2	−0.59	0.36	−0.33	−0.84	116	
WAIS-R Performance IQ	2	−0.59	0.13	−0.55	−0.62	116	
RAVLT trial 1	1	−0.57	–	−0.57	−0.57	56	
WCST perseverative responses	11	0.57	0.29	0.12	1.06	616	
Boston Naming Test	8	−0.54	0.37	−0.14	−1.21	424	
WCST categories achieved	10	−0.52	0.38	0.27	−1.14	510	
WMS-R Paired Associates I	5	−0.51	0.30	−0.19	−0.95	250	
WCST perseverative errors	6	0.51	0.41	−0.03	1.06	300	
CVLT list A trial 1	1	−0.50	–	−0.50	−0.50	49	65.0
CVLT recognition	1	−0.50	–	−0.50	−0.50	49	
WAIS-R Block Design	6	−0.50	0.18	−0.30	−0.82	294	
WAIS-R Verbal IQ	8	−0.50	0.26	−0.17	−0.96	392	
Mini Mental Status Exam	9	−0.49	0.28	−0.10	−1.02	432	
Hooper Visual Organization Test	3	−0.48	0.33	−0.19	−0.85	141	
Paced Auditory Serial Addition Test	2	−0.48	0.18	−0.35	−0.61	94	
Halstead Category Test	3	−0.46	0.29	−0.15	−0.72	135	
Benton Visual Retention Test							
number of errors	2	0.45	0.24	0.42	0.48	88	
WCST nonperseverative errors	4	0.45	0.21	0.20	0.66	176	
CVLT long delay cued recall	1	−0.44	–	−0.44	−0.44	43	
RAVLT total recall trials 1–5	1	−0.43	–	−0.43	−0.43	42	
WAIS-R Similarities	7	−0.43	0.38	−0.18	−1.25	294	
WAIS-R Digit Span backward	13	−0.42	0.42	0.19	−1.11	533	
Trail Making Test Part B	6	−0.41	0.44	0.72	−0.46	240	
CVLT long delay free recall	1	−0.40	–	−0.40	−0.40	39	
WAIS-R Full Scale IQ	4	−0.40	0.73	0.49	−1.29	156	
WAIS-R Vocabulary	7	−0.40	0.24	−0.21	−0.86	273	
CVLT short delay cued recall	1	−0.38	–	−0.38	−0.38	37	
WAIS-R Digit Span forward	15	−0.37	0.40	0.19	−1.11	540	
Right-Left Orientation	1	−0.35	–	−0.35	−0.35	34	
Judgment of Line Orientation	3	−0.33	0.17	−0.16	−0.50	96	
WAIS-R Arithmetic	6	−0.33	0.26	−0.15	−0.74	192	
CVLT list B	1	−0.31	–	−0.31	−0.31	30	
Buschke SRT recognition	2	−0.30	0.29	−0.09	−0.50	58	
Presidents Test-recall	2	−0.30	0.09	−0.23	−0.37	58	
Trail Making Test Part A	5	0.30	0.54	0.85	−0.48	145	

Table continues

Table 10.4. (continued)

Neuropsychological Test/ Test Variable	N d	M d	SD d	Min. d	Max. d	Nfs	OL % (approx.)
WAIS-R Comprehension	5	−0.30	0.18	−0.19	−0.60	145	
Token Test	1	−0.29	–	−0.29	−0.29	28	
WAIS-R Picture Arrangement	3	−0.28	0.10	−0.25	−0.32	81	
WCST failure to maintain set	3	0.25	0.25	0.00	0.50	72	
WAIS-R Information	5	−0.23	−0.15	0.06	−0.50	110	
Corsi Block Tapping	2	−0.22	0.21	−0.07	−0.36	42	
WAIS-R Picture Completion	4	−0.21	0.15	0.00	−0.33	80	
Rey-Osterrieth Complex Figure copy	2	−0.11	0.54	0.50	−0.27	20	
National Adult Reading Test	1	−0.04	–	−0.04	−0.04	3	
Presidents Test-recognition	1	−0.01	–	−0.01	−0.01	–	>95.0

Note. Nd = number of effect sizes; Md = mean effect size; SDd = standard deviation around the effect size; Min.d = smallest effect size obtained; Max.d = largest effect size obtained; Nfs = Fail Safe N; SRT = Selective Reminding Test; DRS = Dementia Rating Scale; CVLT = California Verbal Learning Test; RAVLT = Rey Auditory Verbal Learning Test; WAIS-R = Wechsler Adult Intelligence Scale-Revised; WMS-R = Wechsler Memory Scale-Revised; COWAT = Controlled Oral Word Association Task; WCST = Wisconsin Card Sorting Test.

Table 10.5.   Effect Size Results in Rank Order for Patients with Chronic-Progressive Multiple Sclerosis.

Neuropsychological Test/ Test Variable	N d	M d	SD d	Min. d	Max. d	Nfs	OL % (approx.)Beck
Depression Inventory	2	3.56	2.09	1.36	5.73	710	<5.0
WAIS-R Digit Symbol	1	−2.23	–	−2.23	−2.23	222	25.0
Blessed Dementia Rating Scale	1	1.53	–	1.53	1.53	152	30.0
Symbol Digit Modalities Test	1	−1.36	–	−1.36	−1.36	135	
Semantic fluency	2	−1.29	0.00	−1.29	−1.29	256	
Purdue Pegboard bilateral	1	1.21	–	1.21	1.21	120	
Rey-Osterrieth Complex Figure delayed reproduction	1	−1.10	–	−1.10	−1.10	109	
WCST perseverative errors	1	1.07	–	1.07	1.07	108	45.0
WAIS-R Similarities	2	−0.91	0.49	−0.56	−1.25	180	
COWAT	5	−0.87	0.44	−0.23	−1.36	430	
Famous Persons Test	1	−0.87	–	−0.87	−0.87	86	
WAIS-R Block Design	1	−0.82	–	−0.82	−0.82	81	
WAIS-R Verbal IQ	2	−0.78	0.26	−0.59	−0.96	154	
WAIS-R Digit Span backward	2	−0.77	0.37	−0.51	−1.03	152	
Buschke SRT delayed recall	1	−0.75	–	−0.75	−0.75	74	
Trail Making Test Part A	1	0.72	–	0.72	0.72	71	
WAIS-R Digit Span forward	2	−0.70	0.47	−0.36	−1.03	138	
Benton Facial Recognition	1	−0.68	–	−0.68	−0.68	67	
WCST perseverative responses	3	0.68	–	0.39	1.06	201	

Table continues

Table 10.5. (continued)

Neuropsychological Test/ Test Variable	N d	M d	SD d	Min. d	Max. d	Nfs	OL % (approx.)
Boston Naming Test	3	−0.67	0.47	−0.40	−1.12	198	
Zung Depression Inventory	1	0.65	–	0.65	0.65	64	
Raven's Progressive Matrices	1	−0.63	–	−0.63	−0.63	62	
Stroop interference	1	0.62	–	0.62	0.62	61	
WCST categories achieved	3	−0.62	0.29	−0.37	−0.94	183	
WAIS-R Comprehension	1	−0.60	–	−0.60	−0.60	59	
Trail Making Test Part B	1	0.59	–	0.59	0.59	58	
Mini Mental State Exam	6	−0.57	0.30	−0.13	−1.02	336	
WAIS-R Arithmetic	1	−0.55	–	−0.55	−0.55	54	
Halstead Category Test	1	−0.52	–	−0.52	−0.52	51	
Judgment of Line Orientation	1	−0.50	–	−0.50	−0.50	49	65.0
WAIS-R Information	1	−0.50	–	−0.50	−0.50	49	
WAIS-R Vocabulary	2	−0.50	0.14	−0.39	−0.60	100	
Hooper Visual Organization Test	1	−0.39	–	−0.39	−0.39	38	
Benton Right-Left Orientation	1	−0.35	–	−0.35	−0.35	34	
WCST nonperseverative errors	1	0.33	–	0.33	0.33	32	
WCST failure to maintain set	1	0.25	–	0.25	0.25	24	
Presidents Test-recognition	1	−0.01	–	−0.01	−0.01	–	>95.0

Note. Nd = number of effect sizes; Md = mean effect size; SDd = standard deviation around the effect size; Min.d = smallest effect size obtained; Max.d = largest effect size obtained; Nfs = Fail Safe N; SRT = Selective Reminding Test; DRS = Dementia Rating Scale; CVLT = California Verbal Learning Test; WAIS-R = Wechsler Adult Intelligence Scale-Revised; COWAT = Controlled Oral Word Association Task; WCST = Wisconsin Card Sorting Test.

Table 10.6. Effect Size Results in Rank Order for Patients with Relapse-Remitting Multiple Sclerosis.

Neuropsychological Test/ Test Variable	N d	M d	SD d	Min. d	Max. d	Nfs	OL % (approx.)
RAVLT delayed recall	1	−1.06	–	−1.06	−1.06	105	
Finger Tapping Test right hand	2	−1.02	0.16	−0.90	−1.13	202	
Beck Depression Inventory	1	1.00	–	1.00	1.00	99	45.0
CVLT short delay free recall	1	−1.00	–	1.00	1.00	99	
WAIS-R Digit Symbol	4	−0.93	0.29	−0.57	−1.27	368	
WMS-R Logical Memory II delayed recall	1	−0.91	–	−0.91	−0.91	90	
WCST categories achieved	2	−0.90	0.34	−0.65	−1.14	180	
Finger Tapping Test left hand	2	−0.88	0.11	−0.80	−0.96	174	
CVLT list A trial 5	1	−0.84	–	−0.84	−0.84	83	
RAVLT trial 5	1	−0.79	–	−0.79	−0.79	78	
Grooved Pegboard right hand	2	−0.76	0.05	−0.74	−0.78	150	
Grooved Pegboard left hand	2	−0.74	0.10	−0.70	−0.78	146	
Boston Naming Test	2	−0.69	0.38	−0.42	−0.96	136	

Table continues

Table 10.6. (continued)

Neuropsychological Test/ Test Variable	N d	M d	SD d	Min. d	Max. d	Nfs	OL % (approx.)
CVLT total recall trials 1–5	1	−0.68	–	−0.68	−0.68	67	
Rey-Osterrieth Complex Figure							
immediate reproduction	2	−0.67	0.01	−0.66	−0.67	132	
Semantic fluency	2	−0.66	0.18	−0.53	−0.79	130	
WCST perseverative responses	3	0.65	0.33	0.36	1.02	192	
Raven's Progressive Matrices	2	−0.63	0.13	−0.53	−0.72	124	
WCST perseverative errors	1	0.61	–	0.61	0.61	60	
WMS-R Logical Memory I							
immediate recall	2	−0.61	0.49	−0.26	−0.95	120	
WCST nonperseverative errors	1	0.60	–	0.60	0.60	59	
WAIS-R Object Assembly	2	−0.59	0.01	−0.58	−0.59	116	
WAIS-R Performance IQ	2	−0.59	0.16	−0.55	−0.62	116	
Benton Facial Recognition	1	−0.58	–	−0.58	−0.58	57	
COWAT	6	−0.57	0.15	−0.38	−0.73	336	
CVLT list A trial 1	1	−0.50	–	−0.50	−0.50	49	65.0
CVLT recognition	1	−0.50	–	−0.50	−0.50	49	
Benton Visual Retention Test							
number of errors	1	0.48	–	0.48	0.48	47	
Paced Auditory Serial							
Test	2	−0.48	0.18	−0.35	−0.61	94	
WAIS-R Full Scale IQ	2	−0.47	0.11	−0.44	−0.49	92	
WAIS-R Block Design	3	−0.45	0.14	−0.30	−0.56	132	
CVLT long delay cued recall	1	−0.44	–	−0.44	−0.44	43	
RAVLT total recall trials 1–5	1	−0.43	–	−0.43	−0.43	42	
Mini Mental State Exam	1	−0.42	–	−0.42	−0.42	41	
CVLT long delay free recall	1	−0.40	–	−0.40	−0.40	39	
Trail Making Test Part B	4	0.37	0.56	0.72	−0.46	144	
CVLT short delay cued recall	1	−0.38	–	−0.38	−0.38	37	
RAVLT recognition	1	−0.33	–	−0.33	−0.33	32	
Rey-Osterreith Complex Figure							
delayed reproduction	1	−0.32	–	−0.32	−0.32	31	
CVLT list B	1	−0.31	–	−0.31	−0.31	30	
Token Test	1	−0.29	–	−0.29	−0.29	28	
WAIS-R Digit Span backward	7	−0.28	0.45	0.19	−1.11	189	
WAIS-R Similarities	3	−0.28	0.19	−0.55	−0.62	84	
WAIS-R Digit Span forward	8	−0.27	0.42	0.19	−1.11	208	
WAIS-R Picture Arrangement	2	−0.26	0.01	−0.25	−0.26	50	
WAIS-R Comprehension	2	−0.25	0.14	−0.19	−0.30	48	
WMS-R Paired Associates I	2	−0.24	0.20	−0.19	−0.30	46	
WAIS-R Vocabulary	3	−0.24	0.08	−0.21	−0.27	69	
Corsi Block Tapping Test	2	−0.22	0.21	−0.07	−0.36	42	
WAIS-R Picture Completion	3	−0.21	0.19	0.00	−0.33	60	
WAIS-R Verbal IQ	2	−0.18	0.01	−0.17	−0.19	34	
Judgment of Line Orientation	1	−0.16	–	−0.16	−0.16	15	
WAIS-R Arithmetic	3	−0.16	0.04	−0.15	−0.18	45	
National Adult Reading Test	1	−0.04	–	−0.04	−0.04	3	>95
WAIS-R Information	3	0.02	0.02	0.00	0.06	1	

Table continues

Table 10.6. (continued)

Neuropsychological Test/ Test Variable	N d	M d	SD d	Min. d	Max. d	Nfs	OL % (approx.)
	——Patients do better than controls——						
Rey-Osterreith Complex Figure							
copy	2	0.11	0.54	0.50	−0.2720		
Trail Making Test Part A	3	0.13	0.67	0.85	−0.48	36	

Note. N*d* = number of effect sizes; M*d* = mean effect size; SD*d* = standard deviation around the effect size; Min.*d* = smallest effect size obtained; Max.*d* = largest effect size obtained; Nfs = Fail Safe N; SRT = Selective Reminding Test; DRS = Dementia Rating Scale; CVLT = California Verbal Learning Test; RAVLT = Rey Auditory Verbal Learning Test; WAIS-R = Wechsler Adult Intelligence Scale-Revised; WMS-R = Wechsler Memory Scale-Revised; COWAT = Controlled Oral Word Association Task; WCST = Wisconsin Card Sorting Test.

Safe N (Nfs) for the number of additional studies that would be necessary to reverse the overall probability obtained from our obtained effect size to a value higher than our critical value for statistical significance, which was set at .01 (see Wolf, 1986 for an elaboration). Chapter 15 [Table 15.8] includes similar statistics for the composite neuropsychological domains. The following description of cognitive task and test variable effect sizes are not grouped by domain and are not presented in the order of most to least impaired in MS because both subtypes are considered and they do not have the same order. A "general intelligence" section is also first included to help articulate the differences between relapse-remitting and chronic-progressive patients.

General intelligence measures

With respect to the entire sample of patients with MS (see Table 10.4), general intelligence as measured with standardized tests such as the Wechsler Adult Intelligence Scale-Revised (WAIS-R; Wechsler, 1981) and National Adult Reading Test (NART; Nelson, 1982) show modest differences between patients with MS and controls. The largest effect size was obtained for WAIS-R Performance IQ ($d = -0.59$) which corresponds to an OL% statistic of 62. The obtained effect sizes were consistent with previous findings that differences in WAIS-R Performance IQ between patients and controls are larger in magnitude compared to WAIS-R Verbal IQ effects (see Rao, 1986). Because response speed and the integrity of sensory and motor functions contribute more to the Performance IQ than to the Verbal IQ, it is not possible to determine whether visuospatial functions are more vulnerable to loss than are verbal abilities (Beatty, 1996). The obtained effect size for the WAIS-R Full Scale IQ was even less sensitive to discriminating patients with MS from controls, as the corresponding OL% statistic is 73 ($d = -0.40$) indicating that 73% of patients cannot be differentiated from controls based on WAIS-R Full Scale IQ scores.

Finally, the obtained effect size ($d = -0.04$) for the NART confirms that the residual vocabulary of patients with MS may be the best indicator of premorbid mental ability (see Lezak, 1995, pp. 551–552), as the corresponding overlap of NART scores between patients with MS and controls is greater than 97%.

Patients with chronic-progressive MS (see Table 10.5) tend to show modest differences in WAIS-R Verbal IQ as compared to controls ($d = -0.78$ OL% = 55), albeit larger than those obtained by patients with relapse-remitting MS ($d = -0.18$ OL% = 85). No studies reported a Performance IQ for patients with chronic-progressive MS only. Consequently, it is not known whether significant differences exist between effects for Verbal and Performance IQ for this subtype of MS. For patients with relapse-remitting MS, however, a substantial difference was found between Performance IQ ($d = -0.59$) and Verbal IQ ($d = -0.18$).

Verbal skill
Deficits in verbal fluency were found in patients with MS, with semantic fluency ($d = -0.99$) being more sensitive to MS than phonemic fluency ($d = -0.78$). The corresponding overlap in score distribution (OL% = 45 semantic fluency), however, could only discriminate about half the patients with MS from controls. These effects were larger in the chronic-progressive subtype ($d = -1.29$ semantic fluency; $d = -0.87$ phonemic fluency) compared to the relapse-remitting subtype ($d = -0.66$ semantic fluency; $d = -0.57$ phonemic fluency). Because age was significantly related to performance on the COWAT ($r = -.81$ $p < .0005$ n 10), as was duration of illness (r .61 p .05 n = 12), the differences in magnitude on COWAT performance between subtypes may further support the suggestion that more selective distribution of demyelinating lesions tend to cluster on frontal structures as the disease progresses.

A modest deficit in confrontation naming as indexed with the Boston Naming Test (Kaplan, Goodglass, & Weintraub, 1983) was found ($d = -0.54$) that corresponded to approximately 64% overlap between MS and control scores. No differences with respect to magnitude were found between patients with chronic-progressive MS ($d = -0.67$) and relapse-remitting MS ($d = -0.69$) on the Boston Naming Test. On tests of comprehension such as the WAIS-R Comprehension subtest (Wechsler, 1981), a small effect was obtained ($d = -0.30$ OL% = 79) for all patients with MS. This effect was smaller in patients with relapse-remitting MS ($d = -0.25$ OL% = 82) compared to patients with chronic-progressive MS ($d = -0.60$ OL% = 62), suggesting a greater deficit in verbal comprehension in the chronic-progressive subtype.

Attention/Concentration
Attention and concentration were most often indexed with the Digit Span subtest of the WAIS-R (Wechsler, 1981) in primary studies. The obtained effect sizes for all patients with MS was small ($d = -0.42$ backward; $d = -0.37$ forward) in comparison to the other neuropsychological test effect sizes. The discrepancy in magnitude of effect between forward and backward Digit Span may indicate no significant difficulties involving the manipulation of information in

immediate memory in comparison to simple attentional difficulties as measured with forward span. This is in contrast to previous reports (Rao et al., 1991) that indicate significant deficits on digits backward, but not on digits forward. This discrepancy also holds true in the chronic-progressive and relapse-remitting subtypes, although a large difference was found between subtypes. The obtained effect size for Digit Span backward ($d = -0.77$ OL% = 55) and forward ($d = -0.70$ OL% = 57) for the chronic-progressive subtype was more sensitive to discriminating patients with this subtype of MS from controls compared to the obtained mean effect size for backward ($d = -0.28$ OL% = 78) and forward span ($d = -0.27$ OL% = 80) in the relapse-remitting subtype.

Information processing speed deficits were indexed with the Symbol Digit Modalities Test (SDMT; Smith, 1982), the Digit Symbol subtest from the WAIS-R (Wechsler, 1981) and the Paced Auditory Serial Addition Test (PASAT; Gronwall, 1977). The SDMT was more sensitive to discriminating all patients with MS from controls ($d = -1.36$ OL% = 32 SDMT; $d = -1.03$ OL% = 44 Digit Symbol; $d = -0.48$ OL% = 65 PASAT) compared to scores obtained on the PASAT and Digit Symbol subtest of the WAIS-R. Together these tests were also more sensitive at indexing attentional difficulties in MS compared to WAIS-R Digit Span tasks. Moreover, in the chronic-progressive subtype, WAIS-R Digit Symbol performance was significantly more impaired than performance on the SDMT. That is, a very large effect ($d = -2.23$ OL% = 14) was obtained on the WAIS-R Digit Symbol test. This effect suggests that nearly all patients with chronic-progressive MS can be discriminated from healthy controls as the associated overlap approaches complete separation (OL% = 15) of test scores. Slowed information processing, however, as revealed by the Digit Symbol subtest of the WAIS-R, SDMT or the PASAT, could reflect central influences, peripheral influences, or both (Beatty, 1996; Kaplan, Fein, Morris, & Delis, 1991). Thus, it would be hard to argue that poor performance on the WAIS-R Digit Symbol task can act as a neuropsychological marker for chronic-progressive MS.

WAIS-R Digit Symbol performance in patients with relapse-remitting MS was also more sensitive to MS-control differences in comparison to other tasks of attention and information-processing speed. That is, the obtained effect size ($d = -0.93$ OL% = 48) for WAIS-R Digit Symbol was larger than that obtained for the PASAT ($d = -0.48$ OL% = 68) and WAIS-R Digit Span subtests, although not as large as those evinced in the chronic-progressive subtype.

Memory acquisition and delayed recall

A number of studies have demonstrated that various aspects of memory are differentially affected by MS (e.g., Fischer, Foley, Aikens, Ericson, Rao, & Schindell, 1994; Grafman, Rao, & Litvan, 1990; Rao, Graffman et al., 1993), with some memory processes evidencing substantial loss and others remaining wholly or partially intact (see Thornton & Raz, 1997). Despite the equivocal findings, some general conclusions can be drawn from the results presented in Tables 10.4, 10.5, 10.6.

With respect to all patients with MS, the general pattern suggests that delayed recall is more impaired [$d = -1.44$ OL% = 30 Selective Reminding Test delayed recall (SRT; Buschke & Fuld, 1974)] than immediate recall [$d = -0.43$ OL% = 72 Rey Auditory Verbal Learning Test total recall trials 1–5 (RAVLT; Rey, 1964)] for both verbal [SRT; California Verbal Learning Test (CVLT; Delis, Kramer, Kaplan, & Ober, 1987)] and non-verbal indices (Rey-Osterrieth Complex Figure; ROCF; Rey, 1941; Osterrieth, 1944). The composite Wechsler Memory Scale (WMS-R; Wechsler, 1974) Memory Quotient, however, a measure of immediate and delayed recall, does correspond to an effect size ($d = -1.29$ (OL% = 35) greater than some tasks of delayed recall exclusively. This may reflect the accumulated poor performance across WMS immediate recall subtests. Verbal recall (CVLT, SRT) is more impaired than non-verbal recall (ROCF) for both immediate and delayed recall. With recognition procedures, impairments are generally less severe and may not be evident at all [e.g. Presidents Test (Hamsher & Roberts, 1985)], except among patients with severe global cognitive impairment (see Beatty, 1996; Beatty, Goodkin, Monson, Beatty, & Hertsgaard,1988; Rao, 1986; Thornton & Raz, 1997). Finally, remote memory as indexed with the Famous Persons Test (Albert, Butters & Levin, 1979) and Presidents Test was comparatively impaired to performance on delayed recall tasks when taken together to represent dysfunction in very long-term memory. The magnitude of deficit on the remote memory tasks was also greater than that obtained on recognition memory tasks.

Overall, the present findings suggest impairment across verbal and non-verbal recall tasks with relatively preserved recognition. This may in turn support a retrieval-based account of long-term memory dysfunction in patients with MS. That is, long term memory in MS is affected primarily during retrieval but not during encoding and storage operations. Compared with free recall, recognition presumably imposes less demand on retrieval while nevertheless taxing encoding and storage capacity. Therefore, it appears that patients with MS initially register information into memory but retrieve information less consistently than controls. This conclusion is in contrast to Thornton and Raz's (1997) quantitative review of memory impairment in MS that found a more global pattern of memory deficits in MS. Perhaps the inclusion of newer studies and the exclusion of older studies in the present review (i.e., this review's literature search span 1983–1997 versus Thornton & Raz's 1966–1995 literature search span), can account for the discrepancies in the interpretation of memory impairment in MS. This discrepancy might be solved with further experimentation and eventually, an updated meta-analytic review of memory impairment in MS.

For patients with chronic-progressive MS, a slightly different memory profile was obtained. That is, non-verbal memory measures were slightly more sensitive to MS-control differences (ROCF delayed recall) than verbal measures ($d = -0.75$ OL% = 55 SRT delayed recall), while remote memory as indexed with the Famous Persons Test (Albert, Butters, & Levin, 1979), was also more sensitive than tasks measuring delayed recall of recently learned information (i.e., SRT). Moreover, effects for recall for both verbal and non-verbal tasks were larger in patients with chronic-progressive MS compared to recognition effects ($d = -0.37$ OL% = 75 Presidents Test recognition). This may lend further support to a retrieval-based hypothesis of long term memory dysfunction in patients with MS. No studies, however, reported immediate recall data for patients with chronic-progressive MS only.

On measures of memory function in patients with relapse-remitting MS, neuropsychological deficits are prominent in comparison to other cognitive functions (see Table 10.6). The particular pattern of memory deficits obtained is distinct from patients with chronic-progressive MS. Verbal recall is more impaired than non-verbal recall. Delayed recall is more impaired than immediate recall for verbal tasks but not on visual tasks (see above, and/or Table 10.6). Recall is more impaired than recognition which further supports the retrieval-based hypothesis of long term memory dysfunction. And finally, on tests of remote memory, patients with relapse-remitting MS actually performed better than controls on the Information subtest of the WAIS-R ($d = 0.02$ OL% > 95).

Cognitive flexibility and abstraction

On tests of conceptual function, such as the Category Test (Halstead, 1947; Reitan & Wolfson, 1993), Raven's Matrices (Raven, 1960), the Stroop interference score (Stoop, 1935), Trail Making Test (Part B) (Lezak, 1995, pp. 381–384), Similarities subtest of the WAIS-R, and the Wisconsin Card Sorting Test (WCST; Heaton, 1981), patients with MS display moderate impairment. The most sensitive tasks to MS was Raven's Progressive Matrices ($d = -0.63$ OL% = 60), followed by the Stroop Interference score ($d = 0.62$ OL% = 61), followed by WCST scores ($d = 0.57$ OL% = 64 WCST perseverative responses; $d = -0.52$ OL% = 66 WCST categories achieved). The Category Test and Trail Making Test (Part B) were capable of discriminating 32% and 29% of patients with MS from controls, respectively, whereas the Similarities subtest from the WAIS-R was similar with respect to discriminability (OL% = 70). Moreover, the obtained effect sizes confirm Rao's (1986) observation that the degree of impairment on the Similarities subtest of the WAIS-R is no greater than on the Vocabulary subtest of the WAIS-R when all patients with MS are tested as a group. When subtypes are defined and tested separately, however, the degree of impairment on the Similarities subtest of the WAIS-R for patients with chronic-progressive MS ($d = -0.91$) is greater than that obtained on the Vocabulary subtest of the WAIS-R ($d = -0.50$) by these same patients. Rao's observation, however, does hold true in the relapse-remitting subtype (see Table 10.6).

For patients with chronic-progressive MS, some significant differences in magnitude of effect sizes compared to patients with relapse-remitting MS were obtained. For example, the two most sensitive neuropsychological measures to patients with chronic-progressive MS were the WCST perseverative error score ($d = 1.07$ OL% = 42) and the WAIS-R Similarities subtest ($d = -0.91$ OL% = 48). The corresponding effect sizes for the patients with relapse-remitting MS ($d = 0.61$ OL% = 61 WCST perseverative errors; $d = -0.28$ OL% = 80 WAIS-R Similarities) were the least sensitive to patients. Moreover, the differences in magnitude on WCST performance between subtypes might also lend further support to the suggestion that more selective distribution of demyelinating lesions cluster on frontal structures as the disease progresses with the number of perseverative errors on the WCST providing a good index of focal frontal pathology (Stuss, 1996).

Overall, the implication of these findings is that patients with chronic-progressive MS exhibit a primary deficit in concept formation and perseverative tendencies while patients with relapse-remitting MS do not. When patients with MS are studied as one group, the specificity of this finding is muddled, and the interpretation of findings is equivocal.

Performance skill

Although it has been reported that patients with MS often exhibit deficits on tests of visuoperceptual and visuospatial processing (Rao et al., 1991), when the magnitude of these deficits is taken into consideration as indexed in effect sizes, these deficits can be considered minimal or non-existent. For instance, performance on the Hooper Visual Organization Test (HVOT; Hooper, 1983) corresponded to an OL% statistic of 70. That is, the distribution of scores between patients with MS and controls on the HVOT cannot be discriminated in 70% of cases. Even more overlap was obtained on other measures of visuoperceptual and visuospatial processing (e.g., $d = -0.33$ OL% = 78 Judgment of Line Orientation [Benton et al, 1983]; $d = -0.50$ OL% = 67 WAIS-R Block Design), while copy of the ROCF was reproduced better by patients than controls ($d = 0.11$).

In patients with chronic-progressive MS, the magnitude of effect for WAIS-R Block Design was large ($d = -0.82$ OL% = 50), but may be an artifact of timing rules and slowed performance rather than a true visuospatial deficit. When other obtained effects are taken into consideration that index visuospatial ability (e.g., $d = -0.50$ OL% = 67 Judgment of Line Orientation) and motor speed ($d = 1.21$ OL% = 37 Purdue Pegboard bilateral condition; Lezak, 1995), it is likely that poor performance on the WAIS-R Block Design does indeed reflect slowed performance.

Visuoperceptual and visuospatial deficits in patients with relapse-remitting MS are even smaller. Benton's et al., (1983) Facial Recognition task corresponded to an effect size of –0.58 (OL% = 63). Performance on Judgment of Line Orientation was not able to discriminate more than 15% of patients with relapse-remitting MS from controls ($d = -0.16$ OL% = 87), while copy of the ROCF could not discriminate any patients from controls ($d = 0.11$), as patients performed better than controls. These impairments are minimal, and it is likely that visuoperceptual processing impairments (if present at all) arise from simple defects in speed dependent tasks rather than from higher level disturbances in visuoperceptual and visuospatial processes (see Benton & Tranel, 1993).

Manual dexterity

For all patients with MS, the largest effect sizes for neuropsychological tasks were obtained on tests of manual dexterity and motor speed. The effect sizes range from

−1.76 (Purdue Pegboard left hand) to −0.74 (Grooved Pegboard left hand; Klove, 1963), corresponding respectively to overlap percentages of 23% and 55% (see Table 10.4). Moreover, motor speed is more impaired than manual dexterity in MS, as effect sizes were larger for Purdue Pegboard performance and Finger Tapping Test (Reitan & Wolfson, 1993; Spreen & Strauss, 1998) speed than Grooved Pegboard performance. Lateralizing indices were generally non-existent, although right hand performance was slightly more impaired than left hand performance with the exception of Purdue Pegboard performance (see Table 10.4).

Patients with chronic-progressive MS showed a large effect on Purdue Pegboard bilateral performance (d = 1.21 OL% = 37). Unfortunately, other measures of manual dexterity and motor speed have not been used to study impairment in this particular subtype of patients with MS even though such a large effect exists.

In patients with relapse-remitting MS, lateralizing indices are more evident as Finger Tapping performance with the right hand was significantly more impaired (d = −1.02 OL% = 44) than left hand performance (d = −0.88 OL% = 49). Moreover, motor speed is more impaired than coordinated manual dexterity (Finger Tapping effects > Grooved Pegboard effects) in patients with relapse-remitting MS as Grooved Pegboard performance adds a dimension of complex coordination (Lezak, 1995).

Considering the magnitude of impairment on tasks of manual dexterity and motor speed, and their sensitivity to discriminating patients with MS from controls, it is recommended that documentation of these skills be made in light of the formal neuropsychological instruments mentioned in future research. This might not only document a primary defect in many patients with MS, but also, help in the interpretation of other neuropsychological data where poor performance can be attributed to either slowed performance or to the cognitive construct being measured (e.g., visuospatial function).

A note on affect

Personality alterations, mood disturbances, and psychotic episodes may occur during the course of MS (Cummings & Benson, 1992). Given the requirement of a control group in the computation of an effect size, only mood, or more specifically, depression, was measured in patients with MS and controls in the published literature [most often with the Beck Depression Inventory (BDI; Beck, 1987)]. For all patients with MS, the effect size obtained for the BDI (d = 1.98) corresponds to 19% overlap in the distribution of BDI scores. This is consistent with the clinical observation that depression may be the presenting feature of the disorder, and is more common in multiple sclerosis than it is in many other chronic neurological disorders (Cummings & Benson, 1992; Goodstein & Ferrell, 1977; White, 1990). When patients with MS are parsed into their constituent subtypes, an even more dramatic effect size is obtained in patients with chronic-progressive MS. The BDI effect size (d = 3.56) corresponds to virtually complete separation in BDI scores (OL% < 5). This effect is considerably smaller in patients with relapse-remitting MS (d = 1.00 OL% = 45). It is difficult to determine whether the elevated BDI score is a consequence of frequent clinical exacerbations with accumulating neurological deficit, however.

Summary

The meta-analytic results indicate that cognitive impairment is indeed evident in patients with MS on several cognitive tasks and test variables (see Tables 10.4, 10.5, 10.6). Significant cognitive differences are apparent in the neuropsychological test profiles of chronic-progressive and relapse-remitting subtypes of MS. These differences are not only found in magnitude of deficit, but in the pattern of cognitive [dys]function. Moreover, relations between neuropsychological impairment and clinical and demographic attributes of patients with MS were revealed. These relationships show that patients with chronic-progressive MS present with more executive impairment and hence, suggest a greater tendency for demyelinating lesions to cluster on frontal structures. On the other hand, patients with relapse-remitting MS present with more memory related dysfunction. They do not present with the type of severe episodic memory loss as that seen in dementia of the Alzheimer's type (DAT) that is often attributable to cortical lesions of the temporal-hippocampal formation. The difference in magnitude of effect between patients with MS and DAT confirms this clinical observation (see Chapter 4). More specifically, a retrieval based deficit characterized by generally intact remote and recognition memory was found in the analysis of memory measure effect sizes for all patients with MS.

In conclusion, the synthesis indicates that a large proportion of this patient population is impaired on standard neuropsychological tests. Specifically patients with chronic progressive MS display maximal deficits on frontal-executive tasks whereas patients with relapse-remitting MS present with maximal impairments on tasks of memory function. This finding underscores the need to examine cognitive deficits separately in subtypes of MS which may account for why substantial numbers of patients are indistinguishable from controls on many tests in primary studies of MS.

Chapter 11

MAJOR DEPRESSIVE DISORDER

Most clinical investigators now accept the general notion that major depressive disorder is associated with cognitive abnormalities, but there are many unresolved questions and controversies regarding their magnitude (severity), quality (pattern), and whether purported deficits are indicative of disturbed brain function (Bieliauskas, 1993; Christensen, Griffiths, Mackinnon, & Jacomb, 1997; Grossman, Kaufman, Mednitsky, & Scharff, 1994; Kaufman, Grossman, & Kaufman, 1994; Kinderman & Brown, 1997; King & Caine, 1996; Miller, Faustman, Moses, & Csernansky, 1991; Veiel, 1997). That is, most empirical investigations of neuropsychological function in major depressive disorder have demonstrated mental slowing, inattention, and deficient free recall, within the context of intact naming and cued memory, implicating dysfunction of subcortical brain structures (Caine, 1981; Cummings & Benson, 1984; King & Caine, 1990). Cognitive function in patients with depression, however, range from virtually intact to extremely impaired, making it difficult to describe reliably aspects of cognitive [dys]function that might distinguish the patient with depression from an irreversible cause of dementia such as Alzheimer's disease (e.g., Bornstein, Baker, & Douglass, 1991; Burt, Zembar, & Niederehe, 1995; Caine, 1986; Deptula, Manevitz, & Yozawitz, 1991; Folstein & McHugh, 1978; Johnson & Margo, 1987; Kiloh, 1961).

To make matters worse, most empirical studies do not give due consideration to the quantitative performance of patients with depression on a voluminous battery of cognitive measures – understandably. As such, the nature of cognitive function in depression in most empirical studies can only be articulated on the basis of

the dependent variable(s) in the context of a qualitative review of previous findings (e.g., Cassens, Wolfe, & Zola, 1990; Crews & Harrison, 1995; Golinkoff &
Seeney, 1989; King & Caine, 1990; Massman, Delis, Butters, Supont, & Gillin,
1992). For example, King, Cox, Lyness, Conwell, & Caine (1998) conclude from
their empirical study that elderly depressed inpatients have significant deficits in a
range of explicit verbal learning functions on the CVLT. Notwithstanding, might
additional quantitative evidence of cognition on a wide assortment of similar and
differing tasks and test variables be of value that would help articulate further the
nature of this deficit? Moreover, how large is this impairment of explicit verbal
learning in comparison to other noted cognitive abnormalities in patients with
depression? With these questions in mind, King and Caine (1996) noted that the
neuropsychology of major depressive disorder remained poorly understood, but
that the existing evidence indicated that cognitive disturbances in depression were
related to disturbed cerebral functioning and not to ". . . an epiphenomenon of
disordered mood or distracting ruminations. . ." (p. 213). Accordingly, it seemed
appropriate to integrate this variable literature by way of meta-analysis.

The diagnosis of major depressive disorder and study inclusion criteria

The diagnosis of depression in primary studies must have been made based on
Diagnostic and Statistical Manual [third revised or fourth edition] criteria for
unipolar major depressive disorder which is characterized by at least two weeks
of depressed mood or loss of interest accompanied by at least four additional
symptoms of depression (see fourth edition of the American Psychiatric
Association Diagnostic and Statistical Manual criteria). Studies that included
patients with Dysthymic or Bipolar I or II disorders were not included in our
review.

The review

Twenty-two studies published between 1980 and 1997 met criteria for inclusion
in the present review. In total, cognitive test results from 726 patients with major
depressive disorder and 795 healthy normal controls were recorded across primary studies.
   Descriptive demographic and clinical variable data available from primary
studies from the published literature are presented in Table 11.1. The table
reflects patient samples that are approximately 55 years of age and have completed 13 years of education. The patient with depression was just as likely to
be male or female. When medication regimen was described (n = 5), approximately 45% of patients in study samples were on various types of pharmacotherapies (typically flouxetine) to reduce depressive symptomatology. None
of the demographic or clinical variables correlated significantly with the effect
sizes obtained for any of the cognitive variables. Burt, Zembar, and Niederehe

Table 11.1. Descriptive Statistics for Major Depressive Disorder Cognitive Studies.

Clinical and Demographic Variable	Mdn	M	SD	Range	N
Sample size					
Depressed samples	28	34	24	12–100	22
Control samples	24	36	30	12–118	22
Patient's age	57	55	11	34–72	22
Onset age	50	50	4	47–53	2
Duration of illness (in years)	8.6	8.6	9.1	2–15	2
Percentage of males	42	44	12	22–66	16
Patient's education (in years)	13.7	13.1	2.0	8.5–15.8	20
Percentage on medication	48	42	27	0–75	5

Note. Mdn. = median; M = mean; SD = standard deviation of the mean; N = number of studies in which the variable was reported.

(1995), however, found that demographic and descriptive factors such as age, inpatient versus outpatient status, medication status, depressed subtype (mixed versus unipolar major depressive disorder), and test characteristics (e.g., retention interval, verbal versus visual stimuli) have significant effects on cognition in patients with depression. Further, case studies have provided a careful description of related cognitive impairments with basic clinical and demographic variables (see Albert, Duffy, & Naeser, 1987; Boone, Miller, & Lesser, 1990; Freeman, Galaburda, Cabal, & Geschwind, 1985; Rediess & Caine, 1993).

Cognitive deficits in major depressive disorder

Effect size summaries are presented for specific cognitive tasks and test variables in Table 11.2. Mean d's presented in the column are raw effect sizes. Test variables are presented according to the rank order of the effect size. Effect sizes are included along with the corresponding standard deviation and the number of effect sizes the mean d was based on. To help describe the dispersion of effect sizes, a minimum and maximum d value are also presented. The table also includes the Fail Safe N (Nfs) for the number of additional studies that would be necessary to reverse the overall probability obtained from our obtained effect size to a value higher than our critical value for statistical significance, which was set at.01 (see Wolf, 1986 for an elaboration). Chapter 15 [Table 15.9] includes similar statistics for the composite neuropsychological domains. The following description of cognitive task and test variable effect sizes are grouped by domain and presented in the order of most to least impaired in patients with major depressive disorder.

Delayed recall
Taken together measures of delayed recall correspond to the most impaired neuropsychological domain in patients with depression (see Chapter 15, Table

Table 11.2. Effect Size Results in Rank Order for Patients with Major Depressive Disorder.

Neuropsychological Test/ Test Variable	N d	M d	SD d	Min. d	Max. d	Nfs	OL % (approx.)
Hamilton Depression Rating Scale	5	4.04	1.42	2.24	5.66	2015	<2.0
Brief Psychiatric Rating Scale	1	3.60	–	3.60	3.60	359	<5.0
RAVLT list A trial 5	1	–1.93	–	–1.93	–1.93	192	
RAVLT long delay free recall	1	–1.77	–	–1.77	–1.77	176	
RAVLT short delay free recall	1	–1.52	–	–1.52	–1.52	151	30.0
RAVLT list A total	2	–1.43	0.23	–1.27	–1.59	284	
Wechsler Memory Scale-Revised Memory Quotient	1	–1.42	–	–1.42	–1.42	141	
RAVLT list A trial 1	1	–1.25	–	–1.25	–1.25	124	
RAVLT delayed recognition	1	–1.24	–	–1.24	–1.24	123	
Mattis DRS Initiation/ Perseveration scale	1	–1.07	–	–1.07	–1.07	106	
Mattis DRS Memory scale	1	–1.03	–	–1.03	–1.03	102	
Mini Mental State Examination	6	–1.03	0.38	–0.51	–1.52	612	
Rey-Osterrieth Complex Figure immediate reproduction	2	–1.02	0.20	–0.88	–1.16	202	45.0
Semantic fluency	2	–0.97	0.45	–0.65	–1.28	192	
Letter Cancellation	1	–0.97	–	–0.97	–0.97	96	
WAIS-R Arithmetic	3	–0.89	1.21	–0.13	–2.29	264	
WMS-R Paired Associates I	2	–0.80	0.93	–0.14	–1.46	158	
Trail Making Test Part B	5	0.77	0.70	–0.18	1.67	380	
WMS-R Visual Reproduction I immediate recall	3	–0.71	0.43	–0.46	–1.21	210	
Stroop interference	2	0.69	0.15	0.40	0.97	136	
Buschke SRT delayed recall	1	–0.69	–	–0.69	–0.69	68	
Mattis DRS Total Score	3	–0.68	0.92	0.38	–1.26	201	
WMS-R Visual Reproduction II delayed recall	2	–0.67	0.25	–0.49	–0.84	132	
CVLT discriminability	2	–0.66	0.40	–0.38	–0.95	130	
CVLT long delay free recall	3	–0.66	0.21	–0.56	–0.87	195	
Stroop word reading	3	0.66	0.56	0.11	1.22	195	
Rey-Osterrieth Complex Figure delayed reproduction	4	–0.63	0.40	–0.17	–1.10	248	
WAIS-R Comprehension	3	–0.63	0.75	–0.13	–1.50	186	
WAIS-R Digit Symbol	7	–0.63	0.49	–0.21	–1.45	434	
CVLT list A trial 5	3	–0.62	0.35	–0.23	–0.88	183	
COWAT	7	–0.61	0.26	–0.29	–1.14	420	
WMS-R Logical Memory II delayed recall	7	–0.60	0.70	0.08	–2.07	413	
Warrington Facial Recognition	1	–0.58	–	–0.58	–0.58	57	
WAIS-R Block Design	4	–0.58	0.16	–0.34	–0.70	228	
WMS-R Attention/Concentration	1	–0.57	–	–0.57	–0.57	56	
Benton Facial Recognition	1	–0.54	–	–0.54	–0.54	53	
WAIS-R Performance IQ	6	–0.52	0.25	–0.18	–0.80	306	
WAIS-R Vocabulary	6	–0.52	0.69	–0.06	–1.90	306	
RAVLT list B	1	–0.51	–	–0.51	–0.51	51	

Table continues

Table 11.2. (continued)

Neuropsychological Test/ Test Variable	N d	M d	SD d	Min. d	Max. d	Nfs	OL % (approx.)
CVLT short delay recall	1	−0.50	–	−0.50	−0.50	49	65.0
Mattis DRS Attention scale	1	−0.49	–	−0.49	−0.49	48	
Buschke SRT trials	1	−0.45	–	−0.45	−0.45	44	
WAIS-R Picture Completion	2	−0.45	0.08	−0.40	−0.49	88	
Hooper Visual Organization Test	1	−0.44	–	−0.44	−0.44	43	
Stroop color naming	2	0.44	0.39	0.16	0.72	86	
WCST categories achieved	2	−0.44	0.36	−0.40	−0.49	86	
CVLT list A trials 1–5	2	−0.43	0.74	0.09	−0.95	84	
WAIS-R Digit Span forward	10	−0.43	0.55	0.22	−1.77	420	
Finger Tapping Test-left	1	−0.42	–	−0.42	−0.42	41	
National Adult Reading Test	2	−0.42	0.02	−0.36	−0.48	82	
Raven's Progressive Matrices	1	−0.41	–	−0.41	−0.41	40	
WAIS-R Picture Arrangement	2	−0.40	0.15	−0.29	−0.50	78	
Benton Visual Retention Test number of errors	1	0.39	–	0.39	0.39	38	
Boston Naming Test	6	−0.39	0.43	0.37	−0.84	228	
Mattis DRS Construction scale	1	−0.39	–	−0.39	−0.39	38	
Rey-Osterrieth Complex Figure copy	6	−0.39	0.25	0.11	−0.56	228	
Wide Range Achievement Test Reading	1	−0.38	–	−0.38	0.38	37	
WMS-R Logical Memory I immediate recall	6	−0.35	0.20	−0.09	−0.63	204	
CVLT short delay cued recall	1	−0.34	–	−0.34	−0.34	33	
Finger Tapping Test-right	1	−0.34	–	−0.34	−0.34	33	
WCST perseverations	3	0.32	0.23	0.27	0.40	93	
Paced Auditory Serial Addition Test	3	−0.31	0.15	−0.22	−0.39	90	
WAIS-R Digit Span backward	10	−0.31	0.35	0.22	−0.79	300	
WAIS-R Object Assembly	2	−0.30	0.23	−0.14	−0.47	58	
WAIS-R Information	3	−0.26	0.21	−0.11	−0.50	75	
Consonant Trigrams	2	−0.22	0.08	−0.18	−0.26	42	
WAIS-R Full Scale IQ	6	−0.22	0.13	−0.07	−0.34	126	
CVLT list A trial 1	3	−0.20	0.64	0.45	−0.83	57	
CVLT list B	1	−0.19	–	−0.19	−0.19	18	
Trail Making Test Part A	3	0.18	0.47	−0.20	0.70	51	
WAIS-R Similarities	2	−0.18	0.21	−0.03	−0.32	34	
WAIS-R Verbal IQ	8	0.10	0.16	0.07	−0.35	72	
Buschke SRT total score	2	0.05	0.05	0.03	0.08	8	
Mattis DRS Conceptualization	1	0.00	–	0.00	0.00	–	100.0

Note. Nd = number of effect sizes; Md = mean effect size; SDd = standard deviation around the effect size; Min.d = smallest effect size obtained; Max.d = largest effect size obtained; Nfs = Fail Safe N; SRT = Selective Reminding Test; DRS = Dementia Rating Scale; CVLT = California Verbal Learning Test; RAVLT = Rey Auditory Verbal Learning Test; WAIS-R = Wechsler Adult Intelligence Scale-Revised; WMS-R = Wechsler Memory Scale-Revised; COWAT = Controlled Oral Word Association Task; WCST = Wisconsin Card Sorting Test.

15.9). An important double dissociation of effects is evident, which may aid in the differentiation of depression from probable Alzheimer's disease in keeping with the cognitive profiles. That is, the RAVLT long delay free recall effect size of −1.77 (OL% = 23), is three times as large as that obtained for the CVLT long delay free recall effect size ($d = -0.56$ OL% = 63). This pattern of dissociation (RAVLT effects. CVLT effects) holds true for all RAVLT and CVLT test variables (see Table 11.2). Thus, because no such dissociation of RAVLT and CVLT effects exist in the Alzheimer's disease cognitive profile, in the differential diagnosis of Alzheimer's disease and major depressive disorder a significantly poorer RAVLT performance compared to CVLT performance would suggest a dementing etiology rather than a depressive episode (see Zakzanis, Leach, & Kaplan, 1998; also see Summary – this chapter).

When recognition measures were employed within the same task (i.e., RAVLT), the magnitude of effect was smaller (e.g., $d = -1.24$ OL% = 36) compared to delayed recall effects (e.g., $d = -1.77$ OL% = 23). Moreover, it has been noted elsewhere that patients with depression make few intrusion errors and retain over long delay periods most of the information they had managed to learn initially (Kopelman, 1986). This pattern of memory test performance closely parallels that displayed by patients with subcortical dementia where patients have difficulties initiating systematic retrieval of short- and long-term memory. It has also been noted, however, that the subcortical dysfunction hypothesis of memory deficits in depression is viable, but only for a subgroup of patients as greater than normal heterogeneity in the learning and memory abilities of patients with depression were found which could not be accounted for based on the cumulative effects of aging or repeated depressive episodes. (see Massman, Delis, Butters, Dupont, & Gillin, 1992).

Finally, a verbal-nonverbal delayed recall dissociation is not evident based on the magnitude of effects for the WMS-R Logical Memory and Visual Reproduction subtests. That is, both measures were able to discriminate approximately an equal number of patients with major depressive disorder from healthy normal controls (i.e., $d = -0.67$ OL% = 59 Visual Reproduction vs. $d = -0.60$ OL% = 62 Logical Memory).

Memory acquisition

In keeping with the pattern of patient performance on delayed recall and recognition measures that support a retrieval based impairment, milder encoding deficits in patients with depression are also evident based on the rank order of the effect sizes. As such, measures of memory acquisition correspond to the next most impaired neuropsychological domain in patients with major depressive disorder (see Chapter 15, Table 15.9).

Again, RAVLT effect sizes were greater in magnitude to those obtained for the CVLT across learning trials (e.g., $d = -1.43$ OL% = 30 RAVLT list A total; $d = -0.43$ OL% = 70 CVLT list A trials 1–5), and for short delay free recall (e.g., $d = -1.52$ OL% = 29 RAVLT short delay free recall; $d = -0.50$ OL% = 67 CVLT short delay free recall). A rather large verbal-nonverbal discrepancy, however, between WMS-R Logical Memory and Visual Reproduction immediate recall effects is evident ($d = -0.71$ OL% = 56 Visual Reproduction immediate recall vs. $d = -0.35$ OL% = 75 Logical Memory immediate recall). The discrepant magnitude of these effects would suggest that patients with major depressive disorder have more difficulty immediately recalling visual stimuli compared to verbal stimuli. If encoding of visual rather than verbal stimuli is more taxing, and in keeping with the noted deficits in effortful processing in depression (see King & Caine, 1993), perhaps patients perform more poorly on nonverbal recall measures because of the added attentional demanding qualities needed to encode and recall visual (or non-verbalizable) compared to verbal stimuli. This discrepancy of verbal-nonverbal effects, however, is not evident on WMS-R long delay recall measures. Further experimentation will likely elucidate further the nature and pattern of this dissociation.

Finally, forward and backward span as indexed with the WAIS-R subtest, was able to discriminate no more than approximately 30% of patients from controls. That is, an effect size of -0.43 corresponding to 70% overlap in forward span score distribution between patients and controls was obtained. A smaller effect size of -0.31 (OL% = 78%) was obtained on backward span.

Attention/Concentration
Measures of attention and concentration correspond to the next most impaired neuropsychological domain in patients with major depressive disorder (see Chapter 15, Table 15.9). More specifically, letter cancellation was the most sensitive attentional measure to the presence of major depressive disorder ($d = -0.97$ OL% = 46). Deficient performance on letter cancellation in patients with depression, however, is not associated with spatial neglect deficits as that seen in patients with right hemisphere lesions (see Heilman, Watson, & Valenstein, 1993). Rather, poor performance likely reflects slowed temporal processing of information. Other attention/concentration effect sizes were generally able to discriminate no more than one third of patients with depression from healthy normal controls. For example, Stroop word and color reading effects correspond to effect sizes of 0.66 (OL% = 59) and 0.44 (OL% = 70), respectively. Similarly, attention subtests from the WMS-R and the Mattis DRS correspond to effect sizes of -0.57 (OL% = 64) and -0.49 (OL% = 67). Further, the PASAT, which has been shown to be a very sensitive measure to deficits in information processing ability (Gronwall & Wrightson, 1981), was found to be minimally impaired, and hardly sensitive, in patients with major depressive disorder.

In addition, we calculated effect sizes for effort-demanding and superficial processing conditions using data provided by Weingartner (1986) to test the hypothesis that patients with major depressive disorder were selectively deficient in effortful (i.e., attention-demanding) processing (also see Golinkoff & Seeney, 1989; Hasher & Zacks, 1979). Weingartner's (1986) study was not included in the overall meta-analysis because it did not meet the inclusion criteria of diagnostic specification. Table 11.3 however, includes the effect size and percent overlap for both conditions. Effort demanding tasks yield an effect size that is

Table 11.3. Effect Sizes for Effort-Demanding and Superficial Processing Conditions in Patients with Major Depressive Disorder.

Condition	Effect Size	%Overlap	N. Dep.	N. Con.
Effort Demanding	2.63	10.7	10	10
Superficial Processing	0.42	73.0	10	10

Note. Original raw data taken from Weingartner (1986)
%Overlap = percentage of score overlap distribution between patients with depression and normal controls on condition.
N. Dep. = number of patients with depression; N. Con. = number of healthy normal controls.

almost capable of discriminating patients with depression from controls (i.e., OL% = 10.7), whereas the magnitude of effect from automatic or superficial processing tasks is not a reliable discriminator (i.e., OL% = 73). This dissociation is elaborated in the Summary section of this chapter.

Cognitive flexibility and abstraction

The magnitude of effect for measures of cognitive flexibility and abstraction was quite variable when taken together. For example, an effect size of -1.07 (OL% = 42) was obtained on the Mattis DRS Initiation/Perseveration subscale, although total score on the subscale can be largely attributed to poor word generation on semantic fluency. Conversely, on a test of verbal concept formation, patients did not differ from controls in their ability to explain what each of a pair of words has in common (i.e., $d = -0.18$ OL% = 88; WAIS-R Similarities). Within the range of these effects, cognitive flexibility measures where successful performance is time dependent, such as Trail Making Test Part B or Stroop interference task, tend to be more sensitive to major depressive disorder compared to untimed measures of cognitive flexibility such as the WCST (e.g., $d = 0.77$ OL% = 54 Trail Making Test Part B; $d = 0.32$ OL% = 77 WCST perseverations). This implies that poor performance on measures sensitive to frontal-executive functioning might be largely attributed to slowed cognitive and motoric central processing rather than some presumed structural lesion of the frontal lobes. Whether this impairment on frontal-executive tasks is further exacerbated by medication effects is difficult to tell in keeping with the detailed underreporting of medication status of patients in the primary studies reviewed. Given the paucity of research, it remains important for future experimental studies to assess the possible impact of psychotropic medications on measures sensitive to frontal-executive function before, during, and after standardized treatments.

Performance skill

Measures of performance skill including tasks requiring visuospatial, visuoperceptual, and visuoconstructional ability are by no means consistently impaired in patients with depression. When time dependent tasks, however, are parsed from untimed tasks, the effect sizes are relatively more homogenous in magnitude. For example, when taken together the timed WAIS-R performance subtests including Digit Symbol and Block Design, and the composite WAIS-R Performance IQ were able to discriminate approximately 40% of patients from controls. Conversely, the untimed copy of the ROCF was able to discriminate approximately 25% of patients from controls. Moreover, the pattern of impairment from our profile revealed a trend that suggested a generalized slowing of cognition. Of the 19 tests that were dependent on time as the principle measurement, or that were time limited, 12 tests fell above the median effect size and 7 fell below. The distributions of the mean effect sizes between the timed and untimed tests, however, were not significantly different from one another (see Zakzanis, Leach, & Kaplan, 1998). This pattern of impairment would suggest the absence of a higher-order visuospatial or visuoperceptual impairment and support a generalized slowing of cognitive processing hypothesis in depression.

Also apparent from the table is a large dissociation in composite IQ scores. That is, the WAIS-R Performance IQ is greater than that obtained for the WAIS-R Verbal IQ ($d = -0.52$ OL% = 66 Performance IQ vs. $d = 0.10$ OL% = 92 Verbal IQ). In fact, Verbal IQ estimates ranged from being higher in patients with depression (min. $d = 0.07$) to mild deficits compared to controls (max. $d = -0.35$).

Verbal skill

The magnitude of effect obtained on measures of verbal skill may also aid in the differential diagnosis of depression from Alzheimer's disease and primary progressive aphasia as the corresponding sensitivity of these measures to depression were generally modest. More specifically, naming to confrontation, as indexed with the Boston Naming Test, corresponds to a minimal effect of -0.39 (OL% = 73). This is smaller than the effect obtained for this same measure in patients with Alzheimer's disease or primary progressive aphasia (see Chapter's 4 & 6). Moreover, reading ability was also equally minimally impaired in patients with depression (e.g., $d = -0.42$ OL% = 71 NART; $d = -0.38$ OL% = 73 WRAT reading), as was vocabulary ($d = -0.52$ OL% = 65). Fluency measures on the other hand, were generally more sensitive to the presence of major depressive disorder. That is, semantic fluency effects were able to discriminate approximately half of the patients with depression from healthy normal controls ($d = -0.97$ OL% = 46). Moreover, semantic fluency effects were generally larger than those obtained for phonemic fluency ($d = -0.97$ semantic fluency vs. $d = -0.61$ phonemic fluency). Finally, WAIS-R Comprehension scores were able to discriminate approximately 40% of patients with depression from healthy normal controls ($d = -0.63$ OL% = 60). It may be possible, however, that the impairment in comprehension was secondary to verbal memory deficits in keeping with the rank order of effect sizes (also see Caine, Yerevanian, & Bamford, 1984).

Manual dexterity

Measures of manual dexterity correspond to the least sensitive measures to the presence of major depressive disorder (see Chapter 15, Table 15.9). Only Finger

Tapping Test performance, however, was documented in the literature by way of formal experimentation. Effect sizes correspond to 72% ($d = -0.42$) and 76% ($d = -0.34$) overlap in test score distribution for left and right hand finger tapping scores, respectively. Thus, no asymmetrical deficit is apparent in keeping with the obtained magnitude of effects.

A note on affect

As expected, maximal differences between patients with depression and healthy normal controls were found on the Hamilton Depression Rating Scale ($d = 4.04$ OL%, 5), and the Brief Psychiatric Rating Scale ($d = 3.60$ OL%, 5). These effect sizes correspond to less than 5% overlap. That is, patients with major depressive disorder can be completely discriminated from healthy normal controls based on Hamilton Depression and Brief Psychiatric Rating Scale score dispersion. As such, highly elevated scores on the Hamilton Depression Rating Scale or on the depression related questions of the Brief Psychiatric Rating scale should give rise to the inclusion of major depressive disorder in a differential diagnosis.

Summary

The results of our meta-analysis indicate that cognitive impairment is indeed evident in patients who meet diagnostic criteria for major depressive disorder. More specifically, depression had the largest effect on tests of episodic, declarative memory. Other groups of tests, whose effect sizes fell above the median effect size included tests of verbal fluency and tests of attention. Effect sizes that fell below the median were found on tests of semantic memory, conceptual reasoning, primary memory, working memory, motor speed, and visual-perceptual conceptualization.

In keeping with the pattern of test deficits, we ask then, is this "core" deficit on tests of episodic recall a generalized effect or due to a specific cognitive process? The meta-analysis revealed that tests sensitive to attention are among those with the greatest effect sizes. Faulty attention may contribute to poor memory performance by decreasing efficiency of the encoding process. The effect sizes, however, were larger for tests of episodic recall than for attention which argues against the memory deficit being secondary to the attention deficit. This does not rule out the possibility that faulty attention does indeed influence memory processes but it does argue against faulty attention being the sole source of the memory impairment. Moreover, poor retrieval could account for poor memory performance. Tests of word generation, such as the Controlled Oral Word Association Test (COWAT) or semantic fluency task were also among the tests with the largest effect sizes, but again these effect sizes fell well below those seen on tests of episodic recall. Also, not all tests of episodic recall resulted in equivalent effect sizes. For example, the effect sizes of measures taken from the CVLT or the Buschke Selective Reminding Test (BSRT), both tests of verbal learning capacity, fell below those obtained on the RAVLT. The CVLT and the BSRT differ from the RAVLT in the support given to encoding processes. In the CVLT, words are categorized into four semantic categories which can aid encoding strategies. On the BSRT recall is cued by semantic category if free recall fails, this can also aid performance by facilitating encoding of the words. The RAVLT, on the other hand, consists of 16 non-related words; it does not support encoding strategies and any encoding strategies utilized during the test are examinee dependent. The differences in the magnitude of effect that depression affords on the RAVLT versus the CVLT and BSRT suggests that depression has a selective effect on encoding processes in episodic memory (Zakzanis, Leach, & Kaplan, 1998).

Indeed, Weingartner (1986) tested the hypothesis that patients with depression were deficient in effortful or attention demanding processes (also see Hartlage, Alloy, Vazquez, & Dykman, 1993; Rohling & Scogin, 1993). To-be-recalled words were studied under two conditions. One condition, the effortful cognitive processing condition, required the subject to generate a word that was related in meaning to the target word. The second condition, the acoustic, superficial cognitive processing condition, required the subjects to generate a word that sounded like the target word. Table 11.3 includes the effect size and percent overlap from Weingartner's study. Effort demanding tasks yielded an effect size that was almost capable of discriminating completely patients with depression from controls (i.e., OL% = 10.7), whereas the magnitude of effect between automatic and superficial processing tasks was not a valid discriminator (i.e., OL% = 73.0). It could be argued that the greater effect on effortful memory processes is due to the fact that patients with depression have difficulty engaging in any mental activity that requires effort. The examination of the rank order of effect sizes, however, does not support this hypothesis of a general effect of mental effort on cognitive performance. For example, two of the most demanding tests in terms of mental effort, the PASAT and the Brown-Peterson Consonant Trigrams test, fell near the bottom of the rank order of effect sizes. Therefore, it appears that the effect of effort is specific to memory encoding processes and not a general effect of effortful mental activity.

Indeed, only the RAVLT provided measures that were most sensitive to discriminating patients with major depressive disorder from healthy normal controls. Of the RAVLT measures, recall of items after the fifth trial and the long delayed recall scores was able to discriminate more than 80% of patients from controls. This level of sensitivity would be of some clinical utility if the task was to confirm the subjective reports of memory difficulty in an individual with suspected major depressive disorder. If, however, the aim is to differentiate memory deficits due to depression from an underlying neurological dysfunction, for example dementia, then the use of the RAVLT may yield in a false positive result. That is, the individual with depression may be identified as having a dementing disorder. As such, the clinician would be in a better position to differentiate depression from dementia on the basis of CVLT scores, particularly the number of intrusions (Delis, 1989).

Chapter 12

SCHIZOPHRENIA

Schizophrenia is without doubt a perplexing, enigmatic disease of the brain with a putatively identifiable neuropathophysiology (Andreasen et al., 1994; Heinrichs, 1993; Levin, Yurgelun-Todd, & Craft, 1989; Mesulam, 1990; Randolph, Goldberg, & Weinberger, 1993). Several studies have indeed found conflicting evidence of abnormal structure, function, and physiology in most unimodal, heteromodal, and paralimbic areas of the brain in patients with the disease (Buchsbaum, 1990; Franzen & Ingvar, 1975; McKenna & Chua, 1995; Randolph, Goldberg, & Weinberger, 1993; Seidman, 1983). As such, schizophrenia has come to be understood as a heterogeneous disease charac-terized by neurobiologic alterations (Blanchard & Neale, 1994; Buchsbaum, 1990; Crow, 1990; Flor-Henry, 1976; Jeste & Lohr, 1989; Raz & Raz, 1990; Suddath, Casanova, Goldberg, Daniel, Kelsoe, & Weinberger, 1989; Zakzanis & Heinrichs, 1997, 1999) and disturbed psychiatric symptomatology (Carson & Sanislow, 1992; David & Cutting, 1994; Straube, & Oades, 1992; Young et al., 1998).

From a neurobehavioral perspective there is currently broad agreement that schizophrenia produces impairment of neuropsychological function. Although a number of narrative reviews have described and integrated cognitive findings in schizophrenia (e.g., Heaton & Crowley, 1981; Heinrichs, 1993; Randolph, Goldberg, & Weinberger, 1993), until recently there had been no comprehen-sive quantitative evaluations of this literature. In view of the increasing use of cognitive measures in schizophrenia research and the accumulation of empirical evidence, Heinrichs and Zakzanis (1998) undertook to carry out such an evaluation. They found that schizophrenia is characterized by a very broadly-based cognitive impairment with varying degrees of deficit in all ability domains measured by standard clinical tests. More specifically, they found evidence of impairment in attention and concentration (also see Braff, 1993; Cornblatt & Keilp, 1994), cognitive flexibility and abstraction (also see Gruzelier et al. 1988; Heinrichs, 1990; Van der Does & Van den Bosch, 1992; Weinberger et al. 1986), manual dexterity (also see Goldstein & Zubin, 1990; Schwartz, 1990), visuospatial or performance skill (also see Green, 1985; Raine, 1992; Stuss, 1984), verbal skill (also see Barr, Bilder, Goldberg, Kaplan, & Mukherjee, 1989; Crawford et al. 1993), memory acquisition (also see Goldberg, Gold, Greenberg, & Griffin, 1993; Paulsen et al. 1995), and delayed recall (also see Randolph et al. 1994; Saykin et al. 1991).

From a symptomatology perspective individuals with schizophrenia commonly present with auditory, and less often, visual, hallucinations and most often with delusional ideation that often characterizes their disturbed thought content. While abnormalities in form of thought are seen in such symptoms as loosening of association, tangential speech, thought blocking, and neologistic speech, additional characteristics can include flattened or inappropriate affect, lack of motivation, poor social interaction, as well as idiosyncratic mannerisms and behaviors (Goldman, Axelrod, & Taylor, 1996). There is some evidence to suggest a relationship between schizophrenic symptomatology and cognitive deficit (see Zakzanis, 1998d), but inherent properties of a single disease model of schizophrenia and task difficulty have confounded the validity and reliability of such relationships (see Chapman & Chapman, 1973, 1978, 1989; Goldstein, 1986, 1990; Heinrichs, 1993; Miller, Chapman, Chapman, & Collins, 1995; Seidman, 1983).

The diagnosis of schizophrenia and study inclusion criteria

Schizophrenia usually manifests itself between the ages of 18 and 25. It has a lifetime prevalence ranging from 0.5% to 1.0% of the population (American Psychiatric Association, 1994). DSM-IV defines schizophrenia as a disturbance that lasts for at least 6 months and includes at least 1 month of active-phase symptoms [i.e., two (or more) of the following: delusions, hallucinations, disorganized speech, grossly disorganized or catatonic behavior, negative symptoms] that have been present for a significant portion of time during the 1-month period or for a shorter duration if successfully treated (American Psychiatric Association, 1994).

To be included in the review patients must have met diagnostic criteria of the Diagnostic and Statistical Manual of Mental Disorders (DSM-III or later) for schizophrenia, and have satisfied these criteria on the basis of a structured clinical interview. Study samples that included patients with schizophreniform or schizoaffective disorder were not included in the review. Accordingly, the year 1980 was chosen as a year of publication criterion because it corresponded roughly to the introduction and use of more systematic and reliable diagnostic criteria for schizophrenia (e.g., DSM III).

The review

Two hundred four studies published since 1980 met criteria for inclusion in the present analysis. In total, cognitive test results from 7,420 patients with schizophrenia, and 5,865 normal healthy controls were recorded across primary studies.

Descriptive data available for demographic and clinical variables are presented in Table 12.1. In terms of gender composition, the published literature reflects samples that are overwhelmingly male (82.4%), and fairly chronic in terms of the length of illness history. Most patients underwent initial psychiatric hospitalization in their early twenties and almost 78% were medicated at the time of cognitive testing. The percent of patients with schizophrenia on medication is also presented in Table 12.1. This statistic is more informative than the Clorapromazine (CPZ) equivalent daily dose because of infrequent neuroleptic dose reporting in the published literature. In addition, Clozapine and Respiridone dosages are not convertible into CPZ daily doses. All anti-psychotic medication, however, is reflected in the binary medication variable. Out of 204 studies only 13, or 6%, reported data on unmedicated patient samples. The possible influence of medication on cognitive test performance has been recognized for many years (see Goldman, Axelrod, & Taylor, 1996; Spohn & Strauss, 1989), but convincing evidence for this influence has been lacking and clinicians face ethical constraints in removing patients from treatment for research purposes. Thus apart from some exceptions (e.g., Cleghorn, Kaplan, Szechtman, Szechtman, & Brown, 1990), researchers relied largely on medicated patient samples during the period between 1980 and 1997.

Table 12.1. Descriptive Statistics for Schizophrenia Cognitive Studies.

Variables	M	SD	Range	N
Sample size				
Schizophrenia samples	37	29.7	5–819	166
Control samples				
Patients' age	34.2	9.4	18.1–56.5	162
Onset age	22.4	3.2	17.5–28.0	31
Duration of illness (years)	12.8	7.5	3.0–29.6	30
Hospital admissions	3.9	7.5	2.1–9.5	25
Percentage of males	83.1	64.4	25.0–100.0	143
Patients' education (years)	11.9	1.1	9.0–15.3	109
Medication percentage on neuroleptics	79.9	38.1	0.0–100.0	89
Cpz. eq. daily dose in mg.	538.0	318.6	0.0–1771.9	52

Note. M = mean; SD = standard deviation of the mean; N = number of studies in which the variable was reported; Cpz. eq. = Chlorpromazine equivalent daily dosage in milligrams.

Cognitive deficits in schizophrenia

Effect size summaries are presented for specific cognitive tasks and test variables in Table 12.2. Mean d's presented in the column are raw effect sizes. Test variables are presented according to the rank order of the effect size. Effect sizes are included along with the corresponding standard deviation and the number of effect sizes the mean d was based on. To help describe the dispersion of effect sizes, a minimum and maximum d value are also presented. The table also includes the Fail Safe N (Nfs) for the number of additional studies that would be necessary to reverse the overall probability obtained from our obtained effect size to a value higher than our critical value for statistical significance, which was set at .01 (see Wolf, 1986 for an elaboration). Chapter 15 [Table 15.10] includes similar statistics for the composite neuropsychological domains. The following description of cognitive task and test variable effect sizes are grouped by domain and presented in the order of most to least impaired in schizophrenia.

Table 12.2. Effect Size Results in Rank Order for Patients with Schizophrenia.

Neuropsychological Test/ Test Variable	N d	M d	SD d	Min. d	Max. d	Nfs	OL % (approx.)
WMS-R Visual Reproduction II delayed recall	1	−2.17	−	−2.17	−2.17	216	
RAVLT trial 5	1	−2.10	−	−2.10	−2.10	209	
RAVLT short delay	1	−2.00	−	−2.00	−2.00	199	20.0
WMS-R Memory Quotient	4	−1.83	0.67	−1.16	−2.40	728	
CVLT list A trials 1–5	4	−1.68	0.81	−0.60	−2.30	668	
Rey-Osterrieth Complex Figure delayed reproduction	3	−1.65	0.19	−1.50	−1.86	492	
RAVLT long delay	5	−1.62	0.78	−0.40	−2.40	805	
CVLT list A trial 5	1	−1.54	−	−1.54	−1.54	153	
Purdue Pegboard bilateral	4	−1.53	0.22	−1.30	−1.80	608	
CVLT short delay cued recall	1	−1.52	−	−1.52	−1.52	151	
Semantic fluency	4	−1.52	1.20	−0.80	−2.00	604	30.0
CVLT long delay free recall	4	−1.48	0.94	−0.60	−2.80	588	
Grooved pegboard right hand	2	−1.45	0.50	−1.10	−1.80	288	
WAIS-R Performance IQ	14	−1.44	0.80	−0.50	−3.30	2002	
Benton Finger Localization	16	−1.39	1.90	−0.20	−8.30	2208	
Rey-Osterrieth Complex Figure immediate recall	3	−1.39	0.61	−0.70	−1.86	414	
Token Test	7	−1.35	0.94	−0.18	−2.70	938	
WAIS-R Full Scale IQ	23	−1.33	0.84	−0.11	−3.20	3036	
Grooved Pegboard left hand	2	−1.30	0.57	−0.90	−1.70	258	
CVLT short delay free recall	2	−1.27	0.38	−1.00	−1.54	252	
WMS-R Logical Memory I immediate recall	6	−1.23	0.80	−0.40	−2.40	732	
CVLT long delay cued recall	1	−1.20	−	−1.20	−1.20	119	

Table continues

Table 12.2. (continued)

Neuropsychological Test/ Test Variable	N d	M d	SD d	Min. d	Max. d	Nfs	OL % (approx.)
Buschke's SRT total recall	2	−1.20	0.57	−0.80	−1.60	238	
COWAT	17	−1.19	0.52	−0.20	−6.40	2006	
CVLT intrusions	2	1.18	0.34	0.80	2.00	234	
Continuous Performance Test	12	−1.14	0.48	−0.40	−1.90	1356	
Trail Making Test Part B	13	1.11	0.43	0.50	1.88	1430	
WAIS-R Digit Symbol	4	−1.11	0.40	0.55	1.80	440	
Judgment of Line Orientation	4	−1.10	0.62	−0.30	−1.80	436	
Luria-Nebraska Memory scale	1	−1.10	−	−1.10	−1.10	109	
Mattis DRS Memory scale	1	−1.10	−	−1.10	−1.10	109	
WMS-R Logical Memory II delayed recall	5	−1.10	0.82	−0.10	−2.20	545	
WMS-R Paired Associates I	1	−1.10	−	−1.10	−1.10	109	
WCST perseverative responses	10	1.08	0.53	0.20	1.96	1070	
WCST categories achieved	24	−1.06	0.50	−0.10	−2.20	2520	
Stroop interference	7	−1.04	0.94	−0.20	−2.50	721	
WAIS-R Similarities	1	−1.03	−	−1.03	−1.03	102	
WCST perseverative errors	23	1.01	0.37	0.60	1.30	2300	
Peabody Picture Vocabulary Test	2	−1.00	0.42	−0.70	−1.30	198	45.0
WAIS-R Comprehension	3	−0.99	0.59	−0.60	−1.67	294	
WAIS-R Verbal IQ	24	−0.99	0.68	0.00	−2.80	2352	
WCST correct responses	12	−0.98	0.57	0.00	1.70	1164	
Trail Making Test Part A	10	0.95	0.32	0.40	1.30	910	
WCST total errors	15	0.95	0.20	0.60	1.30	1410	
Benton Facial Recognition	7	−0.93	0.46	−0.10	−1.93	644	
Tower of Hanoi	4	0.93	0.35	0.50	1.30	368	
RAVLT trial 1	2	−0.90	0.42	−0.60	−1.20	178	
CVLT list B	1	−0.89	−	−0.89	−0.89	88	
WAIS-R Digit Span backward	7	−0.82	0.32	−0.30	−1.25	567	
Finger Tapping Test right hand	4	−0.80	0.37	−0.40	−1.20	316	
WAIS-R Block Design	10	−0.79	0.64	−0.10	−2.10	780	
WAIS-R Picture Completion	1	−0.79	−	−0.79	−0.79	78	
WCST non-perseverative errors	9	0.79	0.30	0.20	1.10	702	
CVLT recognition-discriminability	2	−0.77	0.30	−0.55	−0.98	152	
Purdue Pegboard left hand	2	−0.75	0.07	−0.70	−0.80	148	
Raven's Progressive Matrices	2	−0.75	0.50	−0.40	−1.10	148	
CVLT list A trial 1	2	−0.73	0.39	−0.45	−1.00	144	
Finger Tapping Test left hand	4	−0.73	0.33	−0.50	−1.20	288	
National Adult Reading Test	16	−0.73	0.48	0.00	−1.60	1152	
WMS-R Visual Reproduction I immediate recall	2	−0.70	0.28	−0.50	−0.90	138	
WAIS-R Digit Span forward	10	−0.69	0.44	−0.10	−1.01	680	
WAIS-R Vocabulary	28	−0.67	0.47	0.10	1.20	1848	
WCST failure to maintain set	6	0.67	0.32	0.00	0.70	396	
Benton Visual Retention Test number of errors	4	0.62	0.51	0.10	1.30	244	

Table continues

Table 12.2. (continued)

Neuropsychological Test/ Test Variable	N d	M d	SD d	Min. d	Max. d	Nfs	OL % (approx.)
WAIS-R Picture Completion	2	–0.60	0.42	–0.25	–0.86	118	
Rey-Osterrieth Complex Figure							
copy	2	–0.60	0.05	–0.58	–0.63	118	
Mill-Hill Vocabulary	5	–0.58	0.39	–0.05	–0.90	285	
Purdue Pegboard right hand	2	–0.55	0.07	–0.50	–0.60	108	
Shipley	9	–0.53	0.30	–0.10	–0.96	468	
Luria-Nebraska Comprehension							
scale	2	–0.50	0.28	–0.30	–0.70	98	65.0
Stroop color reading	2	–0.50	0.57	–0.10	–0.90	98	
Stroop word reading	2	–0.50	0.57	–0.10	–0.90	98	
WAIS-R Object Assembly	1	–0.42	–	–0.42	–0.42	41	
Wide Range Achievement Test	1	–0.30	–	–0.30	–0.30	29	
Boston Naming Test	3	–0.25	0.15	–0.05	–0.40	72	
WAIS-R Information	1	–0.20	–	–0.20	–0.20	19	
Wonderlic	2	–0.10	0.00	–0.10	–0.10	18	>95.0

Note. Nd = number of effect sizes; Md = mean effect size; SDd = standard deviation around the effect size; Min.d = smallest effect size obtained; Max.d = largest effect size obtained; Nfs = Fail Safe N; DRS = Dementia Rating Scale; CVLT = California Verbal Learning Test; RAVLT = Rey Auditory Verbal Learning Test; WAIS-R = Wechsler Adult Intelligence Scale-Revised; WMS-R = Wechsler Memory Scale-Revised; COWAT = Controlled Oral Word Association Task; WCST = Wisconsin Card Sorting Test.

Delayed recall

Measures of delayed recall correspond to the most impaired neuropsychological domain in patients with schizophrenia (see Chapter 15, Table 15.10). Even the most sensitive measure to the presence of schizophrenia however, (i.e., WMS-R Visual Reproduction delayed recall), did not meet heuristic benchmark criteria (i.e., $d > 3.0$ OL% < 5). Indeed, 17% of patients could not be discriminated from healthy normal controls based on dispersion of WMS-R delayed recall scores. Other measures of delayed recall correspond to a range of effect sizes of –1.65 (OL% = 25 ROCF delayed recall) to –1.10 (OL% = 41 WMS-R delayed recall). Further, a significantly smaller effect size of –0.77 (OL% = 54) was obtained for the CVLT recognition-discriminability measure in comparison to the effect size of –1.48 (OL% = 30) obtained for long delay free recall on the CVLT. This dissociation would support the notion that poor performance on delayed recall measures in patients with schizophrenia results from defective retrieval and not a disturbance in encoding.

Moreover, effect sizes for the nonverbal measures of delayed recall are larger in magnitude compared to the effect sizes obtained for the verbal measures of delayed recall ($d = -1.91$ visual measures vs. $d = -1.35$ verbal measures). In keeping with previous mention that most studies have failed to find differences between visual/verbal modalities despite the suggestion of greater left hemisphere neuroanatomic abnormality (see Calev, Korin, Kugelmass, & Lerer, 1987; Heinrichs, 1993), the present review also found verbal measures of delayed recall to show more heterogeneity of effects across studies and thus, it appears to be a less reliable finding than nonverbal delayed recall deficits.

Finally, semantic memory as indexed with the Information subtest from the WAIS-R corresponds to a smaller effect size of −0.20 (OL% = 85) suggesting relatively little impairment in the retrieval of over-learned information that is part of one's general fund of knowledge and is no longer dependent upon temporal and spatial contextual cues for retrieval (Martin, 1992).

In terms of possible moderator variables, there were no significant product-moment correlations between basic demographic and clinical variables and the delayed recall-related effect sizes. With a limited number of studies reporting, however, non-significant correlation trends with several variables have been described elsewhere (see Heinrichs & Zakzanis, 1998).

Manual dexterity

Measures of manual dexterity were next most impaired in patients with schizophrenia (see Chapter 15, Table 15.10). Although the number of studies reporting bilateral motor results was very small, the most sensitive measure of manual dexterity to the presence of schizophrenia was bilateral Purdue Pegboard performance (d = −1.53 OL% = 28). Indeed, this effect was significantly larger than the unilateral Purdue Pegboard effects (i.e., d = −0.75 OL% = 55 left hand; d = −0.55 OL% = 64 right hand). Unilateral Grooved pegboard performance, which adds a dimension of complex coordination, corresponds to effect sizes that were comparable in magnitude to bilateral Purdue Pegboard effects (e.g., d = −1.45 OL% = 31 right hand; d = −1.30 OL% = 35 left hand), and thus, were more sensitive than unilateral Purdue Pegboard effect sizes. Moreover, Finger Tapping Test effect sizes (d = −0.80 OL% = 53 right hand; d = −0.73 OL% = 56 left hand) were less sensitive than Grooved Pegboard measures, but more sensitive than unilateral Purdue Pegboard measures. Taken together, a comparison of unilateral effect sizes does not support any asymmetrical deficit in manual dexterity in patients with schizophrenia.

Results of tests where patients have to identify and discriminate tactile stimuli showed a mean effect size of −1.39 (OL% = 32; i.e., Benton's Finger Localization). At the same time, the results were very heterogeneous, indicating the existence of patient samples with extensive overlap as well as samples with extensive non-overlap with control distributions.

There were no significant moderator correlations in the manual dexterity effects, although a number of narrative review articles (e.g., Cassens, Inglis, Appelbaum, & Gutheil, 1990; King, 1990; Spohn & Strauss, 1989) have noted that neuroleptic medication is generally associated with decreased motor abilities in the acute (i.e., 1 to 3 months) phase of treatment (Goldman, Axelrod, & Taylor, 1996).

Performance skill

Performance skill effect sizes from visuospatial, visuoperceptual, and constructional ability measures constitute the next most impaired neuropsychological domain in patients with schizophrenia (see Chapter 15, Table 15.10). Results pertaining to tests of performance skill are presented in Table 12.2. The available data suggest moderate overlap values, suggesting that perhaps half of the patients and controls are indistinguishable in terms of performance skill measures.

In keeping with the composite WAIS-R IQ indexes, a discrepancy between Performance and Verbal IQ's is apparent in terms of effect size magnitude. That is, an effect size of –1.44 (OL% = 30) was obtained for the WAIS-R Performance IQ, whereas a significantly smaller effect size of –0.99 (OL% = 45) was obtained for the WAIS-R Verbal IQ index.

On more specific measures of performance skill, the Digit Symbol subtest from the WAIS-R and Judgment of Line Orientation task were capable of discriminating 60% of patients with schizophrenia from normal healthy controls. Benton's Facial Recognition, the Block Design and Picture Completion subtests from the WAIS-R were able to discriminate about 50% of the patients, whereas copy of the Rey-Osterrieth Complex Figure and the Picture Completion and Object Assembly subtests from the WAIS-R were able to discriminate approximately 35% of patients.

Cognitive flexibility and abstraction

The next most impaired neuropsychological domain was that which included measures of cognitive flexibility and abstraction (see Chapter 15, Table 15.10). Measures of cognitive flexibility and abstraction are commonly employed in primary studies of neuropsychological function in schizophrenia as evidence from neurobiological and neuropsychological studies has revived interest in schizophrenia as a disease that arises, at least in part, from the frontal lobes of the brain (Franzen & Ingvar, 1975; Levin, 1984; Randolph, Goldberg, & Weinberger, 1993; Seidman, 1983; Taylor, 1995; Weinberger, 1984, 1988; Weinberger, Berman, & Daniel, 1991). That is, frontal-executive problems observed in patients with schizophrenia and in patients with frontal lobe damage include poor planning, aspontaneity, mental rigidity, and impaired social judgment (Benson & Miller, 1997; Damasio & Anderson, 1993; Stuss, Alexander, & Benson, 1997; Stuss & Benson, 1984, 1986). While the phenomenologic similarity between some features of patients with schizophrenia and of patients with prefrontal injury is circumstantial evidence of prefrontal dysfunction in the former case, it is not direct and certainly not conclusive evidence (Weinberger, Berman, & Daniel, 1991). Nevertheless, these observations have spurred the use of neuropsychological measures like the WCST and phonemic fluency tasks such as the COWAT in the schizophrenia patient population. As such, an effect size of –1.19 (OL% = 38) based on 17 studies of phonemic fluency (i.e., COWAT) was obtained. Similar effects equally based on a large number of studies were demonstrated for each of the WCST variables. Taken together, the WCST effect sizes show a moderately large and reliable impairment of WCST performance in schizophrenia samples, with roughly half of the patients separated from normal control subjects (OL% = 45). The large number of studies reporting WCST results allowed for analysis of moderator variables, but only the correlation with number of hospitalizations approached significance (see Heinrichs & Zakzanis, 1998). In addition, a large number of studies reported WCST results along with WAIS-R IQ results. This allowed for an examination of possible relations between general intellectual levels in schizophrenia samples and the WCST effect size in the same sample. There was a significant relationship between WCST effect size and IQ score, and between WCST effects and IQ effects (Heinrichs & Zakzanis, 1998). This implies that patient samples are likely to differ from control samples on the WCST if they also differ in terms of IQ. Thus impaired WCST scores in schizophrenia may be, in part, a reflection of low general intellectual abilities (also see Axelrod, Goldman, Tompkins, & Jiron, 1994; Heinrichs, 1990).

Moreover, on a simulated task of problem solving where stacks of blocks have to be moved into a new configuration in a minimum number of moves, patients with schizophrenia were again moderately impaired as the obtained effect size of 0.93 (OL% = 48) on the Tower of Hanoi task was also able to discriminate approximately half of the patients from the normal controls based on test score dispersion. Further, an effect size of −1.03 (OL% = 44) was obtained on the Similarities subtest of the WAIS-R which requires the patient to formulate verbal concept similarities for word pairs. Similarly, an effect size of −1.04 (OL% = 11) was obtained on the interference trial of the Stroop task where the patient is required to inhibit reading the color word and instead must name the dissonant color of the ink the word is printed in. Finally, an effect size of 1.11 (OL% = 41) was obtained for Part B of the Trail Making Test.

Taken together, performance of patients with schizophrenia on measures of cognitive flexibility and abstraction suggests that researchers may have over-estimated the importance and involvement of the executive-system and the frontal brain region in the pathophysiology and behavior of schizophrenia (Zakzanis & Heinrichs, 1999). The average magnitude of difference between patients with schizophrenia and healthy control subjects is generally too modest to support the idea that frontal brain dysfunction is a necessary component of schizophrenia. This modesty is most apparent in the average effects obtained for the measures of cognitive flexibility and abstraction. The magnitude of effect for neuropsychological measures of cognitive flexibility and abstraction indicates that the literature is distinguished by heterogeneity whereby most patients show normative frontal function, a minority shows diminished values and some patients demonstrate augmented function rather than deficit. It has been noted elsewhere (see Heinrichs & Zakzanis, 1998; Zakzanis & Heinrichs, 1999) that these effects are hard to incorporate within single disease models that propose major involvement of the frontal system in keeping with the relative specificity of neuropsychological tasks to frontal lobe deficit. Further, quantitative evidence also suggests that cognitive tasks are more sensitive than structural and functional neuroimaging measures to schizophrenic disease (i.e., cognitive effect sizes

> neurobiological effect sizes), but are also less specific and valid indicators of frontal brain system integrity (Zakzanis & Heinrichs, 1999).

Attention/Concentration

The next most impaired neuropsychological domain in schizophrenia was that of attention and concentration (see Chapter 15, Table 15.10). Surprisingly, the magnitude of effect on most measures of attention and concentration did not correspond to the most sensitive measures in keeping with the notion that impaired attention in patients with schizophrenia has been described since the initial descriptions of schizophrenia by Kraepelin (1919) and Bleuler (1911, 1950) and the strong face validity that this deficit bears. As such, moderate effects were obtained in studies using versions of the Continuous Performance Test ($d = -1.14$ OL% = 40) which taps the process of vigilance or maintenance of attention over time (van Zomeren & Brouwer, 1994). More specifically, this task requires the subject to monitor a continuous presentation of "noise" stimuli for a specific target (e.g., as A followed by an X) in a string of letters presented visually or auditorily (Goldman, Axelrod, & Taylor, 1996). Overall, the Continuous Performance Test and Trail Making Test Part A seem to be about equally sensitive to schizophrenia, yielding effect sizes that separate approximately half of the patient and control distributions.

The two effect sizes for the Trail Making Task (Part A and B) are also informative because they represent a situation where a simple and more complex and demanding version of a cognitive task can be studied. If task difficulty and task complexity rather than specific cognitive functions like visual scanning and sequencing contribute to schizophrenia-control differences, more demanding versions of the same basic test should yield significantly larger effect sizes than less demanding versions. Thus Trail Making Test Part B should produce a larger effect size than Trail Making Test Part A when applied to the same sample of patients and controls. That is, Trail Making Test Part A requires rapid sequential connection of numbers in a paper and pencil format, whereas Trail Making Test Part B requires alternation between alphabetic and numeric sequences. Fossum, Holmberg and Reinvang (1992) have shown that the spatial arrangement and dual symbol systems of Trail Making Test Part B underlie the slower Part B completion times. Accordingly, a comparison of Trail Making effect sizes did not reveal a significant difference of effect ($d = 1.11$ Part B vs. $d = 0.95$ Part A). Hence, it appears likely that task difficulty and complexity are less important than the more specific attention and scanning-related cognitive processes elicited by this particular test. Alternatively, since both alphabetic and numeric sequences are probably over-learned information, the differences in processing demands between Trail Making A and B may be minimal (see Heinrichs & Zakzanis, 1998).

Finally, on the more simple color and word reading Stroop tasks, an effect size of -0.50 (OL% = 66) was obtained. These measures are not able to discriminate more than 40% of patients with schizophrenia from controls. When the patient is required to name the color in which the color names are printed and disregard their verbal content (i.e., Stroop interference; see Spreen & Strauss, 1998), however, a substantial increase in effect size magnitude is found. This most likely reflects the additional stress on the frontal-executive system which is required for successful performance (Spreen & Strauss, 1998). Indeed, even with the most restrictive and well-defined usage, the process of attention requires highly integrated, widely distributed central nervous system (CNS) functioning and is thus susceptible to a multitude of local and generalized impairments of the CNS (Goldman, Axelrod, & Taylor, 1996).

Memory acquisition

The magnitude of effect for measures of memory acquisition was quite variable as the mean task or test variable effect sizes ranged from –2.10 (RAVLT) to 0.62 (BVRT). As such, the composite neuropsychological domain of memory acquisition was the next most impaired domain in schizophrenia (see Chapter 15, Table 15.10).

The most frequently reported memory acquisition-related test variable was WAIS-R Digit Span. The task simply involves the repetition of a string of numbers or digits in forward and reverse order. The obtained effects ($d = -0.82$ Digit Span backward & $d = -0.69$ Digit Span forward) were generally smaller in magnitude when compared to other tasks of memory acquisition (e.g., RAVLT, CVLT, and WMS-R immediate recall measures). The overall effect size for WAIS-R Digit Span measures of 0.75 represents a hypothetical overlap with control distributions of about 55%, suggesting a fairly modest degree of discrimination.

The magnitude of effects show that defective total verbal learning over trials (e.g., CVLT list A trials 1–5; CVLT and RAVLT trial 5), or similar summary scores (e.g., WMS-R Logical Memory immediate recall), is a reliable finding in the schizophrenia literature, with a schizophrenia-control distribution overlap of somewhat more than 25% (e.g., $d = -1.68$ OL% = 25 CVLT list A trials 1–5). At the same time, there is some evidence to suggest a disproportionate impairment on verbal measures relative to visual indices of memory acquisition (e.g., $d = -1.23$ OL% = 37 WMS-R Logical Memory immediate recall vs. $d = -0.70$ OL% = 57 WMS-R Visual Reproduction immediate recall). Although Randolph, Goldberg, and Weinberger (1993) have noted in their narrative review of the neuropsychology of schizophrenia that both visual and verbal WMS-R indexes were equally impaired in patients with the disease, when the magnitude of effect and not the statistical significance is taken into account there is indeed evidence to suggest a more specific pattern of impairment on WMS-R indexes. That is, the magnitude of effects imply greater left hemisphere dysfunction on measures of memory acquisition (i.e., WMS-R Logical Memory and Visual Reproduction immediate recall measures) and greater right hemisphere dysfunction on measures of delayed recall (i.e., WMS-R Logical Memory and Visual Reproduction delayed recall). When these effects are taken together, the evidence does indeed favor bilateral dysfunction of medial temporal lobe systems involved in mnemonic processing.

Verbal skill

The least impaired neuropsychological domain in patients with schizophrenia was that domain that included measures of verbal and language skill (see Chapter 15, Table 15.10).

The Token test ($d = -1.35$), however, which is primarily an auditory comprehension measure, and semantic fluency ($d = -1.52$), corresponds to about 1/3 overlap between schizophrenia and control distributions. This evidence is qualified by the relatively large standard deviations which imply considerable dispersion and hence heterogeneity of effect sizes in both the semantic fluency and Token test data. Also note the considerably smaller effect size magnitude obtained on the Comprehension subtest of the Luria-Nebraska battery ($d = -0.50$ OL% = 66).

In contrast, a more moderate average effect size was obtained for Vocabulary tests (e.g., $d = -0.67$ OL% = 60 WAIS-R Vocabulary; $d = -0.58$ OL% = 62 Mill Hill; $d = -0.53$ OL% = 65 Shipley). Heinrichs and Zakzanis (1998) demonstrated that there was no significant difference between the average effect size generated by WAIS-R and non-WAIS-R-based vocabulary tests and that none of the effect sizes correlated significantly with potential demographic or clinical moderators. They also noted that there was a strong trend for highly medicated samples to yield smaller word fluency differences relative to control samples (see Heinrichs & Zakzanis, 1998).

The ability to name to confrontation as indexed with the Boston Naming Test was generally intact in keeping with the magnitude of the effect size ($d = -0.25$) and the percent overlap of test scores (OL% = 82). Perseveration of response to previously named items on the Boston Naming Test, however, has been found (see Barr, Bilder, Goldberg, Kaplan, & Mukherjee, 1989). Given that naming ability is impaired (i.e., greater effects) in cortical degeneration such as that seen in DAT, and PPA, the relative intact ability to name in schizophrenia can certainly assist in the differential diagnosis.

Finally, on a test of premorbid ability, roughly half of the patients with schizophrenia could be discriminated from normal controls based on NART score dispersion ($d = -0.70$ OL% = 55). There is a considerable degree of dispersion around the NART mean and individual study effects ranged from -1.85 to $+.91$, however, which raises questions of reliability in the use of this measure to index premorbid ability levels. Moreover, the data suggest that putative tests of verbal skill and general intellectual function are not interchangeable (i.e., WAIS-R, NART, WRAT) and may vary in sensitivity to schizophrenic illness.

Summary

In our quantitative review, we found cognitive deficit to be a reliable finding in schizophrenia. In addition, it is clear that deficit exists in relation to most cognitive tasks in common use. Moreover, although there is variability in the magnitude of deficit, no single test or cognitive construct completely discriminates patients with schizophrenia from healthy normal controls. In terms of discriminability between schizophrenia and control distributions, these effects are associated with 30%–40% overlap. The smallest effects, like those obtained for the WAIS-R Block Design, Vocabulary, and non-WAIS-R IQ correspond to approximately 60%–70% overlap. Therefore, cognitive impairment cannot be considered a defining characteristic of each case of schizophrenia. Indeed, there is convergent evidence that substantial numbers of patients with schizophrenia are neuropsychologically normal (Heaton & Palmer, 1998; Heinrichs & Awad, 1993; Heinrichs, Ruttan, Zakzanis, & Case, 1997; Palmer et al., 1997). Significant impairment is common and often highly prevalent in schizophrenia, however, and it equals or exceeds the magnitude of deficit found in some neurological disorders (e.g., multiple sclerosis, see Chapter 10).

Accordingly, Heinrichs and Zakzanis (1998) have come to understand the reliable and large, but not inclusive, deficit rates in schizophrenia in terms of a continuum of cognitive function. Patients with the illness may vary from a mild decline in function, to moderate declines, to the kind of severe dysfunction seen in many neurological diseases (also see Goldberg & Gold, 1995; Weinberger, 1995). At the mild end, a patient's cognitive dysfunction is relative to their own potential and may overlap with levels of function obtained by many healthy individuals. At the severe extreme, a patient may have cognitive and neurological abnormalities that are completely distinguished from normal control values. The limitations of this kind of explanation, however, include its testability. There are practical difficulties involved in assessing accurately premorbid cognitive potential in large numbers of schizophrenia patients. Moreover, the continuum argument must assume that patients who show "average" cognitive function – roughly half of those with the illness – have nevertheless undergone a relative decline. Therefore, the same proportion of patients must have been slightly "above average" by normative performance standards prior to illness onset (Heinrichs & Zakzanis, 1998).

Heinrichs and Zakzanis (1998) offer an alternative explanation for the large overlap in cognitive deficit rate in their quantitative review. They claim that such deficit is secondary, peripheral, rather than central to the illness. That is, most diseases have peripheral features that are tied only modestly and indirectly to the primary pathology. For example, overall brain volume reductions are less prevalent in Alzheimer's disease than volume reductions in a specific structure, the hippocampus (see Zakzanis, 1998e). Presumably, this reflects the primary locus of pathology in the hippocampus and other specific structures and the less direct relation of this focal pathology to general changes in brain volume in patients with Alzheimer's disease. Hence, the functions measured by standard cognitive tests in patients with schizophrenia may also be relatively peripheral to the still unknown primary dysfunction (Heinrichs, 1993).

Finally, Heinrichs and Zakzanis (1998) speculate whether substantial, but not absolute (e.g., $d > 3.0$ OL% < 5) effect sizes reflect the existence of cognitively intact and impaired sub-populations of patients (also see Heinrichs, 1993; Heinrichs & Awad, 1993; Heinrichs, Ruttan, Zakzanis, & Case, 1997; Heinrichs & Zakzanis, 1998; Zakzanis & Heinrichs, 1999). In addition, several tests and constructs are characterized by large dispersion of individual effects around their means (see Table 12.2). Such dispersion also implies the existence of impaired and normal subgroups of patients. This is inimical to the continuum view of cognitive deficit, which argues for a single disease process with variable expression. In contrast, a strong form of the heterogeneity argument is the contention that multiple disease processes underpin schizophrenia (see Carpenter, Buchanan, Kirkpatrick, & Tamminga, 1993; Heinrichs, 1993; Liddle & Barnes, 1990). Advocates of the single disease-continuum model can point to brain features like ventricle size to show that patients with schizophrenia are normally distributed on such measures, with little evidence of the kind of bimodality that might indicate sub-populations (David, Goldberg, Gibbon & Weinberger, 1991). On the other hand, there is clear evidence of bimodal distributions in schizophrenia on some psychophysiological measures, like smooth pursuit eye movements (Clementz, Grove, Iacono, & Sweeney, 1992; Iacono, Moreau, Beiser, Heming, & Liu, (1992). Meta-analytic evidence cannot resolve this debate, but it does underscore forcefully the need to develop testable illness models that take heterogeneity into account and extend the search for evidence of multiple disease processes (see Heinrichs & Zakzanis, 1998).

In summary our quantitative synthesis is consistent with Heinrichs and Zakzanis (1998) in that it confirms that a large proportion of this patient population is impaired on standard cognitive tests. The evidence suggests that any "selective" deficits in functions like delayed recall are relative and exist against a background of general dysfunction. This picture is complicated by the need to improve reporting of potential moderator variables, and by the need to develop testable illness models that can account for why substantial numbers of patients are indistinguishable from controls on many tests.

Chapter 13

OBSESSIVE-COMPULSIVE DISORDER

Obsessive-compulsive disorder (OCD) refers to the presence of recurrent obsessions or compulsions severe enough to cause marked distress or interfere with the person's optimal functioning with regard to occupation, social activities, and interpersonal relationships (Baer & Jenike, 1990; Steingard & Dillon-Stout, 1992). Its course usually begins in adolescence or early adulthood, but it may begin in childhood with a gradual onset across all age spans (Rasmussen & Eisen, 1990; Turner, Beidel, & Nathan, 1985). Although OCD was previously thought to be relatively rare in the general population, recent community studies have estimated a lifetime prevalence of 2.5% and 1-year prevalence of 1.5%–2.1% (American Psychiatric Association, 1994).

As its name implies, this neuropsychiatric disease is characterized by obsessions and compulsions. Obsessions are persistent ideas, thoughts, impulses, or images that are experienced, at least initially, as intrusive and senseless. The person typically attempts to ignore or suppress such thoughts or impulses or to neutralize them with some other thought or action. The person recognizes that the obsessions are the product of his or her own mind and are not imposed from without. Compulsions on the other hand, are repetitive, purposeful, and intentional behaviors that are performed in response to an obsession, according to certain rules or in a stereotyped fashion. The behavior is designed to prevent discomfort or some dreaded event or situation. Either the activity is not related in a realistic fashion with what it is designed to prevent, however, or it is clearly excessive. The act is performed with a sense of subjective compulsion that is coupled with a desire to resist the compulsion. The person recognizes that his or her behavior is excessive or unreasonable and does not usually derive pleasure from carrying out the activity, although it provides a release of tension (Jenike, Baer, & Minichiello, 1990).

In keeping with the nature of the disorder itself and the findings associating OCD with both specific pathophysiology and nonspecific neurologic abnormalities, a number of brain-behavior relationships have been described over the past decade (e.g., Hollander, Cohen, Richards, Mullen, DeCaria, & Stern, 1993; Nelson, Early, & Haller, 1993; Otto, 1992; Swoboda & Jenike, 1995). Current neurobiological models of OCD, based on both in vivo structural (Behar et al., 1984; Garber, Ananth, Chiu, Griswold, & Oldendorf, 1989; Luxenburg, Swedo, Flament, & Friedland, 1988) and functional (Baxter, 1992; Baxter, Phelps, Mazziotta, Guze, Schwartz, & Selin, 1987; Laplane, Levasseur, & Pillon, 1989; McGuire, 1995; Nordahl, Benkelfat, Semple, Bross, King, & Cohen, 1989) brain imaging studies implicate the frontal-basal-ganglia-thalamocortical circuits in the pathophysiology of OCD (also see Cummings, 1993; Insel, 1992; Malloy, 1987; Zald & Kim, 1996). That is, most positron emission tomography and single-photon emission computed tomography studies have documented aberrant hyperactivity within circuits involving the orbitofrontal gyrus, basal ganglia, and anterior cingulate cortex in both left and right cerebral hemispheres. Further, structural magnetic resonance imaging studies, even those performed using quantitative volumetric evaluations, have found either subtle morphologic changes of macroscopic brain pathology in patients with OCD in the orbital frontal cortex (Berthier, Kulisevsky, Gironell, & Heras, 1996).

From a neuropsychological perspective, evidence has accumulated to support the hypothesis of fronto-subcortical dysfunction in OCD. Most studies have found deficits in cognitive measures sensitive to frontal-executive function and/or structures involved in subcortical processing such as the basal ganglia, although there are also other noted cognitive impairments suggesting that other structures (i.e., temporal lobe) besides the fronto-basal-ganglia region are involved (Berthier et al., 1996). For example, Aronowitz, Hollander, DeCaria, Cohen, Saoud, Stein, Liebowitz, and Rosen, (1994) found specific deficits in visuospatial and visuoconstructional capacities and immediate visual recall and generalized performance on measures of sustained attention and suppression of interference from irrelevant stimulus properties. Moreover, Zielinski, Taylor, and Jurwin (1991) observed impairments on tests of visual-spatial recall, recognition, and sequencing, consistent with nonverbal, perhaps nondominant hemisphere or subcortical processing deficits. Their patients with OCD, however, also scored equal to or somewhat better than normal controls on most verbal tasks and measures of frontal lobe functioning. Even further, Berthier, Kulisevsky, Gironell, and Heras (1996) found patients with OCD to show cognitive deficits affecting attention, intellectual function, memory, word retrieval, and motor and executive function. Finally, Boone, Ananth, Philpott, Kaur, and Djenderedjian (1991) revealed subtle deficits in visual spatial and visual memory functioning in their patients, but no deficits in frontal lobe skills, verbal memory, attention, or intelligence. On the basis of their findings, they note that the observed cognitive deficits would be consistent with basal ganglia and/or right hemisphere disturbance.

Finally, it should be noted that neuropsychological methodologies and the comprehensiveness of assessments vary widely among investigations which may partially account for their variable conclusions. In general neuropsychological studies of OCD are few, sample sizes are variable or small, and the use of appropriate controls and neuropsychological measures are inconsistent, resulting in limited generalizability of findings (Aronowitz, Hollander, DeCaria, Cohen, Saoud, Stein, Liebowitz, & Rosen, 1994).

The diagnosis of obsessive compulsive disorder and study inclusion criteria

The essential features in meeting a diagnosis of OCD according to DSM criteria include recurrent obsessions or compulsions that are severe enough to be time consuming (i.e., they take more than 1 hour a day) or cause marked distress or significant impairment. Moreover, the patient must also recognize that the obsessions or compulsions are excessive or unreasonable (see Diagnostic and Statistical Manual of Mental Disorders Fourth Edition, 1994). Accordingly, patient samples from primary studies must have met DSM-III, III-R, or IV criteria for obsessive-compulsive disorder to be included in our review.

The review

Twelve studies published between 1980 and 1997 met criteria for inclusion in the present analysis. In total, neuropsychological test results from 340 patients with OCD and 268 normal healthy controls were recorded across primary studies.

Descriptive demographic and clinical variable data available from primary studies from the published literature are presented in Table 13.1 for the patients with OCD. The table reflects patient samples that were approximately 35 years of age, and had completed approximately 14 years of formal education. Patients were, on average, diagnosed with OCD at the age of 23 and had a mean disease duration of 13 years, and on average 27% were medicated. Males and females were just as likely to be included in patients samples (i.e., percentage of males in patient samples = 55). Finally, the mean score of patient samples on the Yale-Brown Obsessive Compulsive Scale (Y-BOCS; Goodman, Price, & Rasmussen, (1989a, b) was 24 (also see Jenike, Baer, & Minichiello, 1990).

In terms of possible moderator variables, none of the demographic and clinical variables correlated significantly with the cognitive tasks. This likely reflects the limited power in keeping with the small sample size of primary studies. It has been noted elsewhere (Jenike, Baer, & Minichiello, 1990), however, that there are a few notable trends in the demographic pattern of OCD and its relationship to cognitive function.

Table 13.1. Descriptive Statistics for Obsessive Compulsive Cognitive Studies.

Variables	M	SD	Range	N
Sample size				
OCD samples	28	15	15–65	12
Control samples	22	6	15–32	12
Patients' age	35	3.0	29–38	12
Onset age	23	0.6	22–23	2
Duration of illness (yrs.)	13	3.1	7.9–17.5	6
Percentage of males	55	11	28–67	11
Patients' education (yrs.)	14.2	1.8	10.4–15.8	7
Percentage on medication	27	39	0–100	7
Y-BOCS	24	3.1	18.4–27.4	7

Note. M = mean; SD = standard deviation of the mean; N = number of studies in which the variable was reported; Y-BOCS = Yale-Brown Obsessive Compulsive Scale.

Cognitive deficits in obsessive compulsive disorder

Effect size summaries are presented for specific cognitive tasks and test variables in Table 13.2. Mean d's presented in the column are raw effect sizes. Test variables are presented according to the rank order of the effect size. Effect sizes are included along with the corresponding standard deviation and the number of effect sizes the mean d was based on. To help describe the dispersion of effect sizes, a minimum and maximum d value are also presented. The table also includes the Fail Safe N (Nfs) for the number of additional studies that would be necessary to reverse the overall probability obtained from our obtained effect size to a value higher than our critical value for statistical significance, which was set at .01 (see Wolf, 1986 for an elaboration). Chapter 15 [Table 15.11] includes similar statistics for the composite neuropsychological domains. The following description of cognitive task and test variable effect sizes are grouped by domain and presented in the order of most to least impaired in OCD.

Performance skill
Measures of performance skill, cognitive flexibility and abstraction, and memory were the most sensitive tasks to OCD as the composite magnitude of effects differed insignificantly between these neuropsychological domains (see Chapter 15, Table 15.11). Indeed, patient impairment on the Benton Visual Retention Test, which corresponds to one of the most sensitive measures to OCD, is suggestive of deficits in visuospatial analysis and synthesis, visual recall, and visual discrimination. This finding implicates limbic/right hemispheric or temporoparietal cerebral structures. The relative magnitude of effects across all neuropsychological domains, however, was small relative to effects gathered for the cortico-subcortical dementias.

In terms of performance skill measure sensitivity, the composite WAIS-R Performance IQ was also sensitive ($d = -0.84$ OL% = 50) to the presence of

Table 13.2.   Effect Size Results in Rank Order for Patients with Obsessive Compulsive
Disorder.

Neuropsychological Test/ Test Variable	N d	M d	SD d	Min. d	Max. d	Nfs	OL % (approx.)
Tactual Performance Test	1	1.15	–	1.15	1.15	114	
Benton Visual Retention Test number of errors	2	0.99	0.13	0.90	1.08	196	45.0
Halstead Category Test number of errors	1	0.91	–	0.91	0.91	90	
WAIS-R Performance IQ	1	–0.84	–	–0.84	–0.84	83	
Benton Visual Retention Test correct responses	1	–0.83	–	–0.83	–0.83	82	
CVLT intrusions	1	0.81	–	0.81	0.81	80	
Corsi spatial span	1	–0.70	–	–0.70	–0.70	69	
CVLT list A trial 1	1	–0.63	–	–0.63	–0.63	62	
Trail Making Test B-A	2	0.61	0.11	0.53	0.69	120	
Trail Making Test Part B	3	0.60	0.28	0.29	0.82	177	
CVLT long delay free recall	2	–0.58	0.37	–0.32	–0.84	114	
WCST perseverative responses	3	0.58	0.42	0.23	1.05	171	
WAIS-R Digit Symbol	2	–0.57	0.12	–0.52	–0.61	112	
WAIS-R Information	2	–0.57	0.12	–0.52	–0.61	112	
Rey-Osterrieth Complex Figure delayed reproduction	1	–0.54	–	–0.54	–0.54	53	
WAIS-R Full Scale IQ	1	–0.54	–	–0.54	–0.54	53	
CVLT short delay free recall	2	–0.52	0.74	0.00	–1.04	102	
CVLT short delay cued recall	1	–0.50	–	–0.50	–0.50	49	65.0
WAIS-R Object Assembly	1	–0.50	–	–0.50	–0.50	49	
WAIS-R Block Design	5	–0.49	0.17	–0.32	–0.73	240	
WMS-R Paired Associates I & II	1	0.46	–	0.46	0.46	45	
WMS-R Visual Reproduction II delayed recall	2	–0.46	0.77	0.09	–1.00	90	
COWAT	4	–0.44	0.39	0.13	–0.73	172	
Purdue Pegboard right hand	1	0.43	–	0.43	0.43	42	
Trail Making Test Part A	3	0.37	0.23	0.15	0.61	108	
WCST categories achieved	3	–0.36	0.24	–0.17	–0.63	105	
WCST errors	1	0.35	–	0.35	0.35	34	
Stroop interference	3	–0.33	0.24	–0.15	–0.60	96	
CVLT long delay cued recall	1	–0.32	–	–0.32	–0.32	31	
CVLT recognition	2	–0.26	0.10	–0.19	–0.32	50	
Hooper Visual Organization Test	1	–0.24	–	–0.24	–0.24	23	
Consonant Trigrams	1	0.23	– 0.23	0.23	22		
Purdue Pegboard left hand	1	–0.20	–	–0.20	–0.20	19	
Stroop color reading	2	–0.19	0.30	0.02	–0.40	36	
WMS-R Visual Reproduction I immediate recall	1	–0.19	–	–0.19	–0.19	18	
CVLT list B	1	–0.17	–	–0.17	–0.17	16	
Design fluency	2	–0.17	0.24	0.00	–0.34	32	
CVLT total recall trials 1–5	1	–0.16	–	–0.16	–0.16	15	
WMS-R Logical Memory I							

Table continues

Table 13.2. (continued)

Neuropsychological Test/ Test Variable	N d	M d	SD d	Min. d	Max. d	Nfs	OL % (approx.)
immediate recall	1	−0.16	–	−0.16	−0.16	15	
Stroop word reading	2	−0.16	0.37	0.10	−0.42	30	
WAIS-R Digit Span backward	4	−0.14	0.10	−0.04	−0.25	52	
WAIS-R Comprehension	1	−0.13	–	−0.13	−0.13	12	
Semantic fluency	1	−0.12	–	−0.12	−0.12	11	
WMS-R Logical Memory II							
delayed recall	1	0.09	–	0.09	0.09	8	
WAIS-R Verbal IQ	3	−0.08	0.11	−0.03	−0.14	21	
Porteus Mazes	1	0.07	–	0.07	0.07	6	
Rey-Osterrieth Complex Figure							
copy	1	−0.07	–	−0.07	−0.07	6	
WAIS-R Digit Span forward	4	−0.06	0.02	−0.05	−0.07	20	
WAIS-R Similarities	1	−0.03	–	−0.03	−0.03	2	
WAIS-R Vocabulary	2	−0.01	0.37	0.26	−0.27	–	>95.0

Note. Nd = number of effect sizes; Md = mean effect size; SDd = standard deviation around the effect size; Min.d = smallest effect size obtained; Max.d = largest effect size obtained; Nfs = Fail Safe N; DRS = Dementia Rating Scale; CVLT = California Verbal Learning Test; WAIS-R = Wechsler Adult Intelligence Scale-Revised; WMS-R = Wechsler Memory Scale-Revised; COWAT = Controlled Oral Word Association Task; WCST = Wisconsin Card Sorting Test.

OCD, as the corresponding test score distribution could discriminate roughly half of the patients from normal healthy controls. Note that the WAIS-R Performance IQ effect is significantly larger than that obtained for the WAIS-R Verbal IQ effect.

According to the rank-order of effects, the next most sensitive performance skill measures were the WAIS-R performance subtest effects. These included Digit Symbol (d = −0.57 OL% = 63), Object Assembly (d = −0.50 OL% = 67), and Block Design (d = −0.49 OL% = 68) subtests. Because poor performance on these measures can be attributed to either a visuospatial-visuoconstructional impairment or slowed response times, it is important to consider the magnitude of effect on an untimed visuospatial task. Thus, the obtained effect for copy of the ROCF – an untimed measure of visuospatial-visuoconstructional ability – was minimal (d = −0.07 OL% > 95), suggesting poor performance on WAIS-R performance subtests to be secondary to slowed responding and not to a higher order impairment in visuospatial-visuoconstructional ability. As Christensen, Kim, Dysken, and Hoover (1992) note, patients with OCD evidence poorer performances relative to controls when temporal factors are introduced into tasks. Thus impaired performance on such tasks as the Block Design and Digit Symbol subtest may be a function of the increased time required by patients in order to ensure accurate performance, particularly when indecisiveness, doubting, undoing, and checking obsessions and compulsions intrude into task performance (Aronowitz et al., 1994).

Cognitive flexibility and abstraction

Taken together putative measures of frontal-executive function were also the most sensitive tasks to OCD (see Chapter 15, Table 15.11). There is considerable variability, however, in keeping with the magnitude of independent effects for such tasks. For example, Category Test (number or errors) scores could discriminate roughly half of the patients with OCD from healthy normal controls ($d = 0.91$ OL% = 48), whereas patients were indistinguishable from normals in keeping with WAIS-R Similarities effects ($d = -0.03$ OL% > 95).

Other large effects included those obtained for the Trail Making Test Part B ($d = 0.60$ OL% = 62) and for Trail Making Test B-A ($d = 0.61$ OL% = 61). This latter Trail Making Test index refers to a difference score (Part B – Part A) that essentially removes the speed element from the test evaluation (Lezak, 1995). The number of perseverative responses on the WCST also served well as a sensitive measure to OCD ($d = 0.58$ OL% = 63). Because this particular WCST variable is most sensitive to frontal-executive integrity (Stuss, 1996), the magnitude of effect for the remaining WCST variables (categories achieved; errors) which have been found to be sensitive to deficits beyond the prefrontal cortex (see Anderson, Damasio, Jones, & Tranel, 1991) would support greater frontal-brain system impairment than diffuse cerebral dysfunction in OCD.

Intermediate effect sizes included phonemic fluency effects, which were generally more sensitive to OCD than semantic fluency effects ($d = -0.44$ OL% = 70 phonemic fluency (COWAT) vs. $d = -0.12$ OL% = 90 semantic fluency). Heterogeneity, however, is also evident within the range of phonemic fluency effects as one OCD patient sample actually performed slightly better on the task compared to controls. On the other hand, the upper value in the range suggests that approximately 40% of a different patient sample was impaired relative to control performance. Moreover, phonemic fluency effects were generally two-fold in comparison to design fluency effects. That is, the associated overlap for design fluency could discriminate approximately 10% of patients from controls ($d = -0.17$ OL% = 88). In keeping with the sensitivity of phonemic fluency to left frontal-brain function, and design fluency to right frontal-brain function (see Jones-Gotman & Milner, 1977; Lezak, 1995; Stuss et al., 1998), this dissociation in magnitude of effects would argue against neuropsychiatric models that propose predominately right anterior hemisphere dysfunction in OCD based on neuropsychological specificity.

This argument is further supported with our minimal effect obtained for Porteus Mazes ($d = 0.07$ OL% >95). This is a task that requires the patient to choose, try, reject or adopt alternative courses to successfully solve a complex maze (Porteus, 1959). Porteus Maze test scores did not differentiate more than 5% of patients from controls.

Delayed recall

As a composite neuropsychological domain, those tasks and test variables that were classified as measures of delayed recall correspond to a mean effect size comparable to the mean effects obtained for the performance skill and cognitive flexibility and abstraction neuropsychological domains (see Chapter 15, Table 15.11). More specifically, the most sensitive delayed recall test variable was CVLT long delay free recall ($d = -0.58$ OL% = 63). When long delay recall was semantically cued, smaller effects were obtained ($d = -0.32$ OL% = 77 CVLT long delay cued recall). Hence, patient performance on delayed recall improved. Moreover, delayed recall by recognition is superior to free recall but similar to cued recall (e.g., $d = -0.26$ OL% = 81 CVLT recognition). This pattern of effects would therefore support a retrieval based memory impairment in OCD.

Nonverbal measures of delayed recall correspond to effect sizes similar in magnitude to those obtained for verbal measures of free recall. For example, test scores for delayed reproduction of the ROCF could discriminate roughly one third of the patients with OCD from normal healthy controls ($d = -0.54$ OL% = 64).

Finally, semantic memory as indexed with the Information subtest from the WAIS-R corresponds to a similar effect size of -0.57 (OL% = 63). The magnitude of this effect suggests comparably impaired (compared to episodic memory) retrieval of overlearned information that is part of one's general fund of knowledge and is no longer dependent upon temporal and spatial contextual cues for retrieval (Martin, 1992). Performance on the WAIS-R Information subtest, however, is largely influenced by age and educational achievement (Lezak, 1995; Wechsler, 1981), and is therefore, not a preferable measure of semantic memory. Moreover, as WAIS-R Vocabulary can also be used to index semantic memory, the obtained magnitude of effect for this measure in our table ($d = -0.01$ OL% > 95) would suggest intact semantic memory. What is needed to partial out an explanation for these disparate effects is a greater number of studies reporting WAIS-R Information and Vocabulary test performances along with basic demographic variables such as age and education. This would allow a correlational analysis of possible moderator variables on WAIS-R Information and Vocabulary performance in future meta-analyses.

Memory acquisition

In keeping with a retrieval based memory impairment, measures of memory acquisition were generally less sensitive to OCD than measures of delayed recall (see Chapter 15, Table 15.11). Considerable variability of effects, however, is evident across independent measures and memory acquisition measures. That is the domain of memory acquisition would be the most impaired domain in OCD if digit span effect sizes were removed from this domain. For example, the most sensitive measure to OCD in our table is the Tactual Performance Test ($d = 1.15$ OL% = 41). This task requires the patient to place shapes in a board while blindfolded. It is a tactile memory test but its score is based on time to completion or on a "memory score" (Halstead, 1947). Together, these scores were used to derive our effect size. As such, perhaps memory "per se" is not to blame for the large obtained effect, but response speed in keeping with the rank-order of effects; although a specific tactual-spatial deficit cannot be ruled out. Thus, this effect could have easily contributed to the performance skill neuropsychological domain composite effect size in keeping with its non-specific neuropsychological parameters.

Purer measures of memory acquisition lend support to a retrieval based memory impairment. For example, total recall across 5 learning trials on the CVLT corresponds to an effect size of −0.16 (OL% = 87). This is significantly smaller than the effect obtained on CVLT delayed recall. Moreover, reproduction of the WMS-R figures (i.e., WMS-R Visual Reproduction subtest) was performed better immediately after exposure (d = −0.19 OL% = 86) compared to reproduction after a delay (d = −0.46 OL% = 68).

Effects for measures of span differed significantly between verbal and non-verbal tasks. That is, Corsi Block Tapping Span could discriminate approximately 40% of patients with OCD from normal healthy controls (d = −0.70 OL% = 57), whereas the forward WAIS-R Digit Span subtest could discriminate no more than 5% of patients (−0.06 OL% > 95). Such dissociation in magnitude reflects the differences that are subsumed under the domain of memory acquisition, and hence, highlights the need to present independent effects.

Manual dexterity
Measures of manual dexterity correspond to the next most sensitive measures to OCD (see Chapter 15, Table 15.11). Only Purdue Pegboard performance, however, was documented in the literature by way of control group experimentation. Effect sizes correspond to 71% (d = −0.43) and 85% (d = −0.20) overlap in test score distribution for right and left hand scores, respectively. Thus, in keeping with the magnitude of effect, there is preliminary evidence to suggest an asymmetrical deficit where left hemisphere dysfunction might be greater than right. If such a dissociation holds true in future experimental findings, it would also argue against neuropsychiatric models that propose predominately right hemisphere dysfunction in OCD.

Attention/Concentration
Although the sensitivity of attention and concentration measures were poor, taken together they were next most sensitive to OCD (see Chapter 15, Table 15.11). More specifically, Trail Making Test Part A effect sizes were most sensitive (d = 0.37 OL% = 75) followed by Stroop color (d = −0.19 OL% = 86) and word (d = −0.16 OL% = 88) naming and reading effects.

Verbal skill
The magnitude of effect for measures of verbal skill suggest that this neuropsychological domain is entirely within normal limits. That is, a composite effect size of 0.08 was obtained which has an associated overlap in test score distribution of 95% (see Chapter 15, Table 15.11). Indeed, the range of WAIS-R Vocabulary effects suggests patient samples can obtain higher scores than normal control comparisons. Moreover, WAIS-R Comprehension and semantic fluency test scores could not discriminate more than 10% of patients from controls (d = −0.13 OL% = 90 WAIS-R Comprehension; d = −0.12 OL% = 91 semantic fluency). Finally,

as already noted, a large dissociation in WAIS-R Verbal and Performance IQ effects is evident. Whereas the WAIS-R Verbal IQ could not discriminate more than 5% of the patients from controls ($d = -0.08$ OL% >95), Performance IQ effects could discriminate roughly half of the patients ($d = -0.84$ OL% = 50).

Summary

The results indicate that patients with OCD are most deficient on tests of performance skill, cognitive flexibility and abstraction, and delayed recall, followed by performance on measures of memory acquisition, attention/concentration, manual dexterity, and verbal skill. More specifically our review of the literature found greater impairment in time-dependent visuospatial and visuoconstructional capacities and immediate visual recall. Indeed, patients with OCD evidence poorer performances relative to controls when temporal factors are introduced into tasks. Thus, the question is of whether such performance decrements are reflective of true organic pathology or are indicative of more functional impairment. The converse interpretation that psychiatric variables and ruminative response styles are epiphenomena of a primary underlying deficit is an equally defensible hypothesis. In keeping with this latter interpretation, slowed response times as a result of ruminative response styles in OCD would itself be evidence of such generalized cortical dysfunction, with actual qualitative task performance playing a secondary role (Aronowitz, et al., 1994).

Our review of the literature also found considerable heterogeneity of effects. It is recognized that various explanations may account for the heterogeneity of effect sizes in patients with OCD. For instance, OCD may be a heterogeneous disorder characterized by various homogenous subtypes. In keeping with the neuroanatomy of OCD, the heterogeneity of the functions subserved by the orbital frontal cortex is consistent with the dramatic differences in cytoarchitecture and connections that distinguish the multiple orbital frontal cortex subregions (Zald & Kim, 1996). Accordingly, OCD samples should be stratified according to type, frequency and severity of OCD symptomatology and presence of neurological signs and symptoms in order to assess differential neuropsychological performance or possible subtypes according to psychiatric as well as neurological factors (Aronowitz, et al., 1994).

Finally, it has been noted (Christensen, Kim, Dysken, & Hoover, 1992) that comparison of the cognitive performance of patients with OCD with that of patients with other psychiatric disorders will be required before any constellation of deficits can be considered specific to OCD (see Cohen et al., 1996; Martin, Pigott, Lalonde, Dalton, Dubbert, & Murphy, 1993). Hence, the use of our tables might indeed make this task simpler for the interested researcher.

Chapter 14

MILD TRAUMATIC BRAIN INJURY

Mild head injury, or traumatic brain injury (TBI), broadly refers to any injury to the head that engenders a change in consciousness, however brief, that is typically the result of contact forces or acceleration/deceleration trauma (Williamson, Scott, & Adams, 1996). The primary neuropathology of mild TBI is diffuse axonal injury caused by shearing forces generated in the brain (Alexander, 1987, 1995; Povlishock, Becker, & Cheng, 1986). Secondary brain insults that may lead to ischemic brain damage are extremely common after brain injuries of all grades and severity, although the absence of hematoma, intracranial hypertension, brain swelling/edema, and the absence of focal signs help confirm the diagnosis of mild TBI (see Miller, 1993).

Moreover, the severity of TBI must be defined by the acute injury characteristics and not by the severity of symptoms at random points after trauma (see Alexander, 1995), because the vast majority of patients with mild TBI make considerable neurobehavioral recovery within the first 3–6 months and then plateau at approximately 2 years post injury (Jones, 1992). Mild TBI, however, can sometimes cause persisting brain damage (Binder, 1986; 1997), albeit mild and rarely disabling (Gualtieri, 1995). Earlier reviews of this literature did not specify how frequent or severe the persisting impairment might be (e.g., Binder, 1986), although more recently, quantitative reviews of this literature (e.g., Binder, Rohling, & Larrabee, 1997) along with experimental studies (e.g., Batchelor, Harvey, & Bryant, 1995) have concluded that persistent mild TBI impairment most often manifests itself clinically as impaired attention and concentration.

More specifically, Binder, Rohling, and Larrabee's (1997) meta-analytic review of eight published neuropsychological studies of mild head trauma, revealed evidence of generalized impairment across supraordinate cognitive domains including attention/concentration, memory, manual dexterity, performance skills, cognitive flexibility and abstraction, and verbal skills, with the attention/concentration domain effect size yielding the largest magnitude of difference between patients and controls. This quantitative review, however, did not consider the more qualitative aspects of neuropsychological function by including independent effect sizes for specific task variables. Accordingly, we include here such independent effects in our cognitive profile to elucidate further the residual neuropsychological mechanisms and there relation to cognitive deficit after mild TBI.

The diagnosis of mild traumatic brain injury and study inclusion criteria

The diagnosis of mild TBI must have been made based on Glascow Coma Scale scores of 13–15, post traumatic amnesia of less than 24 hours, loss of consciousness of less than 20 minutes, and a normal neurological exam and/or no evidence of hematoma on imaging scans if available. If patient samples from the primary studies met these diagnostic criteria, the study was included in our review.

The review

Twelve studies published between 1980 and 1997 met criteria for inclusion in the present analysis. In total, neuropsychological test results from 952 patients with mild TBI, and 495 normal healthy controls were recorded across primary studies.

Descriptive demographic and clinical variable data available from primary studies from the published literature are presented in Table 14.1 for the patients with mild TBI. The table reflects patient samples that are typically male which is consistent with previous prevalence reports that estimate males to be twice as likely as females to suffer a TBI (Dikmen, Machamer, Winn, & Temkin, 1995). Patients were approximately 35 years of age, and had completed approximately 12 years of formal education. Moreover, the mean time elapsed from the initial brain injury to the time of assessment was approximately 11 months.

In terms of possible moderator variables, none of the demographic and clinical variables correlated significantly to the cognitive tasks. This likely reflects the limited power in keeping with the small sample size of primary studies. It has been noted elsewhere (Williamson, Scott, & Adams, 1996), however, that there are a few notable trends in the demographic pattern of TBI and its relationship to cognitive function (also see Lezak, 1979, 1986, 1987a, b)

Table 14.1. Descriptive Statistics for Mild Traumatic Brain Injury Cognitive Studies.

Variables	M	SD	Range	N
Sample size				
Mild TBI samples	79	122	12–436	12
Control samples	41	36	12–132	12
Patients' age	35	12	26–70	12
Percentage of males	64	21	36–90	6
Patients' education (years)	12.4	1.4	9.0–13.9	11
Time post injury to assessment (months)	11.2	9.8	1.0–29.0	6

Note. Med. = median; *M* = mean; *SD* = standard deviation of the mean; *N* = number of studies in which the variable was reported.

Cognitive deficits in mild head injury

Effect size summaries are presented for specific cognitive tasks and test variables in Table 14.2. Mean *d*'s presented in the column are raw effect sizes. Test variables are presented according to the rank order of the effect size. Effect sizes are included along with the corresponding standard deviation and the number of effect sizes the mean *d* was based on. To help describe the dispersion of effect sizes, a minimum and maximum *d* value are also presented. The table also includes the Fail Safe N (Nfs) for the number of additional studies that would be necessary to reverse the overall probability obtained from our obtained effect size to a value higher than our critical value for statistical significance, which was set at.01 (see Wolf, 1986 for an elaboration). Chapter 15 [Table 15.12] includes similar statistics for the composite neuropsychological domains. The following description of cognitive task and test variable effect sizes are grouped by domain and presented in the order of most to least impaired in mild TBI.

Cognitive flexibility and abstraction

As a composite neuropsychological index, cognitive flexibility and abstraction measures were generally most sensitive to the cognitive sequelae of mild TBI. Note that the magnitude of the composite effect sizes for the domains of cognitive flexibility and abstraction, delayed recall, and memory acquisition, however, were generally similar and did not differ significantly (see Chapter 15, Table 15.12).

Performance on measures such as phonemic fluency were found to be most impaired in patients with mild TBI (*d* = –1.22 OL% = 37). Note however, that semantic fluency effect sizes were generally similar in magnitude (*d* = –1.08 OL% = 42). On the nonverbal counterpart to phonemic fluency, design fluency test scores were capable of discriminating approximately 50% of patients with mild TBI from healthy normal controls (*d* = –0.77 OL% = 54).

Wisconsin Card Sorting Test effect sizes for the perseverative scores (*d* = 0.83 OL% = 51 perseverative errors; *d* = 0.81 OL% = 52 perseverative responses)

Table 14.2. Effect Size Results in Rank Order for Patients with Mild Traumatic Brain Injury.

Neuropsychological Test/ Test Variable	N d	M d	SD d	Min. d	Max. d	Nfs	OL % (approx.)
COWAT	3	−1.22	0.80	−0.62	−2.13	363	
RAVLT short delay recall	1	−1.09	–	−1.09	−1.09	108	
Semantic fluency	1	−1.08	–	−1.08	−1.08	107	
WMS-R Logical Memory II delayed recall	2	−1.06	0.78	−0.50	−1.61	210	45.0
WMS-R Logical Memory I immediate recall	2	−0.99	0.81	−0.42	−1.56	196	
WMS-R Paired Associates II	1	−0.96	–	−0.96	−0.96	95	
Mini Mental State Exam	1	−0.94	–	−0.94	−0.94	93	
WMS-R Paired Associates I	1	−0.90	–	−0.90	−0.90	89	
Trail Making Test Part A	3	0.85	0.67	0.36	1.53	252	
RAVLT long delay recall	1	−0.85	–	−0.85	−0.85	84	
WCST perseverative errors	1	0.83	–	0.83	0.83	82	
CVLT total recall trial 1–5	1	−0.82	–	−0.82	−0.82	81	
Rey-Osterrieth Complex Figure copy	1	−0.81	–	−0.81	−0.8	180	
WCST perseverative responses	1	0.81	–	0.81	0.81	80	
Design fluency	1	−0.77	–	−0.77	−0.77	76	
Beck Depression Inventory	1	0.73	–	0.73	0.73	72	
WCST total errors	1	0.69	–	0.69	0.69	68	
State-Trait Anxiety Scale state anxiety	1	0.68	–	0.68	0.68	67	
Stroop color reading	1	0.68	–	0.68	0.68	67	
Stroop word reading	1	0.67	–	0.67	0.67	66	
RAVLT total recall trials 1–5	2	−0.65	0.36	−0.39	−0.90	128	
WAIS-R Information	1	−0.65	–	−0.65	−0.65	64	
RAVLT total recall trial 5	1	−0.63	–	−0.63	−0.63	62	
Halstead Category Test	2	0.63	0.51	0.27	0.99	124	
Paced Auditory Serial Addition Test	1	−0.60	–	−0.60	−0.60	59	
Finger Tapping Test right hand	1	−0.54	–	−0.54	−0.54	53	
Buschke SRT delayed recall (30 minutes)	1	−0.54	–	−0.54	−0.54	53	
Rey-Osterrieth Complex Figure delayed reproduction	1	−0.53	–	−0.53	−0.53	52	
WAIS-R Vocabulary	2	−0.53	0.24	−0.36	−0.70	104	
Buschke SRT total recall	1	−0.51	–	−0.51	−0.51	50	65.0
WAIS-R Performance IQ	1	−0.49	–	−0.49	−0.49	48	
Finger Tapping Test left hand	1	−0.47	–	−0.47	−0.47	46	
Trail Making Test Part B	3	0.47	0.24	0.31	0.74	138	
Stroop interference	2	0.46	0.08	0.43	0.49	90	
Buschke SRT delayed recall (4 hours)	1	−0.44	–	−0.44	−0.44	43	
WAIS-R Full Scale IQ	3	−0.41	0.37	0.00	−0.70	120	
Seashore Rhythm Test	1	−0.37	–	−0.37	−0.37	36	

Table continues

Table 14.2. (continued)

Neuropsychological Test/ Test Variable	N d	M d	SD d	Min. d	Max. d	Nfs	OL % (approx.)
WCST categories achieved	1	−0.37	−	−0.37	−0.37	36	
CVLT intrusions	1	0.34	−	0.34	0.34	33	
Tower of Hanoi correct items	1	−0.33	−	−0.33	−0.33	32	
Tactile Performance Test	1	0.32	−	0.32	0.32	31	
WAIS-R Verbal IQ	1	−0.32	−	−0.32	−0.32	31	
Tower of Hanoi errors	1	−0.28	−	−0.28	−0.28	27	
WMS-R Visual Reproduction II delayed recall	1	−0.24	−	−0.24	−0.24	23	
WMS-R Visual Reproduction I immediate recall	1	−0.21	−	−0.21	−0.21	20	
State-Trait Anxiety Scale trait anxiety	1	0.18	−	0.18	0.18	17	
CVLT perseverations	1	0.14	−	0.14	0.14	13	
WAIS-R Digit Span backward	1	−0.14	−	−0.14	−0.14	13	
WAIS-R Block Design	1	−0.11	−	−0.11	−0.11	10	
Stem completion	1	0.00	−	0.00	0.00	−	100.0

Note. Nd = number of effect sizes; Md = mean effect size; SDd = standard deviation around the effect size; Min.d = smallest effect size obtained; Max.d = largest effect size obtained; Nfs = Fail Safe N; SRT = Selective Reminding Test; DRS = Dementia Rating Scale; CVLT = California Verbal Learning Test; RAVLT = Rey Auditory Verbal Learning Test; WAIS-R = Wechsler Adult Intelligence Scale-Revised; WMS-R = Wechsler Memory Scale-Revised; COWAT = Controlled Oral Word Association Task; WCST = Wisconsin Card Sorting Test.

were considerably larger than that obtained for the categories achieved WCST variable (d = −0.37 OL% = 75). Moreover, the obtained effect size for the Category Test was capable of discriminating 40% (d = 0.63) of patients from controls. Similarly, effect sizes gathered for Trail Making Test Part B and for the Stroop interference trial were both generally more sensitive than the number of categories achieved on the WCST as the associated overlap on these measures could discriminate approximately 30% of patients from controls.

Finally, the Tower of Hanoi task, where patients are required to rearrange three colored rings or beads from their initial position on two of three upright columns to a new set of predetermined positions on one or more of the columns in the most direct (fewest moves) manner (Shallice, 1982; Shallice & Burgess, 1991), was not sensitive to patients with mild TBI as the magnitude of effect was minimal (d = −0.33 OL% = 77 Tower of Hanoi correct items; d = −0.28 OL% = 80 Tower of Hanoi errors).

Delayed recall
Measures of delayed recall were the next most sensitive tasks to mild TBI (see Chapter 15, Table 15.12). More specifically, WMS-R Logical Memory delayed recall performance was most impaired in patients with TBI relative to healthy normal controls. The associated overlap could discriminate approximately 55% of patients from controls based on test score dispersion (d = −1.06 OL% = 43).

Delayed recall of WMS-R Paired Associate learning – a word-learning test with built-in cueing – was also capable of discriminating the same number of patients from controls ($d = -0.96$ OL% = 47). This discriminability was also somewhat true in keeping with RAVLT long delay free recall effect sizes ($d = -0.85$ OL% = 50).

The largest effect obtained for a measure of nonverbal long delay recall was that obtained for the ROCF ($d = -0.53$ OL% = 65). Moreover, the magnitude of effect obtained for long delay WMS-R Visual Reproduction was considerably smaller ($d = -0.24$ OL% = 83). Taken together, the nonverbal long delay recall measures are significantly less sensitive to mild TBI compared to the verbal long delay recall measures (see Table 14.2).

Remote memory, as indexed with the WAIS-R Information subtest, is less impaired in patients with mild TBI ($d = -0.65$ OL% = 59) compared to the ability to recall recently learned information (e.g., RAVLT effects). Also, there is no significant evidence to suggest decay of stored information once it has been encoded ($d = -0.54$ Buschke's SRT 30 minute delayed recall vs. $d = -0.44$ Buschke's SRT 4 hour delayed recall). Unfortunately, no measure of recognition discriminability from such tests as the CVLT have been reported in primary studies that met inclusion criteria.

Memory acquisition

As a neuropsychological domain, memory acquisition was next most impaired in patients with mild TBI (see Chapter 15, Table 15.12). Short delay recall on Rey's AVLT is the most sensitive measure of memory acquisition ($d = -1.09$ OL% = 41), followed closely by immediate recall of the WMS-R Logical Memory stories ($d = -0.99$ OL% = 45) and WMS-R Paired Associates ($d = -0.96$ OL% = 46). Conversely, WAIS-R Digit Span performance in patients with mild TBI was generally within normal limits in keeping with test score dispersion (e.g., $d = -0.14$ OL% = 89). Further, nonverbal memory acquisition measures were again generally less sensitive than verbal measures (e.g., $d = -0.21$ OL% = 85 WMS-R Visual Reproduction immediate recall).

Performance of patients with mild TBI and normal controls on stem completion (see Moscovitch, 1992) is completely indistinguishable. That is, the obtained effect size of 0.00 corresponds to 100% overlap of test score distribution, suggesting that the implicit memory system is spared in most, if not all, cases of mild TBI that have been reported in primary studies included in our review.

Attention/Concentration

On cognitive measures of attention and concentration, patients with mild TBI are considerably less impaired in comparison to tasks sensitive to cognitive flexibility and abstraction and memory function (see Chapter 15, Table 15.12). Effect sizes ranged from 0.68 (OL% = 58) for color word reading on the Stroop task to –0.37 (OL% = 74) on the Seashore Rhythm Test. Patients were comparably impaired ($d = -0.60$ OL% = 62) on the PASAT where the patient is required to add 60 pairs of randomized digits so that each is added to the digit immediately preceding it (see Lezak, 1995, p. 372). Moreover, although not a pure measure of attention and concentration, the magnitude of effect for Trail Making Test Part A performance was most sensitive in indexing attention and concentration deficit in patients with mild TBI ($d = 0.85$ OL% = 50).

Verbal skill

Measures of verbal skill correspond to the next most sensitive tasks to the presence of mild TBI largely because of the inclusion of semantic fluency effects in the composite neuropsychological domain. Although not as large as phonemic fluency effects, semantic fluency effects were capable of discriminating approximately 60% of patients from controls ($d = -1.08$ OL% = 42).

Vocabulary level in patients with mild TBI was documented with the WAIS-R Vocabulary subtest. This individually administered vocabulary test consists of 35 words arranged in order of difficulty (see Wechsler, 1981). The obtained effect was moderately capable of discriminating patients from controls ($d = -0.53$ OL% = 64). As total score on the test, which was used to derive the effect sizes, can reflect both the extent of recall vocabulary and the effectiveness of speaking vocabulary, it is likely that poor recall vocabulary contributed most to the obtained effect size in keeping with the rank order and magnitude of memory related effects (e.g., WAIS-R Information) and verbally related effects (e.g., WAIS-R Verbal IQ). As such, WAIS-R Verbal IQ effects were smaller in magnitude ($d = -0.32$ OL% = 78) compared to vocabulary effects. Also note that the WAIS-R Verbal IQ effect size was smaller in magnitude than the effect obtained for the WAIS-R Performance IQ.

Performance skill

Performance skill measures that index visuospatial and visuoconstructional ability were the next most sensitive tasks to the presence of mild TBI (see Chapter 15, Table 15.12). Of the small number of tasks, copy of the ROCF was found to be most impaired in patients with mild TBI ($d = -0.81$ OL% = 52). Conversely, patient performance on the WAIS-R Block Design subtest was hardly distinguishable from normal controls as test score overlap was considerable ($d = -0.11$ OL% = 92).

As already noted, the WAIS-R Performance IQ effect size was larger, and therefore more sensitive, compared to that obtained for the WAIS-R Verbal IQ. The WAIS-R Performance IQ obtained effect of -0.49 (OL% = 67) was capable of discriminating approximately 30% of patients from controls, whereas the WAIS-R Verbal IQ effect size of -0.32 (OL% = 77) could discriminate approximately 20% of patients.

Manual dexterity

Measures of manual dexterity correspond to the least sensitive measures to the presence of mild TBI (see Chapter 15, Table 15.12). Only Finger Tapping Test performance, however, was documented in the literature by way of control group experimentation. Effect sizes correspond to 64% ($d = -0.54$) and 69% ($d = -0.47$) overlap in test score distribution for right and left hand finger tapping scores, respectively. Thus, no asymmetrical deficit is apparent in keeping with the obtained magnitude of effects.

A note on affect

A considerable effect size ($d = 0.73$) was obtained on the BDI suggesting that approximately 45% of patients with mild TBI have significantly elevated BDI scores. Interestingly, elevated anxiety scores obtained on the State-Trait Anxiety Scale can be attributed to state anxiety ($d = 0.68$ OL% = 58) rather than trait anxiety ($d = 0.18$ OL% = 86). This discrepancy may underscore the development of anxiety as a reaction to the TBI rather than a premorbid personality characteristic.

Summary

Our review of the literature revealed that neuropsychological impairment is indeed evident in patients with mild TBI on a host of cognitive tasks and test variables. More specifically, the neuropsychological profile of mild TBI is consistent with "frontal dysfunction" (see Stuss & Gow, 1992). That is, the large obtained effect size for phonemic fluency can be understood to indicate frontal-executive pathology, as frontal lesions tend to depress phonemic fluency scores, with left frontal lesions resulting in lower word production than right frontal ones (Lezak, 1995; Perret, 1974; Stuss et al., 1998). Further support for the selectivity of frontal dysfunction stems from the large effect sizes obtained on design fluency and the WCST perseverative variables. That is, measures of perseveration on the WCST provide a good index of focal frontal pathology (Anderson, Damasio, & Tranel, 1990; Stuss, 1996), as does design fluency (Lezak, 1995).

The present findings also revealed evidence of impaired cognition with respect to encoding and retrieval from declarative memory. Because the type of memory impairment in patients with mild TBI does not resemble the severe episodic memory loss of a patient with an anterograde memory impairment, such as that seen in the patient with dementia of the Alzheimer's type, there is little evidence to assume dysfunction of temporal-hippocampal cortices. Rather, the type of memory failures in patients with mild TBI appear to reflect faulty encoding strategies (see Stuss & Gow, 1992). As positron emission tomography studies have shown that left prefrontal lobe systems are most active during encoding while right prefrontal lobe systems are most active during the retrieval stage on memory tasks in healthy normals (see Wheeler, Stuss, & Tulving, 1995, 1997), the large obtained effect sizes on memory tasks further supports the caveat that damage to the frontal lobes may be foremost in mild TBI despite the implausibility of a discrete locus of damage after closed head injury (see Newcombe, 1982).

Given the predominant high-end loading of frontal-executive and memory related neuropsychological tasks and test variables in the neuropsychological profile of mild TBI, the results suggest that damage to the frontal lobes may be foremost against the background of diffuse brain damage. Although "frontal dysfunction" after mild TBI may be more important than previously considered (i.e., more prominent than attention/concentration; see Binder, Rohling, & Larrabee, 1997), it may not be solely due to localized frontal damage. Many of the deficits in mild TBI attributed to frontal damage may be secondary to diffuse axonal injury (see Alexander, 1995; Stuss & Gow, 1992). Nonetheless, commonly employed putative neuropsychological measures of frontal-executive dysfunction, whether secondary to diffuse axonal injury or not, are most sensitive to mild TBI-control differences followed closely by measures of delayed recall and memory acquisition. This conclusion is in contrast to previous quantitative reviews that suggest attentional/concentration measures (e.g., digit span, Stroop task, Trail Making Test, and the PASAT) to be most impaired in patients with mild TBI (see Binder, Rohling, & Larrabee, 1997).

Chapter 15

SUMMARY

A review of the magnitude of neuropsychological deficits due to differing neurological and neuropsychiatric disorders would not be complete without a discussion of the comparative differences between the disorders. Hence, the reader will find here such a discussion. In this chapter we also provide a quantitative summary of the previous twelve chapters. The reader will find here summary tables, each corresponding to the specific profiles described and presented in Chapters 4–14. Each table is organized by neuropsychological domain according to the order in which the domain is most to least impaired for a specific syndrome. Each table provides a mean effect size and corresponding standard deviation for each neuropsychological domain. The mean effect size for each neuropsychological domain is based on the independent cognitive task and test variable effect sizes that defined the neuropsychological domain (see Chapter 3). The number of effect sizes (N) and the largest and smallest obtained effect sizes for each neuropsychological domain is also presented.

Comparative summary

One of the underlying tenants of neuropsychology is the idea that brain dysfunction results in behavioral, perceptual and cognitive impairments. Moreover, cerebral diseases have unique and characteristic distributions of pathology within the brain and do not affect the brain uniformly (Black, 1996; Cummings & Benson, 1992; Snowden, Neary, & Mann, 1996). As noted, since psychological processes are regionally organized rather than equipotentially distributed, it necessarily follows that retention of specific cognitive functions contrasting with the deterioration of others leads to identifiable and differentiable patterns of disorder and characteristic neuropsychological syndromes (Bondi, Salmon, & Kaszniak, 1996; Derix, 1994). To facilitate the discussion of the comparisons across disorders the mean effect sizes of the various neuropsychological domains represented in Tables 15.1 through 15.12 are presented graphically in Figure 15.1. For each domain represented on the abscissa, the effect size relative to the control group is represented on the ordinate.

Dementia of the Alzheimer's type (DAT)

Figure 15.1 demonstrates that DAT is associated principally with an impairment on tests of delayed recall. The nature of the tests that constitute the delayed recall domain would classify this as an impairment of declarative, episodic memory. The second most affected domain of functioning is memory acquisition. This domain consists primarily of test results representing immediate recall on

Table 15.1.   Effect Sizes Grouped by Neuropsychological Domain for Patients with Dementia of the Alzheimer's Type.

Function	Mean d	SDd	N	Min. d	Max. d
Delayed Recall	3.23	1.46	74	0.42	7.72
Memory Acquisition	2.10	1.19	189	0.00	5.16
Verbal Skill	1.64	0.93	149	0.00	4.66
Performance Skill	1.58	1.04	107	0.00	6.29
Cognitive Flexibility and Abstraction	1.49	0.77	122	0.07	3.42
Attention/Concentration	1.47	1.00	69	0.15	6.32
Manual Dexterity	0.85	0.36	8	0.53	1.38

Note. Mean d = mean effect size; SDd = standard deviation of effect size; N = number of effect sizes; Min. d = smallest effect in calculated mean; Max. d = largest effect in calculated mean. Effect sizes are represented in absolute values.

Table 15.2.   Effect Sizes Grouped by Neuropsychological Domain for Patients with Fronto-temporal Dementia.

Neuropsychological Domain	Mean d	SDd	N	Min.d.	Max.d.
Cognitive Flexibility and Abstraction	2.28	0.98	12	1.16	4.14
Performance Skill	1.42	0.91	6	0.36	2.52
Memory Acquisition	1.29	0.83	14	0.13	2.50
Attention/Concentration	1.19	0.57	4	0.44	1.81
Delayed Recall	1.08	0.78	10	0.18	2.95
Verbal Skill	0.81	0.39	6	0.42	1.44
Manual Dexterity	–	–	–	–	–

Note. Mean d = mean effect size; SDd = standard deviation of effect size; N = number of effect sizes; Min. d = smallest effect in calculated mean; Max. d = largest effect in calculated mean. Effect sizes are represented in absolute values.

Table 15.3. Effect Sizes Grouped by Neuropsychological Domain for Patients with Primary Progressive Aphasia.

Neuropsychological Domain	Mean d	Sd d	N	Min.d.	Max.d.
Verbal Skill	2.33	2.77	33	0.67	−10.69
Delayed Recall	1.53	2.62	10	2.92	−5.00
Cognitive Flexibility and Abstraction	1.26	1.12	17	0.60	−3.13
Memory Acquisition	1.18	1.44	27	2.53	−3.85
Attention/Concentration	0.47	1.20	7	1.26	−2.00
Performance Skill	0.01	0.95	43	2.33	−2.33
Manual Dexterity	−	−	−	−	−

Note. Mean d = mean effect size; SDd = standard deviation of effect size; N = number of effect sizes; Min. d = smallest effect in calculated mean; Max. d = largest effect in calculated mean. Effect sizes are represented in absolute values.

Table 15.4. Effect Sizes Grouped by Neuropsychological Domain for Patients with Progressive Supranuclear Palsy.

Function	Mean d	SDd	N	Min. d	Max. d
Attention/Concentration	4.00	0.54	3	3.41	4.46
Performance Skill	3.54	0.74	2	3.02	4.07
Manual Dexterity	2.73	1.06	7	1.28	4.01
Cognitive Flexibility and Abstraction	2.52	1.26	19	1.18	5.75
Verbal Skill	2.11	1.01	10	0.43	3.85
Delayed Recall	1.43	0.51	3	1.12	2.02
Memory Acquisition	1.28	0.86	7	0.09	2.77

Note. Mean d = mean effect size; SDd = standard deviation of effect size; N = number of effect sizes; Min. d = smallest effect in calculated mean; Max. d = largest effect in calculated mean. Effect sizes are represented in absolute values.

Table 15.5. Effect Size Results in Rank Order for Nondemented Patients with Parkinson's Disease by Neuropsychological Domain.

Neuropsychological Domain	Mean d	SDd	N	Min.d	Max.d
Delayed Recall	1.26	1.01	24	0.17	4.87
Manual Dexterity	0.78	0.29	12	0.37	1.35
Performance Skill	0.63	0.42	43	0.03	1.68
Attention/Concentration	0.62	0.45	10	0.00	1.36
Cognitive Flexibility and Abstraction	0.61	0.75	100	0.00	6.90
Memory Acquisition	0.60	0.49	84	0.00	2.25
Verbal Skill	0.46	0.32	70	0.00	1.46

Note. Mean d = mean effect size; SDd = standard deviation of effect size; N = number of effect sizes; Min. d = smallest effect in calculated mean; Max. d = largest effect in calculated mean. Effect sizes are represented in absolute values.

Table 15.6. Effect Size Results in Rank Order for Demented Patients with Parkinson's Disease by Neuropsychological Domain.

Neuropsychological Domain	Mean d	SDd	N	Min.d	Max.d
Manual Dexterity	2.42	1.07	10	1.33	4.93
Cognitive Flexibility and Abstraction	1.86	0.98	25	0.72	4.31
Delayed Recall	1.82	0.57	2	1.41	2.22
Performance Skill	1.46	0.78	10	0.17	2.72
Memory Acquisition	1.11	1.01	17	0.09	3.81
Verbal Skill	1.00	0.84	17	0.00	3.56
Attention/Concentration	0.88	0.10	4	0.80	1.02

Note. Mean d = mean effect size; SDd = standard deviation of effect size; N = number of effect sizes; Min. d = smallest effect in calculated mean; Max. d = largest effect in calculated mean. Effect sizes are represented in absolute values.

Table 15.7. Effect Sizes Grouped by Neuropsychological Domain for Patients with Huntington's Disease.

Function	Mean d	SDd	N	Min. d	Max. d
Delayed Recall	2.61	1.41	4	1.01	4.04
Memory Acquisition	2.35	0.72	10	1.39	3.55
Cognitive Flexibility and Abstraction	1.98	0.58	11	0.78	2.55
Manual Dexterity	1.78	0.75	15	3.11	1.78
Attention/Concentration	1.62	1.04	13	0.23	4.00
Performance Skills	1.58	0.55	23	0.43	2.51
Verbal Skills	1.07	0.63	21	0.04	2.12

Note. Mean d = mean effect size; SDd = standard deviation of effect size; N = number of effect sizes; Min. d = smallest effect in calculated mean; Max. d = largest effect in calculated mean. Effect sizes are represented in absolute values.

Table 15.8. Effect Sizes Grouped by Neuropsychological Domain for Patients with Multiple Sclerosis.

Function	Mean d	SDd	N	Min. d	Max. d
Manual Dexterity	1.01	0.42	15	0.64	1.81
Delayed Recall	0.65	0.56	21	0.01	2.63
Performance Skill	0.62	0.39	42	0.00	2.23
Cognitive Flexibility and Abstraction	0.58	0.33	66	0.00	1.36
Verbal Skill	0.54	0.34	50	0.04	1.29
Attention/Concentration	0.53	0.23	11	0.03	0.85
Memory Acquisition	0.49	0.35	47	0.03	1.11

Note. Mean d = mean effect size; SDd = standard deviation of effect size; N = number of effect sizes; Min. d = smallest effect in calculated mean; Max. d = largest effect in calculated mean. Effect sizes are represented in absolute values.

Table 15.9.   Effect Sizes Grouped by Neuropsychological Domain for Patients with
             Major Depressive Disorder.

Function	Mean d	SDd	N	Min. d	Max. d
Delayed Recall	0.73	0.50	21	0.08	2.07
Memory Acquisition	0.60	0.47	57	0.03	1.93
Attention/Concentration	0.59	0.45	18	0.03	1.67
Cognitive Flexibility and Abstraction	0.52	0.29	18	0.03	1.14
Performance Skill	0.51	0.28	32	0.11	1.45
Verbal Skill	0.48	0.55	31	0.01	2.29
Manual Dexterity	0.38	0.10	2	0.34	0.42

Note. Mean d = mean effect size; SDd = standard deviation of effect size; N = number of effect
sizes; Min. d = smallest effect in calculated mean; Max. d = largest effect in calculated mean.
Effect sizes are represented in absolute values.

Table 15.10. Effect Sizes Grouped by Neuropsychological Domain for Patients with
             Schizophrenia.

Neuropsychological Domain	Mean d	SDd	N	Min.d.	Max.d.
Delayed Recall	1.39	0.65	28	0.10	2.80
Manual Dexterity	1.18	1.31	36	0.20	8.30
Performance Skill	1.08	0.73	38	0.10	3.30
Cognitive Flexibility and Abstraction	1.07	0.78	140	0.00	8.40
Attention/Concentration	1.01	0.44	47	0.10	1.90
Memory Acquisition	0.99	0.61	45	0.07	2.40
Verbal Skill	0.89	0.60	82	0.00	2.80

Note. Mean d = mean effect size; SDd = standard deviation of effect size; N = number of effect
sizes; Min. d = smallest effect in calculated mean; Max. d = largest effect in calculated mean.
Effect sizes are represented in absolute values.

Table 15.11. Effect Sizes Grouped by Neuropsychological Domain for Patients with
             Obsessive Compulsive Disorder.

Function	Mean d	SDd	N	Min. d	Max. d
Performance Skill	0.46	0.24	11	0.07	0.84
Cognitive Flexibility and Abstraction	0.45	0.29	19	0.00	1.05
Delayed Recall	0.44	0.29	11	0.09	1.00
Memory Acquisition	0.37	0.33	23	0.00	1.15
Manual Dexterity	0.31	0.16	2	0.20	0.43
Attention/Concentration	0.28	0.20	7	0.02	0.61
Verbal Skill	0.08	0.12	7	0.00	0.13

Note. Mean d = mean effect size; SDd = standard deviation of effect size; N = number of effect
sizes; Min. d = smallest effect in calculated mean; Max. d = largest effect in calculated mean.
Effect sizes are represented in absolute values.

Table 15.12. Effect Sizes Grouped by Neuropsychological Domain for Patients with Mild
Head Injury.

Function	Mean d	SDd	N	Min. d	Max. d
Cognitive Flexibility and Abstraction	0.72	0.48	14	0.27	2.13
Delayed Recall	0.71	0.43	8	0.24	1.61
Memory Acquisition	0.69	0.42	11	0.14	1.56
Attention/Concentration	0.63	0.36	10	0.31	1.53
Verbal Skill	0.62	0.35	4	0.32	1.08
Performance Skill	0.47	0.35	3	0.11	0.81
Manual Dexterity	0.44	0.11	3	0.32	0.54

Note. Mean d = mean effect size; SDd = standard deviation of effect size; N = number of effect
sizes; Min. d = smallest effect in calculated mean; Max. d = largest effect in calculated mean.
Effect sizes are represented in absolute values.

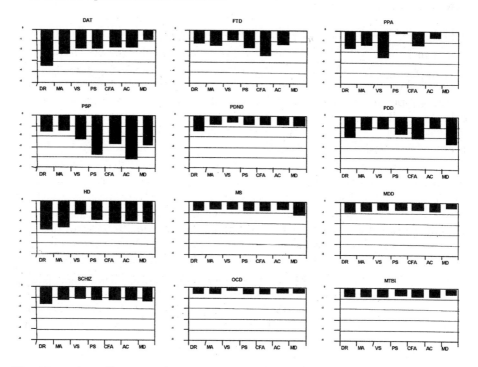

Fig. 15.1.   Overall Pattern of Neurocognitive Function by Neuropsychological Domain
for Each Neurological and Neuropsychiatric Syndrome. Abbreviations: DAT
= Dementia of the Alzheimer's type; FTD = frontal-temporal dementia; PPA
= primary progressive aphasia; PSP = progressive supranuclear palsy; PDND
= non-demented Parkinson's disease; PDD = demented Parkinson's disease;
HD = Huntington's disease; MS = multiple sclerosis; MDD = major depressive disorder; SCHZ = schizophrenia; OCD = obsessive compulsive disorder; MTBI = mild traumatic brain injury; DR = Delayed Recall; MA =
Memory Acquisition; VS = Verbal Skill; PS = Performance Skill; CFA =
Cognitive Flexibility and Abstraction; AC = Attention/Concentration; MD
= Manual Dexterity.

information. This represents a rather homogeneous collection of test results that consist of primary memory (e.g., digit span forwards, consonant trigrams) and encoding (e.g., CVLT list A, Trial 1 and RAVLT trial 1). Moreover, the domains of verbal skills, performance skills, cognitive flexibility and abstraction, and attention and concentration are relatively equivalent in the severity of impairment. The least effected domain is manual dexterity.

The relative order of disability is consistent with the pattern of neuropsychological impairment reported in various qualitative reviews of DAT (Cummings & Benson, 1992; Zec, 1993). That is, the earliest and most frequent symptom of Alzheimer's disease is memory impairment characterized by rapid forgetting and relatively preserved declarative memory for past events as compared to obvious and severe memory for more recent events. Word-finding difficulties and impaired semantic fluency contribute to the verbal skills deterioration and perceptual and visuoconstructional impairment contribute to deterioration in performance skills.

Fronto-temporal dementia (FTD)
The neuropsychological deficits of FTD are greatest in the domain of cognitive flexibility and abstraction. This is in keeping with the recognized importance of frontal lobe functioning on tests of this domain. The second most affected domain is performance skills. In contrast to DAT, FTD has far less effect on delayed recall and memory acquisition and even less effect on verbal skills.

Primary progressive aphasia (PPA)
Primary progressive aphasia exerts its greatest effect on verbal skills as would be expected. Moderate effects are also present on delayed memory and cognitive flexibility and abstraction, but these are due to relatively selective effects on verbal as opposed to non-verbal tests. For example, compare the difference in the magnitude of effect size of PPA on the RAVLT delayed free recall of -4.42 to that on the delayed reproduction of the Rey Osterreith Complex Figure of $+0.81$, or the effect size of -1.99 on the COWAT to that of the number of categories achieved on the WCST of $+0.10$. Furthermore, the overall effect of PPA on verbal skills is attested to by comparing the effect size on the WAIS-R Verbal IQ of -1.14 to that on the WAIS-R Performance IQ of -0.15. Finally, in comparison to both DAT and FTD, PPA has virtually no effect on performance skills.

Progressive supranuclear palsy (PSP)
Of the neurological disorders reviewed, PSP, somewhat unexpectedly, yielded the largest absolute effect sizes. In addition, in terms of overall impairment, PSP easily rivaled that of DAT, although the pattern of impairment was quite distinct from that displayed by patients with DAT. PSP had the largest effect on attention and concentration, performance skills, manual dexterity and cognitive flexibility and abstraction. Verbal skills were more moderately affected but this represents relatively large effects on semantic fluency as well as on the WAIS-R

Verbal IQ (see Table 7.2 Chapter 7). Additionally, PSP also had a moderate effect on delayed recall and memory acquisition but certainly not to the magnitude as that displayed by patients with DAT.

Parkinson's disease without dementia

Parkinson's disease, when not accompanied by a generalized decline in cognitive functioning, exerted its primary influence on delayed recall. The effect on delayed recall was moderate and comparable to that due to progressive primary aphasia and certainly not characteristic of the pattern of delayed recall displayed by patients with DAT. The second most affected domain was manual dexterity, which happens to be the least impaired neuropsychological domain in patients with DAT, PPA, and FTD. The relative effect size difference between delayed recall and manual dexterity is surprising given that motor symptoms such as tremor, rigidity and bradykinesia tend to predominate in Parkinson's disease.

Parkinson's disease with dementia

When Parkinson's disease is accompanied with a decline in cognitive function, the most severe effects are found on manual dexterity, cognitive flexibility and abstraction and delayed recall. A more moderate effect is also found on performance skills. The overall severity of effect on the neuropsychological domains is far less than what we found with PSP, however. In addition, Parkinson's disease with dementia exerts less effect on attention and concentration and on performance skills. Much of the effect of Parkinson's disease may be due to bradyphrenia. That is, examination of the rank order of effect sizes of the individual tests revealed that the majority of the largest effect sizes came from tests that either had a time limit to complete or the test measure was based on time to complete the test.

Huntington's disease (HD)

Huntington's disease exerted the largest effects on delayed recall and memory acquisition. The effect of HD on memory recall approached the effect that patients with DAT exerted. Huntington's disease had a greater effect than DAT had on memory acquisition, however. Huntington's disease also exerted moderate effects on cognitive flexibility and abstraction, manual dexterity, attention/concentration and performance skills. HD appeared to be second only to PSP in terms of its overall negative impact on neuropsychological functioning.

Multiple sclerosis (MS)

When considering the effects of MS on neuropsychological functioning, regardless of type (i.e., chronic/progressive or relapsing/remitting), MS has the greatest effect on manual dexterity. Although there are apparent differences in the presentation of the MS neuropsychological profiles between the two types (see Chapter 10), the general effect on functioning is relatively mild. In fact, except for the decrement in manual dexterity there is very little of a profile that would help differentiate MS based on cognitive test scores alone.

Major depressive disorder

Depression appears to exert its greatest effect on delayed recall. The effect is moderate to small but it is consistent with the subjective complaints of individuals suffering from a major depressive episode. Like MS, the neuropsychological profile is minimal. That is, depression appears to exert a relatively mild decrement in numerous neuropsychological domains. In comparison to MS, however, depression has the least effect on manual dexterity.

Schizophrenia

Schizophrenia exerts moderate effects on all neuropsychological domains reviewed. Our review indicates that schizophrenia is characterized by a very broadly-based cognitive impairment with varying degrees of deficit in all ability domains measured by standard clinical tests. At the same time, cognitive deficit is not an inclusive feature of the illness. The average magnitude of effect sizes suggests that a substantial proportion of any given schizophrenia sample will be indistinguishable from healthy control subjects on any given cognitive test.

Obsessive compulsive disorder (OCD)

From the standpoint of clinical interpretation, OCD appears to result in the least neuropsychological impairment of any of the neurological or neuropsychiatric disorders reviewed. The largest effects were noted, however, on performance skills, cognitive flexibility and abstraction, delayed recall and memory acquisition.

Mild traumatic brain injury (mild TBI)

Mild traumatic brain injury has its greatest effects on cognitive flexibility and abstraction, delayed recall, memory acquisition, attention/concentration and verbal skills. Minimal effects were noted on performance skills and manual dexterity. In relationship to other disorders discussed, mild TBI appears to result in similar, but slightly greater cognitive impairment than that caused by major depressive disorder and multiple sclerosis.

On the concept of cortical vs. subcortical dementia

Albert, Feldman and Willis (1974) described the pattern of forgetfulness, slowness of thought process, behavioral change (primarily apathy and depression) and "impaired ability to manipulate acquired knowledge" that accompanied PSP. McHugh and Folstein (1975) described the dementia syndrome of HD as a generalized inefficiency of all thought processes, including memory and gradual loss of initiative. Both Albert et al. (1974) and McHugh and Folstein (1975) emphasized that both conditions were related to subcortical degeneration. McHugh and Folstein stressed that the dementia differed from that associated with cortical degeneration in that the latter was accompanied by an amnesic disturbance, aphasia, apraxia, alexia or agnosia. Thus began the dichotomy of subcortical and cortical dementias. Although there has been considerable debate over the distinction, the concept nevertheless lingers. Whatever the difference in opinion in terms of the clinical validity and usefulness of the cortical-subcortical dementia controversy, the debate did not diminish the importance of recognizing that different neuropathological disorders can result in different patterns of neuropsychological impairment.

Hence, our analysis of effect sizes supports the concept that different patterns of neuropsychological impairment reflect different pathologies although support for the cortical-subcortical framework proposed by Albert et al.(1974) and McHugh and Folstein (1975) is not generally supported with cognitive tests. If one examines Figure 15.2 and compares the pattern of impairment of the "cortical dementias" of DAT, FTD and PPA against that of the subcortical dementias of PSP, Parkinson's disease (PD) and HD, it appears that the variability between the different cortical dementias is as great as the difference between the cortical dementias and the subcortical dementias. For example, DAT and HD are associated with a severe memory impairment to a far greater degree than that found with FTD, PPA, PSP or PD. If there is a pattern of neuropsychological impairment that is most common with "subcortical dementia", it is impairment of manual dexterity, performance skills and cognitive flexibility and abstraction. This pattern of impairment may be viewed as coinciding with the slowness of mentation and impaired "manipulation of acquired knowledge", but HD deviates significantly in the nature of the memory impairment of the other subcortical dementias.

Amongst the cortical dementias, there is a reasonable pattern of neuropsychological impairment that may facilitate differential diagnosis, however. Dementia of the Alzheimer's type is characterized by severe delayed memory impairment and a moderate impairment of memory acquisition skills. In FTD delayed recall and memory acquisition are relatively spared but there is a much greater impairment of cognitive flexibility and abstraction than that encountered in either DAT or PPA. Primary progressive aphasia, on the other hand, is characterized by a severe impairment of verbal skills, a lesser degree of impairment of delayed recall and memory acquisition and performance skills that are well within normal range.

With these considerations in mind, given the questionable validity, yet useful framework of cortical versus subcortical dementia, a diagnosis of dementia should be more than just "cortical" or "subcortical". That is, the neuropsychological literature that has amassed in recent years allows the neuropsychologist to make finer diagnostic discriminations within the cortical-subcortical model. Simply stating that a degenerative condition is "cortical" or "subcortical" does not do justice to the vast contributions made in our field. Hence, we hope that our compendium of neuropsychological profiles will aid the clinician in arriving at a more finer diagnosis of dementia when called upon.

On neurological vs. psychiatric differentiation

One of the most common referral requests for neuropsychological assessment is to determine if an individual's cognitive dysfunction has an "organic" (i.e., neurological) or "functional" (i.e., psychiatric) basis. Examination of the profiles of neuropsychological impairment of depression and OCD reveals at best a mild, generalized performance decrement across most neuropsychological domains. Of the psychiatric disorders reviewed, schizophrenia appears most like a neurological disorder, and in fact, appears to affect neuropsychological status to a greater degree than MS and Parkinson's disease without dementia. Therefore, if a differential diagnosis involves either OCD or depression, then a neuropsychological assessment should be able to conclude that cognitive complaints are not due to neurological dysfunction. If, however, the differential diagnosis involves schizophrenia, then neuropsychological test results may be indistinguishable from those obtained from a number of neurological disorders unless the clinician uses the more qualitative neuropsychological profiles to search for

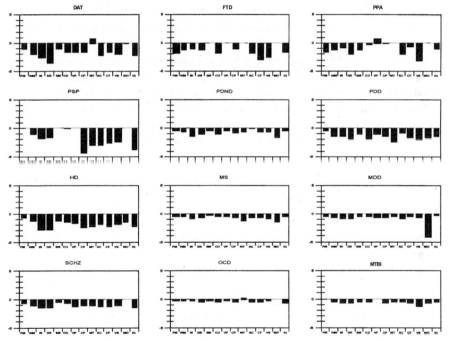

Fig. 15.2.   Pattern of Performance on Proposed Neuropsychological Battery Test Domains for Each Neurological and Neuropsychiatric Syndrome. Abbreviations: DAT = Dementia of the Alzheimer's type; FTD = frontal-temporal dementia; PPA = primary progressive aphasia; PSP = progressive supranuclear palsy; PDND = non-demented Parkinson's disease; PDD = demented Parkinson's disease; HD = Huntington's disease; MS = multiple sclerosis; MDD = major depressive disorder; SCHZ = schizophrenia; OCD = obsessive compulsive disorder; MTBI = mild traumatic brain injury; PM = primary memory; WM = working memory; IR = immediate recall; DR = delayed recall; SM = semantic memory; CO = constructional skills; VP = visuoperceptual abilities; CP = complex psychomotor functioning; MT = motor skills; AC = attention/concentration; CF = conceptual flexibility; VS = verbal skills; MO = mood; IQ = intellectual functioning.

markers (i.e., $d > 3.0$ OL% < 5) and makes double dissociations of effects between the disorders to be differentiated.

Proposed battery for differential diagnosis

Our meta-analyses can be applied to help design a battery of tests that can be used to differentiate between several cognitive etiologies. Given the wide variety of tests available, the meta-analyses are useful because they provide a useful means for comparing effect sizes for given tests across different etiologies. Based on our analysis we chose a battery of tests that could be used to help differentiate the various disorders discussed in this book.

The first step in choosing tests involves inspection of the tables for effect sizes for individual tests. As a heuristic to choosing tests, the following criteria were applied: (1) *Magnitude of effect size*. As we have argued, the effect size for critical tests should exceed 3.0. Exceptions would have to be allowed but at the least, the effect size for a given test should be above the median effect size, and preferably in the upper quartile for one of the conditions being considered in a differential. (2) *Standardization*. A set of standardized norms should be available for a given test. Ideally the test should meet the requirements for standardized tests established by the American Psychological Association. (3) *Availability*. The tests should be readily available in a standard format. Unfortunately, this eliminates the general use of many tests with some promise (e.g., Buschke's Selective Reminding Procedure, Tower of Hanoi or London) because they are not readily available in a standardized format nor do they have publicly available norms. (4) *Consistency of use across different etiologies*. Ideally the tests should have been applied to all etiologies we surveyed in our analysis. Unfortunately, this was not possible in all cases but the majority of tests we will discuss met this criterion. In addition, wherever possible we chose at least two or more tests that would fall within the cognitive domains we described in Chapter 2.

The decision to choose more than one test for each domain stems from an attempt to increase reliability of the data and to provide alternate tests for the same function. There is a caveat that must be acknowledged, however. Many of the tests are multifactorial in nature and any two tests that have prima facie validity as a measure of a given ability, may in fact, be measuring different processes that lead to the same outcome (see Kaplan, 1988). As an example, consider the Block Design subtest of the Wechsler scales. The score for each design is based on correct reproduction of the target design within specified time limits. Two individuals may obtain the same score, but they may have used a different process to obtain the score. Consider a score of zero. One individual may have the ability to grasp the relationships among the elements and have the ability to execute the necessary steps and movements to complete the task but due to severe mental slowing, fail to place the final block within the time limit. Another individual may have spent the entire time attempting to place a single block in a given position. If one considers the quality of their work, the first case would clearly be superior to the second yet they would have obtained the same score.

The tests chosen for our battery are presented in Table 15.13. The tests are categorized according to neuropsychological domains that will, in all hope, facilitate clinical interpretation. The domains presented in Table 15.13 differ from those used throughout the book in that they allow for finer gradations in cognitive functions. For example, the domain of Memory Acquisition has been subdivided into Primary Memory, Working Memory and Immediate Memory. Delayed Recall has been subdivided into Delayed Memory, which primarily reflects episodic recall, and Semantic Memory which represent declarative memory for factual information or skill. In addition to the new divisions of neuropsychological domains, we also include the domains of Mood and Intellectual functioning.

Primary Memory. This consists of tests that historically have been considered to be tests of short-term memory. It is a memory of limited capacity and short duration. Digit span forwards represent a measure of capacity and the consonant trigrams test represents a measure of the durability of the trace.

Working Memory. This set of tests represents the processes necessary to hold information in immediate memory in order to manipulate it to yield a desired output. Digit span backwards requires the individual to retain a sequence of digits in primary memory and to manipulate it in order to recall the digits in reverse sequence. The Paced Auditory Serial Addition Test (PASAT) requires the individual to retain information presented in order to generate the sums of successive digits. The WAIS-R Arithmetic requires performing mental computations of varying levels of difficulty.

Immediate Memory. This domain consists of tests that assess recall of information immediately after it is presented. It differs from primary memory in that the amount of information exceeds the maximum capacity of the primary memory buffer. In effect it constitutes recall from secondary memory at a very short delay. Together with Delayed Memory scores it provides a measure by which information is encoded into categorical memory for episodic recall. Comparing the amount of information recalled in supraspan lists such as the Rey Auditory Verbal Learning Test (RAVLT) or the California Verbal Learning Test (CVLT) to the primary memory span yields an estimate of encoding ability. Utilizing word lists and recall of narrative prose material such as the Logical Memory stories from the Wechsler Memory Scale can also evaluate an individual's ability to code apparently unrelated material (word lists) and related information.

Note, if the differential diagnosis is very early Alzheimer's disease vs. memory complaint associated with major depressive disorder, then the CVLT should be opted for because it is less sensitive to depression and is therefore less likely to give a false positive in favor of Alzheimer disease.

Delayed Memory. This domain consists of tests that evaluate recall of information after delays of twenty or more minutes after immediate memory of the same information has been tested. Comparison of the amount of information recalled after a delay relative to the amount recalled after immediate recall provides a measure of the consolidation of information in secondary memory. This comparison is particularly useful when evaluating conditions characterized by severe anterograde amnesia such as Alzheimer's disease.

Table 15.13. Neuropsychological Test Battery.

Domain Name	Test	Domain Name	Test
Primary Memory	WAIS-R Digit Span Forwards Consonant Trigrams	Immediate Memory	CVLT Trial 5 Total RAVLT Trial 5 Total
Working Memory	WAIS-R Digit Span Backwards PASAT WAIS-R Arithmetic		WMS-R Logical Memory I WMS-R Visual Reproduction I ROCF Immediate Reproduction
Visuoconstructional Skills	WAIS-R Block Design WAIS-R Object Assembly ROCF Copy	Delayed Memory	CVLT Delayed Free Recall CVLT Delayed Cued Recall CVLT Delayed Recognition
Visuoperceptual Abilities	Facial Recognition (Benton) Hooper Visual Organization Test Judge of Line Orientation WAIS-R Picture Completion		RAVLT Delayed Free RecallW RAVLT Delayed Recognition WMS-R Logical Memory II WMS-R Visual Reproduction II
Cognitive Flexibility/ Abstraction	WAIS-R Similarities WCST – Number of Categories WCST Perseverative Responses	Complex Psychomotor Skills	WAIS-R Digit Symbol Stroop Color Naming Test Stroop Word Reading Test
Verbal Skills	COWAT Semantic Fluency Boston Naming Test	Simple Motor Skills	Trail Making Test – Form A Finger Tapping Test Grooved Pegboard Test
Mood	Beck Depression Inventory Hamilton Depression Rating Scale	Attention/Concentration	Purdue Pegboard Test Stroop Color-word Interference Test
Intellectual Functioning	WAIS-R Full IQ		

Semantic Memory. This domain of tests represents knowledge for factual information or performance of a learned skill that is independent of conscious recollection of a specific time or place. All three can be viewed as representing acquired knowledge but the set of tests is not homogeneous in content or ability. The WAIS-R Information subtest evaluates factual knowledge, the WAIS-R Vocabulary represents word knowledge and the National Adult Reading Test (NART) represents reading of single words with either irregular or rule-governed spelling. These three tests correlate highly with general intelligence and with verbal intelligence. They also represent approximations of pre-morbid functioning although there is reason to use caution when doing so.

Constructional Skills. This set of tests evaluates an individual's capacity to reproduce an object or drawing. This set of tests is crucial for determining the presence of constructional apraxia, the inability to translate a visual pattern into the appropriate actions in order to reproduce the pattern. The WAIS-R Block Design requires the assembly of colored blocks into a novel geometric pattern. The WAIS-R Object Assembly requires assembly of a representation of a real object using jig-saw-like pieces. The Rey-Osterrieth Complex Figure (ROCF) Copy condition requires the individual to copy a novel-complex figure using pencil and paper. Utilization of all three will help the examiner determine the underlying cause of constructional difficulties. The Block Design and ROCF utilize novel stimuli therefore placing a greater demand on visual analysis and synthesis. The ROCF places even greater demand on planning and organization of the output and various scoring schemes have been devised to help define these aspects of construction. The Object Assembly test places a demand on the examinee's internal representation of objects and the knowledge of how the parts are related to the whole object.

Visuoperceptual Abilities. This domain includes tests that require recognition of a visual stimulus but does not require a complex manual response. The Facial Recognition Test, Hooper Visual Organization Test and the WAIS-R evaluate various aspects of visual perception from matching of stimuli or recognition from memory. The Judgment of Line Orientation evaluates visual spatial appreciation and discernment.

Complex Psychomotor Skills. This domain consists of tests that assess the speed by which a task can be completed or how many responses can be completed within a set time limit. The tasks vary in form of output; the Trail Making and Digit Symbol tests require a manual output and the Stroop Color Naming and Word Reading require verbal output. The complexity arises from the need to selectively respond to a visual stimulus.

Simple Motor Tests. This domain consists of tests of relatively simple motor responses. All three, finger tapping, grooved pegboard and the Purdue pegboard can provide information with regards to lateralized motor deficits. The two pegboard tests include an extra component of hand-eye coordination and demand greater attention.

Attention/Concentration. This domain includes tests that involve several dimensions of attention. Stroop Color-Word interference task requires controlled, selective attention in order to suppress the automatic dominant response. Form B of the Trail Making test also requires control over a dominant response and in addition demands switching attention between two automatic responses. The Failure to maintain set measure of the Wisconsin Card Sorting Test evaluates the ability to sustain attention on a given response.

Conceptual Reasoning/Cognitive Flexibility. This domain evaluates the ability to develop or recognize conceptual or semantic relationships among stimuli. The WAIS-R Similarities evaluates the individual's capacity to formulate broad general categories between to items. This is dependent on prior experience and can be influenced by education. The Wisconsin Card Sorting Test (WCST) evaluates several aspects of problem solving. The WCST requires inductive reasoning and the ability of an individual to utilize feedback in order to modify their responses. It also evaluates cognitive flexibility by requiring that an individual switch their response.

Verbal Skills. This domain consists of three subtests that evaluate word retrieval. Two of the tests, the Controlled Oral Word Association Test (COWAT) and the semantic fluency test, require production of words for specified time (usually one minute intervals). The COWAT and semantic fluency tests have been shown to be dissociable, however and therefore do not reflect a unitary process. For example, individuals in the early stages of Alzheimer's disease will show a greater decrement in production under the semantic fluency condition than on the COWAT. The Boston Naming Test evaluates the ability to retrieve the names of objects depicted in line drawings. It tends to be the single most sensitive test to an aphasic disturbance, and is also an early symptom of Alzheimer disease.

Mood. Although this does not technically constitute a neuropsychological domain, it is common in clinical practice to determine the potential effects of mood on cognitive performance. The Beck Depression Inventory and Hamilton Depression Rating Scale are both self-report inventories. Both can provide useful information with regards to type and severity of depressive complaints.

Intellectual Functioning. The measure of general intellectual function is useful as a means of evaluating expected abilities; particularly memory. It is common practice to assess performance on tests of learning and recall with respect to general intellectual functioning; a significantly lower score on the memory test being interpreted as representing a specific memory deficit. On the other hand, because general intellectual functioning can be expected to show a significant decline with many disorders the measure will also provide a measure of general cognitive functioning.

Evaluation of the test battery. To evaluate the usefulness of the battery in identifying patterns of impairment among the various etiologies, we have graphed the mean effect size for the domains for each disorder in Figure 15.2. The division of the Memory Acquisition domain into Working Memory, Primary Memory and Immediate Memory yield additional information with respect to differences among etiologies. Working memory was more affected than primary memory in Alzheimer disease but the opposite pattern was noted in frontal-temporal lobe dementia and in primary progressive aphasia. The removal of tests of semantic memory from the Delayed Recall domain resulted in a more pure assessment of episodic memory and also highlighted specific semantic memory problems found in Alzheimer's disease, primary progressive aphasia, Parkinson's disease with dementia and in Huntington's disease. Placing semantic memory in a separate category also enhanced the degree of the delayed recall deficit found in Huntington's disease.

Addition of the Mood domain highlighted the presence of depressive symptoms in the extrapyramidal diseases and the relative absence of the symptoms in the cortical dementias. The ability to visualize the effect of mood also helps to emphasize the contribution of affective state to cognitive performance. For example, comparing Major Depressive Disorder to Mild Traumatic Brain Injury one can see that severely depressed mood may have a greater effect on immediate and delayed recall measures than the effects of head trauma.

Division of Performance Skill into separate domains of Constructional, Visual-perceptual and Complex Psychomotor Skills also helps clarify the sources of the effects noted in several etiologies. For example, in Huntington's disease as well as in progressive supranuclear palsy the effect size of Performance Skill was due primarily to psychomotor slowing and slowing on tasks of simple motor skills. In Huntington's disease however, visual perceptual functioning is affected to a greater degree than is visuoconstructional capacity.

Conclusions

Our review of the neuropsychological literature could only be systematically integrated with quantitative methodology such as that employed by meta-analysis. We maintain that any derived composite effect size based on a combination of scores from two or more measures of different tasks or same test variables, however, results in loss of data points that can be used to differentiate disorders with cognitive tests (also see Kaplan, 1988, 1990). As already stated, a meta-analytic approach that minimizes the inclusion of specific test variables can result in serious distortions in the interpretations and recommendations drawn from its conclusions. To be neuropsychologicaly meaningful, a meta-analysis should represent as few kinds of behavior or dimensions of cognitive function as possible. Further, should the levels of performance for combined measures differ, the composite effect size which make up the meta-analysis – which will be somewhere between the highest and the lowest of the combined effects – will be misleading. Effect sizes calculated by summing or averaging a set of tasks or even same test variables are removed from the behavior they represent. As such, it is for these reasons that independent effect sizes, based sometimes on one study finding, were included in the profiles. We included a quantitative summary of these profiles, however, to address the methodological issue of reliability and to provide the reader with an organized means to interpreting the profiles and to assist in making a neuropsychological differential diagnosis.

By sometimes including cognitive effect sizes based on a single primary study finding (i.e., $Nd = 1$), however, the magnitude of those effects might be questioned on grounds of reliability. That is, reliability is the degree to which independent meta-analytic effects remain relatively consistent over repeated reviews of the same literature (see Zakzanis, 1998f). It assures the reader that whenever a meta-analytic review is carried out, the results could be replicated if the same literature was reviewed again under similar circumstances. In practical terms, reliability as it relates to our review is the desired consistency or reproducibility of meta-analytic effects. We understand that a "new" primary study's findings might produce an effect size that is different from that presented in our profiles. By then averaging this new primary study's effect with the corresponding cognitive effect presented in our profile, it should be obvious that this might shuffle the rank order of the measures in the given qualitative profile. Does this mean that the profiles are unreliable? We don't think so.

A test of reliability assumes that the results could be replicated if the *same* literature was reviewed again under similar circumstances. The inclusion of new primary study effects averaged into our effects would result in dissimilar circumstances in which reliability was being measured. Thus, we believe the presence of single effects in our profiles are just as valid as the scientist who incorporates a single study finding, or the gist of a narrative review, into his or her epistemology. In other words, a single study effect is valid until proven otherwise. Or, if you like, a scientist's fund of knowledge will not be revised until that knowledge has been falsified in his or her opinion. Popper's falsificationism to say the least.

Accordingly, what we have provided in our profiles are effects derived from our knowledge base i.e., the neuropsychological literature. As this literature grows, our profiles will undoubtedly need revision just as the scientist's general fund of knowledge will when he or she is presented with new findings. Moreover, as the neuropsychological literature replicates and falsifies its findings, the reliability of our knowledge base will never really be known, or ever proven "true", only false. To prove it true would require a halting of research and knowledge as we know it – and even then it could not be *really* proven true, it would only be ensured the test of time. So the best we could do was review the neuropsychological literature for the years 1980 to 1997. Therefore, to test fairly the reliability of our profiles, one would need to conduct a similar literature review using the same methods and procedures as those utilized here. If one were to test the reliability of our profiles by comparing our effects with newly acquired study findings, we believe that this approach would not be a true test of reliability. What it will do is falsify the sensitivity of a given cognitive measure to a specific disorder. Hence, our knowledge of test sensitivity, as represented in the profiles, will need revision.

We emphasize the utilization of the profiles found in chapters 4–14 that include independent effects for three reasons. First, they represent what we currently know about the sensitivity of cognitive tasks and test variables to specific disorders of the brain. Secondly, they provide reason for future research into brain-behavior relations (also see Chapter 1–3). Finally, it should be quite evident that cognitive tests are multifactorial. An immediately obvious implication is the degree to which experts would agree as to which tests should be included within a given neuropsychological domain (see Chapter 3; also see Lezak, 1995). Moreover, the focus on neuropsychological domains does not address the nature and effectiveness of the strategies that an individual may employ enroute to either a successful or unsuccessful overall test score (see Kaplan, 1988, 1990; Lezak, 1995; Milberg, Hebben, & Kaplan, 1996). As such, we believe consideration of the independent test variable effect sizes found in Chapters 4–14 provide more useful information than can be obtained from the more domain focused summary found here in Chapter 15. Taken together, we hope our work will aid in making a neuropsychological differential diagnosis.

REFERENCES

*Studies preceded by an asterisk were included in the meta-analyses

Aarsland, D., Tandberg, E. Larsen, J. P., & Cummings, J. L. (1996). Frequency of dementia in Parkinson's disease. *Archives of Neurology, 53,* 538–542.

*Abbruzzese, M., Bellodi, L., Ferri, S., & Scarone, S. (1995). Frontal lobe dysfunction in schizophrenia and obsessive compulsive disorder: A neuropsychological study. *Brain and Cognition, 27,* 202–212.

Adams, R. D., & Victor, M. (1977). *Principles of neurology.* Toronto: McGraw-Hill.

Adams, R. D., Victor, M., & Ropper, A. H. (1997). *Prinicples of neurology* (6th ed.). Toronto: McGraw-Hill.

Albert, M. L., Feldman, R. G., & Willis, A. L. (1974). The subcortical dementia of progressive supranuclear palsy. *Journal of Neurology, Neurosurgery, and Psychiatry, 37,* 121–130.

*Albert, M. S., Butters, N., Brandt, J. (1981). Development of remote memory loss in patients with Huntington's disease. *Journal of Clinical Neuropsychology, 3,* 1–12.

Albert, M. S., Butters, N., & Levin, J. (1979). Temporal gradients in the retrograde amnesia of patients with alcoholic Korsakoff's disease. *Archives of Neurology, 36,* 211–216.

Albert, M. S., Duffy, F. H., & McAnulty, I. (1990). Electrophysiological comparisons between two groups of patients with Alzheimer's disease. *Archives of Neurology, 47,* 857–863.

Albert, M. S., Duffy, F. H., & Naeser, M. (1987). Nonlinear changes in cognition with age and their neuropsychologic correlates. *Canadian Journal of Psychology, 41,* 141–157.

*Alexander, G. E., Prohovnik, I., Sackheim, H. A., Stern, Y., & Mayeux, R. (1995). Cortical perfusion and gray matter weight in frontal lobe dementia. *Journal of Neuropsychiatry and Clinical Neurosciences, 7,* 188–196.

*Alexander, G. E., Prohovnik, I., Stern, Y., & Mayeux, R. (1994). WAIS-R subtest profile and cortical perfusion in Alzheimer's disease. *Brain and Cognition, 24*, 24–43.

Alexander, M. P. (1987). The role of neurobehavioral syndromes in the rehabilitation and outcome of closed head injury. In H. S. Levin, J. Grafman, & H. M. Eisenberg (Eds.), *Neurobehavioral recovery from head injury*, (pp. 191–205). New York: Oxford University Press.

Alexander, M. P. (1995). Mild traumatic brain injury: Pathophysiology, natural history, and clinical management. *Neurology, 45*, 1253–1260.

*Allen, H. A., Liddle, P. F., & Frith, C. F. (1993). Negative features, retrieval processes, and verbal fluency in schizophrenia. *British Journal of Psychiatry, 163*, 769–775.

*Almkvist, O., & Backman, L. (1993). Progression in Alzheimer's disease: Sequencing of neuropsychological decline. *International Journal of Geriatric Psychiatry, 8*, 755–763.

*Aloia, M. S., Gourovitch, M. L., Weinberger, D. R., & Goldberg, T. E. (1996). An investigation of semantic space in patients with schizophrenia. *Journal of the International Neuropsychological Society, 2*, 267–273.

Alzheimer, A. (1977). A unique illness involving the cerebral cortex. In D. A. Rottenvert & F. H. Hochberg (Eds.), C. N. Hocvhberg, & F. H. Hochberg (tran.), *Neurological classics in modern translation* (pp. 41–43). New York: Haffner Press.

*Amato, M. P., Ponziani, G., Pracucci, G., Bracco, L., Siracusa, G., & Amaducci, L. (1995). Cognitive impairment in early-onset multiple sclerosis: Pattern, predictors, and impact on everyday life in a 4-year follow-up. *Archives of Neurology, 52*, 168–172.

American Psychiatric Association (1994). *Diagnostic and Statistical Manual of Mental Disorders* (4th ed.). *DSM-IV*. Washington, DC: Author.

Ammons, R. B., & Ammons, C. H. (1962). The Quick Test (QT): Provisional manual. *Psychological Reports (Monograph supplement I-VII), 111–161.

Anderson, S. W., Damasio, H., Jones, R. D., & Tranel, D. (1991). Wisconsin Card Sorting Test performance as a measure of frontal lobe damage. *Journal of Clinical and Experimental Neuropsychology, 13*, 909–922.

Anderson, S. W., Damasio, H., & Tranel, D. (1990). Neuropsychological impairments with lesions caused by tumor or stroke. *Archives of Neurology, 47*, 397–405.

Andreasen, N. C., Arndt, S., Swayze, V., Cizaldo, T., Flaum, M., O'Leary, D., Ehrhardt, J. C., & Yuh, W. T. C. (1994). Thalamic abnormalities in schizophrenia visualized through magnetic resonance image averaging. *Science, 266*, 294–298.

Appell, J., Kertesz, A., & Fishman, M. (1982). A study of language functioning in Alzheimer's patients. *Brain and Language, 17*, 73–91.

*Appollonia, I., Grafman, J., Clark, K., Nichelli, P., Zeffiro, T., & Hallett, M. (1994). Implicit and explicit memory in patients with Parkinson's disease with and without dementia. *Archives of Neurology, 51*, 359–367.

*Archer, J., Hay, D. C., & Young, A. W. (1992). Face processing in psychiatric conditions. *British Journal of Clinical Psychology, 31*, 45–61.

*Aronowitz, B. R., Hollander, E., DeCaria, C., Cohen, L., Saoud, J. B., Stein, D., Liebowitz, M. R., & Rosen, W. G. (1994). Neuropsychology of obsessive compulsive disorder: Preliminary findings. *Neuropsychiatry, Neuropsychology, and Behavioral Neurology, 7*, 81–86.

*Atack, J. R., Litvan, I., Thal, L. J., May, C., Rapoport, S. I., & Chase, T. N. (1991). Cerebrospinal fluid acetylcholinseterase activity relative to normal subjects and lack of inhibition by oral physostigmine. *Journal of Neurology, Neurosurgery, and Psychiatry, 54*, 832–835.

Axelrod, B. N., Goldman, R. S., Tompkins, L. M., & Jiron, C. C. (1994). Differential patterns of performance on the Wisconsin Card Sorting Test in schizophrenia, mood disorder, and traumatic brain injury. *Neuropsychiatry, Neuropsychology, and Behavioral Neurology, 7,* 20–24.

*Axelrod, B. N., Goldman, R. S., Tompkins, L. M., & Jiron, C. C. (1994). Poor differential performance on the Wisconsin Card Sorting Test in schizophrenia, mood disorders, and traumatic brain injury. *Neuropsychiatry, Neuropsychology, and Behavioral Neurology, 7,* 20–24.

*Auriacombe, A., Grossman, Carveh, S., Gollomp, S., Stern, M. B., & Hurig, H. I. (1993). Verbal fluency deficits in Parkinson's disease. *Neuropsychology, 7,* 182–192.

*Austin, M. P., Ross, M., Murray, C., O'Carroll, R. E., Ebmeier, K. P., & Goodwin, G.M. (1992). Cognitive function in major depression. *Journal of Affective Disorder, 25,* 21–30.

*Azuma, T., Bayles, K. A., Cruz, R. F., Tomoeda, C. K., Wood, J. A., McGeaugh, A., & Montgomery Jr., E.B. (1997). Comparing the difficulty of letter, semantic and name fluency tasks for normal elderly and patients with Parkinson's disease. *Neuropsychology, 11,* 488–497.

Baer, L., & Jenike, M. A. (1990). Introduction. In M. A. Jenike, L. Baer, & Minichiello, W. E. (Eds.), *Obsessive compulsive disorders: Theory and managment.* (pp. 3–9). Chicago: Year Book Medical Publishers, Inc..

Bak, T. H., & Hodges, J. R. (1998). The neuropsychology of progressive supranuclear palsy. *Neurocase, 4,* 89–94.

Bakan, D. (1966). The test of significance in psychological research. *Psychological Bulletin, 66,* 1–29.

Baldereschi, M., Amato, M. P., Nencini, P., Pracucci, G., Lippi, A., Amaducci, L., Gauthier, S., Beatty, L., Quiroga, P., Klassen, G., Galea, A., Muscat, P., Osuntokun, B., Ogunniyi, A., Portera-Sanchez, A., Bermejo, F., Hendrie, H., Burdine, V., Brashear, A., Farlow, M., Maggi, S., & Katzman, R. (1994). Cross-national interrater agreement on the clinical diagnostic criteria for dementia. *Neurology, 44,* 239–242.

*Balota, D. A., & Ferraro, F. R. (1996). Lexical, sublexical, and implicit memory processes in healthy young and healthy older adults and in individuals with dementia of the Alzheimer's type. *Neuropsychology, 10,* 82–95.

*Barba, G. D., & Wong, C. (1995). Encoding specificity and intrusion in Alzheimer's disease and amnesia. *Brain and Cognition, 27,* 1–16.

*Barr, A., & Brandt, J. (1996). Word-list generation deficits in dementia. *Journal of Clinical and Experimental Neuropsychology, 18,* 810–822.

Barr, W. B., Bilder, R. M., Goldberg, E., Kaplan, E., & Mukherjee, S. (1989). The neuropsychology of schizophrenic speech. *Journal of Cummunication Disorders, 22,* 327–349.

*Bartfai, A., Wirson, A., Levander, S., & Schalling, D. (1989). Smooth pursuit eye tracking and neuropsychological performance in healthy volunteers. *Acta Psychiatrica Scandinavica, 80,* 479–486.

*Batchelor, J., Harvey, A. G., & Bryant, R. A. (1995). Stroop color word test as a measure of attentional deficit following mild head injury. *The Clinical Neuropsychologist, 9,* 180–186.

Baum, H. M., & Rothschild, B. B. (1981). The incidence and prevalence of reported multiple sclerosis. *Annals of Neurology, 10,* 420–428.

Baxter, Jr., L. R. (1992). Neuroimaging studies of obsessive-compulsive disorder. *Psychiatric Clinics of North America, 15,* 871–884.

Baxter Jr., L. R., Phelps, M. E., Mazziotta, J. C., Guze, B. H., Schwartz, J. M., & Selin, C. E. (1987). *Archives of General Psychiatry, 44,* 211–218.

*Bayles, K. A. (1991). Age at onset of Alzheimer's disease. *Archives of Neurology, 48,* 155–159.

Beatty, W. W. (1996). Multiple sclerosis. In R. L. Adams, O. A. Parsons, J. L. Culbertson, & S. J. Nixon (Eds.), *Neuropsychology for clinical practice: Etiology, assessment, and treatment of common neurological disorders.* (pp. 225–242). Washington: American Psychological Association.

Beatty, W. W., & Gange, J. J. (1977). Neuropsychological aspects of multiple sclerosis. *Journal of Nervous and Mental Disease, 164,* 42–50.

*Beatty, W. W., Goodkin, D. E., Beatty, P. A., & Monson, N. (1989). Frontal lobe dysfunction and memory impairment in patients with chronic progressive multiple sclerosis. *Brain and Cognition, 11,* 73–86.

*Beatty, W. W., Goodkin, D. E., Monson, N., & Beatty, P. A. (1989). Cognitive disturbances in patients with relapse-remitting multiple sclerosis. *Archives of Neurology, 46,* 1113–1119.

*Beatty, W. W., Goodkin, D. E., Monson, N., Beatty, P. A., & Hertsgaard, D. (1988). Anterograde and retrograde amnesia in patients with chronic progressive multiple sclerosis. *Archives of Neurology, 45,* 611–619.

*Beatty, W. W., Jocic, Z., Monson, N., & Katzung, V. M. (1994). Problem solving by schizophrenic and schizoaffective patients on the Wisconsin and California card sorting tests. *Neuropsychology, 8,* 49–54.

*Beatty, W. W., Jocic, Z., Monson, N., & Staton, D. (1993). Memory and frontal lobe dysfunction in schizophrenia and schizoaffective disorder. *The Journal of Nervous and Mental Disease, 181,* 448–453.

*Beatty, W. W. Hames, K. A., Blanco, C. R., Paul, R. H., & Wilbanks, S. L. (1995). Verbal abstraction deficit in multiple sclerosis. *Neuropsychology, 9,* 198–205.

*Beatty, W. W., & Monson, N. (1991). Metamemory in multiple sclerosis. *Journal of Clinical and Experimental Neuropsychology, 13,* 309–327.

*Beatty, W. W., & Monson, N. (1994). Picture and motor sequencing in multiple sclerosis. *Journal of Clinical and Experimental Neuropsychology, 16,* 165–172.

*Beatty, W. W., & Monson, N. (1996). Problem solving by patients with multiple sclerosis: Comparison of performance on the Wisconsin and California card sorting tests. *Journal of the International Neuropsychological Society, 2,* 134–140.

*Beatty, W. W., Paul, R. H., Wilbanks, S. L., Hames, K. A., Blanco, C. R., & Goodkin, D. E. (1995). Identifying multiple sclerosis patients with mild or global cognitive impairment using the screening examination for cognitive impairment. *Neurology, 45,* 718–723.

Beck, A. T. (1987). *Beck Depression Inventory.* San Antonio, TX: The Psychological Corporation.

*Becker, J. T. (1988). Working memory and secondary memory deficits in Alzheimer's disease. *Journal of Clinical and Experimental Neuropsychology, 10,* 739–753.

*Becker, J. T., Boller, F., Lopez, O. L., Saxton, J., & McGonigle, K. L. (1994). The natural history of Alzheimer's disease: Description of study cohort and accuracy of diagnosis. *Archives of Neurology, 51,* 585–594.

*Becker, J. T., Huff, J., Nebes, R. D., Holland, A., & Boller, F. (1988). Neuropsychological function in Alzheimer's disease. *Archives of Neurology, 45,* 263–268.

*Becker, J. T., Lopez, O. L., & Wess, J. (1992). Material-specific memory loss in probable Alzheimer's disease. *Journal of Neurology, Neurosurgery, and Psychiatry, 55*, 1177–1181.

*Becker, J. T., Wess, J., Hunkin, N. M., & Parkin, A. J. (1993). Use of temporal context information in Alzheimer's disease. *Neuropsychologia, 31*, 137–143.

Behar, D., Rapoport, J. L., Berg, C. J., Denckla, M. B., Mann, L., Cox, C., Fedio, P., Zahn, T., & Wolfman, M. G. (1984). Computerized tomography and neuropsychological test measures in adolescents with obsessive-compulsive disorder. *American Journal of Psychiatry, 141*, 363–369.

*Belano, R., & Ska, B. (1992). Interaction between verbal and gestural language in progressive aphasia: A longitudinal case study. *Brain and Language, 43*, 355–385.

*Bellini, L., Abbruzzese, M., Gambini, O., Rossi, A., Stratta, P., & Scarone, S. (1991). Frontal and callosal neuropsychological performances in schizophrenia: Further evidence of possible attention and mnesic dysfunctions. *Schizophrenia Research, 5*, 115–121.

Bem, D. J. (1995). Writing a review article for Psychological Bulletin. *Psychological Bulletin, 118*, 172–177.

Bender, L. (1938). A visual motor Gestalt test and its clinical use. *American Orthopsychiatric Association, Research Monographs*, No. 3.

Benson, D. F. (1979). Neurologic correlates of anomia. In H. Whitaker & H. A. Whitaker (Eds.), *Studies in neurolinguistics*. (Vol. 4, pp. 298–328). New York: Academic Press.

Benson, D. F. (1993). Aphasia. In K. M. Heilman & E. Valenstein (Eds.), *Clinical neuropsychology* (pp. 17–36). 3rd ed. New York: Oxford University Press.

Benson, D. F. (1994). *The neurology of thinking*. New York: Oxford University Press.

Benson, D. F., & Ardila, A. (1996). *Aphasia: A clinical perspective*. New York: Oxford University Press.

Benson, D. F., & Miller, B. L. (1997). Frontal lobes: Clinical and anatomic aspects. In T. E. Feinberg, & M. J. Farah (Eds.), *Behavioral neurology and neuropsychology*. (pp. 401–408). New York: McGraw-Hill.

*Benson, D. F., & Zaias, B. W. (1991). Progressive aphasia: A case with postmortem correlation. *Neuropsychiatry, Neuropsychology, and Behavioral Neurology, 4*, 215–223.

Benton, A. L. (1974). *Revised Visual Retention Test* (4th ed.). New York: The Psychological Corporation.

Benton, A. L., & Hamsher, K. deS. (1989). *Multilingual Aphasia Examination*. Iowa City: AJA Associates.

Benton, A. L., Hamsher, K. deS., Varney, N. R., & Spreen, O. (1983). *Contributions to neuropsychological assessment*. New York: Oxford University Press.

Benton, A. L., Sivan, A. B., Hamsher, K. deS., Varney, N. R., & Spreen, O. (1994). *Contributions to neuropsychological assessment* (2nd ed.). New York: Oxford University Press.

Benton, A. L., & Tranel, D. (1993). Visuoperceptual, visuospatial, and visuoconstructional disorders. In K. M. Heilman & E. Valenstein (Eds.), *Clinical neuropschology* (pp. 165–213). 3rd ed. New York: Oxford University Press.

Benton, A. L., Varney, N. R., & Hamsher, K. deS. (1978). Visuospatial judgment: A clinical test. *Archives of Neurology, 35*, 364–367.

*Berent, S., Giordani, B., Lehtinen, S., Markel, D., Penney, J. B., Buchtel, H. A., Starosta-Rubinstein, S., Hichwa, R., & Young, A. B. (1988). Positron emission tomographic scan investigations of Huntington's disease: Cerebral metabolic correlates of cognitive function. *Annals of Neurology, 23*, 541–546.

*Berman, K. F., Illowsky, B. P., Weinberger, D. R. (1988). Physiological dysfunction of dorsolateral prefrontal cortex in schizophrenia IV: Further evidence for regional and behavioral specificity. *Archives of General Psychiatry, 45,* 616–622.

*Bernard, L. C., McGarth, M. J., & Houston, W. (1996). The differential effects of simulating malingering, closed head injury, and other CNS pathology on the Wisconsin Card Sorting Test: Support for the "pattern of performance" hypothesis. *Archives of Clinical Neuropsychology, 11,* 231–245.

Berthier, M. L., Kulisevsky, J., Gironell, A., & Heras, J. A. (1996). Obsessive-compulsive disorder associated with brain lesions: Clinical phenomenology, cognitive function, and anatomic correlates. *Neurology, 47,* 353–361.

*Biassou, N. (1995). Phonologic processing deficits in Alzheimer's disease. *Neurology, 45,* 2165–2169.

Bieliauskas, L. A. (1993). Depressed or not depressed? That is the question. *Journal of Clinical and Experimental Neuropsychology, 15,* 119–134.

Bieliauskas, L. A., Fatenau, P. S., Lacey, M. A., & Roper, B. L. (1997). Use of the odds-ratio to translate neuropsychological test scores into real-world outcomes: From statistical significance to clinical significance. *Journal of Clinical and Experimental Neuropsychology, 19,* 889–896.

*Biggins, C. A., Boyd, J. L., Harrop, F. M., Madeley, P. M., Mindham, R. H. S., Randall, J. I., & Spokes, E. G. S. (1992). A controlled, longitudinal study of dementia in Parkinson's disease. *Journal of Neurology, Neurosurgery, and Psychiatry, 55,* 566–571.

*Bilder, R. M., Lipschutz-Broch, L., Reiter, G., Geisler, S. H., Mayeroff, D. I., & Liberman, J. A. (1992). Intellectual deficits in first-episode schizophrenia: Evidence for progressive deterioration. *Schizophrenia Bulletin, 18,* 437–448.

Binder, L. M. (1986). Persisting symptoms after mild head injury. A review of the postconcussive syndrome. *Journal of Clinical and Experimental Neuropsychology, 8,* 323–346.

Binder, L. M. (1997). A review of mild head trauma. Part II: Clinical implications. *Journal of Clinical and Experimental Neuropsychology, 19,* 433–458.

Binder, L. M., Rohling, M. L., & Larrabee, G. J. (1997). A review of mild head trauma. Part I: Meta-analytic review of neuropsychological studies. *Journal of Clinical and Experimental Neuropsychology, 19,* 421–431.

*Binetti, G., Magni, E., Cappa, S. F., Padovani, A., Bianchetti, A., & Trabucci, M. (1995). Semantic memory in Alzheimer's disease: An analysis of category fluency. *Journal of Clinical and Experimental Neuropsychology, 17,* 82–89.

*Binetti, G., Magni, E., Padovani, A., Cappa, S. F., Bianchetti, A., & Trabucci, M. (1995). Release from proactive interference in early Alzheimer's disease. *Neuropsychologia, 33,* 379–384.

*Bird, M., & Luszcz, M. (1993). Enhancing memory performance in Alzheimer's disease: Acquisition assistance and cue effectiveness. *Journal of Clinical and Experimental Neuropsychology, 15,* 921–932.

Black, S. E. (1996). Focal cortical atrophy syndromes. *Brain and Cognition, 31,* 188–229.

Blacker, D., Albert, M. S., Bassett, S. S., Go, R. C. P., Harrell, L. E., & Folstein, M. F. (1994). Reliability and validity of NINCDS-ADRDA criteria for Alzheimer's disease: The National Institute of Mental Health genetics initiative. *Archives of Neurology, 51,* 1198–1204.

*Blanchard, J. J., & Neale, J. M. (1994). The neuropsychological signature of schizophrenia: Generalized or differential deficit. *American Journal of Psychiatry, 151,* 40–48.

Bleuler, E. (1911/1950). *Dementia praecox or the group of schizophrenias* (translated by J. Zinkin). New York: International Universities Press.

Boller, F. (1980). Mental status of patients with Parkinson's disease. *Journal of Clinical Neuropsychology, 2,* 157–172.

Boller, F., Ducyckaerts, C. (1997). Alzheimer disease: Clinical and anatomic aspects. In T. E. Feinberg, & M. J. Farah (Eds.), *Behavioral neurology and neuropsychology.* (pp. 521–544). New York: McGraw-Hill.

*Bondi, M. W., & Kaszniak, A. W. (1991). Implicit and explicit memory in Alzheimer's disease and Parkinson's disease. *Journal of Clinical and Experimental Neuropsychology, 13,* 339–358.

*Bondi, M. W., Kaszniak, A. W., Bayles, K. A., & Vance, K. T. (1993). Contributions of frontal system dysfunction to memory and perceptual abilities in Parkinson's disease. *Neuropsychology, 7,* 89–102.

*Bondi, M. W., Kaszniak, A. W., Rapcsak, S. Z., & Butters, N. (1993). Implicit and explicit memory following anterior communicating artery aneurysm rupture. *Brain and Cognition, 22,* 213–229.

*Bondi, M. W., Monsch, A. U., Galasko, D., Butters, N., Salmon, D. P., & Delis, D. C. (1994). Preclinical cognitive markers of dementia of the Alzheimer's type. *Neuropsychology, 8,* 374–384.

Bondi, M. W., Salmon, D. P., & Kaszniak, A. W. (1996). The neuropsychology of dementia. In I. Grant & K. M. Adams (Eds.), *Neuropsychological assessment of neuropsychiatric disorders* (pp. 164–199). 2nd ed. New York: Oxford University Press.

*Bonilla, J. L., & Johnson, M. K. (1995). Semantic space in Alzheimer's disease patients. *Neuropsychology, 9,* 345–353.

*Boone, K. B., Ananth, J., Philpott, L., Kaur, A., & Djenderedjian, A. (1991). Neuropsychological characteristics of nondepressed adults with obsessive compulsive disorder. *Neuropsychiatry, Neuropsychology, and Behavioral Neurology, 4,* 96–109.

*Boone, K. B., Lesser, I. M., Miller, B. L., Wohl, M., Berman, N., & Lee, A. (1995). Cognitive functioning in older depressed outpatients: Relationship of presence and severity of depression to neuropsychological test scores. *Neuropsychology, 9,* 390–398.

*Boone, K. B., Lesser, I., Wohl, M., Berman, N., Lee, A., & Palmer, B. (1994). Cognitive functioning in a mildly to moderately depressed geriatric sample: Relationship to chronological age. *Journal of Neuropsychiatry and Clinical Neurosciences, 6,* 267–272.

Boone, K. B., Miller, B. L., & Lesser, I. M. (1990). Performance on frontal lobe tests in healthy, older individuals. *Developmental Neuropsychology, 6,* 215–224.

Bornstein, R. A., Baker, G. B., & Douglass, A. B. (1991). Depression and memory in major depressive disorder. *Journal of Neuropsychiatry and Clinical Neurosciences, 3,* 78–80.

Bornstein, R. A., & Chelune, G. J. (1988). Factor structure of the Wechsler Memory Scale—Revised. *The Clinical Neuropsychologist, 2,* 107–115.

Bornstein, R. A., & Chelune, G. J. (1989). Factor structure of the Wechsler memory Scale—Revised in relation to age and education level. *Archives of Clinical Neuropsychology, 4,* 15–24.

*Bornstein, R. A., Nasrallah, H. A., Olson, S. C., Coffman, J. A., Torello, M., & Schwarzkopf, S. B. (1990). Neuropsychological deficit in schizophrenic subtypes: Paranoid, nonparanoid, and schizoaffective subgroups. *Psychiatry Research, 31,* 15–24.

*Borod, J. C., Martin, C. C., Alpert, M., Brozgold, A., & Welkowitz, J. (1993). Perception of facial emotion in schizophrenic and right brain-damaged patients. *The Journal of Nervous and Mental Disease, 181,* 494–502.

Bouillaud, J. B. (1825). Recherches cliniques propres a demontrer que la perte de la parole correspond a la lesion de lobules anterieurs du cerveau, et a confirmer l'opinion de M. Gall sur le siege de l'organe du langage articule. *Archives of General Medicine, 8,* 25–45.

Bowers, D., Bauer, R. M., & Heilman, K. M. (1993). The nonverbal affect lexicon: Theoretical perspectives from neuropsychological studies of affect perception. *Neuropsychology, 7,* 433–444.

*Bradshaw, J. L., Phillips, J. G., Dennis, C., Mattingley, J. B., Andrews, D., Chiu, E., Pierson, J. M., & Bradshaw, J. A. (1992). Initiation and execution of movement sequences in those suffering from and at-risk of developing Huntington's disease. *Journal of Clinical and Experimental Neuropsychology, 14,* 179–192.

Braff, D. L. (1993). Information processing and attention dysfunctions in schizophenia. *Schizophrenia Bulletin, 19,* 233–259.

*Braff, D. L., Glick, I. D., Johnson, M. H., & Zissok, S. (1988). The clinical significance of thought disorder across time in psychiatric patients. *The Journal of Nervous and Mental Disease, 176,* 213–220.

*Braff, D. L., Heaton, R. K., Kuck, J., Cullum, C. M., Moranville, J., Grant, I., & Zisook, S. (1991). The generalized pattern of neuropsychological deficits in outpatients with chronic schizophrenia with heterogeneous Wisconsin Card Sorting Test results. *Archives of General Psychiatry, 48,* 891–898.

Brandt, J., & Butters, N. (1986). The neuropsychology of Huntington's disease. *Trends in Neuroscience, 9,* 118–120.

Brandt, J., & Butters, N. (1996). Neuropsychological characteristics of Huntington's disease. In I. Grant & K. M. Adams (Eds.), *Neuropsychological assessment of neuropsychiatric disorders.* (pp. 312–341). New York: Oxford University Press.

Brandt, J., & Bylsma, F. W. (1993). The dementia of Huntington's disease. In, R. W. Parks, R. F. Zec, & R. S. Wilson (Eds.), *Neuropsychology of Alzheimer's disease and other dementias.* New York: Oxford University Press.

Brandt, J., & Rich, J. B. (1995). Memory disorders in the dementias. In A. D. Baddeley, B. A. Wilson, & F. N. Watts (Eds.), *Handbook of memory disorders.* Chichester, England: John Wiley and Sons.

*Brandt, J., Spencer, M., & Folstein, M. (1988). The telephone interview for cognitive status. *Neuropsychiatry, Neuropsychology, and Behavioral Neurology, 1,* 111–117.

Broca, P. (1865). Sur la faculte du langage articule. *Bulletin de Sociology et Anthropology de Paris, 6,* 337–393.

*Brown, K. W., White, T., & Palmer, D. (1992). Movement disorders and psychological tests of frontal lobe function in schizophrenic patients. *Psychological Medicine, 22,* 69–77.

*Brown, R. G., Jahanshahi, M., & Marsden, C. D. (1990). Sexual function in patients with Parkinson's disease and their partners. *Journal of Neurology, Neurosurgery, and Psychiatry, 53,* 480–486.

*Brown, R. G., Jahanshahi, M., & Marsden, C. D. (1993). The execution of bimanual movements in patients with Parkinson's, Huntington's, and cerebellar disease. *Journal of Neurology, Neurosurgery, and Psychiatry, 56,* 295–297.

Brown, R. G., & Marsden, C. D. (1986). Visuospatial function in Parkinson's disease. *Brain, 109,* 987–1002.

*Brown, R. G., Scott, L. C., Bench, C. J., Dolan, R. J. (1994). Cognitive function in depression: Its relationship to the presence and severity of intellectual decline. *Psychological Medicine, 24,* 829–847.

*Brown, R. G., Shahi, M. J., & Marsden, C. D. (1993). The execution of bimanual movements in patients with Parkinson's, Huntington's and cerebellar disease. *Journal of Neurology, Neurosurgery, and Psychiatry, 56,* 295–297.

*Brugger, P., Monsch, A. U., Salmon, D. P., & Butters, N. (1996). Random number generation in dementia of the Alzheimer's type: A test of frontal executive function. *Neuropsychologia, 34,* 97–103.

Brun, A. (1987). Frontal lobe degeneration of the non-Alzheimer type I. Neuropathology. *Archives of Gernontology and Geriatric Psychiatry, 6,* 193–208.

Brun, A. (1993). Frontal lobe degeneration of the non Alzheimer type revisited. *Dementia, 4,* 126–131.

Brun, A., & Gustafson, L. (1976). Distribution of cerebral degeneration in Alzheimer's disease. *Archiv fur Psychiatrie und Nervenkrankheiten, 223,* 15–33.

*Buchanan, R. W., Strauss, M. E., Brier, A., Kirkpatrick, & Carpenter, W. T. (1997). Attentional impairments in deficit and nondeficit forms of schizophrenia. *American Journal of Psychiatry, 154,* 363–370.

Buchsbaum, M. S. (1990). The frontal lobes, basal ganglia, and temporal lobe as sites for schizophrenia. *Schizophrenia Bulletin, 16,* 379–390.

*Buckwalter, J. G., Sobel, E., Dunn, M. E., Diz, M. M., & Hendersen, V. W. (1993). Gender differences on a brief measure of cognitive functioning in Alzheimer's disease. *Archives of Neurology, 50,* 757–760.

Burt, D. B., Zembar, M. J., Niederehe, G. (1995). Depression and memory impairment: A meta-analysis of the association, its pattern, and specificity. *Psychological Bulletin, 117,* 285–305.

Buschke, H., & Fuld, P. A. (1974). Evaluation of storage, retention, and retrieval in disordered memory and learning. *Neurology, 11,* 1019–1025.

*Butler, R. W., Jenkins, M. A., Sprock, J., & Braff, D. L. (1992). Wisconsin Card Sorting Test deficits in chronic paranoid schizophrenia: Evidence for a relatively discrete subgroup? *Schizophrenia Research, 7,* 169–176.

*Butters, M. A., Lopez, O. L., & Becker, J. T. (1996). Focal temporal lobe dysfunction in probable Alzheimer's disease predicts a slow rate of cognitive decline. *Neurology, 46,* 687–692.

Butters, N., Delis, D. C., & Lucas, J. A. (1995). Clincal assessment of memory disorders in amnesia and dementia. *Annual Review of Psychology, 46,* 493–523.

*Butters, N., Granholm, E., Salmon, D. P., & Grant, I. (1987). Episodic and semantic memory: A comparison of amnesic and demented patients. *Journal of Clinical and Experimental Neuropsychology, 9,* 479–497.

Butters, N., Wolfe, J., Granholm, E., & Martone, M. (1986). An assessment of verbal recall, recognition and fluency abilities in patients with Huntington's disease. *Cortex, 22,* 11–32.

*Buytenhuijs, E. L., Berger, H. J. C., Van Spaendonck, K. P. M., Horstink, M. W. I. M., Borm, G. F., & Cools, A. R. (1994). Memory and learning strategies in patients with Parkinson's disease. *Neuropsychologia, 32*, 335–342.

*Cadieux, N. L., & Greve, K. W. (1997). Emotion processing in Alzheimer's disease. *Journal of the International Neuropsychological Society, 3*, 411–419.

*Caekebeke, J. F. V., Jennekens-Schinkel, A., Van der Linden, M. E., Buruma, O. J. S., & Roos, R. A. C. (1991). The interpretation of dysprosody in patients with Parkinson's disease. *Journal of Neurology, Neurosurgery, and Psychiatry, 54*, 145–148.

*Caffarra, P., Riggio, L., Malvezzi, L., Scaglioni, A., & Freedman, M. (1997). Orienting of visual attention in Alzheimer's disease: It's implication in favor of the interhemispheric balance. *Neuropsychiatry, Neuropsychology, and Behavioral Neurology, 10*, 90–95.

*Cahn, D. A., Salmon, D. P., Bondi, M. W., Butters, N., Johnson, S. A., Wiederholt, W. C., & Barrett-Connor, E. (1997). A population-based analysis of qualitative features of the neuropsychological test performance of individuals with dementia of the Alzheimer's types: Implications for individuals with questionable dementia. *Journal of the International Neuropsychological Society, 3*, 387–393.

*Cahn, D. A., Salmon, D. P., Butters, N., Wiederholt, W. C., Corey-Bloom, J., Edelstein, S. L., & Barrett-Connor, E. (1995). Detection of dementia of the Alzheimer type in a population-based sample: Neuropsychological test performance. *Journal of the International Neuropsychological Society, 1*, 252–260.

*Cahn, D. A., Salmon, D. P., Monsch, A. U., Butters, N., Wiederholt, W. C., Corey-Bloom, J., & Barrett-Connor, E. (1996). Screening for dementia of the Alzheimer's type in the community: The utility of the clock drawing test. *Archives of Clinical Neuropsychology, 11*, 529–539.

Caine, E. D. (1981). Pseudodementia: Current concepts and future directions. *Archives of General Psychiatry, 38*, 1359–1364.

Caine, E. D. (1986). The neuropsychology of depression: The pseudodementia syndrome. In I. Grant & K. M. Adams (Eds.), *Neuropsychological assessment of neuropsychiatric disorders.* New York: Oxford University Press.

Caine, E. D., Yerevanian, B. I., & Bamford, K. A. (1984). Cognitive function and the dexamethasone suppresion test in depression. *American Journal of Psychiatry, 141*, 116–118.

*Calev, A. (1984). Recall and recognition in mildly disturbed schizophrenics: The use of matched tasks. *Psychological Medicine, 14*, 425–429.

*Calev, A., Edelist, S., Kugelmass, S., & Lerer, B. (1991). Performance of long-stay schizophrenics on matched verbal and visuospatial recall tasks. *Psychological Medicine, 21*, 655–660.

Calev, A., Korin, Y., Kugelmass, S., & Lerer, B. (1987). Performance of chronic schizophrenics on matched word and design recall tasks. *Biological Psychiatry, 22*, 699–709.

*Calev, A., Venables, P. H., & Monk, A. F. (1983). Evidence for distinct verbal memory pathologies in severely and mildly disturbed schizophrenics. *Schizophrenia Bulletin, 9*, 247–264.

Calne, D. B., Snow, B. J., & Lee, C. (1992). Criteria for diagnosing Parkinson's disease. *Annals of Neurology, 32*, S125-S127.

*Camicioli, R., Howieson, D., Lehmann, S., & Kaye, J. (1997). Talking while walking: The effect of a dual task in aging and Alzheimer's disease. *Neurology, 48*, 955–958.

*Caplan, R., & Guthrie, D. (1994). Blink rate in childhood schizophrenia spectrum disorder. *Biological Psychiatry, 35*, 228–234.

*Carew, T., Lamar, M., Cloud, B. S., Grossman, M., & Libon, D. J. (1997). Impairment in category fluency in ischemic vascular dementia. *Neuropsychology, 11*, 400–412.

*Carlesimo, G. A., Fadda, L., Marfia, G. A., Caltagirone, C. (1995). Explicit memory and repetition priming in dementia: Evidence for a common basic mechanism underlying conscious and unconscious retrieval deficits. *Journal of Clinical and Experimental Neuropsychology, 17*, 44–57.

Carpenter, W. T., Buchanan, R. W., Kirkpatrick, B., & Tamminga, C. (1993). Strong inference, theory testing, and the neuroanatomy of schizophrenia. *Archives of General Psychiatry, 50*, 825–831.

*Carr, S. A. (1980). Interhemispheric transfer of stereognostic information in chronic schizophrenics. *British Journal of Psychiatry, 136*, 53–58.

*Carrigan, P. W., & Green, M. F. (1991). Signal detection analysis of short-term recall in schizophrenia. *The Journal of Nervous and Mental Disease, 179*, 495–498.

Carson, R. C., & Sanislow III, C. A. (1992). The schizophrenias. In H. E. Adams & P. B. Sutker (Eds.), *Comprehensive handbook of psychopathology*. New York: Plenum.

*Carter, C. S., Robertson, L. C., & Nordahl, T. E. (1992). Abnormal processing of irrelevant information in chronic schizophrenia: Selective enhancement of Stroop facilitation. *Psychiatry Research, 41*, 137–146.

Carver, R. P. (1978). The case against statistical significance testing. *Harvard Educational Review, 48*, 378–399.

*Caselli, R. J., Windebank, A. J., Peterson, R. C., Komori, T., Parisi, J. E., Okazaki, H., Kokmen, E., Iverson, R., Dinaploi, R. P., Graff-Radford, N. R., & Stein, S. D. (1993). Rapidly progressive aphasic dementia and motor neuron disease. *Annals of Neurology, 33*, 200–207.

Cassens, G. C., Wolfe, L., & Zola, M. (1990). The neuropsychology of depression. *Journal of Neuropsychiatry and Clinical Neurosciences, 2*, 202–213.

Cassens, G., Inglis, A. K., Appelbaum, P. S., & Gutheil, T. G. (1990). Neuroleptics: Effects on neuropsychological function in chronic schizophrenic patients. *Schizophrenia Bulletin, 16*, 477–499.

*Chan, A. S., Butters, N., Salmon, D. P., Johnson, S. A., Paulsen, J. S., & Swenson, M. R. (1995). Comparison of the semantic networks in patients with dementia and amnesia. *Neuropsychology, 9*, 177–186.

*Chan, A. S., Salmon, D. P., Butters, N., & Johnson, S. A. (1995). Semantic network abnormality predicts rate of cognitive decline in patients with probable Alzheimer's disease. *Journal of the International Neuropsychological Society, 1*, 297–303.

*Channon, S., Jones, M-C., & Stephenson, S. (1993). Cognitive strategies and hypothesis testing during discrimination learning in Parkinson's disease. *Neuropsychologia, 31*, 75–81.

Chapman, L. J., & Chapman, J. P. (1973). Problems in the measurement of cognitive deficit. *Psychological Bulletin, 79*, 380–385.

Chapman, L. J., & Chapman, J. P. (1978). When should schizophrenic and normal groups be compared? *Journal of Psychiatric Research, 14*, 321–325.

Chapman, L. J., & Chapman, J. P. (1989). Strategies for resolving the heterogeneity of schizophrenics and their relatives using cognitive measures. *Journal of Abnormal Psychology, 98*, 357–366.

Charcot, J. M. (1875). *Lesons sur les maladies du systeme nerveux* 2nd ed. Paris: Delahaye et Lecrosnier.

*Cherry, B. J., Buckwalter, J. G., & Henderson, V. W. (1996). Memory span procedures in Alzheimer's disease. *Neuropsychology, 10,* 286–293.

*Chertkow, H., Bub, D., Bergman, H., Bruemmer, A., Merling, A., & Rothfleisch, J. (1994). Increased semantic priming in patients with dementia of the Alzheimer's type. *Journal of Clinical and Experimental Neuropsychology, 16,* 608–622.

*Chiacchio, L., Grossi, D., Stanlone, M., & Trojano, L. (1993). Slowly progressive aphasia associated with surface dyslexia. *Cortex, 29,* 145–152.

Christensen, H., Griffiths, K., Mackinnon, A., & Jacomb, P. (1997). A quantitative review of cognitive deficits in depression and Alzheimer-type dementia. *Journal of the International Neuropsychological Society, 3,* 631–651.

Christensen, H., Hadzi-Pavlovic, D., & Jacomb, P. (1991). The psychometric differentiation of dementia from normal aging: A meta-analysis. *Journal of Consulting and Clinical Psychology, 3,* 147–155.

*Christensen, K. J., Kim, S. W., Dysken, M. W., & Hoover, K. M. (1992). Neuropsychological performance in obsessive compulsive disorder. *Biological Psychiatry, 31,* 4–18.

*Clark, C. M., Jacova, C., Klonoff, H., Kremer, B., Hayden, M., & Paty, D. (1997). Pathological association and dissociation of functional systems in multiple sclerosis and Huntington's disease. *Journal of Clinical and Experimental Neuropsychology, 19,* 63–76.

*Claus, J. J., Ludwig, C., Mohr, E., Giuffra, M., Blin, J., & Chase, T. N. (1991). Nootropic drugs in Alzheimer's disease: Symptomatic treatment with pramiracetam. *Neurology, 41,* 570–574.

*Cleghorn, J. M. (1989). Increased frontal and reduced parietal glucose metabolism in acute untreated schizophrenia. *Psychiatry Research, 28,* 119–133.

*Cleghorn, J. M., Garnett, E. S., Nahmias, C., Brown, G. M., Kaplan, R. D., Szechtman, H., Szechtman, B., Franco, S., Deimer, S. W., & Cook, P. (1990). Regional brain metabolism during auditory hallucinations in chronic schizophrenia. *British Journal of Psychiatry, 157,* 562–570.

Cleghorn, J. M., Kaplan, R. D., Szechtman, B., Szechtman, H., & Brown, G. M. (1990). Neuroleptic drug effects on cognitive function in schizophrenia. *Schizophrenia Research, 3,* 211–219.

Clementz, B. A., Grove, W. W., Iacono, W. G., & Sweeney, J. A. (1992). Smooth-pursuit eye movement dysfunction and liability for schizophrenia: Implications for genetic modeling. *Journal of Abnormal Psychology, 101,* 117–129.

Coffey, C., Cummings, J. L., Lovell, M. R., & Pearlson, G. D. (Eds.), *The American Psychiatric Press textbook of geriatric neuropsychiatry.* Washington: American Psychiatric Press.

*Cohen, H., Bouchard, S., Scherzer, P., & Whitaker, H. (1994). Language and verbal reasoning in Parkinson's disease. *Neuropsychiatry, neuropsychology, and Behavioral Neurology, 7,* 166–175.

Cohen, J. (1957). Factor analytically based rationale for Wechsler Adult Intelligence Scale. *Journal of Consulting Psychology, 21,* 451–457.

Cohen, J. (1988). *Statistical power analysis for the behavioral sciences* (2nd. ed.). New York: Academic Press.

Cohen, J. (1994). The earth is round (p < .05). *American Psychologist, 49,* 997–1003.

*Cohen, L., Benoit, N., Van Eackhout, P., Ducarne, B., & Brunet, P. (1993). Pure progressive aphemia. *Journal of Neurology, Neurosurgery, and Psychiatry, 56,* 923–924.

*Cohen, L. J., Hollander, E., Decaria, C. M., Stein, D. J., Simeon, D., Liebowitz, M. R., & Aronowitz, B. R. (1996). Specificity of neuropsychological impairment in obsessive compulsive disorder: A comparison with social phobic and normal control subjects. *Journal of Neuropsychiatry and Clinical Neurosciences, 8,* 82–85.

*Cohen, R. A., & Fisher, M. (1989). Amantadine treatment of fatigue associated with multiple sclerosis. *Archives of Neurology, 46,* 676–680.

*Condray, R., Steinhauer, S. R., & Goldstein, G. (1992). Language comprehension in schizophrenics and their brothers. *Biological Psychiatry, 32,* 790–802.

*Condray, R., Steinhauer, S. R., Van Kammen, D. P., & Kasparek, A. (1996). Working memory capacity predicts language comprehension in schizophrenic patients. *Schizophrenia Research, 20,* 1–13.

*Coolidge, F. L., Middleton, P. A., Griego, J. A., & Schmidt, M. M. (1996). The effects of interference on verbal learning in multiple sclerosis. *Archives of Clinical Neuropsychology, 11,* 605–611.

Cooper, H. M. (1979). Statistically combining independent studies: A meta-analysis of sex diffferences in conformity research. *Journal of Personality and Social Psychology, 37,* 131–146.

Cooper, H. M., & Hedges, L. V. (1994). *The handbook of research synthesis.* New York: Russel Sage Foundation.

*Corcoran, R., Mercer, G., & Frith, C. D. (1995). Schizophrenia, symptomatology and social inference: Investigating "theory of mind" in people with schizophrenia. *Schizophrenia Research, 17,* 5–13.

Corey-Bloom, J., Thal, L. J., Galasko, D., Folstein, M., Drachman, D., Raskind, M., & Lanska, M. D. (1995). Diagnosis and evaluation of dementia. *Neurology, 45,* 211–218.

Cornblatt, B. A., & Keilp, J. G. (1994). Impaired attention, genetics, and the pathophysiology of schizophrenia. *Schizophrenia Bulletin, 20,* 31–46.

*Cornblatt, B. A., Lenzenwger, M. F., & Kimling, L. E. (1989). The continuous performance test; identical pairs version II: Contrasting attentional profiles in schizophrenic and depressed patients. *Psychiatry Research, 29,* 65–85.

Cornford, M. E., Chang, L., & Miller, B. L. (1995). The neuropathology of Parkinsonism: An overview. *Brain and Cognition, 28,* 321–341.

Corsellis, J. A. N. (1976). Aging and the dementias. In W. Blackwood & J. A. N. Corsellis (Eds.), *Greenfield's neuropathology.* (pp. 796–848). Chicago: Year Book Medical Publishers.

Cowles, M. (1989). *Statistics in psychology: An historical perspective.* Lawrence Erlbaum Associates.

Craenhals, A., Raison-van Ruymbeke, A. M., Rectum, D., Seron, X., & Laterre, E. C. (1990). Is slowly progressive aphasia actually a new clinical entity? *Aphasiology, 4,* 485–509.

*Craft, S., Willerman, L., & Bigler, E. D. (1987). Callosal dysfunction in schizophrenia and schizo-affective disorder. *Journal of Abnormal Psychology, 96,* 205–213.

*Crawford, J. R., Besson, J. A. O., Bremmer, M., Ebmeler, K. P., Cochrane, R. H. B., & Kirkwood, K. (1992). Estimation of premorbid intelligence in schizophrenia. *British Journal of Psychiatry, 161,* 69–74.

*Crawford, J. R., Obonsawin, M. C., & Bremner, M. (1993). Frontal lobe impairment in schizophrenia: Relationship to intellectual functioning. *Psychological Medicine, 23,* 787–790.

Crews, JR., W. D., & Harrison, D. W. (1995). The neuropsychology of depression and its implications for cognitive therapy. *Neuropsychology Review, 5*, 81–123.

*Cronin-Golomb, A., & Braun, A. E. (1997). Visuospatial dysfunction and problem solving in Parkinson's disease. *Neuropsychology, 11*, 44–52.

*Crossley, M., D'Arcy, C., Rawson, N. S. B. (1997). Letter and category fluency in community-dwelling Canadian seniors: A comparison of normal participants to those with dementia of the Alzheimer or vascular type. *Journal of Clinical and Experimental Neuropsychology, 19*, 52–62.

Crosson, B. (1992). *Subcortical functions in language and memory.* New York: The Guilford Press.

Crow, T. J. (1990). Temporal lobe asymmetries as the key to the etiology of schizophrenia. *Schizophenia Bulleitn, 16*, 433–443.

*Cullum, C. M., Filley, C. M., & Kozora, E. (1995). Episodic memory function in advanced aging and early Alzheimer's disease. *Journal of the International Neuropsychological Society, 1*, 100–103.

*Cullum, C. M., Harris, J. G., Waldo, M. C., Smernoff, E., Madison, A., Nagamato, H. T., Griffith, J., Adler, L. E., & Freedman, R. (1993). Neurophysiological and neuropsychological evidence for attentional dysfunction in schizophrenia. *Schizophrenia Research, 10*, 131–141.

*Culver, C. L., Kunen, S., & Zinkgraf, S. A. (1986). Patterns of recall in schizophrenics and normal subjects. *The Journal of Nervous and Mental Disease, 174*, 620–623.

Cummings, J. L. (1990). *Subcortical dementia.* New York: Oxford University Press.

Cummings, J. L. (1993). Frontal-subcortical circuits and human behavior. *Archives of Neurology, 50*, 873–880.

Cummings, J. L., & Benson, D. F. (1984). Subcortical dementia: Review of an emerging concept. *Archives of Neurology, 41*, 874–879.

Cummings, J. L., & Benson, D. F. (1992). *Dementia: A clinical approach.* Boston: Butterworth-Heinemann.

Cummings, J. L., Benson, D. F., Hill, M., & Read, S. (1985). Aphasia in dementia of the Alzheimer type. *Neurology, 35*, 394–397.

Cummings, J. L., & Kaufer, D. (1996). Neuropsychiatric aspects of Alzheimer's disease: The cholinergic hypothesis revistited. *Neurology, 47*, 876–883.

Cummings, J. L., & Khachaturian, Z. (1996). Definitions and diagnostic criteria. In S. Gauthier & M. Dunitz (Eds.), *Clinical diagnosis and management of Alzheimer's disease.* (pp. 3–13). Boston, MA: Butterworth-Heinemann.

*Cutmore, T. R. H., & Beninger, R. J. (1990). Do neuroleptics impair learning in schizophrenic patients? *Schizophrenia Research, 3*, 173–186.

*Dabson, D. J. G., & Neufeld, R. W. J. (1987). Span of apprehension among remitted schizophrenics using small visual angles. *The Journal of Nervous and Mental Disease, 175*, 362–370.

*Dalby, J. T., & Williams, R. (1986). Preserved reading and spelling ability in psychotic disorders. *Psychological Medicine, 16*, 171–175.

*Dalla-Barba, G., & Goldblum, M. C. (1996). The influence of semantic encoding on recognition memory in Alzheimer's disease. *Neuropsychologia, 34*, 1181–1186.

*Dalla-Barba, G., Parlato, V., Iavarone, A., & Boller, F. (1995). Anosognosia, intrusions and "frontal" functions in Alzheimer's disease and depression. *Neuropsychologia, 33*, 247–259.

Damasio, A. R. (1994). *Descartes' error: Emotion, reason, and the human brain.* New York: A Grossman / Putnam.

Damasio, A. R., & Anderson, S. W. (1993). The frontal lobes. In K. M. Heilman & E. Valenstein (Eds.), *Clinical neuropsychology* (3rd ed.). New York: Oxford University Press.

Damasio, H., & Damasio, A. R. (1989). *Lesion analysis in neuropsychology*. New York: Oxford University Press.

*Daum, I., Riesch, G., Sartori, G., & Birbaumer, N. (1996). Semantic memory impairment in Alzheimer's disease. *Journal of Clinical and Experimental Neuropsychology, 18*, 648–665.

*David, A. S. (1993). Callosal transfer in schizophrenia: Too much or too little. *Journal of Abnormal Psychology, 102*, 573–579.

*David, A. S. (1993). Spatial and selective attention in the cerebral hemispheres in depression, mania, and schizophrenia. *Brain & Cognition, 23*, 166–180.

David, A. S., & Cutting, J.C. (1994). *The neuropsychology of schizophrenia*. Hillsdale NJ: Lawerence Erlbaum Associates.

*David, A. S., & Cutting, J. C. (1992). Visual imagery and visual semantics in the cerebral hemispheres in schizophrenia. *Schizophrenia Research, 8*, 263–271.

David, D. G., Goldberg, T. E., Gibbon, R., & Weinberger, D. R. (1991). Lack of a bimodal distribution of ventricular size in schizophrenia: a Gaussian mixture analysis of 1056 cases and controls. *Biological Psychiatry, 30*, 887–903.

*Davidson, O. R., & Knight, R. G. (1995). Speed of semantic reasoning and mental rotation in patients with Parkinson's disease without dementia. *Neuropsychiatry, Neuropsychology, and Behavioral Neurology, 8*, 182–188.

*de Bonis, M., de Boeck, P., Lida-Pulik, H., & Feline, A. (1995). Identity disturbances and self-other differentiation in schizophrenics, borderlines, and normal controls. *Comprehensive Psychiatry, 36*, 362–366.

*Dean, R. S., Gray, J. W., & Seretny, M. L. (1987). Cognitive aspects of schizophrenia and primary affective depression. *International Journal of Clinical Psychology, 9*, 33–36.

*Defebvre, L., Le Couffe, P., Destee, A., Houdart, P., & Steinling, M. (1995). Tomographic measurments of regional cerebral blood flow in progressive supranuclear palsy and Parkinson's disease. *Acta Neurologica Scandinavica, 92*, 235–241.

Delecluse, F., Andersen, A. R., & Waldemar, G. (1990). Cerebral blood flow in progressice aphasia without dementia. *Brain, 113*, 1395–1404.

Delis, D. C. (1989). Neuropsychological assessment of learning and memory. In F. Boller, & J. Grafman (Eds.), *Handbook of neuropsychology* (Vol. 3, pp.3–33). Amsterdam, The Netherlands: Elsevier Science Publishers.

Delis, D. C., Kramer, J. H., Kaplan, E., & Ober, B. A. (1987). *California verbal learning test: Adult version*. San Antonio, TX: The Psychological Corporation.

Delis, D. C., Massman, P. J., Butters, N., Salmon, D. P., Cermak, L. S., & Kramer, J. H. (1991). Profiles of demented and amnesic patients on the California Verbal Learning Test: Implications for the assessment of memory disorders. *Psychological Assessment, 3*, 19–26.

*Delis, D. C., Massman, P. J., Butters, N., Salmon, D. P., Shear, P. K., Demadura, T., & Filoteo, J. V. (1992). Spatial cognition in Alzheimer's disease: Subtypes of global local impairment. *Journal of Clinical and Experimental Neuropsychology, 14*, 463–477.

*DeLuca, J., Johnson, S. K., Beldowicz, D., & Natelson, B. H. (1995). Neuropsychological impairment in chronic fatigue syndrome, multiple sclerosis, and depression. *Journal of Neurology, Neurosurgery and Psychiatry, 58*, 38–43.

*DeLuca, J., Johnson, S. K., & Natelson, B. H. (1993). Information processing efficiency in chronic fatigue syndrome and multiple sclerosis. *Archives of Neurology, 50,* 301–304.

*Del Ser, T., Gonzalez-Montalvo, J. I., Martinez-Espinoza, S., Delgado-Villapalos, C., & Bermejo, F. (1997). Estimation of premorbid intelligence in Spanish people with the word accentuation test and its application to the diagnosis of dementia. *Brain and Cognition, 33,* 343–356.

*DeMyer, M. K., Gilmor, R. L., Hendrie, H. C., DeMyer, W. E., Augustyn, G. T., & Jackson, R. K. (1988). Magnetic resonance brain images in schizophrenic and normal subjects: Influence of diagnosis and education. *Schizophrenia Bulletin, 14,* 21–37.

*Deptula, D., Manevitz, A., & Yozawitz, A. (1991). Asymmetry of recall in depression. *Journal of Clinical and Experimental Neuropsychology, 13,* 854–870.

De Renzi, E., & Faglioni, P. (1978). Normative data and screening power of a shortened version of the token test. *Cortex, 14,* 41–49.

De Renzi, E., & Vignolo, L. A. (1962). The token test: A sensitive test to detect disturbances in aphasics. *Brain, 85,* 665–678.

Derix, M. M. A. (1994). *Neuropsychological differentiation of dementia syndromes.* Lisse: Swets & Zeitlinger.

*D'Esposito, M., Onishi, K., Thompson, H., Robinson, K., Armstrong, C., & Grossman, M. (1996). Working memory impairments in multiple sclerosis: Evidence from a dual-task paradigm. *Neuropsychology, 10,* 51–56.

*Deweer, B., Pillon, B., Michon, A., & Dubois, B. (1993). Mirror reading in Alzheimer's disease: Normal skill learning and acquisition of item-specific information. *Journal of Clinical and Experimental Neuropsychology, 15,* 789–804.

*Dewick, H. C., Hanley, J. R., Davies, A. D. M., Flayfer, S., & Turnbull, C. (1991). Perception and memory for faces in Parkinson's disease. *Neuropsychologia, 29,* 785–802.

*Dick, M. B., Nielson, K. A., Beth, R. E., Shankle, W. R., Cotman, C. W. (1995). Acquisition and long-term retention of a fine motor skill in Alzheimer's disease. *Brain and Cognition, 29,* 294–306.

*Dieci, M., Vita, A., Silenzi, C., Caputo, A., Comazzi, M., Ferrari, L., Ghiringhelli, L., Mezzetti, M., Tenconi, F., & Invernizzi, G. (1997). Non-selective impairment of Wisconsin Card Sorting Test performance in patients with schizophrenia. *Schizophrenia Research, 25,* 33–42.

*Diesfeldt, H. F. A. (1990). Recognition memory for words and faces in primary degenerative dementia of the Alzheimer type and normal old age. *Journal of Clinical and Experimental Neuropsychology, 12,* 931–945.

*Dikmen, S. S., Machamer, J. E., Winn, H. R., & Temkin, N. (1995). Neuropsychological outcome at 1-year post head injury. *Neuropsychology, 9,* 80–90.

Diller, L., Ben-Yishay, Y., & Gerstman, L. J. (1974). *Studies in cognition and rehabilitation in hemiplegia.* (Rehabilitation Monograph No. 50). New York: New York University Medical Center Institute of Rehabilitation Medicine.

*Direnfeld, L. K., Albert, M. L., Volicer, L., Langlais, P. J., Marquis, J., & Kaplan, E. (1984). The possible relationship of laterality to dementia and neurochemical findings. *Archives of Neurology, 41,* 935–941.

*Ditchfield, H., & Hemsley, D. R. (1990). Interhemispheric transfer of information and schizophrenia. *European Archives of Psychiatry and Neurological Sciences, 239,* 309–313.

Dom, R., Malfroid, M., & Baro, F. (1976). Neuropathology of Huntington's chorea: Studies of the venrobasal complex of the thalamus. *Neurology, 26,* 64–68.

*Downes, J. J., Roberts, A. C., Sahakian, B. J., Evenden, J. L., Morris, R. G., & Robbins, T. W. (1989). Impaired extra-dimensional shift performance in medicated and unmedicated Parkinson's disease: Evidence for a specific attentional dysfunction. *Neuropsychologia, 27,* 1329–1342.

Drachman, D. A., O'Donnell, B. F., Lew, R. A., & Swearer, J. M. (1990). The prognosis in Alzheimer's disease: 'How far' rather than 'how fast' best predicts the course. *Archives of Neurology, 47,* 851–856.

Dreese, M. J., & Netsky, M. G. (1968). Degenerative disorders of the basal ganglia. In J. Minckler (Ed.), *Pathology of the nervous system.* New York: McGraw Hill.

*Dubois, B., Daze, F., Pillon, B., Cusiman, G., Lhermitte, F., & Agid, Y. (1987). Cholinergic-dependent cognitive deficits in Parkinson's disease. *Annals of Neurology, 22,* 26–30.

*Dubois, B., Pillon, B., Legault, F., Agid, Y., & Lhermitte, F. (1988). Slowing of cognitive processing in progressive supranuclear palsy: a comparison with Parkinson's disease. *Archives of Neurology, 45,* 1194–1199.

*Dubois, B., Pillon, B., Sternic, N., Lhermitte, F., & Agid, Y. (1990). Age-induced cognitive disturbances in Parkinson's disease. *Neurology, 40,* 38–41.

*Duchek, J. M., Balota, D. A., & Ferraro, F. R. (1994). Component analysis of a rhythmic finger tapping task in individuals with senile dementia of the Alzheimer's type and in individuals with Parkinson's disease. *Neuropsychology, 8,* 218–226.

Duffy, J. R., & Petersen, R. C. (1992). Primary progressive aphasia. *Aphasiology, 6,* 1–15.

Dunn, L. M., & Dunn, L. M. (1981). *Peabody Picture Vocabulary Test—Revised.* Circle Pines, MN: American Guidance Service.

Duvoisin, R. C. (1992). Clinical diagnosis. In I. Litvan & Y. Agid (Eds.), *Progressive supranuclear palsy: Clincal and research approaches.* (pp. 15–33). New York: Oxford University Press.

*Earle-Boyer, E. A., Serper, M. R., Davidson, M., & Harvey, P. D. (1991). Continuous performance tests in schizophrenic patients: Stimulus and medication effects on performance. *Psychiatry Research, 37,* 47–56.

*Eberling, J. L., Reed, B. R., Baker, M. G., & Jagust, W. J. (1993). Cognitive correlates of regional cerebral blood flow in Alzheimer's disease. *Archives of Neurology, 50,* 761–766.

*Eikmeier, G., Lodemann, E., Zerbin, D., & Gastpar, M. (1992). P300, clinical symptoms, and neuropsychological parameters in acute and remitted schizophrenia: A preliminary report. *Biological Psychiatry, 31,* 1065–1069.

Elfgren, C., Passant, U., & Risberg, J. (1993). Neuropsychological findings in frontal lobe dementia. *Dementia, 4,* 214–219.

Englund, E., & Brun, A. (1987). Frontal lobe degeneration of the non-Alzheimer type IV. White matter changes. *Archives of Gerontology and Geriatric Psychiatry, 6,* 235–243.

*Epelbaum, J., Javoy-Agid, F., Hirsch, E., Hann, J. J., Kordon, C., Krantic, S., & Agid, Y. (1987). Brain somatostatin concentrations do not decrease in progressive supranuclear palsy. *Journal of Neurology, Neurosurgery, and Psychiatry, 50,* 1526–1528.

Ernst, J., Warner, M. H., Hochberg, M. T., & Townes, B. (1988). Factor analysis of the Halstead-Reitan Neuropsychological Battery including the WAIS and replications using the WAIS-R. *International Journal of Neuropsychology 10,* 103–105.

Farrer, L. A., Cupples, L. A., Blackburn, B. A., Kiely, M. A., Auerbach, A., Growdon, M. D., Connor-Lacke, M. P. H., Karlinsky, H., Thibert, A., Burke, J. R., Utley, C., Chui, H., Ireland, A., Duara, R., Lopez-Alberola, R., Larson, E. B., O'Connell, S., & Kukull, W. A. (1994). Interrater agreement for diagnosis of Alzheimer's disease: The MIRAGE study. *Neurology, 44, 652–656.*

*Faust, M. E., & Balota, D. A. (1997). Inhibition of return and visuospatial attention in healthy older adults and individuals with dementia of the Alzheimer type. *Neuropsychology, 11*, 13–29.

*Fautsman, W. O., Moses, J. A., Ringo, D. L., & Newcomer, J. W. (1991). Left-handedness in male schizophrenic patients is associated with increased impairment on the Luria-Nebraska neuropsychological battery. *Biological Psychiatry, 30*, 326–334.

*Feher, E. P., Doody, R. S., Whitehead, J., & Pirozzoto, F. J. (1991). Progressive nonfluent aphasia with dementia: A case report. *Journal of Geriatric Psychiatry and Neurology, 4*, 236–240.

*Fennema-Notestne, C., Butters, N., Heindel, W. C., & Salmon, D. P. (1994). Semantic homophone priming in patients with dementia of the Alzheimer's type. *Neuropsychology, 8*, 579–587.

Filley, C. M., & Cullum, C. M. (1997). Education and cognitive function in Alzheimer's disease. *Neuropsychiatry, Neuropsychology, and Behavioral Neurology, 10*, 48–51.

*Filley, C. M., Davis, K. A., Schmitz, S. P., Stears, J. C., Heaton, R. K., Kelley, J., Culig, K. M., & Scherzinger, A. L. (1989). Neuropsychological performance and magnetic resonance imaging in Alzheimer's disease and normal aging. *Neuropsychiatry, Neuropsychology, and Behavioral Neurology, 2*, 81–91.

*Filoteo, J. V., Delis, D. C., Massman, P. J., Demadura, T., Butters, N., & Salmon, D. P. (1992). Directed and divided attention in Alzheimer's disease: Impairment in shifting of attention to global and local stimuli. *Journal of Clinical and Experimental Neuropsychology, 14*, 871–883.

*Filoteo, J. V., Delis, D. C., Roman, M. J., Demadura, T., Ford, E., Butters, N., Salmon, D. P., Paulsen, J., Shults, C. W., Swenson, M., & Swerdlow, N. (1995). Visual attention and perception in patients with Huntington's disease: Comparisons with other subcortical and cortical dementias. *Journal of Clinical and Experimental Neuropsychology, 17*, 654–667.

Fischer, J. S., Foley, F. W., Aikens, J. E., Ericson, G. D., Rao, S. M., & Shindell, S. (1994). What do we really know about cognitive dysfunction, affective disorders, and stress in multiple sclerosis? A practitioner's guide. *Journal of Neurological Rehabilitation, 8*, 151–164.

*Fisher, L. M., Freed, D. M., & Corkin, S. (1990). Stroop color-word test performance in patients with Alzheimer's disease. *Journal of Clinical and Experimental Neuropsychology, 12*, 745–758.

*Fisher, P., Gatterer, G., Marterer, A., & Danielczyk, W. (1988). Nonspecificity of semantic impairment in dementia of Alzheimer's type. *Archives of Neurology, 45*, 1341–1343.

*Fleischman, D. A., Gabrieli, J. D. E., Reminger, S., Rinaldi, J., Morrell, F., & Wilson, R. (1995). Conceptual priming in perceptual identification for patients with Alzheimer's disease and a patient with right occipital lobectomy. *Neuropsychology, 9*, 187–197.

Fleming, K., Goldberg, T. E., & Gold, J. M. (1994). Applying working memory constructs to schizophrenic cognitive impairment. In A. S. David & J. C. Cutting (Eds.),

The neuropsychology of schizophrenia. (pp. 197–213). Hillsdale NJ: Lawerence Erlbaum.

Flor-Henry, P. (1976). Lateralized temporal-limbic dysfucntion and psychopathology. *Annals of the New York Academy of Science, 280,* 777–795.

*Fogliani, A. M., Parisi, R., Fogliani-Messina, T. M., & Rapisarda, V. (1985). Interhemispheric transfer of visual information in schizophrenia. *Perceptual and Motor Skills, 60,* 867–870.

Folstein, M. F., Folstein, S. E., & McHugh, P. R. (1975). "Mini-mental state": A practical method for grading the mental state of patients for the clinician. *Journal of Psychiatric Research, 12,* 189–198.

Folstein, M. F., & McHugh, P. R. (1978). Dementia syndrome of depression. In R. Katzman, R. D. Terry, & K. L. Bick (Eds.), *Alzheimer's disease: Senile dementia and related disorders.* New York: Raven Press.

*Foroud, T., Siemers, E., Kleindorfer, D., Bill, D. J., Hodes, M. E., Norton, J. A., Conneally, P. M., & Christan, J. C. (1995). Cognitive scores in carriers of Huntington's disease gene compared to non carriers. *Annals of Neurology, 37,* 657–664.

Fossum, B., Homberg, H., & Reinvang, I. (1992). Spatial and symbolic factors in performance on the Trail Making Test. *Neuropsychology, 6,* 71–75.

*Fowler, K. S., Saling, M. M., Conway, E. L., Semple, J. M., & Louis, W. J. (1997). Computerized neuropsychological tests in the early detection of dementia: Prospective findings. *Journal of the International Neuropsychological Society, 3,* 139–146.

*Frame, C. L., & Oltmanns, T. F. (1982). Serial recall by schizophrenic and affective patients during and after psychotic episodes. *Journal of Abnormal Psychology, 91,* 311–318.

'Franke, P., Maier, W., Hahn, C., & Klinger, T. (1992). Wisconsin Card Sorting Test. An indicator of vulnerability to schizophrenia? *Schizophrenia Research, 6,* 243–249.

*Franke, P., Maier, W., Hardt, J., Frieboes, R., Lichtermann, D., & Hain, C. (1993). Assessment of frontal lobe functioning in schizophrenia and unipolar major depression. *Psychopathology, 26,* 76–84.

*Franke, P., Maier, W., Hardt, J., & Hain, C. (1993). Cognitive functioning and anhedonia in subjects at risk for schizophrenia. *Schizophrenia Research, 10,* 77–84.

*Franklin, G. M., Heaton, R. K., Nelson, L. M., Filley, C. M., & Seibert, C. (1988). Correlation of neuropsychological and MRI findings in chronic / progressive multiple sclerosis. *Neurology, 38,* 1826–1829.

Franzen, G., & Ingvar, D. H. (1975). Absence of activation in frontal structures during psychological testing of chronic schizophrenics. *Journal of Neurology, Neurosurgery, and Psychiatry, 38,* 1027–1032.

*Fraser, W. I., King, K. M., Thomas, P., & Kendell, R. E. (1986). The diagnosis of schizophrenia by language analysis. *British Journal of Psychiatry, 148,* 275–278.

*Freedman, M. (1990). Object alternation and orbitofrontal system dysfunction in Alzheimer's and Parkinson's disease. *Brain and Cognition, 14,* 134–143.

Freedman, M. (1990). Parkinson's disease. In J. L. Cummings (Ed.), *Subcortical dementia.* New York: Oxford University Press.

*Freedman, M. (1994). Frontal and parietal lobe dysfunction in depression: Delayed alternation and tactile learning deficits. *Neuropsychologia, 32,* 1015–1025.

Freedman, M., & Albert, M. L. (1985). Subcortical dementia. In J. A. M. Frederiks (Ed.), *Handbook of clinical neurology, Vol. 2. (46): Neurobehavioural disorders.* U.K.: Elsevier Science Publishers.

Freedman, M., Leach, L., Kaplan, E., Winocur, G., Shulman, K. I., & Delis, D. C. (1994). *Clock drawing: A neuropsychological analysis*. New York: Oxford University Press.

*Freedman, M., & Oscar-Berman, M. (1997). Breakdown of cross-modal function in dementia. *Neuropsychiatry, Neuropsychology, and Behavioral Neurology, 10,* 102–106.

*Freedman, M., Rivoira, P., Butters, N., Sax, D. S., & Feldman, R. G. (1984). Retrograde amnesia in Parkinson's disease. *Canadian Journal of Neurological Science, 11,* 297–301.

Freeman, R. L., Galaburda, A. M., Cabal, R. D., & Geschwind, N. (1985). The neurology of depression: Cognitive and behavioral deficits with focal findings in depression and resolution after electroconvulsive therpay. *Archives of Neurology, 42,* 289–291.

Frick, R. W. (1996). The appropriate use of null hypothesis testing. *Psychological Methods, 1,* 379–390.

Friedland, R. P. (1993). Alzheimer's disease: Clinical features and differential diagnosis. *Neurology, 43* (suppl. 4), S45-S51.

*Frisoni, G. B., Beltramello, A., Geroldi, C., Weiss, C., Bianchetti, A., & Trabucci, M. (1996). Brain atrophy in fronto-temporal dementia. *Journal of Neurology, Neurosurgery and Psychiatry, 61,* 157–165.

*Frisoni, G. B., Pizzolato, G., Geroldi, C., Rossato, A., Bianchetti, A., & Trabucchi, M. (1995). Dementia of the frontal type: neuropsychological and (99Tc)-HM-PAO SPET features. *Journal of Geriatric Psychiatry and Neurology, 8,* 42–48.

*Frith, C. D., Friston, K. J., Herold, S., Silberweig, D., Fletcher, P., Camila, C., Dolan, R. J., Frackowiak, F. S. J., & Liddle, P. F. (1995). Regional brain activity in chronic schizophrenic patients during the performance of a verbal fluency task. *British Journal of Psychiatry, 167,* 343–349.

*Fuh, J. L., Liao, K. K., Wang, S. J., & Lin, K. N. (1994). Swallowing difficulty in primary progressive aphasia: A case report. *Cortex, 30,* 701–705.

*Furey-Kurkjian, M. L., Pietrini, P., Graft-Radford, N. R., Alexander, G. E., Freo, U., Szczepanik, J., & Schapiro, M. B. (1996). Visual variant of Alzheimer disease: Distinctive neuropsychological features. *Neuropsychology, 10,* 294–300.

*Gabrieli, J. D. E., Singh, J., Stebbins, G. T., & Goetz, C. G. (1996). Reduced working memory span in Parkinson's disease: Evidence for the role of a frontostriatal system in working and strategic memory. *Neuropsychology, 10,* 322–332.

*Gabrieli, J. D. E., Stebbins, G. T., Singh, J., Willingham, D. B., & Goetz, C. G. (1997). Intact mirror-tracing and impaired rotary-pursuit skill learning in patients with Huntington's disease: Evidence for dissociable memory systems in skill learning. *Neuropsychology, 11,* 272–281.

*Gainotti, G., Parlato, V., Monteleone, D., & Carlomagno, S. (1992). Neuropsychological markers of dementia on visual-spatial tasks: A comparison between Alzheimer's type and vascular forms of dementia. *Journal of Clinical and Experimental Neuropsychology, 14,* 239–252.

*Galasko, D., Clark, C., Chang, L., Miller, B., Green, R. C., Motter, R., & Seubert, P. (1997). Assessment of CSF levels of tau protein in mildly demented patients with Alzheimer's disease. *Neurology, 48,* 632–635.

*Galasko, D., Kwo-on-Yen, P. F., Klauber, M. R., & Thal, L. J. (1990). Neurological findings in Alzheimer's disease and normal aging. *Archives of Neurology, 47,* 625–627.

*Galasko, D., Klauber, M. R., Hofstetter, R., Salmon, D. P., Lasker, B., & Thal, L. J. (1990). The mini-mental state examination in the early diagnosis of Alzheimer's disease. *Archives of Neurology, 47*, 49–52.

*Galynker, I. I., & Harvey, P. D. (1992). Neuropsychological screening in the psychiatric emergency room. *Comprehensive Psychiatry, 33*, 291–295.

*Gambini, O., Abbruzzese, M., & Scarone, S. (1993). Smooth pursuit and saccadic eye movements and Wisconsin Card Sorting Test performance in obsessive compulsive disorder. *Psychiatry Research, 48*, 191–200.

Garber, J. H., Ananth, J. V., Chiu, L. C., Griswold, V. J., & Oldendorf, W. H. (1989). Nuclear magnetic resonance study of obsessive-compulsive disorder. *American Journal of Psychiatry, 146*, 1001–1005.

*Garety, P. A., Phil, M., Hemsley, D. R., & Wessely, S. (1991). Reasoning in deluded schizophrenic and paranoid patients. *The Journal of Nervous and Mental Disease, 179*, 194–201.

*Gaudino, E. A., Masur, D. M., Kaufman, L. D., Sliwinski M., & Krupp, L. B. (1995). Depression and neuropsychological performance in Eosinophilia Myalgia Syndrome: A comprehensive analysis of cognitive function in a chronic illness. *Neuropsychiatry, Neuropsychology, and Behavioral Neurology, 8*, 118–126.

*Georgiou, N., Bradshaw, J. L., & Phillips, J. G. (1997). Effect of directed attention in Huntington's disease. *Journal of Clinical and Experimental Neuropsychology, 19*, 367–377.

Geschwind, N. (1965). Disconnexion syndromes in animals and man. I and II. *Brain, 88*, 237–294; 585–644.

*Giordani, B., Berent, S., Boivin, M. J., Penney, J. B., Lehtinen, S., Markel, D. S., Hollingsworth, Z., Butterbaugh, G., Hichwa, R. D., Gusella, J. F., & Young, A. B. (1995). Longitudinal neuropsychological and genetic linkage analysis of persons at risk for Huntington's disease. *Archives of Neurology, 52*, 59–64.

Glass, G. V., McGaw, B., & Smith, M. L. (1981). *Meta-analysis in social research*. Beverly Hills: Sage.

*Gnanalingham, K. K., Byrne, E. J., Thornton, A., Sambrook, M. A., & Bannister, P. (1997). Motor and cognitive function in Lewy body dementia: Comparison with Alzheimer's and Parkinson's diseases. *Journal of Neurology, Neurosurgery, and Psychiatry, 62*, 243–252.

*Goffinet, A. M., De Volder, A. G., Gillain, C., Rectem, D., Bol, A., Michel, C., Cogneau, M., & Laterre, C. (1989). Positron tomography demonstrates frontal lobe hypometabolism in progressive supranuclear palsy. *Annals of Neurology, 25*, 131–139.

Golbe, L., Davis, P., Schcenberg, B., & Duvoisin, R. (1988). Prevalence and natural history of progressive supranuclear palsy. *Neurology, 38*, 1031–1034.

*Gold, J. M., Herman, B. P., Randolph, C., Wyler, A. R., Goldberg, T. E., & Weinberger, D. R. (1994). Schizophrenia and temporal lobe epilepsy: A neuropsychological analysis. *Archives of General Psychiatry, 51*, 265–272.

*Gold, J. M., Randolph, C., Carpenter, C. J., Goldberg, T. E., & Weinberger, D. R. (1992). Forms of memory failure in schizophrenia. *Journal of Abnormal Psychology, 101*, 487–494.

Goldberg, T. E., & Gold, J. M. (1995). Neurocognitive deficits in schizophrenia. In S. R. Hirsch & D. R. Weinberger (Eds.), *Schizophrenia*. Oxford: Blackwell Science.

Goldberg, T. E., Gold, J. M., Greenberg, R., & Griffin, S. (1993). Contrasts between patients with affective disorders and patients with schizophrenia on a neuropsychological test battery. *American Journal of Psychiatry, 150*, 1355–1362.

Goldberg, T. E., Kelsoe, J. R., Weinberger, D. R., Pliskin, N. H., Kirwin, P. D., & Berman, K. F. (1988). Performance of schizophrenia patients on putative neuropsychological tests of frontal lobe function. *International Journal of Neuroscience, 42*, 51–58.

*Goldberg, T. E., Ragland, D. R.., Gold, J. M., Bigelow, L. B., Torrey, E. F., & Weinberger, D. R. (1990). Neuropsychological assessment of monozygotic twins disconcordant for schizophrenia. *Archives of General Psychiatry, 47*, 1066–1072.

*Goldberg, T. E., Saint-Cyr, J. A., & Weinberger, D. R. (1990). Assessment of procedural learning and problem solving in schizophrenic patients by tower of Hanoi type tasks. *Journal of Neuropsychiatry and Clinical Neurosciences, 2*, 165–173.

Goldberg, T.E., Weinberger, D.R., Pliskin, N.H., Berman, K.F., & Plodd, M.H. (1987). Further evidence for dementia of the prefrontal type in schizophrenia? *Archives of General Psychiatry, 44*, 1043–1051.

*Goldberg, T. E., Weinberger, D. R., Pliskin, N. H., Berman, K. F., & Plodd, M. H. (1989). Recall memory deficit in schizophrenia: A possible manifestation of prefrontal dysfunction. *Schizophrenia Research, 2*, 251–257.

Goldman, R. S., Axelrod, B. N., & Taylor, S. F. (1996). Neuropsychological aspects of schizophrenia. In I. Grant & K. M. Adams (Eds.), *Neuropsychological assessment of neuropsychiatric disorders*. (pp. 504–525). New York: Oxford University Press.

*Goldstein, F. C., Levin, H. S., Roberts, V. J., Goldman, W. P., Kalechstein, A. S., Winslow, M., & Goldstein, S. J. (1996). Neuropsychological effects of closed head injury in older adults: A comparison with Alzheimer's disease. *Neuropsychology, 10*, 147–154.

Goldstein, G. (1984) Comprehensive neuropsychological assessment batteries. In G. Goldstein, & M. Hersen (Eds.), *Handbook of psychological assessment*. (pp. 181–210). New York: Pergamon Press.

Goldstein, G. (1986). The neuropsychology of schizophrenia. In I. Grant & K. M. Adams (Eds.), *Neuropsychological assessment of neuropsychiatric disorders*. New York: Oxford University Press.

Goldstein, G. (1990). Neuropsychological heterogeneity in schizophrenia: A consideration of abstraction and problem-solving abilities. *Archives of Clinical Neuropsychology, 5*, 251–264.

*Goldstein, G., & Zubin, J. (1990). Neuropsychological differences between young and old schizophrenics with and without associated neurological dysfunction. *Schizophrenia Research, 3*, 117–126.

*Goldstein, P. C., Rosenbaum, G., & Taylor, M. A. (1997). Assessment of differential attention mechanisms in seizure disorders and schizophrenia. *Neuropsychology, 11*, 309–317.

Golinkoff, M., & Seeney, J. A. (1989). Cognitive impairments in depression. *Journal of Affective Disorders, 17*, 105–112.

Goodglass, H., & Kaplan, E. (1983a). *Boston Diagnostic Aphasia Examination (BDAE)*. Philadelphia: Lea and Febiger. Odessa, FL: Psychological Assessment Resources.

Goodglass, H., & Kaplan, E. (1983b). *The assessment of aphasia and related disorders* (2nd ed.). Philadelphia, PA: Lea and Febiger.

Goodman, L. (1953). Alzheimer's disease. A clinico-paphologic analysis of twenty-three cases with a theory on causation. *Journal of Nervous and Mental Disease, 117*, 97–130.

Goodman, W. K., Price, L. H., & Rasmussen, S. A. (1989a). The Yale-Brown Obsessive Compulsive Scale: I. Development, use and reliability. *Archives of General Psychiatry, 46*, 1006–1011.

Goodman, W. K., Price, L. H., & Rasmussen, S. A. (1989b). The Yale-Brown Obessive Compulsive Scale II: Validity. *Archives of General Psychiatry, 46*, 1012–1016.

Goodstein, R. K., & Ferrell, R. B. (1977). Multiple sclerosis presenting as depressive illness. *Disorders of the Nervous System, 38*, 127–131.

*Gourovitch, M. L., Goldberg, T. E., & Weinberger, D. R. (1996). Verbal fluency deficits in patients with schizophrenia: Semantic fluency is differentially impaired as compared with phonologic fluency. *Neuropsychology, 10*, 573–577.

Grady, C. L., Haxby, J. V., Horwitz, B., Sundaram, M., Berg, G., Schapiro, M., Friedland, R. P., & Rapoport, S. I. (1988). Longitudinal study of the early neuropsychological and cerebral metabolic changes in dementia of the Alzheimer type. *Journal of Clinical and Experimental Neuropsychology, 10*, 576–596.

*Graff-Radford, N. R., Damasio, A. R., Hyman, B. T., Hart, M. N., Tranel, D., Damasio, H., Van Hoesen, G. W., & Rezai, K. (1990). Progressive aphasia in a patient with Pick's disease: A neuropsychological, radiologic, and anatomic study. *Neurology, 40*, 620–626.

*Grafman, J., Litvan, I., Gomez, C., & Chase, T. N. (1990). Frontal lobe function in progressive supranuclear palsy. *Archives of Neurology, 47*, 553–558.

Grafman, J., Litvan, I., & Stark, M. (1995). Neuropsychological features of progressive supranuclear palsy. *Brain & Cognition, 28*, 311–320.

*Grafman, J., Rao, S. M., Bernardin, L., & Leo, G. J. (1991). Automatic memory processes in patients with multiple sclerosis. *Archives of Neurology, 48*, 1072–1075.

Grafman, J., Rao, S. M., & Litvan, I. (1990). Disorders of memory. In S.M. Rao (Ed.), *Neurobehavioral aspects of multiple sclerosis* (pp. 102–117). New York: Oxford University Press.

*Grafman, J., Weingartner, H., Newhouse, P. A., Thompson, K., Lalonde, F., Litvan, I., & Molechan, S. (1990). Implicit learning in patients with Alzheimer's disease. *Pharmacopsychiatry, 23*, 94–101.

*Graham, K. S., & Hodges, J. R. (1997). Differentiating the roles of the hippocampal complex and the neocortex in long-term memory storage: Evidence from the study of semantic dementia and Alzheimer's disease. *Neuropsychology, 11*, 77–89.

*Graham, K. S., Hodges, J. R., & Patterson, K. (1994). The relationship between comprehension and oral reading in progresseve fluent aphasia. *Neuropsychologia, 32*, 299–316.

*Granholm, E., & Butters, N. (1988). Associative encoding and retrieval in Alzheimer's and Huntington's disease. *Brain and Cognition, 7*, 335–347.

Green, B. F., & Hall, J. A. (1984). Quantitative methods for literature reviews. *Annual review of psychology, 35*, 37–53.

*Green, J., Morris, J. C., Sandson, J., McKeel Jr., D. W., & Miller, J.W. (1990). Progressive aphasia: A precursor or global dementia? *Neurology, 40*, 423–429.

*Green, J. D. W., Hodges, J. R., & Baddeley, A. D. (1995). Autobiographical memory and executive function in early dementia of Alzheimer type. *Neuropsychologia, 33*, 1647–1670.

*Green, M., & Walker, E. (1985). Neuropsychological performance and positive and negative symptoms in schizophrenia. *Journal of Abnormal Psychology, 94*, 460–469.

*Green, M., & Walker, E. (1986). Attentional performance in positive and negative symptom schizophrenia. *The Journal of Nervous and Mental Disease, 174*, 208–213.

*Greenwood, P. M., Parasuraman, R., & Alexander, G. E. (1997). Controlling the focus of spatial attention during visual search: Effects of advanced aging and Alzheimer disease. *Neuropsychology, 11*, 3–12.

*Greiffenstein, M., Milberg, W., Lewis, R., & Rosenbaum, G. (1981). Temporal lobe epilepsy and schizophrenia: Comparison of reaction time deficits. *Journal of Abnormal Psychology, 90,* 105–112.

Gronwall, D. M. A. (1977). Paced auditory serial-addition task: A measure of recovery from concussion. *Perceptual and Motor Skill, 44,* 367–373.

Gronwall, D. M. A., & Wrightson, P. (1981). Memory and information processing capacity after mild head injury. *Journal of Clinical Neuropsychology, 2,* 51–60.

*Grosse, D. A., & Wilson, R. S. (1991). Maze learning in Alzheimer disease. *Brain and Cognition, 15,* 1–9.

Grossman, I., Kaufman, A. S., Mednitsky, S., & Scharff, L. (1994). Neurocognitive abilities for a clinically depressed sample versus a mathced control group of normal individuals. *Psychiatry Research, 51,* 231–244.

*Grossman, M., Carvelli, S., Gollomp, S., Stern, M. B., Vernon, G., & Hurtig, H. I. (1991). Sentence comprehension and praxis deficits in Parkinson's disease. *Neurology, 41,* 1620–1626.

*Grossman, M., Carvelli, S., Peltzer, L., Stern, M. B., Gollomp, S., & Hurtig, H. I. (1993). Visual construction impairments in Parkinson's disease. *Neuropsychology, 7,* 536–547.

*Grossman, M., Mickanin, J., Onishi, K., & Hughes, E. (1995). An aspect of sentence processing in Alzheimer's disease: Quantifier-noun agreement. *Neurology, 45,* 85–91.

*Grossman, M., Mickanin, J., Onishi, K., Robinson, K. M., & D'Esposito, M. (1996). Freehand drawing impairments in probable Alzheimer's disease. *Journal of the International Neuropsychological Society, 2,* 226–235.

*Grundman, M., Corey-Bloom, S., Jernigan, T., Archibald, S., & Thal, L. J. (1996). Low body weight in Alzheimer's disease is associated with mesial temporal cortex atrophy. *Neurology, 46,* 1585–1592.

*Gruzelier, J., Liddiard, D., Davis, L., & Wilson, L. (1990). Topographical EEG differences between schizophrenic patients and controls during neuropsychological functional activation. *International Journal of Psychophysiology, 8,* 275–282.

*Gruzelier, J., Seymour, K., Wilson, L., Jolley, A., & Hirsch, S. (1988). Impairments on neuropsychological tests of temporo-hippocampal and frontohippocampal functions and word fluency in remitting schizophrenia and affective disorders. *Archives of General Psychiatry, 45,* 623–629.

Gualtieri, C. T. (1995). The problem of mild brain injury. *Neuropsychiatry, Neuropsychology, and Behavioral Neurology, 8,* 127–136.

*Guich, S. M., Buchsbaum, M. S., Burgwald, L., Wu, J., Haier, R., Asarnow, R., Nuechterlein, K., & Patkin, S. (1989). Effect of attention on frontal distribution of delta activity and cerebral metabolic rate in schizophrenia. *Schizophrenia Research, 2,* 439–448.

*Guilmette, T. J., & Rasile, D. (1995). Sensitivity, specificity, and diagnostic accuracy of verbal memory measures in the assessment of mild head injury. *Neuropsychology, 9,* 338–344.

*Gur, R. C., Saykin, A. J., Blonder, L. X., & Gur, R. E. (1987). "Behavioral imaging":II. Application of the quantitative algorithm to hypothesis testing in a population of hemiparkinsonian patients. *Neuropsychiatry, Neuropsychology, and Behavioral Neurology, 1,* 87–96.

Gur, R. E. (1977). Motoric laterality imbalance in schizophrenia. *Archives of General Psychiatry, 34,* 33–37.

Gur, R. E. (1978). Left hemisphere dysfunction and left hemisphere overactivation in schizophrenia. *Journal of Abnormal Psychology*, 87, 226–238.

Gusella, J. F., MacDonald, M. E., Ambrose, C. M., & Duyao, M. P. (1993). Molecular genetics of Huntington's disease. *Archives of Neurology*, 50, 1157–1163.

Gusella, J. F., Wexler, N. S., Conneally, P. M., Naylor, S. L., Anderson, M. A., Tanzi, R. E., Watkins, P. C., Ottina, K. Wallace, M. R., Sakaguchi, A. Y., Young, A. B., Shoulson, I., Bonilla, E., & Martin, J. B. (1983). A polymorphic DNA marker genetically linked to Huntington's disease. *Nature, 306*, 234–238.

Gusella, J. F., MacDonald, M. E., Ambrose, C. M., Duyao, M. P. (1993). Molecular genetics of Huntington's disease. *Archives of Neurology*, 50, 1157–1163.

Gusella, J. F., Wexler, N. S., Conneally, P. M., Naylor, S. L., Anderson, M. A., Tanzi, R. E., Watkins, P. C., Ottina, K., Wallace, M. R., Sakaguchi, A. Y., Young, A. B., Shoulson, I., Bonilla, E., & Martin, J. B. (1983). A polymorphic DNA marker genetically linked to Huntington's Disease. *Nature, 306*, 234–238.

Gustafson, L. (1987). Frontal lobe degeneration of the non-Alzheimer type II. Clinical picture and differential diagnosis. *Archives of Gerontology and Geriatric Psychiatry*, 6, 209–233.

Gustafson, L. (1993). Clinical picture of frontal lobe degeneration of non-Alzheimer type. *Dementia*, 4, 143–148.

Guttman, L. (1985). The illogic of statistical inference for cumulative science. *Applied Stochastic Models and Data Analysis, 1*, 3–10.

*Haaland, K. Y., Harrington, D. L., O'Brien, S., & Hermanowicz, N. (1997). Cognitive-motor learning in Parkinson's disease. *Neuropsychology*, 11, 180–186.

Hachinski, V. C. (1997). Frontotemporal degeneration, Pick's disease, and corticobasal degeneration. Archives of Neurology, 54, 1429.

Hachinski, V. C., Iliff, L. D., & Zilhka, E. (1975). Cerebral blood flow in dementia. *Archives of Neurology*, 32, 632–637.

*Hagger, C., Buckley, P., Kenny, J. T., Friedman, L., Ubogy, D., & Meltzer, H. Y. (1993). Improvement in cognitive functions and psychiatric symptoms in treating-refractory schizophrenic patients receiving clozapine. *Biological Psychiatry, 34*, 702–712.

*Hain, C., Maier, W., Klinger, T., & Frankle, P. (1993). Positive/negative symptomatology and experimental measures of attention in schizophrenic patients. *Psychopathology, 26*, 62–69.

Halstead, W. C. (1947). *Brain and intelligence*. Chicago: University of Chicago Press.

Hamsher, K. deS., & Roberts, R. J. (1985). Memory for recent US presidents in patients with cerebral disease. *Journal of Clinical and Experimental Neuropsychology, 7*, 1–13.

*Hanes, K. R., Andrewes, D. G., & Pantelis, C. (1995). Cognitive flexibility and complex integration in Parkinson's disease, Huntington's disease and schizophrenia. *Journal of the International Neuropsychological Society, 1*, 545–553.

*Hanes, K. R., Andrewes, D. G., Smith, D. J., & Pantelis, C. (1996). A brief assessment of executive control dysfunction: Discriminant validity and homogeneity of planning, set shift, and fluency measures. *Archives of Clinical Neuropsychology, 11*, 185–191.

*Harrell, L. E., Duvall, E., Folks, D. G., Duke, L., Bartolucci, A., Conboy, T., Callaway, R., & Kerns, D. (1991). The relationship of high-intensity signals on magnetic resonance images to cognitive and psychiatric state in Alzheimer's disease. *Archives of Neurology, 48*, 1136–1140.

*Harrington, D. L., Haaland, K. Y., Yeo, R. A., & Marder, E. (1990). Procedural memory in Parkinson's disease: Impaired motor but not visuospatial learning. *Journal of Clinical and Experimental Neuropsychology, 12,* 323–339.

*Harris, J. G., Adler, L. E., Young, D. A., Cullum, C. M., Rilling, L. M., Cicerello, A., Intermann, P. M., & Freedman, R. (1996). Neuropsychological dysfunction in parents of schizophrenics. *Schizophrenia Research, 20,* 253–260.

Hartlage, S., Alloy, L. B., Vazquez, C., & Dykman, B. (1993). Automatic and effortful processing in depression. *Psychological Bulletin, 113,* 247–278.

*Hartman, M. (1991). The use of semantic knowledge in Alzheimer's disease: Evidence for impairments of attention. *Neuropsychologia, 29,* 213–228.

Haser, L., & Zacks, R. T. (1979). Automatic and effortful processes in memory. *Journal of Experimental Psychology: General, 108,* 356–388.

Hauser, S. L., Dawson, D. M., Lehrich, J. R., Beal, M. F., Devy, S. V., Propper, R. D., Mills, J. A., & Weiner, H. L. (1983). Intensive immunosuppression in progressive multiple sclerosis. *New England Journal of Medicine, 308,* 173–180.

Hauw, J. J., Daniel, S. E., Dickson, D., Horoupian, D. S., Jellinger, K., Lantos, P., McKee, A., Tabaton, M., & Litvan, I. (1994). Preliminary NINDS neuropathologic criteria for Steele-Richardson-Olszewski syndrome (progressive supranuclear palsy). *Neurology, 44,* 2015–2019.

*Haxby, J. V., Grady, C. L., Koss, E., Horwitz, B., Heston, L., Schapiro, M., Friedland, R. P., & Rappoport, S. I. (1990). Longitudinal study of cerebral metabolic asymmetries and associated neuropsychological patterns in early dementia of the Alzheimer type. *Archives of Neurology, 47,* 753–760.

*Haxby, J. V., Grady, C. L., Koss, E., Horwitz, B., Schapiro, M., Friedland, R. P., & Rapoport, S. I. (1988). Heterogeneous anterior-posterior metabolic patterns in dementia of the Alzheimer's type. *Neurology, 38,* 1853–1863.

*Harvey, P. D. (1983). Speech competence in manic and schizophrenic psychoses: The association between clinically rated thought disorder and cohesion and reference performance. *Journal of Abnormal Psychology, 92,* 368–377.

*Harvey, P. D., Earle-Boyer, E. A., Wielgus, M. S., & Levinson, J. C. (1986). Encoding, memory, and thought disorder in schizophrenia and mania. *Schizophrenia Bulletin, 12,* 252–261.

*Harvey, P. D., Keefe, R. S. E., Moskowitz, J., Putrram, K. M., Mohs, R. C., & Davis, K. L. (1990). Attentional markers of vulnerability to schizophrenia: Performance of medicated and unmedicated patients and normals. *Psychiatry Research, 33,* 179–188.

*Harvey, S. A., Nelson, E., Haller, J. W., & Early, T. S. (1993). Lateralized attentional abnormality in schizophrenia is correlated with severity of symptoms. *Biological Psychiatry, 33,* 93–99.

Heaton, R. K. (1981). *Wisconsin card sorting test (WCST).* Odessa, FL: Psychological Assessment Resources.

Heaton, R. K., Chelune, G. J., Talley, J., Kay, G. G., & Curtiss, G. (1993). *Wisconsin card sorting test manual—revised and expanded.* Psychological Assessment Resources.

Heaton, R. K., & Crowley, T. J. (1981). Effects of psychiatric disorders and their somatic treatments on neuropsychological test results. In S. B. Filskov & T. J. Boll (Eds.), *Handbook of clinical neuropsychology.* (pp. 481–525). New York: John Wiley and Sons.

Heaton, R. K., & Palmer, B. W. (1998). Neuropsychologically normal schizoprhenia. *Journal of the International Neuropsychological Society, 4,* 220.

*Heaton, R. K., Paulsen, J. S., McAdams, L. A., Kuck, J., Zisook, S., Braff, D., Harris, M. J., & Jeste, D. V. (1994). Neuropsychological deficits in schizophrenics: Relationship to age, chronicity, and dementia. *Archives of General Psychiatry, 51,* 469–476.

Hedges, L. V., & Olkin, I. (1985). *Statistical methods for meta-analysis.* New York: Academic Press.

Heilman, K. M. (1973). Ideational apraxia—a re-definition. *Brain, 96,* 861–864.

Heilman, K. M. (1997). Handedness. In L. J. G. Rothi & K. M. Heilman (Eds.), *Apraxia: The neuropsychology of action.* (pp. 19–28). UK: Psychology Press.

Heilman, K. M., & Gonzalez Rothi, L. J. (1993). Apraxia. In K. M. Heilman & E. Valenstien (Eds.), *Clinical neuropsychology* (pp. 141–163). (3rd ed.), New York: Oxford University Press.

Heilman, K. M., & Valenstein, E. (1972). Frontal lobe neglect in man. *Neurology, 22,* 660–664.

Heilman, K. M., & Valenstein, E. (1979). Mechanisms underlying hemispatial neglect. *Annals of Neurology, 5,* 166–170.

Heilman, K. M., & Valenstein, E. (1993). *Clinical neuropsychology.* (3rd ed.), New York: Oxford University Press.

Heilman, K. M., Watson, R. T., & Valenstein, E. (1993). Neglect and related disorders. In K. M. Heilman & E. Valenstein (Eds.), *Clinical neuropsychology.* (pp. 279–336). (3rd ed.), New York: Oxford University Press.

Heindel, W. C., Salmon, D. P., & Butters, N. (1989). Neuropsychological differentiation of memory impairments in dementia. In G. Gilmore, P. Whitehouse, & M. Wyke (Eds.), *Memory, aging, and dementia.* New York: Springer.

*Heindel, W. C., Salmon, D. P., & Butters, N. (1990). Pictorial priming and cued recall in Alzheimer's and Huntington's disease. *Brain and Cognition, 13,* 282–295.

*Heindel, W. C., Salmon, D. P., & Butters, N. (1991). The biasing of weight judgment in Alzheimer's and Huntington's disease: A priming or programming phenomenon? *Journal of Clinical and Experimental Neuropsychology, 13,* 189–203.

Heinrichs, R. W. (1990). Variables associated with Wisconsin Card Sorting Test performance in neuropsychiatric patients referred for assessment. *Neuropsychiatry, Neuropsychology, and Behavioral Neurology, 3,* 107–112.

Heinrichs, R. W. (1993). Schizophrenia and the brain: Conditions for a neuropsychology of madness. *American Psychologist, 48,* 221–233.

Heinrichs, R. W. (1994). Performance on tests of diencephalic-hippocampal verbal memory function in schizophrenia, Korsakoff's syndrome and personality disorder. *Schizophrenia Research, 13,* 127–132.

Heinrichs, R. W. (1999). *Searching the brain for Schizoprhenia: The end of madness.* New York: Oxford University Press.

Heinrichs, R. W., & Awad, G. (1993). Neurocognitive subtypes of chronic schizophrenia. *Schizophrenia Research, 13,* 49–58.

Heinrichs, R. W., Ruttan, L. A., Zakzanis, K. K., & Case, D. (1997). Parsing schizophrenia with neurocognitive tests: Evidence of stability and validity. *Brain and Cognition, 35,* 207–224.

Heinrichs, R. W., & Zakzanis, K. K. (1998). Neurocognitive deficit in schizophrenia: A quantitative review of the evidence. *Neuropsychology, 12,* 426–445.

*Henderson, V. W., Buckwalter, J. G., Sobel, E., Freed, D. M., & Diz, M. M. (1992). The agraphia of Alzheimer's disease. *Neurology, 42,* 776–784.

*Herlitz, A., Adolfsson, R., Backman, L., Nilsson, L. G. (1991). Cue utilization following different forms of encoding in mildly, moderately, and severely demented patients with Alzheimer's disease. *Brain and Cognition, 15*, 119–130.

*Hietanen, M., & Teravainen, H. (1988). The effect of age of disease onset on neuropsychological performance in Parkinson's disease. *Journal of Neurology, Neurosurgery, and Psychiatry, 51*, 244–249.

*Highgate-Maynard, S., & Neufeld, R. W. J. (1986). Schizophrenic memory-search performance involving nonverbal stimulus properties. *Journal of Abnormal Psychology, 95*, 67–73.

*Hodges, J. R., & Patterson, K. (1995). Is semantic memory consistently impaired early in the course of Alzheimer's disease? Neuroanatomical and diagnostic implications. *Neuropsychologia, 33*, 441–459.

Hodges, J. R., Patterson, K. E., Oxbury, S., & Funnell, E. (1992). Semantic dementia: Progressive fluent aphasia with temporal lobe atrophy. *Brain, 115*, 1783–1806.

*Hodges, J. R., Salmon, D. P., & Butters, N. (1990). Differential impairment of semantic and episodic memory in Alzheimer's and Huntington's diseases: A controlled prospective study. *Journal of Neurology, Neurosurgery, and Psychiatry, 53*, 1089–1095.

*Hodges, J. R., Salmon, D. P., & Butters, N. (1992). Semantic memory impairment in Alzheimer's disease: Failure of access or degraded knowledge? *Neuropsychologia, 30*, 301–314.

*Hodges, J. R., Salmon, D. P., Butters, N. (1993). Recognition and naming of famous faces in Alzheimer's disease: A cognitive analysis. *Neuropsychologia, 31*, 775–788.

Hoehn, M. M., & Yahr, M. D. (1967). Parkinsonism: Onset, progression and mortality. *Neurology, 17*, 427–442.

*Hollander, E., Cohen, L., Richards, M., Mullen, L., Decaria, C., & Stern, Y. (1993). A pilot study of the neuropsychology of obsessive compulsive disorder and Parkinson's disease: Basic ganglia disorders. *Journal of Neuropsychiatry and Clinical Neurosciences, 5*, 104–107.

*Hollander, E., & Wong, C. M. (1996). The relationship between executive function impairment and serotonergic sensitivity in obsessive compulsive disorder. *Neuropsychiatry, Neuropsychology, and Behavioral Neurology, 9*, 230–233.

*Honig, L. S., Ramsay, E., & Sheremata, W. A. (1992). Event-related potential P300 in multiple sclerosis. *Archives of Neurology, 49*, 44–50.

Hooper, H. E. (1983). *Hooper Visual Organization Test (VOT)*. Los Angeles: Western Psychological Services.

*Holzman, P. S., Shenton, M. E., & Solovay, M. R. (1986). Quality of thought disorder in differential diagnosis. *Schizophrenia Bulletin, 12*, 360–372.

Howard, D., & Patterson, K. E. (1992). *Pyramids and palm trees: A test of semantic access from pictures and words*. Thames Valley Publishing.

*Hua, M. S., & Lu, C. S. (1994). Multiple system atrophy and visuospatial function. *Neuropsychology, 8*, 91–94.

Huber, S. J., & Bornstein, R. A. (1992). Neuropsychological evaluation of Parkinson's disease. In S. J. Huber & J. L. Cummings (Eds.), *Parkinson's disease: Neurobehavioral aspects*. (pp.32–45). New York. Oxford University Press.

*Huber, S. J., Christy, J. A., & Paulson, G. W. (1991). Cognitive heterogeneity associated with clinical subtypes of Parkinson's disease. *Neuropsychiatry, Neuropsychology, and Behavioral Neurology, 4*, 147–157.

Huber, S. J., & Cummings, J. L. (1992). *Parkinson's disease: Neurobehavioral aspects.* New York: Oxford University Press.

*Huber, S. J., Freidenberg, D. L., Shuttleworth, E. C., Paulson, G. W., & Christy, J. A. (1989). Neuropsychological impairments associated with severity of Parkinson's disease. *Journal of Neuropsychiatry and Clinical Neurosciences, 1,* 154–158.

*Huber, S. J., Freidenberg, D. L., Shuttleworth, E. C., Paulson, G. W., & Clapp, L. E. (1989). Neuropsychological similarities in lateralized Parkinsonism. *Cortex, 25,* 461–470.

Huber, S. J., & Paulson, G. W. (1985). The concept of subcortical dementia. *American Journal of Psychiatry, 142,* 1312–1317.

*Huber, S. J., Shuttleworth, E. C., Christy, J. A., Chakeres, D. W., Curtin, A., & Paulson, G. W. (1989). Magnetic resonance imaging in dementia of Parkinson's disease. *Journal of Neurology, Neurosurgery, and Psychiatry, 52,* 1221–1227.

*Huber, S. J., Shuttleworth, E. C., Freidenberg, D. L. (1989). Neuropsychological differences between the dementias of Alzheimer's and Parkinson's disease. *Archives of Neurology, 46,* 1287–1291.

*Huberman, M., Moscovitch, M., Freedman, M. (1994). Comparison of patients with Alzheimer's and Parkinson's disease on different explicit and implicit tests of memory. *Neuropsychiatry, Neuropsychology, and Behavioral Neurology, 7,* 185–193.

*Huff, F. J., Becker, J. T., Belle, S. H., Nebes, R. D., Holland, A. L., & Boller, F. (1987). Cognitive deficits and clinical diagnosis of Alzheimer's disease. *Neurology, 37,* 1119–1124.

Hunter, J. E., & Schmidt, F. L. (1990). *Methods of meta-analysis: Correcting error and bias in research findings.* Newbury Park, CA: Sage.

Hunter, J. E., Schmidt, F. L., & Jackson, G. B. (1982). *Meta-analysis: Cumulating research findings across studies.* Beverly Hills: Sage.

Huntington, G. (1872). On chorea. *Medical Surgical Reporter, 26,* 317–321.

Hyman, B. T., Arriagada, P. V., Van Hoesen, G. W., & Damasio, A. R. (1993). Memory impairment in Alzheimer's disease: An anatomical perspective. In R. W. Parks, R. F. Zec, & R. S. Wilson (Eds.), *Neuropsychology of Alzheimer's disease and other dementias* (pp. 138–150). New York: Oxford University Press.

Hyman, B. T., Van Hoesen, G. W., Damasio, A. R., & Barnes, C. L. (1984). Alzheimer's disease: Cell specific pathology isolates the hippocampal formation. *Science, 225,* 1168–1170.

Iacono, W. G., Moreau, M., Beiser, M., Heming, J. A. E., & Liu, T. Y. (1992). Smooth-pursuit eye tracking in first episode psychotic patients and their relatives. *Journal of Abnormal Psychology, 101,* 104–116.

*Incalzi, R. A., Capparella, O., Gemma, A., Marra, C., & Carbonin, P. U. (1995). Effects of aging and of Alzheimer's disease on verbal memory. *Journal of Clinical and Experimental Neuropsychology, 17,* 580–589.

Insel, T. R. (1992). Toward a neuroanatomy of obsessive-compulsive disorder. *Archives of General Psychiatry, 49,* 739–744.

*Jack, C. R., Peterson, R. C., O' Brien, P. C., & Tangalos, E. G. (1992). MR-based hippocampal volumetry in the diagnosis of Alzheimer's disease. *Neurology, 42,* 183–188.

Jacobson, N. S., & Hollon, S. D. (1996). Cognitive-behavior therapy versus pharmacotherapy: Now that the jury's returned its verdict, it's time to present the rest of the evidence. *Journal of Consulting and Clinical Psychology, 64,* 74–80.

Jastak, S., & Wilkinson, G. S. (1984). *Wide Range Achievement Test—Revised.* Wilmington DE: Jastak Assessment Systems.

*Javitt, D. C., Doneshka, P., Zylberman, I., Ritter, W., Vaughan Jr., H. G. (1993). Impairment of early cortical processing in schizophrenia: An event-related potential confirmation study. *Biological Psychiatry, 33,* 513–519.

Jenike, M. A., Baer, L., & Minichiello, W. E. (1990). *Obsessive compulsive disorders: Theory and management.* Chicago: Year Book Medical Publishers.

Jernigan, T. L., Salmon, D. P., Butters, N., & Hesselink, J. R. (1991). Cerebral structure on MRI, Part II: Specific changes in Alzheimer's and Huntington's diseases. *Biological Psychiatry, 29,* 68–81.

Jeste, D. V., & Lohr, J. B. (1989). Hippocampal pathologic findings in schizophrenia: A morphometric study. *Archives of General Psychiatry, 46,* 1019–1024.

*Jeste, D. V., Wragg, R. E., Salmon, D. P., Harris, M. J., & Thal, L. J. (1992). Cognitive deficits of patients with Alzheimer's disease with and without delusions. *American Journal of Psychiatry, 149,* 184–189.

Johnson, B. T. (1989). *DSTAT: Software for the meta-analytic review of research literatures.* Hillsdale NJ: Lawerence Erlbaum.

*Johnson, D. L., & Kesner, R. P. (1997). Comparison of temporal order memory in early and middle stage Alzheimer's disease. *Journal of Clinical and Experimental Neuropsychology, 19,* 83–100.

Johnson, K. A., Jones, K., Holman, B. L., Becker, J. A., Spiers, P. A., Satlin, A., & Albert, M. S. (1998). Preclinical prediction of Alzheimer's disease using SPECT. *Neurology, 50,* 1563–1571.

*Johnson, M., Bonilla, J. L., & Hermann, A. M. (1997). Effects of relatedness and number of distractors on attribute judgment in Alzheimer's disease. *Neuropsychology, 11,* 392–399.

*Johnson, M., Hermann, A. M., & Bonilla, J. L. (1995). Semantic relations and Alzheimer's disease: Typicality and directions of testing. *Neuropsychology, 9,* 529–536.

Johnson, M. H., & Margo, P. A. (1987). Effects of mood and severity on memory processes in depression and mania. *Psychological Bulletin, 101,* 28–40.

*Johnson, O., & Crockett, D. (1982). Changes in perceptual asymmetries with clinical improvement of depression and schizophrenia. *Journal of Abnormal Psychology, 91,* 45–54.

*Johnson, R., Litvan, F., & Grafman, J. (1991). Progressive supranuclear palsy: Altered sensory processing leads to degraded cognition. *Neurology, 41,* 1257–1262.

Jones, C. L. (19??). Recovery from head trauma: A curvilinear process? In C. J. Long & L. K. Ross (Eds.), *Handbook of head trauma: Acute care to recovery.* (pp. 247–270). New York: Plenum.

*Jones, S. H., Gray, J. A., & Hemsley, D. R. (1992). Loss of the kamin blocking effect in acute but not chronic schizophrenics. *Biological Psychiatry, 32,* 739–755.

*Jones, S. H., Hemsley, D. R., & Gray, J. A. (1991). Contextual effects on choice reaction time and accuracy in acute and chronic schizophrenics: Impairment in selective attention or in the inference of prior learning? *British Journal of Psychiatry, 159,* 415–421.

Jones-Gotman, M., & Milner, B. (1977). Design fluency: The invention of nonsense drawings after focal cortical lesions. *Neuropsychologia, 15,* 653–674.

*Jordan, N., Sagar, H. J., & Cooper, J. A. (1992). A component analysis of the generation and release of isometric force in Parkinson's disease. *Journal of Neurology, Neurosurgery, and Psychiatry, 55,* 572–576.

*Jordan, N., Sagar, H. J., & Cooper, J. A. (1992). Cognitive components of reaction time in Parkinson's disease. *Journal of Neurology, Neurosurgery, and Psychiatry, 55*, 658–664.

*Joyce, E. M., Collinson, S. L., & Crichton, P. (1996). Verbal fluency in schizophrenia: Relationship with executive function, semantic memory and clinical alogia. *Psychological Medicine, 26*, 39–49.

*Kahn, E. M., Weiner, R. D., Coppola, R., Kudler, H. S., & Schultz, K. (1993). Spectral and topographic analysis of EEG in schizophrenic patients. *Biological Psychiatry, 33*, 284–290.

Kaplan, E. (1988). A process approach to neuropsychological assessment. In T. Boll & B. K. Bryant (Eds.), *Clinical neuropsychology and brain function: Research, measurement, and practice*. Washington, D.C.: American Psychological Association.

Kaplan, E. (1990). The process approach to neuropsychological assessment of psychiatric patients. *Journal of Neuropsychiatry, 2*, 72–87.

Kaplan, E., Fein, D., Morris, R., & Delis, D. C. (1991). *WAIS-R as a neuropsychological instrument*. San Antonio, TX: The Psychological Corporation.

Kaplan, E., Gallagher, R., & Glosser, G. (in press). Aphasia-related disorders. In M. Serno (Ed.), *Acquired aphasia* (3rd edn). New York: Academic Press.

Kaplan, E., Goodglass, H., & Weintraub, S. (1983). *Boston Naming Test*. Philadelphia: Lea & Febiger.

Kaplan, H. I., & Saddock, B. J. (1989). *Comprehensive textbook of psychiatry*. (4th ed.). Baltimore: Williams & Wilkins.

*Karbe, H., Kertesz, A., & Polk, M. (1993). Profiles of language impairment in primary progressive aphasia. *Archives of Neurology, 50*, 193–201.

*Kareken, D. A., Gur, R. C., Mozley, P. D., Mozley, L. H., Saykin, A. J., Stasel, D. L., & Gur, R. E. (1995). Cognitive functioning and neuroanatomic volume measures in schizophrenia. *Neuropsychology, 9*, 211–219.

*Kareken, D. A., Moberg, P. J., & Gur, R. C. (1996). Proactive inhibition and semantic organization: Relationship with verbal memory in patients with schizophrenia. *Journal of the International Neuropsychological Society, 2*, 486–493.

*Katsanis, J., Iacono, W. G., & Beiser, M. (1990). Anhedonia and perceptual aberration in first-episode psychotic patients and their relatives. *Journal of Abnormal Psychology, 99*, 202–206.

Katzen, H. L., Levin, B. E., & Llabre, M. L. (1998). Age of disease onset influences cognition in Parkinson's disease. *Journal of the International Neuropsychological Society, 4*, 285–290.

*Kaufer, D. I., Miller, B. L., Itti, L., Fairbanks, L. A., Li, J., Fishman, J., Kushi, J., & Cummings, J. L. (1997). Midline cerebral morphometry distinguishes frontotemporal dementia and Alzheimer's disease. *Neurology, 48*, 978–985.

*Kaufer, D. I., Miller, B. L., Itti, L., Fairbanks, L. A., Li, J., Fishman, J., Kushi, J., & Cummings, J. L. (1997). Midline cerebral morphometry distinguishes frontotemporal dementia and Alzheimer's disease. *Neurology, 48*, 978–985.

Kaufman, A. S., Grossman, I., & Kaufman, N. L. (1994). Comparison of hospitalized depressed patients and matched normal controls on tests that differ in their level of cognitive complexity. *Journal of Psychoeducational-Assessment, 12*, 112–125.

*Kawasaki, Y., Maeda, Y., Suzuki, M., Urato, K., Higashima, M., Kiba, K., Yamaguchi, N., Matsuda, H., & Hisada, K. (1993). SPECT analysis of regional cerebral blood flow changes in patients with schizophrenia during the Wisconsin Card Sorting Test. *Schizophrenia Research, 10*, 109–116.

*Kazmerski, V. A., & Friedman, D. (1997). Effect of multiple presentations of words on event-related potential and reaction time repetition effects in Alzheimer's patients and young and older controls. *Neuropsychiatry, Neuropsychology, and Behavioral Neurology, 10,* 32–47.

*Keefe, R. S. E., & Magaro, P. A. (1980). Creativity and schizophrenia: An equivalence of cognitive processing. *Journal of Abnormal Psychology, 89,* 390–398.

*Keefe, R. S. E., Lees-Roitman, S. E., Harvey, P. D., Blum, C. S., DuPre, R. L., Prieto, P. M., Davidson, M., & Davis, K. L. (1995). A pen-and-paper human analogue of a monkey prefrontal cortex activation task: Spatial working memory in patients with schizophrenia. *Schizophrenia Research, 17,* 25–33.

*Keild, J. G., Alexander, G. E., Stern, Y., & Prohovnik, I. (1996). Inferior parietal perfusion, lateralization, and neuropsychological dysfunction in Alzheimer's disease. *Brain and Cognition, 32,* 365–383.

*Kempler, D., Metter, E. J., Riege, W. H., Jackson, C. A., Benson, D. F., & Hanson, W. R. (1990). Slowly progressive aphasia: Three cases with language, memory, CT and PET data. *Journal of Neurology, Neurosurgery, and Psychiatry, 53,* 987–993.

*Kern, R. S., Van Gorp, W. G., Cummings, J. L., Brown, W. S., & Osato, S. S. (1992). Confabulation in Alzheimer's disease. *Brain and Cognition, 19,* 172–182.

*Kerr, B., Calogero, M., Vitoello, M. V., Prinz, P. N., Williams, D. E., & Wilkie, F. (1992). Letter matching: Effects of age, Alzheimer's disease, and major depression. *Journal of Clinical and Experimental Neuropsychology, 14,* 478–498.

*Kerr, S. L., & Neale, J. M. (1993). Emotion perception in schizophrenia: Specific deficit or further evidence of generalized poor performance. *Journal of Abnormal Psychology, 102,* 312–318.

Kertesz, A. (1979). *Aphasia and associated disorders.* New York: Grune & Stratton.

Kertesz, A. (1982). *The Western Aphasia Battery.* San Antonio, TX: The Psychological Corporation.

Kertesz, A. (1994). *Localization and neuroimaging in neuropsychology.* New York: Academic Press.

Kertesz, A. (1997). Frontotemporal degeneration, Pick's disease, and corticobasal degeneration: One entity or 3? 1. *Archives of Neurology, 54,* 1427–1429.

Kertesz, A., Davidson, W., & McCabe, P. (1998). Primary progressive semantic aphasia: A case study. *Journal of the International Neuropsychological Society, 4,* 388–398.

*Kertzman, C., Robinson, D. L., Litvan, I. (1990). Effects of physotigmine on spatial attention in patients with progressive supranuclear palsy. *Archives of Neurology, 47,* 1346–1350.

*Kessler, J., Herholz, K., Grond, M., & Heiss, W. D. (1991). Impaired metabolic activation in Alzheimer's disease: A PET study during continuous visual recognition. *Neuropsychologia, 29,* 229–243.

Kidron, D., Black, S. E., Stanchev, P., Buck, B., Szalai, J. P., Parker, J., Szekely, C., & Bronskill, M. J. (1997). Quantitative MR volumetry in Alzheimer's disease: Topogrpahic markers and the effects of sex and education. *Neurology, 49,* 1504–1512.

*Killian, G. A., Holzman, P. S., Davis, J. M., & Gibbons, R. (1984). Effects of psychotropic medication on selected cognitive and perceptual measures. *Journal of Abnormal Psychology, 93,* 58–70.

Kiloh, L. G. (1961). Pseudo-dementia. *Acta Psychiatrica Scandinavica, 336*–351.

Kimura, D. (1967). Functional asymmetry of the brain in dichotic listening. *Cortex, 3,* 163–178.

Kinderman, S. S., & Brown, G. B. (1997). Depression and memory in the elderly: A meta-analysis. *Journal of Clinical and Experimental Neuropsychology, 19*, 625–642.

King, D. (1990). The effect of neuroleptics on cognitive and psychomotor function. *British Journal of Psychiatry, 157*, 799–811.

King, D., & Caine, E. D. (1990). Depression. In J. L. Cummings (Ed.), *Subcortical dementia*. New York: Oxford University Press.

King, D., & Caine, E. D. (1996). Cognitive impairment in major depression. In I. Grant, K. M. Adams (Eds.), *Neuropsychological assessment of neuropsychiatric disorders*. (pp. 200–217). New York: Oxford University Press.

*King, D. A., Caine, E. D., Conwell, Y., & Cox, C. (1991). The neuropsychology of depression in the elderly: A comparative study of normal aging and Alzheimer's disease. *The Journal of Neuropsychiatry and Clinical Neurosciences, 3*, 163–168.

*King, D. A., Caine, E. D., & Cox, C. (1993). Influence of depression and age on selected cognitive functions. *Clinical Neuropsychologist, 7*, 443–453.

*King, D. A., Cox, C., Lyness, J. M., & Caine, E. D. (1995). Neuropsychological effects of depression and age in an elderly sample: A confirmatory sample. *Neuropsychology, 9*, 399–408.

King, D. A., Cox, C., Lyness, J. M., Conwell, Y., & Caine, E. D. (1998). Quantitative and qualitative differences in the verbal learning performance of elderly depressives and healthy controls. *Journal of the International Neuropsychological Society, 4*, 115–126.

*Kirshner, H. S., Tanridag, O., Thurman, L., & Whetsell Jr., W. O. (1987). Progressive aphasia without dementia: Two cases with focal spongiform degeneration. *Annals of Neurology, 22*, 527–532.

*Klonoff, H., Clark, C., Oger, J., Paty, D., & Li, D. (1991). Neuropsychological performance in patients with mild multiple sclerosis. *Journal of Nervous and Mental Disease, 179*, 127–131.

Klove, H. (1963). Clinical neuropsychology. In F. M. Forster (Ed.), *The medical clinics of north America*. New York: Saunders.

*Knight, R. A., Elliot, D. S., & Freedman, E. G. (1985). Short-term visual memory in schizophrenics. *Journal of Abnormal Psychology, 94*, 427–442.

*Knight, R. A., Youard, P. J., & Wooles, I. M. (1985). Visual information-processing deficits in chronic schizophrenic subjects using tasks matched for discriminating power. *Journal of Abnormal Psychology, 94*, 454–459.

*Knight, R. G. (1996). Facilitation by semantic priming in Alzheimer's disease and control groups matched for accuracy of word recognition. *Neuropsychology, 10*, 96–100.

*Knopman, D. (1991). Long-term retention of implicitly acquired learning in patients with Alzheimer's disease. *Journal of Clinical and Experimental Neuropsychology, 13*, 880–894.

*Knopman, D., & Nissen, M. J. (1991). Procedural learning is impaired in Huntington's disease: Evidence from the serial reaction time task. *Neuropsychologia, 29*, 245–254.

*Knopman, D., & Ryberg, S. (1989). A verbal memory test with high predictive accuracy for dementia of the Alzheimer's type. *Archives of Neurology, 46*, 141–145.

Knopman, D. S., Mastri, A. R., Frey, W. H., Sung, J. H., Rustan, T. (19??). Dementia lacking distinctive histologic features: A common non-Alzheimer degenerative dementia. *Neurology, 40*, 251–256.

*Knowlton, B. J., Squire, L. R., Paulsen, J. S., Serdlow, N. R., Swenson, M., & Butters, N. (1996). Dissociations within nondeclaritive memory in Huntington's disease. *Neuropsychology, 10*, 538–548.

*Kolb, B., & Whishaw, I. Q. (1983). Performance of schizophrenic patients on tests sensitive to left or right frontal, temporal, or parietal function in neurological patients. *The Journal of Nervous and Mental Disease, 171*, 435–443.

*Kolvisto, M., Portin, R., & Rinne, J. O. (1996). Perceptual priming in Alzheimer's and Parkinson's diseases. *Neuropsychologia, 34*, 449–547.

Kopelman, M. D. (1986). Clinical tests of memory. *British Journal of Psychiatry, 148*, 517–525.

*Kopelman, M. D. (1991). Non-verbal, short-term forgetting in the alcoholic Korsakoff syndrome and Alzheimer-type dementia. *Neuropsychologia, 29*, 737–747.

*Koss, E., Weiffenbach, J. M., Haxby, J. V., & Friedland, R. P. (1988). Olfactory detection and identification performance are dissociated in early Alzheimer's disease. *Neurology, 38*, 1228–1232.

Kraemer, H. C., & Andrews, G. (1982). A nonparametric technique for meta-analysis effect size calculation. *Psychological Bulletin, 94*, 190–192.

Kraepelin, E. (1919). *Dementia praecox and paraphrenia* (pp. 282–329). (translated by R. M. Barclay) (G. M. Robertson, Ed.). Huntington, NY: R. E. Krieger.

*Krakowski, M. I., Convit, A., Jaeger, J., Lin, S., & Volavka, J. (1989). Neurological impairment in violent schizophrenic inpatients. *American Journal of Psychiatry, 146*, 849–853.

*Kremen, W. S., Seidman, L. S., Faraone, S. V., Pepple, J. R. Lyons, M. J., & Tsuang, M. T. (1996). The "3Rs" and neuropsychological function in schizophrenia: An empirical test of the matching fallacy. *Neuropsychology, 10*, 22–31.

Kristensen, M. O. (1985). Progressive supranuclear palsy—20 years later. *Acta Neurologica Scandinavica, 71*, 177–189.

*Krupp, L. B., Sliwinski, M., Masur, D. M., Friedberg, F., & Coyle, P. K. (1994). Cognitive functioning and depression in patients with chronic fatigue syndrome and multiple sclerosis. *Archives of Neurology, 51*, 705–710.

Kukull, W. A., Larson, E. B., Reifler, B. V., Lampe, T. H., Yerby, M., & Hughes, J. (1990). Interrater reliability of Alzheimer's disease diagnosis. *Neurology, 40*, 257–260.

Kurtzke, J. F. (1983). Rating neurological impairment in multiple sclerosis. An Expanded Disability Status Scale (EDSS). *Neurology, 33*, 1444–1452.

Kurtzke, J. F. (1988). Multiple sclerosis: What's in a name? *Neurology, 38*, 309–316.

*Kurylo, D. D., Corkin, S., Rizzo III, J. F., & Growdon, J. H. (1996). Greater relative impairment of object recognition than of visuospatial abilities in Alzheimer's disease. *Neuropsychology, 10*, 74–81.

*Kwapil, T. R., Chapman, L. J., & Chapman, J. P. (1992). Monaural and binaural story recall by schizophrenic subjects. *Journal of Abnormal Psychology, 101*, 709–716.

*Kwapil, T. R., Hegley, D. C., Chapman, L. J., & Chapman, J. P. (1990). Facilitation of word recognition by semantic priming in schizophrenia. *Journal of Abnormal Psychology, 99*, 215–221.

*Laakso, M. P., Partanen, K., Riekkinen Jr., P., Lehtovirta, M., Helkala, E. L., Halillkainen, M., Hanninen, T., Vainio, P., Soininen, H. (1996). *Neurology, 46*, 678–681.

*LaBarge, E., Smith, D. S., Dick, L., Storandt, M. (1992). Agraphia in dementia of the Alzheimer's type. *Archives of Neurology, 49*, 1151–1156.

*Laine, M., Vuorinen, E., Rinne, J. O. (1997). Picture naming deficits in vascular dementia and Alzheimer's disease. *Journal of Clinical and Experimental Neuropsychology, 19*, 126–140.

*Lamberly, G. L., Putnam, S. H., Chatel, D. M., Bieliasuskas, L. A., & Adams, K. M. (1994). Derived trail making test indices: A preliminary report. *Neuropsychiatry, Neuropsychology, and Behavioral Neurology, 7*, 230–234.

*Landro, N. I., Orbeck, A. L., & Rund, B. R. (1993). Memory functioning in chronic and non-chronic schizophrenics, affectively disturbed patients and normal controls. *Schizophrenia Research, 10*, 85–92.

Laplane, D., Levasseur, M., & Pillon, B. (1989). Obsessive-compulsive and other behavioral changes with bilateral basal ganglia lesions: A neuropsychological, magnetic resonance imaging and positron tomography study. *Brain, 112*, 699–725.

*Laplante, L., Everett, J., & Thomas, J. (1992). Inhibition through negative priming with Stroop stimuli in schizophrenia. *British Journal of Clinical Psychology, 31*, 307–326.

*Lapleche, G., & Albert, M. S. (1995). Executive function deficits in mild Alzheimer's disease. *Neuropsychology, 9*, 313–320.

Larrabee, G. J., & Curtis, G. (1992). *Factor structure of an ability-focused neuropsychological battery.* Presented at the Annual Meeting of the International Neuropsychological Society, San Diego, CA.

Larrabee, G. J., & Curtiss, G. (1995). Construct validity of various verbal and visual memory tests. *Journal of Clinical and Experimental Neuropsychology, 17*, 536–547.

Larrabee, G. J., Kane, R. L., Schuck, J. R., & Francis, D. J. (1985). Construct validity of various memory testing procedures. *Journal of Clinical and Experimental Neuropsychology, 7*, 239–250.

*Lawrie, S. M., Abukmeil, S. S., Chiswick, A., Egan, V., Santosh, C. G., & Best, J. J. K. (1997). Qualitative cerebral morphology in schizophrenia: A magnetic resonance imaging study and systematic literature review. *Schizophrenia Research, 25*, 155–166.

Lees, A. J. (1987). The Steele-Richardson-Olszewski syndrome (progressive supranuclear palsy). In C. D. Marsden & S. Fahn, (Eds.), *Movement disorders 2.* (Vol. 13, 272–287). London: Butterworth.

*Lees, A. J., Leigh, P. N., Marsden, C. D., Quinn, N. P., & Summers, B. A. (1994). Cognitive deficits in progressive supranuclear palsy, Parkinson's disease, and multiple system atrophy in tests sensitive to frontal lobe dysfunction. *Journal of Neurology, Neurosurgery, & Psychiatry, 57*, 79–88.

*Lehtovirta, M., Soininen, H., Heliasalini, S., Mannermaa, A., Helkala, E. L., Hartikainen, P., Hanninen, T., Ryynanen, M., & Riekkinen, P. J. (1996). Clinical and neuropsychological characteristics in familial and sporadic Alzheimer's disease: Relation to a polipoprotein E polymorphism. *Neurology, 46*, 413–419.

*Leininger, B. E., Gramling, S. E., Farrell, A. D., Kreutzer, J. S., & Peck III, E. A. (1990). Neuropsychological deficits in symptomatic minor head injury patients after concussion and mild concussion. *Journal of Neurology, Neurosurgery, and Psychiatry, 53*, 293–296.

*Lemsky, C. M., Smith, G., Malec, J. F., & Ivnik, R. J. (1996). Identifying risk for functional impairment using cognitive measures: An application of CART modeling. *Neuropsychology, 10*, 368–375.

Leonberger, F. T., Nicks, S. D., Larrabee, G. J., & Goldfader, P. R. (1992). Factor structure of the Wechsler Memory Scale- Revised within a comprehensive neuropsychological battery. *Neuropsychology, 6*, 239–249.

*Levander, S. E., Bartfai, A., & Schalling, D. (1985). Regional cortical dysfunction in schizophrenic patients studied by computerized neuropsychological methods. *Perceptual and Motor Skills, 61*, 479–495.

*Levin, B. E., Llabre, M. M., Reisman, S., Weiner, W. J., Sanchez-Ramos, J., Singer, C., & Brown, M. C. (1991). Visuospatial impairment in Parkinson's disease. *Neurology, 41*, 365–369.

*Levin, B. E., Llabre, M. M., & Weiner, W. J. (1989). Cognitive impairments associated with early Parkinson's disease. *Neurology, 39*, 557–561.

Levin, B. E., Tomer, R., & Rey, G. J. (1992). Cognitive impairments associated with early Parkinson's disease. *Neurology, 39*, 557–561.

Levin, S. (1984). Frontal lobe dysfunctions in schizophrenia II: Impairments of psychological and brain functions. *Journal of Psychiatric Research, 18*, 57–72.

*Levin, S., Hall, J. A., Knight, R. A., & Alpert, M. (1985). Verbal and nonverbal expression of affect in speech of schizophrenic and depressed patients. *Journal of Abnormal Psychology, 94*, 487–497.

Levin, S., Yurgelun-Todd, D., & Craft, S. (1989). Contributions of clinical neuropsychology to the study of schizophrenia. *Journal of Abnormal Psychology, 98*, 341–356.

*Lewis, S. W., Ford, R. A., Syed, G. M., Reveley, A. M., & Toone, B. K. (1992). A controlled study of 99mTc-HMPAO single-photon emission imaging in chronic schizophrenia. *Psychological Medicine, 22*, 27–35.

*Lewitt, P. A., Foster, N. L., & Newman, R. P. (1984). Blink rates and disorders of movement. *Neurology, 34*, 677–678.

Lezak, M. D. (1979). Recovery of memory and learning functions following traumatic brain injury. *Cortex, 15*, 63–70.

Lezak, M. D. (1982). The problem of assessing executive functions. *International Journal of Psychology, 17*, 281–297.

Lezak, M. D. (1986). Psychological implications of traumatic brain damage for the patients's family. *Rehabilitation Psychology, 31*, 241–250.

Lezak, M. D. (1987a). Making neuropsychological assessment relevant to head injury. In H. S. Levin, J. Grafman, & H. M. Eisenberg (Eds.), *Neurobehavioral recovery from head injury*. New York: Oxford University Press.

Lezak, M. D. (1987b). Relationships between personality disorders, social disturbances, and physical disability following traumatic brain injury. *Journal of Head Trauma Rehabilitation, 2*, 57–69.

Lezak, M. D. (1988). IQ: R. I. P. *Journal of Clinical and Experimental Neuropsychology, 10*, 351–361.

Lezak, M. D. (1995). *Neuropsychological assessment* (3rd ed.). New York: Oxford University Press.

*Libon, D. J., Mattson, R. E., Glosser, G., Kaplan, E., Malamut, B. L., Sands, L. P., Swenson, R., & Cloud, B. S. (1996). A nine-word dementia version of the California Verbal Learning Test. *The Clinical Neuropsychologist, 10*, 237–244.

Lichtheim, L. (1885). On aphasia. *Brain, 7*, 433–484.

Liddle, P. F., & Barnes, T. R. E. (1990). Syndromes of chronic schizophrenia. *British Journal of Psychiatry, 157*, 558–561.

Liepmann, H. (1920). Apraxia. *Ergebnisse der Gesamten Medizin, 1*, 516–543.

Light, R. J., & Pillemer, D. B. (1984). *Summing up: The science of reviewing research*. Cambridge, M.A.: Harvard University Press.

*Lim, K. O., Sullivan, E. V., Zipursky, R. B., & Pfefferbaum, A. (1996). Cortical gray matter volume deficits in schizophrenia: A replication. *Schizophrenia Research, 20*, 157–164.

*Linn, R. T., Wolf, P. A., Backman, D. L., Knoefel, J. E., Cobb, J. L., Belanger, A. J., Kaplan, E., & D' Agostino, R. B. (1995). The "preclinical phase" of probable

Alzheimer's disease: A 13-year prospective study of the Farmingham cohort. *Archives of Neurology, 52,* 485–490.

*Lipinska, B., & Backman, L. (1997). Encoding-retrieval interactions in mild Alzheimer's disease: The role of access to categorical information. *Brain and Cognition, 34,* 274–286.

*Lipinska, B., Backman, L., Mantyla, T., & Vitanen, M. (1994). Effectiveness of self-generated cues in early Alzheimer's disease. *Journal of Clinical and Experimental Neuropsychology, 16,* 809–819.

*Lippa, C. F., Cohen, R., Smith, T. W., & Drachman, D. A. (1991). Primary progressive aphasia with focal neuronal achromasia. *Neurology, 41,* 882–886.

Lipsey, M. W., & Wilson, D. B. (1993). The efficacy of psychological, educational, and behavioral treatment. *American Psychologist, 12,* 1181–1209.

Lishman, W. A. (1978). *Organic psychiatry.* Oxford: Blackwell Scientific Publications.

Lishman, W. A. (1987). *Organic psychiatry* (2nd ed.). Oxford: Blackwell Scientific Publications.

Litvan, I., & Agid, Y. (1992). *Progressive supranuclear palsy: Clinical and research approaches.* Oxford: Oxford University Press.

Litvan, I., Agid, Y., Calne, D., Campbell, G., Dubois, B., Duvoisin, R. C., Goetz, C. G., Golbe, L. I., Grafman, J., Growdon, J. H., Hallet, M., Jankovic, J., Quinn, N. P., Tolosa, E., & Zee, D. S. (1996). Clinical research criteria for the diagnosis of progressive supranuclear palsy (Steele-Richardson-Olszewksi syndrome): report of the NINDS-SPSP international workshop. *Neurology, 47,* 1–9.

Litvan, I., Campbell, G., Mangone, C. A., Verny, M., McKee, A., Chaudhuri, K. R., Jellinger, K., Pearce, R. K., D'Olhaberriague, L. (1997). Which clinical features differentiate progressive supranuclear palsy (Steele-Richardson-Olszewski syndrome) from related disorders? A clinicopathological study. *Brain, 120,* 65–74.

*Litvan, I., Grafman, J., Gomez, C., & Chase, T. N. (1989). Memory impairment in patients with progressive supranuclear palsy. *Archives of Neurology, 46,* 765–767.

*Litvan, I. Grafman, J., Vendrell, P., & Martinez, J.M. (1988). Slowed information processing in multiple sclerosis. *Archives of Neurology, 45,* 281–285.

*Litvan, I., Grafman, J., Vendrell, P., Martinez, J.M., Junque, C., Vendrell, J.M., & Baraquee-Bordas, L. (1988). Multiple memory deficits in patients with multiple sclerosis. *Archives of Neurology, 45,* 607–610.

*Litvan, I., Mohr, E., William, J., Gomez, C., & Chase, T. N. (1991). Differential memory and executive functions in demented patients with Parkinson's and Alzheimer's disease. *Journal of Neurology, Neurosurgery, and Psychiatry, 54,* 25–29.

Loftus, G. R. (1991). On the tyranny of hypothesis testing in the social sciences. *Contemporary Psychology, 36,* 102–105.

Loftus, G. R. (1994). *Why psychology will never be a real science until we change the way we analyze data.* Address presented at the American Psychological Association 102nd annual convention, Los Angeles, CA.

*Logsdon, R. G., Teri, L., Williams, D. E., Vitiello, M. V., & Prinz, P. N. (1989). The WAIS-R profile: A diagnostic tool for Alzheimer's disease. *Journal of Clinical and Experimental Neuropsychology, 11,* 892–898.

*Lopez, O. L., Swihart, A. A., Becker, J. T., Reinmuth, O. M., Reynolds III, C. F., Rezek, D. L., & Daly, F. L. (1990). Reliability of NINCDS-ADRDA clinical criteria for the diagnosis of Alzheimer's disease. *Neurology, 40,* 1517–1522.

Loranger, A. W., Goodell, H., McDowell, F. H., Lee, J. E., & Sweet, R. D. (1972). Intellectual impairment in Parkinson's disease. *Brain, 95,* 405–412.

Luria, A. R. (1973). *The working brain: An introduction to neuropsychology.* New York: Basic Books.

Luxenburg, J. S., Swedo, S. E., Flament, M. F., & Friedland, R. P. (1988). Neuroanatomical abnormalities in obsessive-compulsive disorder detected with quantitative X-ray computed tomography. *American Journal of Psychiatry, 145,* 1089–1093.

*Mack, J. L., & Patterson, M. B. (1995). Executive dysfunction and Alzheimer's disease: Performance on a test of planning ability, the Porteus Maze Test. *Neuropsychology, 9,* 556–564.

*Maddox, W. T., Filoteo, J. V., Delis, D. C., & Salmon, D. P. (1996). Visual selective attention deficits in patients with Parkinson's disease: A quantitative model-based approach. *Neuropsychology, 10,* 197–218.

Mahler, M. E., & Benson, D. F. (1990). Cognitive dysfunction in multiple sclerosis: A subcortical dementia? In S.M. Rao (Ed.), *Neurobehavioral aspects of Multiple Sclerosis* (pp. 88–101). New York: Oxford University Press.

*Mahurin, R. K., & Cooke, N. (1996). Verbal series attention test: Clinical utility in the assessment of dementia. *The Clinical Neuropsychologist, 10,* 43–53.

Mahurin, R. K., Feher, E. P., Nance, M. L., Levy, J. K., & Pirozzolo, F. J. (1993). Cognition in Parkinson's disease and related disorders. In R. W. Parks, R. F. Zec, & R. S. Wilson (Eds.), *Neuropsychology of Alzheimer's disease and other dementias.* (pp. 308–349). New York: Oxford University Press.

*Maki, P. M., & Knopman, D. S. (1996). Limitations of the distinction between conceptual and perceptual implicit memory: A study of Alzheimer's disease. *Neuropsychology, 10,* 464–474.

*Malapani, C., Pillon, B., Dubois, B., & Agid, Y. (1994). Impaired simultaneous cognitive task performance in Parkinson's disease: A dopamine-related dysfunction. *Neurology, 44,* 319–326.

*Maler, W., Franke, P., Hain, C., Kopp, B., & Rist, F. (1992). Neuropsychological indicators of the vulnerability to schizophrenia. *Progress in Neuro-Psychopharmacology and Biological Psychiatry, 16,* 703–715.

*Malessa, S., Gaymard, B., Rivand, S., Levera, P., Hirsch, E., Verney, M., Duyckaerts, C., Agid, Y., & Pierrot-Deseilligny, C. (1994). Role of pontine nuclei damage in smooth pursuit impairment or progressive supranuclear palsy: A clinical pathological study. *Neurology, 44,* 716.

Malloy, P. (1987). Frontal lobe dysfunction in obsessive-compulsive disorder. In E. Perecman (Ed.), *The frontal lobes revisted.* (pp. 207–223). New York: The IRBN Press.

*Mandal, M. K., & Rai, A. (1987). Responses to facial emotion and psychopathology. *Psychiatry Research, 20,* 317–323.

Mann, D. M. A., & South, P. W. (1993). The topographic distribution of brain atrophy in frontal lobe dementia. *Acta Neuropathologica, 85,* 334–340.

Mann, D. M. A., South, P. W., Snowden, J. S., & Neary, D. (1993). Dementia of frontal lobe type: Neuropathology and immunohistochemistry. *Journal of Neurology, Neurosurgery, and Psychiatry, 56,* 605–614.

*Margolin, D. I., Pate, D. S., Friedrich, F. J., & Elia, E. (1990). Dysnomia in dementia and in stroke patients: Different underlying cognitive deficits. *Journal of Clinical and Experimental Neuropsychology, 12,* 597–612.

Marsden, C. D. (1982). The mysterious motor function of the basal ganglia: The Robert Wartenberg lecture. *Neurology, 32,* 514–539.

Marsden, C. D. (1990). Parkinson's disease. *Lancet, 335*, 948–952.

Marsden, C. D. (1994). Parkinson's disease. *Journal of Neurology, Neurosurgery, and Psychiatry, 57*, 672–681.

*Marsh, L., Suddath, R. L., Higgins, N., & Weinberger, D. R. (1994). Medial temporal lobe structures in schizophrenia: Relationship of size to duration of illness. *Schizophrenia Research, 11*, 225–238.

*Marson, D. C., Cody, H. A., Ingram, K. K., & Harrell, L. E. (1995). Neuropsychologic predictors of competency in Alzheimer's disease using a rational reasons legal standard. *Archives of Neurology, 52*, 955–959.

Martin, A. (1987). Representation of semantic and spatial knowledge in Alzheimer's patients: Implications for models of preserved learning in amnesia. *Journal of Clinical and Experimental Neuropsychology, 9*, 191–224.

Martin, A. (1992). Degraded knowledge representation in patients with Alzheimer's disease: Implications for models of semantic and repetition priming. In L. R. Squire & N. Butters (Eds.), *Neuropsychology of memory* (pp. 220–240). (2nd ed.). New York: The Guilford Press.

*Martin, A., Pigott, T. A., Lalonde, F. M., Dalton, I., Dubbert, B., & Murphy, D. L. (1993). Lack of evidence for Huntinton's disease-like cognitive dysfunction in obsessive compulsive disorder. *Biological Psychiatry, 33*, 345–353.

*Martin, A, Wiggs, C. L., Altemus, M., Rubenstein, C., & Murphy, D. L. (1995). Working memory as assessed by subject-ordered tasks in patients with obsessive compulsive disorder. *Journal of Clinical and Experimental Neuropsychology, 17*, 786–792.

Martin, R. C., Loring, D. W., Meador, K. J., & Lee, G. P. (1990). The effects of lateralized temporal lobe dysfunction on formal and semantic word fluency. *Neuropsychologia, 28*, 823–829.

*Martone, M., Butters, N., Trauner, D. (1986). Some analyses of forgetting of pictorial material in amnesic and demented patients. *Journal of Clinical and Experimental Neuropsychology, 8*, 161–178.

*Maruff, P., & Currie, J. (1995). An attentional grasp reflex in patients with Alzheimer's disease. *Neuropsychologia, 33*, 689–701.

Massman, P. J., Delis, D. C., Butters, N., Dupont, R. M., & Gillin, J. C. (1992). The subcortical dysfunction hypothesis of memory deficits in depression: Neuropsychological validation in a subgroup of patients. *Journal of Clinical and Experimental Neuropsychology, 14*, 687–706.

*Massman, P. J., Delis, D. C., Butters, N., Levin, B. E., & Salmon, D. P. (1990). Are all subcortical dementias alike?: Verbal learning and memory in Parkinson's and Huntington's disease patients. *Journal of Clinical and Experimental Neuropsychology, 12*, 729–744.

*Massman, P. J., Delis, D. C., Filoteo, J. V., Butters, N., Salmon, D. P., & Demadura, T. L. (1993). Mechanisms of spatial impairment in Alzheimer's disease subgroups: Differential breakdown of directed attention to global-local stimuli. *Neuropsychology, 7*, 172–181.

*Mather, J. A., Neufeld, R. W. J., Merskey, H., & Russel, N. C. (1992). Disruption of saccade production during oculomotor tracking in schizophrenia and the use of its changes across target velocity as a discriminator of the disorder. *Psychiatry Research, 43*, 93–109.

*Mattes, R., Cohen, R., Berg, P., Canavan, A. G. M., & Hopmann, G. (1991). Slow-cortical potentials (SCPS) in schizophrenic patients during performance of the Wisconsin Card Sorting Test (WCST). *Neuropsychologia, 29,* 195–205.

Mattis, S. (1988). *Dementia Rating Scale (DRS).* Odessa, FL: Psychological Assessment Resuources.

*Mayeux, R., Stern, Y., Sano, M., Cote, L., & Williams, J. B. W. (1987). Clinical and biochemical correlates of bradyphrenia in Parkinson's disease. *Neurology, 37,* 1130–1134.

*McCarley, R. W., Faux, S. F., Shenton, M., LeMay, M., Cane, M., Ballinger, R., & Duffy, F. H. (1989). CT abnormalities in schizophrenia- A preliminary study of their correlations with P300/P200 electrophysiological features and positive/negative symptoms. *Archives of General Psychiatry, 46,* 698–708.

*McDaniel, K. D., Wagner, M. T., & Greenspan, B. S. (1991). The role of brain single photon emission computed tomography in the diagnosis of primary progressive aphasia. *Archives of Neurology, 48,* 1257–1260.

*McDonald, C. M., Brown, G. G., & Gorell, J. M. (1996). Impaired set-shifting in Parkinson's disease: New evidence from a lexical decision task. *Journal of Clinical and Experimental Neuropsychology, 18,* 793–809.

*McElhiney, M. C., Moody, B. J., Steif, B. L., Prudic, J., Devanand, D. P., Nobler, M. S., & Sackeim, H. A. (1995). Autobiographical memory and mood: Effects of electroconvulsive therapy. *Neuropsychology, 9,* 501–517.

McGuire, P. K. (1995). The brain in obsessive-compulsive disorder. *Journal of Neurology, Neurosurgery, and Psychiatry, 59,* 457–459.

*McGuire, P. K., Silbersweig, D. A., Wright, I., Murray, R. M., Frackowiak, R. S. J., & Frith, C. D. (1996). The neural correlates of inner speech and auditory verbal imagery in schizophrenia: Relationship to auditory verbal hallucinations. *British Journal of Psychiatry, 169,* 148–159.

McHugh, P. R. (1989). The neuropsychiatry of basal ganglia disorders: A triadic syndrome and its explanation. *Neuropsychiatry, Neuropsychology, and Behavioral Neurology, 2,* 239–247.

McHugh, P. R., & Folstein, M. F. (1975). Psychiatric syndromes of Huntington's chorea: A clinical and phenomenologic study. In D. F. Benson & D. Blumer (Eds.), *Psychiatric aspects of neurologic disease.* New York: Grune and Stratton.

McHugh, P. R., & Folstein, M. F. (1979). Psychopathology of dementia: Implications for neuropathology. In R. Katzman (Ed.), *Cogenital and acquired cognitive disorders.* New York: Oxford University Press.

McIntosh-Michaelis, S. A., Roberts, M. H., Wilkonson, S. M., Diamond, I. D., McLellan, D. L., Martin, J. P., & Spackman, A. J. (1991). The prevalence of cognitive impairment in a community survey of multiple sclerosis. *British Journal of Clinical Psychology, 30,* 333–348.

McKay, S. E., & Golden, C. J. (1981). The assessment of specific neuropsychological skills using scales derived from factor analysis of the Luria-Nebraska Neuropsychological Battery. *International Journal of Neuroscience, 14,* 189–204.

*McKay, S. E., McKenna, P. J., Bentham, P., Mortimer, A. M., Holbery, A., & Hodges, J. R. (1996). Semantic memory is impaired in schizophrenia. *Biological Psychiatry, 39,* 929–937.

McKenna, P. J., Mortimer, A. M., & Hodges, J. R. (1994). Semantic memory and schizophrenia. In A. S. David & J. C. Cutting (Eds.), *The neuropsychology of schizophrenia.* (pp. 163–178). Hillsdale NJ: Lawerence Erlbaum.

McKhann, G., Drachman, D., Folstein, M., Katzman, R., Price, D., & Stadlin, E. M. (1984). Clinical diagnosis of Alzheimer's disease: Report of the NINCDS-ADRDA work group under the auspices of the Department of Health and Human Services Task Force on Alzheimer's disease, *Neurology, 34*, 939–944.

McPherson, S., & Cummings, J. L. (1996). Neuropsychological aspects of Parkinson's disease and Parkinsonism. In I. Grant & K. M. Adams (Eds.), *Neuropsychological assessment of neuropsychiatric disorders.* (pp. 288–311). New York: Oxford University Press.

Meehl, P. E. (1967). Theory testing in psychology and physics: A methodological paradox. *Philosophy of Science, 34*, 103–115.

Meiran, N., & Jelicic, M. (1995). Implicit memory in Alzheimer's disease: A meta-analysis. *Neuropsychology, 9*, 291–303.

*Meltzer, C. C., Zubieta, J. K., Brandt, J., Tune, L. E., Mayberg, H. S., & Frost, J. J. (1996). Regional hypometabolism in Alzheimer's disease as measured by positron emission tomography after correction for effects of partial volume averaging. *Neurology, 47*, 454–461.

*Mendez, M. F., & Mashla-Mendez, M. (1991). Differences between multi-infarct dementia and Alzheimer's disease on unstructured neuropsychological tasks. *Journal of Clinical and Experimental Neuropsychology, 13*, 923–932.

*Mentis, M. J., Weinstein, E. A., Horwitz, B., McIntosh, A. R., Pietrini, P., Alexander, G. E., Furey, M., & Murphy, D. G. M. (1995). Abnormal brain glucose metabolism in the in the delusional misidentification syndromes: A positron emission tomography study in Alzheimer's disease. *Biological Psychiatry, 38*, 438–449.

*Mesulam, M-M. (1982). Slowly progressive aphasia without generalized dementia. *Annals of Neurology, 11*, 592–598.

Mesulam, M-M. (1985). *Principles of behavioral neurology.* Philadelphia: F. A. Davis Company.

Mesulam, M-M. (1987). Primary progressive aphasia—differentiation from Alzheimer's disease. *Annals of Neurology, 22,* 533–534.

Mesulam, M-M. (1990). Schizophrenia and the brain. *New England Journal of Medicine, 322,* 842–845.

Mesulam, M-M., Johnson, N., Grujic, Z., & Weintraub, S. (1997). Apoliproprotein E genotypes in primary progressive aphasia. *Neurology, 49*, 51–55.

Mesulam, M-M., & Weintraub, S. (1992). Heterogeneity in Alzheimer's disease. In F. Boller, F. Forcette, Z. Khachaturian, M. Poncet, & Y. Christen (Eds.), *Primary progressive aphasia: Sharpening the focus on a clinical syndrome.* (pp. 43–66). Berlin: Springer-Verlag.

Micheli, G., Caltagirone, C., & Gainotti, G, Masullo, C., & Silveri, M. C. (1981). Neuropsychological correlates of localized cerebral lesions in nonaphasic brain-damaged patients. *Journal of Clinical Neuropsychology, 3*, 53–63.

*Michie, P. T., Fox, A. M., Warp, P. B., Catts, S. V., & McConaghy, N. (1990). Event-related potential indices of selective attention and cortical lateralization in schizophrenia. *Psychophysiology, 8,* 234–244.

*Mickanin, J., Grossman, M., Onishi, K., Auriacombe, S., & Clark, C. (1994). Verbal and nonverbal fluency in patients with probable Alzheimer's disease. *Neuropsychology, 8*, 385–394.

Milberg, W. P., Hebben, N., & Kaplan, E. (1996). The Boston process approach. In I. Grant & K. M. Adams (Eds.), *Neuropsychological assessment of neuropsychiatric disorders* (pp. 58–80). (2nd edn). New York: Oxford University Press.

Miller, B., Chapman, J. P., Chapman, L. J., & Collins, J. (1995). Task difficulty and cognitive deficits in schizophrenia. *Journal of Abnormal Psychology, 104,* 251–258.

Miller, B. L., Chang, L., Oropilla, G., Ismael, M. (1994). Alzheimer's disease and frontal lobe dementias. In C. Coffey, J. L. Cummings, M. R. Lovell, & G. D. Pearlson (Eds.), *The American Psychiatric Press textbook of geriatric neuropsychiatry.* (pp. 389–404). Washington: American Psychiatric Press.

*Miller, B. L., Cummings, J. L., Villanurva-Meyer, J., Boone, K., Mehringer, C. M., Lesser, I. M., & Mena, I. (1991). Frontal lobe degeneration: Clinical, neuropsychological, and SPECT characteristics. *Neurology, 41,* 1374–1382.

Miller, E. (1971). On the nature of the memory disorder in presenile dementia. *Neuropsychology, 9,* 75–81.

Miller, E. (1972). Efficiency of coding and the short-term memory defect in presenile dementia. *Neuropsychology, 10,* 133–136.

Miller, J. D. (1993). Head injury. *Journal of Neurology, Neurosurgery, and Psychiatry, 56,* 440–447.

Miller, L. S., Faustman, W. O., Moses, J. A., & Csernansky, J. G. (1991). Evaluating cognitive impairment in depression with the Luria-Nebraska Neuropsychological Battery: Severity correlates and comparisons with nonpsychiatric controls. *Psychiatry Research, 37,* 219–227.

Milner, B. (1963). Effects of different brain lesions on card sorting. *Archives of Neurology, 9,* 90–100.

Milner, B. (1964). Some effects of frontal lobectomy in man. In J.M. Warren & K. Akert (Eds.), *The frontal granular cortex and behavior.* New York: McGraw Hill.

Milner, B. (1971). Interhemispheric differences in the localization of psychological processes in man. *British Medical Bulletin, 27,* 272–277.

*Min, S. K., & On, B. H. (1992). Hemispheric asymmetry in visual recognition of words and motor response in schizophrenic and depressive patients. *Biological Psychiatry, 31,* 255–262.

*Minden, S. L., Moes, E. J., Orav, J., Kaplan, E., & Reich, P. (1990). Memory impairment in multiple sclerosis. *Journal of Clinical and Experimental Neuropsychology, 12,* 566–586.

Mirsky, A. F. (1989). The neuropsychology of attention: Elements of a complex behavior. In E. Perecman (Ed.), *Individual differences in hemispheric specialization.* New York: Plenum Press.

*Mirsky, A. F., Ingraham, L. J., & Kugelmass, S. (1995). Neuropsychological assessment of attention and its pathology in the Israeli cohort. *Schizophrenia Bulletin, 21,* 193–204.

*Mitrushina, M., Drebinf, C., Uchiyama, C., Satz, P., Van Gorp, W., & Chervinsky, A. (1994). The pattern of deficit in different memory components in normal aging and dementia of the Alzheimer's type. *Journal of Clinical Psychology, 50,* 591–596.

*Moffoot, A. P. R., O'Carroll, R. E., Bennie, J., Carroll, C., Dick, N., Ebmeier, K. P., & Goodwin, G. M. (1994). Diurnal variation of mood and neuropsychological function in major depression with melancholia. *Journal of Affective Disorders, 32,* 257–269.

*Mohr, E., Cox, C., Williams, J., Chase, T. N., & Fedio, P. (1990). Impairment of central auditory function in Alzheimer's disease. *Journal of Clinical and Experimental Neuropsychology, 12,* 235–246.

*Mohr, E., Juncos, J., Cox, C., Litvan, I., Fedio, P., & Chase, T. N. (1990). Selective deficits in cognition and memory in high-functioning Parkinsonian patients. *Journal of Neurology, Neurosurgery, and Psychiatry, 53,* 603–606.

*Mohr, E., Schlegel, J., Fabbrini, G., Williams, J., Mouradian, M. M., Mann, W. M., Clause, J. J., Fedio, P., & Chase, T. N. (1989). Clonidine treatment of Alzheimer's disease. *Archives of Neurology, 46,* 376–378.

*Money, E. A., Kirk, R. C., & McNaughton, N. (1992). Alzheimer's dementia produces a loss of discrimination but no increase in rate of memory decay in delayed matching to sample. *Neuropsychologia, 30,* 133–143.

*Monsch, A. U., Bondi, M. W., Butters, N., Paulsen, J. S., Salmon, D. P., Brugger, P., & Swenson, M. R. (1994). A comparison of category and letter fluency in Alzheimer's disease and Huntington's disease. *Neuropsychology, 8,* 25–30.

*Monsch, A. U., Bondi, M. W., Butters, N., Salmon, D. P., Katzman, R., & Thai, L. J. (1992). Comparisons of verbal fluency tasks in the detection of dementia of the Alzheimer type. *Archives of Neurology, 49,* 1253–1258.

*Montaldi, D., Brooks, D. N., McColl, J. H., Wyper, D., Patterson, J., Barron, E., & McCulloch, J. (1990). Measurement of regional cerebral blood flow and cognitive performance in Alzheimer's disease. *Journal of Neurology, Neurosurgery, and Psychiatry, 53,* 33–38.

*Monti, L. A., Gabrieli, J. D. E., Reminger, S. L., Rinaldi, J. A., Wilson, R. S., & Fleischman, D. A. (1996). Differential effects of aging and Alzheimer's disease on conceptual implicit and explicit memory. *Neuropsychology, 10,* 101–112.

*Morgan, C. D., Nordin, S., & Murphy, C. (1995). Odor identification as an early marker for Alzheimer's disease: Impact of lexical functioning and detection sensitivity. *Journal of Clinical and Experimental Neuropsychology, 17,* 793–803.

*Morice, R. (1990). Cognitive inflexibility and pre-frontal dysfunction in schizophrenia and mania. *British Journal of Psychiatry, 157,* 50–54.

*Morice, R., & Delahunty, A. (1996). Frontal/executive impairments in schizophrenia. *Schizophrenia Bulletin, 22,* 125–137.

*Morice, R., & McNicol, D. (1986). Language changes in schizophrenia: A limited replication. *Schizophrenia Bulletin, 12,* 239–251.

*Morris, J. C., Heyman, A., Mohs, R. C., Hughes, J. P., Van Belle, G., Fillenbaum, G., Mellits, E. D., & Clark, C. (1989). The consortium to establish a registry for Alzheimer's disease (CERAD). Part I. Clinical and neuropsychological assessment of Alzheimer's disease. *Neurology, 39,* 1159–1165.

Morris, R. G., & Baddeley, A. D. (1988). Primary and working memory functioning in Alzheimer-type dementia. *Journal of Clinical and Experimental Neuropsychology, 10,* 279–296.

*Morris, R. G., Downes, J. J., Sahakian, B. J., Evenden, J. L., Heald, A., & Robbins, T. W. (1988). Planning and spatial working memory in Parkinson's disease. *Journal of Neurology, Neurosurgery, and Psychiatry, 51,* 757–766.

*Morrison-Stewart, S. L., Williamson, P. C., Corning, W. C., Kutcher, S. P., Snow, W. G., & Merskey, H. (1992). Frontal and non-frontal lobe neuropsychological test performance and clinical symptomatology in schizophrenia. *Psychological Medicine, 22,* 353–359.

Moscovitch, M. (1992). A neuropsychological model of memory and consciousness. In L. R. Squire & N. Butters (Eds.), *Neuropsychology of memory* (pp. 5–22). (2nd ed.). New York: Guilford Press.

Moss, M. B., & Albert, M. S. (1988). Alzheimer's disease and other dementing disorders. In M. S. Albert, & M. B. Moss (Eds.), *Geriatric neuropsychology* (pp. 145–178). New York: Guilford Press.

Moss, M. B., & Albert, M. S. (1992). Neuropsychology of Alzheimer's disease. In R. F. White (Ed.), *Clinical syndromes in adult neuropsychology: The practitioner's handbook.* (pp. 305–343). Amsterdam: Elsevier Science Publishers.

Moss, M. B., Albert, M. S., Butters, N., & Payne, M. (1986). Differential patterns of memory loss among patients with Alzheimer's disease, Huntington's disease, and alcoholic Korsakoff's syndrome. *Archives of Neurology, 43,* 239–246.

*Mueser, K. T., Bellack, A. S., Morrison, R. L., & Wade, J. H. (1990). Gender, social competence, and symptomatology in schizophrenia: A longitudinal analysis. *Journal of Abnormal Psychology, 99,* 138–147.

*Multhaup, K. S., & Balota, D. A. (1997). Generation effect and source memory in healthy older adults and in adults with dementia of the Alzheimer type. *Neuropsychology, 11,* 382–391.

*Mutter, S. A., Howard, J. H., & Howard, D. V. (1994). Serial pattern learning after head injury. *Journal of Clinical and Experimental Neuropsychology, 16,* 271–288.

*Nathaniel-James, D. A., Brown, R., & Ron, M. A. (1996). Memory impairment in schizophrenia: Its relationship to executive function. *Schizophrenia Research, 21,* 85–96.

*Nathaniel-James, D. A., & Frith, C. D. (1996). Confabulation in schizophrenia: Evidence of a new form? *Psychological Medicine, 26,* 391–399.

Neary, D. (1997). Frontotemporal degeneration, Pick disease, and corticobasal degeneration: One entity or 3? 3. *Archives of Neurology, 54,* 1425–1427.

Neary, D., & Snowden, J. S. (1996). Frontal-temporal dementia: Nosology, neuropsychology, and neuropathology. *Brain and Cognition, 34,* 176–187.

Neary, D., Snowden, J. S., Gustafson, L., Passant, U., Stuss, D., Black, S., Freedman, M., Kertesz, A., Robert, P. H., Albert, M., Boone, K., Miller, B. L., Cummings, J., & Benson, D. F. (19??). Frontotemporal lobar degeneration: A consensus on clinical diagnostic criteria. *Neurology, 51,* 1546–1554.

Neary, D., Snowden, J. S., Northem, B., Goulding, P. (1988). Dementia of frontal lobe type. *Journal of Neurology, Neurosurgery, and Psychiatry, 51,* 353–361.

Nebes, R. D., & Brady, C. B. (1992). Generalized cognitive slowing and severity of dementia in Alzheimer's disease: Implications for the interpretation of response-time data. *Journal of Clinical and Experimental Neuropsychology, 14,* 317–326.

*Nelson, E., Early, T. S., & Haller, J. W. (1993). Visual attention in obsessive compulsive disorder. *Psychiatry Research, 49,* 183–196.

Nelson, H. E., (1982). *The National Adult Reading Test (NART): Test manual.* Windsor, Berks, U.K.: NFER-Nelson.

*Nelson, H. E., Pantelis, C., Carruthers, K., Speller, J., Baxendale, S., & Barnes, T. R. E. (1990). Cognitive functioning and symptomatology in chronic schizophrenia. *Psychological Medicine, 20,* 357–365.

*Nestor, P. G., Faux, S. F., McCarley, R. W., Shenton, M. E., & Sands, S. F. (1990). Measurement of visual sustained attention in schizophrenia using signal detection analysis and a newly developed computerized CPT task. *Schizophrenia Research, 3,* 329–332.

Newcombe, F. (1982). The psychological consequences of closed head injury: Assessment and rehabilitation. *Injury, 14,* 111–136.

*Nichelli, P., Appollonto, I., Clark, K., & Grafman, J. (1994). Word frequency monitoring in Parkinson's disease: An analysis of accuracy and precision. *Neuropsychiatry, Neuropsychology, and Behavioral Neurology, 7,* 289–294.

Nixon, S. J. (1996). Alzheimer's disease and vascular dementia. In R. L. Adams, O. A. Parsons, J. L. Culbertson, & S. J. Nixon (Eds.), *Neuropsychology for clinical practice: Etiology, assessment, and treatment of common neurological disorders.* (pp. 65–105). Washington, DC: American Psychological Association.

Nordahl, T. E., Benkelfat, C., Semple, W. E., Bross, M., King, A. C., & Cohen, R. M. (1989). Cerebral glucose metabolic rates in obsessive compulsive disorder. *Neuropsychopharmacology, 2,* 23–28.

*Nordin, S., & Murphy, C. (1996). Impaired sensory and cognitive olfactory function in questionable Alzheimer's disease. *Neuropsychology, 10,* 113–119.

*Nyback, H., Nyman, Blomqvist, G., Sjogren, I., & Ston-Elander, S. (1991). Brain metabolism Alzheimer's dementia: Studies of 11 C-deoxyglucose accumulation, CSF monoamine metabolites and neuropsychological test performance in patients and healthy subjects. *Journal of Neurology, Neurosurgery, and Psychiatry, 54,* 672–678.

*Nyenhuis, D. L., Rao, S. M., Zajecka, J. M., Luchetta, T., Bernardin, L., & Garron, D. C. (1995). Mood disturbance versus other symptoms of depression in multiple sclerosis. *Journal of the International Neuropsychological Society, 1,* 291–296.

Oakes, M. L. (1986). *Statistical inference: A commentary for the social and behavioral sciences.* New York: Wiley.

*Obiols, J. E., Clos, M., Corbero, E., Domingo, M., Trincheria, I., & Domench, E. (1992). Sustained attention deficit in young schizophrenic and schizotypic men. *Psychological Reports, 71,* 1131–1136.

*Obiols, J. E., Marcos, T., & Salamero, M. (1987). Ventricular enlargement and neuropsychological testing in schizophrenia. *Acta Psychiatrica Scandinavica, 76,* 199–202.

O'Brien, J. T. (1995). Is hippocampal atrophy on magnetic resonance imaging a marker for Alzheimer's disease? *International Journal of Geriatric Psychiatry, 10,* 431–435.

*O'Brien, J. T., Eagger, S., Syed, G. M. S., Sahakian, B. J., & Levy, R. (1992). A study of regional cerebral blood flow and cognitive performance in Alzheimer's disease. *Journal of Neurology, Neurosurgery, and Psychiatry, 55,* 1182–1187.

*O'Carrol, R. (1992). Selecting controls for schizophrenia research studies: The use of the National Adult Reading Test (NART) is a measure of premorbid ability. *Schizophrenia Research, 8,* 137–141.

*O'Donnell, B. F., Shenton, M. E., McCarley, R. W., Faux, S. F., Smith, R. S., Salisbury, D. F., Nestor, P. G., Pollack, S. D., Kikinis, R., & Jolesz, F. A. (1993). The auditory N2 component in schizophrenia: Relationship to MRI temporal lobe gray matter and to other ERP abnormalities. *Biological Psychiatry, 34,* 26–40.

Ogden, J. A. (1996). *Fractured minds: A case-study approach to clinical neuropsychology.* New York: Oxford University Press.

*Ogden, J. A., Growdon, J. H., & Corkin, S. (1990). Deficits on visuospatial tests involving forward planning in high functioning Parkinsonians. *Neuropsychiatry, Neuropsychology, and Behavioral Neurology, 3,* 125–139.

Oltmanns, T. F. (1978). Selective attention in schizophrenia and manic psychoses: The effect os distraction on information processing. *Journal of Abnormal Psychology, 87,* 212–225.

*Oltmanns, T. F., Murphy, R., Berenbaum, H., & Dunlop, S. R. (1985). Rating verbal communication impairment in schizophrenia and affective disorders. *Schizophrenia Bulletin, 11,* 292–299.

*Ostergaard, A. L., Heindel, W. C., Paulsen, J. S. (1995). The biasing effect of verbal labels on memory for ambiguous figures in patients with progressive dementia. *Journal of the International Neuropsychological Society, 1*, 271–280.

Osterrieth, P. A. (1944). Le test de copie d'une figure complexe. *Archives de Psychologie, 30*, 206–356.

Otto, M. W. (1992). Normal and abnormal information processing: A neuropsychological perspective on obsessive compulsive disorder. *Psychiatric Clinics of North America, 15*, 825–848.

Overall, J.E., & Gorham, D.R. (1962). The brief psychiatric rating scale. *Psychological Reports, 10*, 799–812.

*Owen, A.M., Beksinska, M., James, M., Leigh, P. N., Summers, B. A., Marsden, C. D., Quinn, N. P., Sahakian, B. J., & Robbins, T. W. (1993). Visuospatial memory deficits at different stages of Parkinson's disease. *Neuropsychologia, 31*, 627–644.

*Owen, A. M., Sahakian, B. J., Hodges, J. R., Summers, B. A., Polkey, C. E., & Robbins, T. W. (1995). Dopamine-dependent frontostriatal planning deficits in early Parkinson's disease. *Neuropsychology, 9*, 126–140.

*Oyanagi, K., Takahashi, H., Wakabayashi, K., & Ikuta, F. (1989). Correlative decrease of large neurons in the neostriatum and basal nucleus meynert in Alzheimer's disease. *Brain Research, 504*, 354–357.

*Pachana, N. A., Boone, K. B., Miller, B. L., Cummings, J. L., & Berman, N. (1996). Comparison of neuropsychological functioning in Alzheimer's disease and frontotemporal dementia. *Journal of the International Neuropsychological Society, 2*, 505–510.

*Padovani, A., Di Piero, V., Bragoni, M., Iacoboni, M., Gualdi, G. F., & Lenzi, G. L. (1995). Patterns of neuropsychological impairment in mild dementia: A comparison between Alzheimer's disease and multi-infarct dementia. *Acta Neurologica Scandinavica, 92*, 433–442.

*Palmer, B. W., Heaton, R. K., Paulsen, J. S., Kuck, J., Braff, D., Harris, M. J., Zisook, S., & Jeste, D. V. (1997). Is it possible to be schizophrenic yet neuropsychologically normal? *Neuropsychology, 11*, 437–446.

*Paolo, A. M., Axelrod, B. N., Troster, A. I., Blackwell, K. T., & Koller, W. C. (1996). Utility of a Wisconsin Card Sorting Test short form in persons with Alzheimer's and Parkinson's disease. *Journal of Clinical and Experimental Neuropsychology, 18*, 892–897.

*Park, S., & Holzman, P. S. (1993). Association of working memory deficit and eye tracking dysfunction in schizophrenia. *Schizophrenia Research, 11*, 55–61.

*Parkin, A. J. (1993). Progressive aphasia without dementia—A clinical and cognitive neuropsychological analysis. *Brain and Language, 44*, 201–220.

Parkinson, J. (1817). *An essay of the shaking palsy*. London: Sherwood, Neely, & Jones.

Parks, R. W., Haxby, J. V., & Grady, C. L. (1993). Positron emission tomography in Alzheimer's disease. In R. W. Parks, R. F. Zec, & R. S. Wilson (Eds.), *Neuropsychology of Alzheimer's disease and other dementias*. (pp. 459–488). New York: Oxford University Press.

Parks, R. W., Zec, R. F., & Wilson, R. S. (1993). *Neuropsychology of Alhzeimer's disease and other dementias*. New York: Oxford University Press.

Parsons, O. A., Vega, Jr., A., & Burn, J. (1969). Differential psychological effects of lateralized brain damage. *Journal of Consulting and Clinical Psychology, 33*, 551–557.

*Partiot, A., Verin, M., Pillon, B., Teixeir-Ferreira, C., Agid, Y., & Dubois, B. (1996). Delayed response tasks in basal ganglia in man: Further evidence for a striato-frontal cooperation in behavioral adaptation. *Neuropsychologia, 34*, 709–721.

*Partridge, F. M., Knight, R. G., & Feeham, M. (1990). Direct and indirect memory performance in patients with senile dementia. *Psychological Medicine, 20,* 111–118.

*Pasquier, F., Lebert, F., Grymonprez, L., & Petit, H. (1995). Verbal fluency in dementia of frontal lobe type and dementia of Alzheimer type. *Journal of Neurology, Neurosurgery, and Psychiatry, 58,* 81–84.

Patten, J. (1995). *Neurological differential diagnosis.* London: Springer.

*Patterson, K., Graham, N., & Hodges, J. R. (1994). Reading in dementia of the Alzheimer's type: A preserved ability. *Neuropsychology, 8,* 395–407.

*Paul, R. H., Blanco, C. R., Hames, K. A., & Beatty, W. W. (1997). Autobiographical memory in multiple sclerosis. *Journal of the International Neuropsychological Society, 3,* 246–251.

*Paulsen, J. S., Butters, N., Salmon, D. P., Heindel, W. C., & Swenson, M. R. (1993). Prism adaptation in Alzheimer's and Huntington's disease. *Neuropsychology, 7,* 73–81.

*Paulsen, J. S., Heaton, R. K., Sadek, J. R., Perry, W., Delis, D. C., Braff, D., Kuck, J., Zisook, S., & Jeste, D. V. (1995). The nature of learning and memory impairments in schizophrenia. *Journal of the International Neuropsychological Society, 1,* 88–99.

*Paus, T. (1991). Two modes of central gaze fixation maintenance and oculomotor distractibility in schizophrenics. *Schizophrenia Research, 5,* 145–152.

*Paus, T. (1989). Oculomotor and electrophysiological signs of distractibility in schizophrenics. *Activitas Nervosa Superior, 32,* 147–148.

*Pearlson, G. D., Harris, G. J., Powers, R. E., Barta, P. E., Camargo, E. E., Chase, G. A., Noga, T., & Tune, L. E. (1992). Quantitative changes in mesial temporal volume, regional cerebral blood flow, and cognition in Alzheimer's disease. *Archives of General Psychiatry, 49,* 402–408.

Perret, E. (1974). The left frontal lobe of man and the suppression of habitual responses in verbal categorical behavior. *Neuropsychologia, 12,* 323–330.

*Petersen, R. C., Smith, G. E., Ivnik, R. J., Kokmen, E., & Tangalos, E. G. (1994). Memory function in very early Alzheimer's disease. *Neurology, 44,* 867–872.

Peterson, L. R., & Peterson, M. J. (1959). Short-term retention of individual verbal items. *Journal of Experimental Psychology, 58,* 193–198.

Peyser, J. M., Rao, S. M., LaRocca, N. G., & Kaplan, E. (1990). Guidelines for neuropsychological research in multiple sclerosis. *Archives of Neurology, 47,* 94–97.

*Phillips, M. L., Woodruff, P. W. R., & David, A. S. (1996). Stroop interference and facilitation in the cerebral hemispheres in schizophrenia. *Schizophrenia Research, 20,* 57–68.

*Pillon, B., Blin, J., Vidailheti, M., Deweer, B., Sirigu, A., Dubois, B., Agid, Y. (1995). The neuropsychological pattern of corticobasal degeneration: Comparison with progressive supranuclear palsy and Alzheimer's disease. *Neurology, 45,* 1477–1483.

*Pillon, B., Dewer, B., Michon, A., Malapani, C., Agid, Y., Dubois, B. (1994). Are explicit memory disorders of progressive supranuclear palsy related to damage to stritofrontal circuits? Comparison with Alzheimer's, Parkinson's, and Huntington's diseases. *Neurology, 44,* 1264–1270.

Pillon, B., & Dubois, B. (1992). Cognitive and behavioral impairments. In, I. Litvan & Y. Agid (Eds.), *Progressive supranuclear palsy: Clinical and research approaches.* Oxford: Oxford University Press.

*Pillon, B., Dubois, B., Lhermitte, F., & Agid, Y. (1986). Heterogeneity of cognitive impairment in progressive supranuclear palsy, Parkinson's disease, and Alzheimer's disease. *Neurology, 36,* 1179–1185.

*Pillon, B., Ertle, S., Deweer, B., Sarazin, M., Agid, Y., & Dubois, B. (1996). Memory for spatial location is affected in Parkinson's disease. *Neuropsychologia, 34,* 77–85.

Pirozzolo, F. J., Hansch, E. C., Mortimer, J. A., Webster, D. D., & Kuskowski, M. A. (1982). Dementia in Parkinson's disease: A neuropsychological analysis. *Brain and Cognition, 1,* 71–83.

*Pishkin, V., & Bourne Jr., L. E. (1981). Abstraction and the use of available information by schizophrenic and normal individuals. *Journal of Abnormal Psychology, 90,* 197–203.

*Pishkin, V., & Williams, W. V. (1983). Cognitive deficit in schizophrenia: Subvocal mediation, rigidity, and complexity parameters. *The Journal of Nervous and Mental Disease, 171,* 24–29.

*Pishkin, V., & Williams, W. V. (1984). Redundancy and complexity of information in cognitive performances of schizophrenic and normal individuals. *Journal of Clinical Psychology, 40,* 648–654.

Poeck, K., & Luzzatti, C. (1988). Slowly progressive aphasia in three patients: The problem of accompanying neuropsychological deficits. *Brain, 111,* 151–168.

*Pogue-Geile, M. F., & Oltmanns, T. F. (1980). Sentence perception and distractibility in schizophrenic, manic, and depressed patients. *Journal of Abnormal Psychology, 89,* 115–124.

Poser, C. M., Paty, D. W., Scheinberg, L., McDonald, W. I., Davis, F. A., Ebers, G. C., Johnson, K. P., Sibley, W. A., Silberberg, D. H., & Tourtellotte, W. W. (1983). New diagnostic criteria for multiple sclerosis: guidelines for research protocols. *Annals of Neurology, 13,* 227–231.

*Poewe, W., Benke, T., Karamat, E., Schelosky, L., Wagner, M., & Sperk, G. (1990). CSF somatostatin-like immunoreactivity in dementia of Parkinson's disease. *Journal of Neurology, Neurosurgery, and Psychiatry, 53,* 1105–1106.

*Poewe, W., Berger, W., Benke, T., & Schelosky, L. (1991). High-speed memory scanning in Parkinson's disease: Adverse effects of levodopa. *Annals of Neurology, 29,* 670–673.

Porteus, S. D. (1959). *The Maze Test and clinical psychology.* Palo Alto, CA: Pacific Books.

Porteus, S. D. (1965). *Porteus Maze Test. Fifty years' application.* New York: Psychological Corporation.

Povlishock, J. T., Becker, D. P., & Cheng, C. L. Y. (1986). Axonal change in minor head injury. *Journal of Neuropathology and Experimental Neurology, 42,* 225–242.

*Pozzi, D., Perracchi, M., Sabe, L., Golimstock, A., Garcia, H., & Starkstein, S. (1995). Quantified electroencephalographic correlates of neuropsychological deficits in Alzheimer's disease. *Journal of Neuropsychiatry, and Clinical Neurosciences, 7,* 61–67.

*Pozzilli, C., Passafiume, D., Bernardi, S., Pantano, P., Incoccia, C., Bastianecco, S., Bozza, L., Lenzi, G. L., & Fieschi, C. (1991). SPECT, MRI and cognitive functions in multiple sclerosis. *Journal of Neurology, Neurosurgery, and Psychiatry, 54,* 110–115.

Purdue Research Foundation (no date). *Purdue Pegboard Test.* Lafayette, IN: Lafayette Instrument Co.

*Ragin, A. B., & Oltmanns, T. F. (1986). Lexical cohesion and formal thought disorder during and after psychotic episodes. *Journal of Abnormal Psychology, 95,* 181–183.

Raine, A. (1992). An evaluation of structual and functional prefrontal deficits in schizophrenia: MRI and neuropsychological measures. *Psychiatry Research, 45,* 123–137.

*Raine, A., Andrews, H., Sheard, C., Walder, C., & Manders, D. (1989). Interhemispheric transfer in schizophrenics, depressives, and normals with schizoid tendencies. *Journal of Abnormal Psychology, 98,* 35–41.

*Raine, A., Harrison, G. N., Reynolds, G. P., Sheard, C., Cooper, J. E., & Medley, I. (1990). Structural and functional characteristics of the corpus callosum in schizophrenics, psychiatric controls, and normal controls- a magnetic resonance imaging and neuropsychological evaluation. *Archives of General Psychiatry, 47,* 1060–1064.

*Ramachandran, G., Marder, K., Tang, M., Schofield, P. W., Chun, M. R., Devanand, D. P., Stern, Y., & Mayeux, R. (1996). A preliminary study of a-polipoprotien E genotype and psychiatric manifestations of Alzheimer's disease. *Neurology, 47,* 256–259.

Randolph, C., Goldberg, T. E., & Weinberger, D. R. (1993). The neuropsychology of schizophrenia. In K. M. Hielman & E. Valenstein (Eds.), *Clinical neuropsychology* (3rd ed.). New York: Oxford University Press.

*Randolph, C., Gold, J. M., Kozora, E., Cullum, C. M., Herman, B. P., & Wyler, A. R. (1994). Estimating memory function: Disparity of Wechsler memory scale- revised and California verbal learning test indices in clinical and normal samples. *Clinical Neuropsychologist, 8,* 99–108.

Rao, S. M. (1986). Neuropsychology of multiple sclerosis: A critical review. *Journal of Clinical and Experimental Neuropsychology, 8,* 503–542.

Rao, S. M. (1990). *Neurobehavioral aspects of multiple sclerosis.* New York: Oxford University Press.

Rao, S. M. (1993). White matter dementias. In R.W. Parks, R.F. Zec, & R.S. Wilson (Eds.), *Neuropsychology of Alzheimer's Disease and Other Dementias.* (pp. 438–456). New York: Oxford University Press.

*Rao, S. M., Grafman, J., DiGiulio, D., Mittenberg, W., Bernardin, L., Leo, G. J., Luchetta, T., & Unverzagt, F. (1993). Memory dysfunction in multiple sclerosis. Its relation to working memory, semantic encoding, and implicit learning. *Neuropsychology, 7,* 364–374.

*Rao, S. M., Hammeke, T. A., Glatt, S., McQuillen, M. P., Khatri, B. O., Rhodes, A. M., & Pollard, S. (1984). Neuropsychological studies in chronic progressive multiple sclerosis. *Annals of the New York Academy of Sciences, 436,* 495–497.

*Rao, S. M., Hammeke, T. A., & Speech, T. J. (1987). Wisconsin Card Sorting Test performance in relapse-remitting and chronic-progressive multiple sclerosis. *Journal of Consulting and Clinical Psychology, 55,* 263–265.

*Rao, S. M., Leo, G. J., Bernardin, L., & Unverzagt, F. (1991). Cognitive dysfunction in multiple sclerosis. I. Frequency, patterns, and prediction. *Neurology, 41,* 685–691.

*Rao, S. M., Leo, G. J., & St. Aubin-Faubert, P. (1989). On the nature of memory disturbance in multiple sclerosis. *Journal of Clinical and Experimental Neuropsychology, 11,* 699–712.

Raskin, S. A., Borod, J. C., & Tweedy, J. R. (1990). Neuropsychological aspects of Parkinson's disease. *Neuropsychology Review, 1,* 185–221.

*Raskin, S. A., Borod, J. C., & Tweedy, J. R. (1992). Set-shifting and spatial orientation in patients with Parkinson's disease. *Journal of Clinical and Experimental Neuropsychology, 14,* 801–824.

*Raskin, S. A., & Rearick, E. (1996). Verbal fluency in individuals with mild traumatic brain injury. *Neuropsychology, 10,* 416–422.

Rasmussen, S. A., & Eisen, J. L. (1990). Epidemiology and clinical features of obsessive-compulsive disorder. In M. A. Jenike, L. Baer, & W. E. Minichiello (Eds.), *Obsessive compulsive disorders: Theory and managment.* (pp. 10–27). Chicago: Year Book Medical Publishers, Inc.

Rasmusson, D. X., Carson, K. A., Brookmeyer, R., Kawas, C., & Brandt, J. (1996). Predicting rate of cognitive decline in probable Alzheimer's disease. *Brain and Cognition, 31,* 133–147.

Raven, J. C. (1960). *Guide to the Standard Progressive Matrices.* London: H.K. Lewis.

Raven, J. C. (1982). *Revised manual for Raven's Progressive Matrices and Vocabulary Scale.* Windsor, U.K.: NFER Nelson.

Raz, S., & Raz, N. (1990). Structural brain abnormalities in the major psychoses: A quantitative review of the evidence from computerized imaging. *Psychological Bulletin, 108,* 93–108.

*Rebok, G., Brandt, J., & Folstein, M. (1990). Longitudinal cognitive decline in patients with Alzheimer's disease. *Journal of Geriatric Psychiatry and Neurology, 3,* 91–97.

Rediess, S., & Caine, E. D. (1993). Aging associated cognitive changes: How do they relate to the diagnosis of dementia? *Current Opinion in Psychiatry, 6,* 531–535.

*Reichard, C. C., Camp, C. J., & Strub, R. L. (1995). Effects of sudden insight on long-term sentence priming in Alzheimer's disease. *Journal of Clinical and Experimental Neuropsychology, 17,* 325–334.

*Reid, W., Broe, G., Creasey, H., Grayson, D., McCusker, E., Bennet, H., Longley, W., & Sulway, M. R. (1996). Age at onset and pattern of neuropsychological impairment in mild early-stage Alzheimer's disease. *Archives of Neurology, 53,* 1056–1061.

Reitan, R. M. (1958). Validity of the Trail Making Test as an indicator of organic brain damage. *Perceptual and Motor Skills, 8,* 271–276.

Reitan, R. M., & Wolfson, D. (1989). The seashore Rhythm Test and brain functions. *The Clinical Neuropsychologist, 3,* 70–78.

Reitan, R. M., & Wolfson, D. (1993). *The Halstead-Reitan neuropsychological test battery: Theory and clinical interpretation.* Tucson, AZ: Neuropsychology Press.

*Revonsuo, A., Portin, R., Kolvikko, L., Rinne, J. O., & Rinne, U. K. (1993). Slowing of information processing in Parkinson's disease. *Brain and Cognition, 21,* 87–110.

Rey, A. (1941). Psychological examination of traumatic encephalopathy. *Archives de Psychologie, 28,* 286–340; sections translated by J. Corwin, & F. W. Bylsma, *The Clinical Neuropsychologist,* 1993, 4–9.

Rey, A. (1964). *L'examen Clinique en Psychologie.* Paris: Presses Universitaires de France.

*Richards, M., Cote, L. J., & Stern, Y. (1993). Executive function in Parkinson's disease: Set shifting or set maintenance? *Journal of Clinical and Experimental Neuropsychology, 15,* 266–279.

*Richards, P. M., & Ruff, R. M. (1989). Motivational effects on neuropsychological functioning: Comparison of depressed versus nondepressed individuals. *Journal of Consulting and Clinical Psychology, 57,* 396–402.

Risberg, J. (1987). Frontal lobe degeneration of the non-Alzheimer type. III. Regional cerebral blood flow. *Archives of Gerontology and Geriatric Psychiatry, 6,* 225–233.

Risberg, J., Passant, U., Warkentin, S., & Gustafson, L. (1993). Regional cerebral blood flow in frontal lobe dementia of non Alzheimer type. *Dementia, 4,* 186–187.

*Rist, F., & Thurm, I. (1984). Effects of intramodal and crossmodal stimulus diversity on the reaction time of chronic schizophrenics. *Journal of Abnormal Psychology, 93,* 331–338.

*Rizzo, L., Danion, J-M., Van Der Linden, M., & Grange, D. (1996). Patients with schizophrenia remember that an event has occurred, but not when. *British Journal of Psychiatry, 168,* 427–431.

*Rizzo, L., Danion, J. M., Van Der Linden, M., Grange, D., & Rohmer, J. G. (1996). Impairment of memory for spatial context in schizophrenia. *Neuropsychology, 10,* 376–384.

Robbins, T. W. (1990). The case for frontostriatal dysfunction in schizophrenia. *Schizophrenia Bulletin, 16,* 391–402.

*Robbins, T. W., James, M., Owen, A. M., Lange, K. W., Lees, A. J., Leigh, P. N., Marsden, C. D., Quinn, N. P., & Summers, B. A. (1994). Cognitive deficits in progressive supranuclear palsy, Parkinson's disease and multiple system atrophy in tests sensitive to frontal lobe dysfunction. *Journal of Neurology, Neurosurgery, and Psychiatry, 57,* 79–88.

*Roberts, V. J., Ingram, S. M., Lamar, M., & Green, R. C. (1996). Prosody impairment and associated affective and behavioral disturbances in Alzheimer's disease. *Neurology, 47,* 1482–1488.

*Robertson, C., Hazelwood, R., & Rawson, M. D. (1996). The effects of Parkinson's disease on the capacity to generate information randomly. *Neuropsychologia, 34,* 1069–1078.

*Robertson, G., Taylor, P. J. (1985). Some cognitive correlates of schizophrenic illness. *Psychological Medicine, 15,* 81–98.

*Robinson, K. M., Grossman, M., White-Devine, T., & D' Esposito, M. (1996). Category specific difficulty naming with verbs in Alzheimer's disease. *Neurology, 47,* 178–182.

Rohling, M. L., & Scogin, F. (1993). Automatic and effortful memory processes in depressed patients. *Journal of Gerontology: Psychological Sciences, 10,* 87–95.

Rosen, W. G., Terry, R. D., Fuld, P. A., Katzman, R., & Peck, A. (1980). Pathological verification of ischemic score in differentiation of dementias. *Annals of Neurology, 7,* 486–488.

*Rosenbaum, G., Chapin, K., & Shore, D. L. (1988). Attention deficit in schizophrenia & schizotypy: Marker versus symptom variables. *Journal of Abnormal Psychology, 97,* 41–47.

Rosenthal, R. (1979). "The 'file drawer' problem and tolerance for null results." *Psychological Bulletin, 86,* 638–641.

Rosenthal, R. (1991). *Meta-analytic procedures for social research.* Beverly Hills, CA: Sage.

Rosenthal, R. (1995). Writing meta-analytic reviews. *Psychological Bulletin, 118,* 183–192.

*Rosser, A., & Hodges, J. R. (1994). Initial letter and semantic category fluency in Alzheimer's disease, Huntington's disease, and progressive supranuclear palsy. *Journal of Neurology, Neurosurgery, and Psychiatry, 57,* 1389–1394.

Rothi, L. J. G., & Heilman, K. M. (1997). *Apraxia: The neuropsychology of action.* UK: Psychology Press.

Rothschild, D. (1934). Alzheimer's disease. *American Journal of Psychiatry, 91,* 485–518.

*Rouleau, I., Salmon, D. P., Butters, N., Kennedy, C., & McGuire, K. (1992). Quantitative and qualitative analyses of clock drawings in Alzheimer's and Huntington's disease. *Brain and Cognition, 18,* 70–87.

*Roxborough, H., Muir, W. J., Blackwood, D. H. R., Walker, M. T., & Blackburn, I. M. (1993). Neuropsychological and P300 abnormalities in schizophrenics and their relatives. *Psychological Medicine, 23,* 305–314.

Roy, E. A. (1996). Hand preference, manual asymmetries and limb apraxia. In D. Elliott & E. A. Roy (Eds.), *Manual asymmetries in motor performance.* (pp. 215–236). Boca Raton, FL: CRC Press.

Roy, E. A., Brown, L., Winchester, T., Square, P., Hall, C., & Black, S. (1993). Memory processes and gestural performance in apraxia. *Adapted Physical Activity Quarterly, 10,* 293–311.

Rozeboom, W. W. (1960). The fallacy of the null hypothesis significance test. *Psychological Bulletin, 57,* 416–428.

*Rund, B. R. (1982). The effect of distraction on focal attention in paranoid and non-paranoid schizophrenic patients compared to normals and non-psychotic psychiatric patients. *Journal of Psychiatric Research, 17,* 241–250.

*Rund, B. R. (1989). Distractibility and recall capability in schizophrenics: A 4 year longitudinal study of stability in cognitive performance. *Schizophrenia Research, 2,* 265–275.

*Rund, B. R., Landro, N. I., & Orbeck, A. L. (1993). Stability in backward masking performance in schizophrenics, affectively disturbed patients, and normal controls. *Journal of Nervous and Mental Disease, 181,* 233–237.

*Rund, B. R., Orbeck, A. L., & Landro, N. I. (1992). Vigilance deficits in schizophrenics and affectively disturbed patients. *Acta Psychiatrica Scandinavica, 86,* 207–212.

*Russel, A. J., Cullum, C. M., Jones, P. B., Hemsley, D. R., & Murray, R. M. (1997). Schizophrenia and the myth of intellectual decline. *American Journal of Psychiatry, 154,* 635–639.

*Russell, P. N., Consedine, C. E., & Knight, R. G. (1980). Visual and memory search by process schizophrenics. *Journal of Abnormal Psychology, 89,* 109–114.

*Ryan, L., Clark, C. M., Klonoff, H., & Paty, D. (1993). Models of cognitive deficit and statistical hypotheses: Multiple sclerosis, an example. *Journal of Clinical and Experimental Neuropsychology, 15,* 563–577.

*Ryan, L., Clark, C. M., Klonoff, H., Li, D., & Paty, D. (1996). Patterns of cognitive impairment in relapsing-remitting multiple sclerosis and their relationship to neuropathology on magnetic resonance images. *Neuropsychology, 10,* 176–193.

*Sabe, L., Jason, L., Juejati, M., Leiguarda, R., & Starkstein, S. E. (1995). Dissociation between declaritive and procedural learning in dementia and depression. *Journal of Clinical and Experimental Neuropsychology, 17,* 841–848.

*Saccuzzo, D. P., & Braff, D. L. (1980). Associative cognitive dysfunction in schizophrenia and old age. *The Journal of Nervous and Mental Disease, 168,* 41–45.

*Sackeim, H. A., Freeman, J., McElhiney, M., Coleman, E., Prudic, J., & Devanand, D. P. (1992). Effects of major depression on estimates of intelligence. *Journal of Clinical and Experimental Neuropsychology, 14,* 268–288.

Sagar, H. J. (1987). Clinical similarities and differences between Alzheimer's disease and Parkinson's disease. In R. J. Wurtman, S. H. Corkin, & J. H. Growdon (Eds.), *Alzheimer's disease: Advances in basic research and therapies.* (pp. 91–107). Cambridge, MA: Center for Brain Sciences and Metabolism Charitable Trust.

*Sagar, H. J., Sullivan, E. V., Cooper, J. A., & Jordan, N. (1991). Normal release from proactive interference in untreated patients with Parkinson's disease. *Neuropsychologia, 20,* 1033–1044.

*Sagawa, K., Kawakatsu, S., Komatani, A., & Totsuka, S. (1990). Frontality, laterality, and cortical-subcoritcal gradient of cerebral blood flow in schizophrenia: Relationship to symptoms and neuropsychological functions. *Neuropsychobiology, 24*, 1–7.

*Sahakian, B. J., Downes, J. J., Eagger, S., Evenden, J. L., Levy, R., Philport, M. P., Roberts, A. C., & Robbins, T. W. (1990). Sparing of attentional relative to mnemonic function in a subgroup of patients with dementia of the Alzheimer type. *Neuropsychologia, 28*, 1197–1213.

*Sahgal, A., Galloway, P. H., McKeith, I. G., Lloyd, S., Cook, J. H., Ferrier, I. N., & Edwardson, J. A. (1992). Matching-to-sample deficits in patients with senile dementias of the Alzheimer and Lewy body types. *Archives of Neurology, 49*, 1043–1046.

*Sahgal, A., McKeith, I. G., Galloway, P. H., Tasker, N., & Steckler, T. (1995). Do differences in visuospatial ability between senile dementias of the Alzheimer and Lewy body types reflect differences solely in mnemonic function. *Journal of Clinical and Experimental Neuropsychology, 17*, 35–43.

Saint-Cyr, J. A., Taylor, A. E., & Lang, A. E. (1993). Neuropsychological and psychiatric side effects in the treatment of Parkinson's disease. *Neurology, 43 (suppl. 6)*, S47-S52.

*Salmon, D. P., Granholm, E., McCullough, D., Butters, N., & Grant, I. (1989). Recognition memory span in mildly and moderately demented patients with Alzheimer's disease. *Journal of Clinical and Experimental Neuropsychology, 11*, 429–443.

*Salmon, D. P., Shimamura, A. P., Butters, N., & Smith, S. (1988). Lexical and semantic priming deficits in patients with Alzheimer's disease. *Journal of Clinical and Experimental Neuropsychology, 10*, 477–494.

*Salmon, E., Meulemans, T., Van der Linden, M., Degueldre, C., & Franck. (1996). Anterior cingulate dysfunction in presenile dementia due to progressive supranuclear palsy. *Acta Neurologica Belgica, 96*, 247–253.

*Salovay, M. R., Shenton, M. E., & Holzman, P. S. (1987). Comparitive studies of thought disorders in mania and schizophrenia. *Archives of General Psychiatry, 44*, 13–20.

Sandson, J., & Albert, M. L. (1987). Perseveration in behavioral neurology. *Neurology, 37*, 1736–1741.

*Sandson, T. A., O' Connor, M., Sperling, R. A., Edelman, R. R., & Warach, S. (1996). Noninvasive perfusion MRI in Alzheimer's disease: A preliminary report. *Neurology, 47*, 1338–1342.

*Sasi, P. T., & Srivastava, A. (1992). Neurocognitive impairment in positive and negative schizophrenia. *Psychological Studies, 37*, 47–56.

*Saykin, A. J., Gur, R. C., Gur, R. E., Mozley, P. D., Mozley, L. H., Resnick, S. M., Kester, D. B., & Stafiniak, P. (1991). Neuropsychological function in schizophrenia: Selective impairment in memory and learning. *Archives of General Psychiatry, 48*, 618–624.

*Saykin, A. J., Shtasel, D. L., Gur, R. E., Kester, B., Mozley, L. H., Stafiniak, P., & Gur, R. C. (1994). Neuropsychological deficits in neuroleptic naive patients with first-episode schizophrenia. *Archives of General Psychiatry, 51*, 124–131.

*Scarone, S., Abbruzzese, M., & Gambini, O. (1993). The Wisconsin Card Sorting Test discriminates schizophrenic patients and their siblings. *Schizophrenia Research, 10*, 103–107.

*Schapiro, M. B., Pietrini, P., Grady, C. L., Bail, M. J., Decarli, C., Kumar, A., Kaye, J. A., & Haxby, J. V. (1993). Reductions in parietal and temporal cerebral metabolic rates for glucose are not specific for Alzheimer's disease. *Journal of Neurology, Neurosurgery, and Psychiatry, 56*, 859–864.

*Scheltens, P. h., Hazenberg, G. J., Lindeboom, J., Valk, J., Wolters, E. C. h. (1990). A case of progressive aphasia without dementia: "temporal" Pick's disease? *Journal of Neurology, Neurosurgery, and Psychiatry, 53*, 79–80.

*Schlosser, D., & Ivison, D. (1989). Assessing memory deterioration with the Wechsler Memory Scale, the National Adult Reading Test and the Schonell Graded Word Reading Test. *Journal of Clinical and Experimental Neuropsychology, 11*, 785–792.

*Schmand, B., Brand, N., & Kuipers, T. (1992). Procedural learning of cognitive and motor skills in psychotic patients. *Schizophrenia Research, 8*, 157–170.

Schmidt, F. L. (1992). What do data really mean? Research findings, meta-analysis, and cumulative knowledge in psychology. *American Psychologist, 47*, 1173–1181.

Schmidt, F. L. (1996). Statistical significance testing and cumulative knowledge in psychology: Implications for training of researchers. *Psychological Methods, 1*, 115–129.

*Schneider, S. G., & Asarnow, R. F. (1987). A comparison of cognitive/neuropsychological impairments of nonretarded autistic and schizophrenic children. *Journal of Abnormal Child Psychology, 15*, 29–46.

*Schoenhuber, R., & Genticini, M. (1988). Anxiety and depression after mild head injury: A case control study. *Journal of Neurology, Neurosurgery, and Psychiatry, 51*, 722–724.

*Scholten, I. M., Kneebone, A. C., Denson, L. A., Field, C. D., & Blumbergs, P. (1995). Primary progressive aphasia: Serial linguistic, neuropsychological and radiological findings with neuropathological results. *Aphasiology, 9*, 495–516.

*Schretlen, D., Brandt, J., Bobholtz, J.H. (1996). Validation of the Brief Test of Attention in patients with Huntington's disease and amnesia. *The Clinical Neuropsychologist, 10*, 90–95.

Schumacher, G. A., Beebe, G., Kibler, R. F., Kurland, L. T., Kurtzke, J. F., McDowell, F., Nagler, B., Sibley, W. A., Tourtelotte, W. W., & Willmon, T. L. (1965). Problems of experimental trials of therapy in multiple sclerosis: Report by the panel on the evaluation of experimental trials of therapy in multiple sclerosis. *Annuals of the the New York Academy of Science, 122*, 552–568.

Schwartz, B., Carr, A., Munich, R. L., & Bartuch, E. (1990). Voluntary motor performance in psychotic disorders. *Psychological Reports, 66*, 1223–1234.

*Schwartz, B., Deutsch, L. H., Cohen, C., Warden, D., Deutsh, S.I. (1991). Memory for temporal order in schizophrenia. *Biological Psychiatry, 29*, 329–339.

*Schwartz, B., Winstead, D. K., & Adinoff, B. (1983). Temporal integration deficit in visual information processing by chronic schizophrenics. *Biological Psychiatry, 18*, 1311–1320.

*Schwartz, B. L., Rosse, R. B., Veazey, C., & Deutsch, S. I. (1996). Impaired motor skill learning in schizophrenia: Implications for corticostriatal dysfunction. *Comprehensive Psychiatry, 39*, 241–248.

Scoville, W. B., & Milner, B. (1957). Loss of recent memory after bilateral hippocampal lesions. *Journal of Neurology, Neurosurgery, and Psychiatry, 20*, 11–21.

Seidman, L. J. (1983). Schizophrenia and brain dysfunction. An integration of recent neurodiagnostic findings. *Psychological Bulletin, 94*, 195–238.

*Seidman, L. J., Oscar-Berman, M., Kalinowski, A. G., Ajilore, O., Kremen, W. S., Faraone, S. V., & Tsuang, M. T. (1995). Experimental and clinical neuropsychological measures of prefrontal dysfunction in schizophrenia. *Neuropsychology, 9*, 481–490.

*Seidman, L. J., Pepple, J. R., Faraone, S. V., Kremen, W.S., Green, A. I., Brown, W. A., & Tsuang, M. T. (1993). Neuropsychological performance in chronic schizophrenia in response to neuroleptic dose reduction. *Biological Psychiatry, 33,* 575–584.

*Seidman, L. J., Talbat, N. L., Kalinowski, A. G., McCarley, R. W., Faraone, S. V., Kremen, W. S., Pepple, J. R., & Tsuang, M. T. (1992). Neuropsychological probes of fronto-limbic system dysfunction in schizophrenia: Olfactory identification and Wisconsin Card Sorting performance. *Schizophrenia Research, 6,* 55–65.

*Sengal R. A., & Lovallo, W. R. (1983). Effects of cueing on immediate and recent memory in schizophrenia. *The Journal of Nervous and Mental Disease, 171,* 426–430.

*Sereno, A. B., & Holzman, P. S. (1996). Spatial selective attention in schizophrenic, affective disorder, and normal subjects. *Schizophrenia Research, 20,* 33–50.

Shallice, T. (1982). Specific impairments of planning. *Philosophical Transactions of the Royal Society of London, 298,* 199–209.

Shallice, T. (1988). *From neuropsychology to mental structure.* Cambridge: Cambridge University Press.

Shallice, T., & Burgess, P. (1991). Higher-order cognitive impairments and frontal lobe lesions in man. In H. S. Levin, H. M. Eisenberg, & A. L. Benton (Eds.), *Frontal lobe function and dysfunction.* (pp. 125–138). New York: Oxford University Press.

*Shear, P. K., Sullivan, E. V., Mathalon, D. H., Lim, K. O., Davis, L. F., Yesavage, J. A., Tinklenberg, J. R., & Pfefferbaum, A. (1995). Longitudinal volumetric computed tomographic analysis of regional brain changes in normal aging and Alzheimer's disease. *Archives of Neurology, 52,* 392–402.

*Shenton, M. E., Kikinis, R., McCarley, R. W., Metcalf, D., Tieman, J., & Jalesz, F. A. (1991). Application of automated MRI volumetric measurement techniques to the ventricular system in schizophrenics and normal controls. *Schizophrenia Research, 5,* 103–113.

*Shoqeirat, M. A., & Mayes, A. R. (1988). Spatiotemporal memory and rate of forgetting in acute schizophrenics. *Psychological Medicine, 18,* 843–853.

Shoulson, I. (1990). Huntington's disease: Cognitice and psychiatric features. *Neuropsychiatry, Neuropsychology, and Behavioral Neurology, 3,* 15–22.

Shoulson, I., & Fah, S. (1979). Huntington's disease: Clinical care and evaluation. *Neurology, 29,* 1–3.

Sim, M., & Sussman, I. (1962). Alzheimer's disease: It's natural history and differential diagnosis. *Journal of Nervous and Mental Disease, 135,* 489–499.

*Simon, E., Leach, L., Winocur, G., & Moscovitch, M. (1994). Intact primary memory in mild to moderate Alzheimer disease: Indices from the California Verbal Learning Test. *Journal of Clinical and Experimental Neuropsychology, 16,* 414–422.

Sjogren, H. (1950). Twenty-four cases of Alzheimer's disease. *Acta Medica Scandinavica, 246,* 225–233.

Sjogren, T., Sjogren, H., & Lindren, Y. (1952). Morbus Alzheimer and morbus Pick, genetic, clinical and patho-anatomical study. *Acta Psychiatrica Scandinavica, 82* (Suppl.), 611–617.

*Ska, B., Poissant, A., & Joanette, Y. (1990). Line orientation judgment in normal elderly and subjects with dementia of Alzheimer's type. *Journal of Clinical and Experimental Neuropsychology, 12,* 695–702.

*Slaghuis, W. L., & Bakker, V. J. (1995). Forward and backward visual masking of contour by light in positive and negative symptom schizophrenia. *Journal of Abnormal Psychology, 104,* 41–54.

Smith, A. (1960). Changes in Porteus Maze scores of brain-operated schizophrenics after an eight year interval. *Journal of Mental Science, 106,* 967–978.

Smith, A. (1968). The Symbol-Digit Modalities Test: A neuropsychologic test for economic screening of learning and other cerebral disorders. *Learning Disorders, 3,* 83–91.

Smith, A. (1982). *Symbol digit modalities test manual.* Los Angeles: Western Psychological Services.

Snowden, J. S., Neary, D., & Mann, D. M. A. (1996). *Fronto-temporal lobar degeneration: Fronto-temporal dementia, progressive aphasia, semantic dementia.* New York: Churchill Livingstone.

*Snowden, J. S., Neary, D., Mann, D. M. A., Goulding, P. J., & Testa, H. J. (1992). Progressive language disorder due to lobar atrophy. *Annals of Neurology, 31,* 174–183.

Snyder, P. J., & Nussbaum, P. D. (1998). *Clinical neuropsychology: A pocket handbook for assessment.* Washington, DC: American Psychological Association.

Sohlberg, M. M., & Mateer, C. A. (1989). *Introduction to cognitive rehabilitation: Theory and practice.* New York: The Guilford Press.

*Solomon, C. M., Holyman, P. S., Levin, S., & Gale, H. J. (1987). The association between eye-tracking dysfunction and thought disorder in psychosis. *Archives of General Psychiatry, 44,* 31–35.

*Sonobe, N. (1993). Eye movements, verbal material recall and negative symptoms in chronic schizophrenia. *International Journal of Psychophysiology, 15,* 73–78.

Soper, H. V., Cicchetti, D. V., Satz, P., Light, R., & Orsini, D. L. (1988). Null hypothesis disrespect in neuropsychology: Dangers of alpha and beta errors. *Journal of Clinical and Experimental Neuropsychology, 10,* 255–270.

Soukup, V. M., & Adams, R. L. (1996). Parkinson's disease. In R. L. Adams, O. A. Parsons, J. L. Culbertson & S. J. Nixon (Eds.), *Neuropsychology for clinical practice: Etiology, assessment, and treatment of common neurological disorders.* (pp. 243–267). Washington, DC: American Psychological Association.

*Souza, V. B. N., Muir, W. J., Walker, M. T., Glabus, M. F., Roxborough, H. M., Sharp, C. W., Dunan, J. R., & Blackwood, D. H. R. (1995). Auditory P300 event-related potentials and neuropsychological performance in schizophrenia and bipolar affective disorder. *Biological Psychiatry, 37,* 300–310.

*Spampinato, U., Habert, M. O., Mas, J. L., Bourdel, M. C., Ziegler, M., de Recondo, J., Askienanzy, J., & Rondot, P. (1991). (99mTC)-HM-PAO SPECT and cognitive impairment in Parkinson's disease: A comparison with dementia of the Alzheimer type. *Journal of Neurology, Neurosurgery, and Psychiatry, 54,* 787–792.

*Speedie, L. J., Brake, N., Folstein, S. E., Bowers, D., & Heilman, K. M. (1990). Comprehension of prosody in Huntington's disease. *Journal of Neurology, Neurosurgery, and Psychiatry, 53,* 607–610.

*Spiler, K. B., Brown, G. G., & Gorell, J. M. (1994). Lexical decision in Parkinson disease: Lack of evidence for generalized bradyphrenia. *Journal of Clinical and Experimental Neuropsychology, 16,* 457–471.

Spohn, H. E., & Strauss, M. E. (1989). Relation of neuroleptic and anti-cholinergic medication to cognitive functions in schizophrenia. *Journal of Abnormal Psychology, 98,* 367–380.

Spreen, O., & Strauss, E. (1991). *A compendium of neuropsychological tests.* New York: Oxford University Press.

Spreen, O., & Strauss, E. (1998). *A compendium of neuropsychological tests* (2nd ed.), New York: Oxford University Press.

*Starkstein, S. E., Migliurelli, R., Teson, A., Sabe, L., Vazquez, S., Turjanski, M., Robinson, R. G., & Leiguarda, R. (1994). Specificity of changes in cerebral blood flow in patients with frontal lobe dementia. *Journal of Neurology, Neurosurgery, and Psychiatry, 57*, 790–796.

Starkstein, S. E., Preziosi, T. J., Berthier, M. L., Bolduc, P. L., Mayberg, H. S., & Robinson, R. G. (1989). Depression and cognitive impairment in Parkinson's disease. *Brain, 112*, 1141–1153.

Starkstein, S. E., Preziosi, T. J., Bolduc, P. L., & Robinson, R. G. (1990). Depression in Parkinson's disease. *Journal of Nervous and Mental Disease, 178*, 27–31.

*Starkstein, S. E., Vazquez, S., Migliorelli, R., Teson, A., Petracca, G., & Leiguardo, R. (1995). A SPECT study of depression in Alzheimer's disease. *Neuropsychiatry, Neuropsychology, and Behavioral Neurology, 8*, 38–43.

Steele, J. C. (1972). Progressive supranuclear palsy. *Brain, 95*, 693–704.

Steele, J. C., Richardson, J. C., & Olszewski, J. (1964). Progressive supranuclear palsy: a heterogeneous degeneration involving the brain stem, basal ganglia, and cerebellum, with vertical gaze and pseudobulbar palsy, nuclear dystonia, and dementia. *Archives of Neurology, 10*, 333–359.

Steingard, R., & Dillon-Stout, D. (1992). Tourette's Syndrom and obsessive compulsive diorder: Clinical aspects. *Psychiatric Clinics of North America, 15*, 849–900.

Stengel, E. (1943). A study of the symptomatology and differential diagnosis of Alzheimer's disease and Pick's disease. *Journal of Mental Science, 89*, 1–20.

*Stern, Y., Andrews, H., Pittman, J., Sano, M., Tatemichi, T., Lantigua, R., & Mayeux, R. (1992). Diagnosis of dementia in a heterogeneous population: Development of a neuropsychological paradigm based diagnosis of dementia and quantified correction for the effects of education. *Archives of Neurology, 49*, 453–460.

Stern, Y., Tang, M.-X., Jacobs, D. M., Sano, M., Marder, K., Bell, K., Dooneief, G., Schofield, P., & Cote, L. (1998). Prospective comparative study of the evolution of probable Alzheimer's disease and Parkinson's disease dementia. *Journal of the International Neuropsychological Society, 4*, 279–284.

*Stirling, J. D., Helkwell, J. S. E., & Hewitt, J. (1997). Verbal memory impairment in schizophrenia: No sparing of short term recall. *Schizophrenia Research, 25*, 85–95.

Storandt, M., Botwinick, J., Danziger, W. L., Berg, L., & Hughes, C. P. (1984). Psychometric differentiation of mild senile dementia of the Alzheimer's type. *Archives of Neurology, 41*, 497–499.

*Storandt, M., Stone, K., & LaBarge, E. (1995). Deficits in reading performance in very mild dementia of the Alzheimer type. *Neuropsychology, 9*, 174–176.

*Strandburg, R. J., Marsh, J. T., Brown, W. S., Asarnow, R. F., Guthrie, D., & Higa, J. (1990). Event-related potential correlates of impaired attention in schizophrenic children. *Biological Psychiatry, 27*, 1103–1115.

Straube, E. R., & Oades, R. D. (1992). *Schizophrenia: Empirical research and findings*. San Diego: Academic Press.

*Strauss, M. E., & Brandt, J. (1986). Attempt at preclinical identification of Huntington's disease using the WAIS. *Journal of Clinical and Experimental Neuropsychology, 8*, 210–218.

Stroop, J. R. (1935). Studies of interference in serial verbal reactions. *Journal of Experimental Psychology, 18*, 643–662.

Strub, R. L., & Black, F. W. (1993). *The mental status examination in neurology.* Philadelphia: F. A. Davis Company.

Stuss, D. T. (1996). Frontal lobes. In J. G. Beaumont, P. M. Kenealy, & M. J. C. Rogers (Eds.), *The Blackwell dictionary of neuropsychology.* (pp. 346–353). Cabridge: Blackwell Publishers.

Stuss, D. T., Alexander, M. P., & Benson, D. F. (1997). Frontal lobe functions. In M. R. Trimble & J. L. Cummings (Eds.), *Contemporary behavioral neurology.* (pp. 169–187). Boston: Butterworth-Heinemann.

Stuss, D. T., Alexander, M. P., Hamer, L., Palumbo, C., Dempster, R., Binns, M., Levine, B., & Izukawa, D. (1998). The effects of focal anterior and posterior brain lesions on verbal fluency. *Journal of the International Neuropsychological Society, 4,* 265–278.

Stuss, D. T., & Benson, D. F. (1984). Neuropsychological studies of the frontal lobes. *Psychological Bulletin, 95,* 3–28.

Stuss, D. T., & Benson, D. F. (1986). *The frontal lobes.* New York: Raven Press.

*Stuss, D. T., Benson, D. F., Kaplan, E. F., Weir, W. S., Naeser, M. A., Liberman, I., & Ferrill, D. (1983). The involvement of orbitofrontal cerebrum in cognitive tasks. *Neuropsychologia, 21,* 235–248.

Stuss, D. T., & Gow, C. A. (1992). "Frontal-dysfunction" after traumatic brain injury. *Neuropsychiatry, Neuropsychology, and Behavioral Neurology, 5,* 272–282.

Suddath, R. L., Casanova, M. F., Goldberg, T. E., Daniel, D. G., Kelsoe, J. R., & Weinberger, D. R. (1989). Temporal lobe pathology in schizophrenia: A quantitative magnetic resonance imaging study. *American Journal of Psychiatry, 146,* 464–472.

Sulkava, R., Wikstrom, J., Aromaa, A., Raitasalo, R., Lehtenen, V., Lehtela, K., & Palo, J. (1985). Prevalence of severe dementia in Finland. *Neurology, 35,* 1025–1029.

*Sullivan, E. V., Mathalon, D. H., Ha, C. N., Zipursky, R. B., & Pfefferbaum, A. (1992). The contribution of constructional accuracy and organizational strategy to nonverbal recall in schizophrenia and chronic alcoholism. *Biological Psychiatry, 32,* 312–333.

*Sullivan, E. V., Mathalon, D. H., Zipursky, R. B., Kersteen-Tucker, Z., Knight, R. T., & Pfefferbaum, A. (1993). Factors of the Wisconsin Card Sorting Test as measures of frontal-lobe function in schizophrenia and in chronic alcoholism. *Psychiatry Research, 46,* 175–199.

*Sullivan, E. V., Shear, P. K., Lim, K. O., Zipursky, R. B., & Pfefferbaum, A. (1996). Cognitive and motor impairments are related to gray matter volume deficits in schizophrenia. *Comprehensive Psychiatry, 39,* 234–240.

*Sullivan, E. V., Shear, P. K., Zipursky, R. B., Sagar, H. J., & Pfefferbaum, A. (1997). Patterns of content, contextual, and working memory impairments in schizophrenia and non amnesic alcoholism. *Neuropsychology, 11,* 195–206.

*Sullivan, M. P., Faust, M. E., & Balota, D. A. (1995). Identity negative priming in older adults and individuals with dementia of the Alzheimer type. *Neuropsychology, 9,* 537–555.

*Swearer, J. M., O' Donnel, B. F., Drachman, D. A., Woodward, B. M. (1992). Neuropsychological features of familial Alzheimer's disease. *Annals of Neurology, 32,* 687–694.

*Swedlon, N. R., Paulsen, J., Braff, D. L., Butters, N., Geyer, M. A., & Swenson, M. R. (1995). Impaired prepulse inhibition of acoustic and tactile startle response in patients with Huntington's disease. *Journal of Neurology, Neurosurgery, and Psychiatry, 58,* 192–200.

Swoboda, K. J., & Jenike, M. A. (1995). Frontal abnormalities in a patient with obsessive-compulsive disorder: The role of structural lesions in obsessive-compulsive behavior. *Neurology, 45,* 2130–2134.

Taylor, A. E., & Saint-Cyr, J. A. (1992). Executive function. In S. J. Huber & J. L. Cummings (Eds.), *Parkinson's disease: Neurobahavioral aspects.* (pp. 74–85). New York: Oxford University Press.

*Taylor, A. E., Saint-Cyr, J. A., & Lang, A. E. (1990). Memory and learning in early in early Parkinson's disease: Evidence for a "frontal-lobe syndrome". *Brain and Cognition, 13,* 211–232.

*Taylor, K. I., Salmon, D. P., Rice, V. A., Bondi, M. W., Hill, L. R., Ernesto, C. R., & Butters, N. (1996). Longitudinal examination of American National Adult Reading Test (AMNART) performance in dementia of the Alzheimer type (DAT): Validation and correction based on degree of cognitive decline. *Journal of Clinical and Experimental Neuropsychology, 18,* 883–891.

Taylor, S. F. (1995). Cerebral blood flow activation and functional lesions in schizophrenia. *Schizophrenia Research, 19,* 129–140.

Teasdale, G., & Jennet, B. (1974). Assessment of coma and impaired consciousness. *Lancet, ii,* 81–84.

*Testa, D., Fetoni, V., Soliveri, P., Musicco, M., Palazzini, E., & Girotti, F. (1993). Cognitive and motor performance in multiple system atrophy and Parkinson's disease compared. *Neuropsychologia, 31,* 207–210.

Teuber, H. L. (1955). Physiological psychology. *Annual Review of Psychology, 6,* 267–296.

The Lund and Manchester Groups (1994). Clinical and neuropathological criteria for frontotemporal dementia. *Journal of Neurology, Neurosurgery, and Psychiatry, 57,* 416–418.

Thornton, A. E., & Raz, N. (1997). Memory impairment in multiple sclerosis: A quantitative review. *Neuropsychology, 11,* 357–366.

Tierney, M. C., Fisher, R. H., Lewis, A. J., Zorzitto, M. L., Snow, W. G., Reid, D. W., & Nieuwstraten, P. (1988). The NINCDS-ADRDA Work Group criteria for the clinical diagnosis of probable Alzheimer's disease: A clinicopathologic study of 57 cases. *Neurology, 38,* 359–364.

Tikofsky, R. S., Hellman, R. S., & Parks, R. W. (1993). Single photon emission computed tomography and applications to dementia. In R. W. Parks, R. F. Zec, & R. S. Wilson (Eds.), *Neuropsychology of Alzheimer's disease and other dementias.* (pp. 489–510). New York: Oxford University Press.

*Trichard, C., Martinot, Alagille, M., Masure, M. C., Hardy, P., Ginestet, D., & Feline, A. (1995). Time course of prefrontal lobe dysfunction in severely depressed inpatients: A longitudinal neuropsychological study. *Psychological Medicine, 25,* 79–85.

*Trojano, L., Chiacchio, L., De Luca, G., & Gross, D. (1994). Exploring visuospatial short-term memory defect in Alzheimer's disease. *Journal of Clinical and Experimental Neuropsychology, 16,* 911–915.

Troster, A. I., Butters, N., Cullum, C. M., & Salmon, D. P. (1989). Differentiating Alzheimer disease from Huntington's disease with the Wechsler Memory Scale-Revised. *Clinical Neuropsychologist, 5,* 611–632.

*Troster, A. I., Butters, N., Salmon, D. P., Cullum, C. M., Jacobs, D., Brandt, J., & White, R. F. (1993). The diagnostic utility of savings scores: Differentiating Alzheimer's and Huntington's diseases with the logical memory and visual reproduction tests. *Journal of Clinical and Experimental Neuropsychology, 15,* 773–788.

*Troster, A. I., Moe, K. E., Vitiello., M. V., & Prinz, P. N. (1994). Predicting long-term outcome in individuals at risk for Alzheimer's disease with the Dementia Rating Scale. *Journal of Neuropsychiatry and Clinical Neurosciences, 6,* 54–57.

*Troster, A. I., Paolo, A. M., Lyons, K. E., Glatt, S. L., Hubble, J. P., Koller, W. C. (1995). The influence of depression on cognition in Parkinson's disease: A pattern of impairment distinguishable from Alzheimer's disease. Neurology. *Neurology, 45,* 672–676.

*Troster, A. I., Stalp, L. D., Paolo, A. M., Fields, J. A., & Koller, W. C. (1995). Neuropsychological impairment in Parkinson's disease with and without depression. *Archives of Neurology, 52,* 1164–1169.

Turner, B. (1968). Pathology of paralysis agitans. In P. J. Vinken, & G. W. Bruyn (Eds.), *Diseasees of the basal ganglia. Vol. 6 Handbook of clinical neurology.* (pp. 212–217). New York: American Elsevier.

Turner, S. M., Beidel, D. C., & Nathan, R. S. (1985). Biological factors in obsessive-compulsive disorders. *Psychological Bulletin, 97,* 430–450.

*Tweedy, J. R., Langer, K. G., & McDowell, F. H. (1982). The effect of semantic relations on the memory deficit associated with Parkinson's disease. *Journal of Clinical Neuropsychology, 4,* 235–247.

Tyrrell, P. J., Warrington, E. K., Frackowiak, R. S., & Rossor, M. N. (1990). Heterogeneity in progressive aphasia due to focal cortical atrophy. *Brain, 113,* 1321–1336.

*Van den Bosch, R. J. (1984). Eye tracking impairment: Attentional and psychometric correlates in psychiatric patients. *Journal of Psychiatric Research, 18,* 277–286.

*Van den Bosch, R. J., Rombouts, R. P., & van Asma, M. J. O. (1996). What determines continuous performance task performance? *Schizophrenia Bulletin, 22,* 643–651.

*Van den Bosch, R. J., Van Asma, M. J. O., Rombauts, R., & Lauwerlens, J. W. (1992). Coping style and cognitive dysfunction in schizophrenic patients. *British Journal of Psychiatry, 161 (suppl. 18),* 123–128.

Van der Does, R., & Van den Bosch, R. J. (1992). What determines Wisconsin Card Sorting performance in schizophrenia? *Clinical Psychology Review, 12,* 567–583.

*Van der Hurk, P. R., & Hodges, J. R. (1995). Episodic and semantic memory in Alzheimer's disease and progressive supranuclear palsy: A comparative study. *Journal of Clinical and Experimental Neuropsychology, 17,* 459–471.

*Van Gorp, W. G., Mitrushina, M., Cummings, J. L., Satz, P., & Modesitt, J. (1989). Normal aging and the subcortical encephalopathy of AIDS: A neuropsychological comparison. *Neuropsychiatry, Neuropsychology, and Behavioral Neurology, 2,* 5–20.

*van Spaendonck, K. P. M., Berger, H. J. C., Horstink, M. W. I. M., Borm, G. F., & Cools, A. R. (1995). Card sorting performance in Parkinson's disease: A comparison between acquisition and shifting performance. *Journal of Clinical and Experimental Neuropsychology, 17,* 918–925.

*van Spaendonck, K. P. M., Berger, H. J. C., Horstink, M. W. I. M., Buytenhuijs, E. L., & Cools, A. R. (1996). Executive functions and disease characteristics in Parkinson's disease. *Neuropsychologia, 34,* 617–626.

van Zomeren, A. H., & Brouwer, W. H. (1994). *Clinical neuropsychology of attention.* New York: Oxford University Press.

*Varney, N. R., Roberts, R. J., Struchen, M. A., Hanson, T. V., Franzen, K. M., & Connell, S. K. (1996). Design fluency among normals and patients with closed head injury. *Archives of Clinical Neuropsychology, 11,* 345–353.

Veiel, H. O. F. (1997). A preliminary profile of neuropsychological deficits associated with major depression. *Journal of Clinical and Experimental Neuropsychology, 19*, 587–603.

*Veltman, J. C., Brouwer, W. H., van Zomeren, A. H., & van Wolffelaar, P. C. (1996). Central executive aspects of attention in subacute and very sever closed head injury patients: Planning, inhibition, flexibility and divided attention. *Neuropsychology, 10*, 357–367.

Verny, M., Jelllinger, K. A., Hauw, J. J., Bancher, C., Litvan, I., & Agid, Y. (1996). Progresssive supranuclear palsy: A clinicopathological study of 21 cases. *Acta Neuropathologica, 91*, 427–31.

*Villardita, C. (1993). Alzheimer's disease compared with cerebrovascular dementia: Neuropsychological similarities and differences. *Acta Neurologica Scandinavica, 87*, 298–308.

*Walker, E., & Marwit, S. J. (1980). A cross-sectional study of emotion recognition in schizophrenics. *Journal of Abnormal Psychology, 89*, 428–436.

Warrington, E. K. (1982). The fractionation of arithmetical skills: A single case study. *Quarterly Journal of Experimental Neuropsychology, 34A*, 31–51.

Warrington, E. K. (1984). *Recognition Memory Test*. Windsor, UK: NFER-Nelson.

Waterfall, M. L., & Crowe, S. F. (1995). Meta-analytic comparison of the components of visual cognition in Parkinson's disease. *Journal of Clinical and Experimental Neuropsychology, 17*, 759–772.

*Watt, S., Jokel, R., & Behrmann, M. (1997). Surface dyslexia in nonfluent progressive aphasia. *Brain and Language, 56*, 211–233.

Wechsler, D. (1981). *Wechsler Adult Intelligence Scale- Revised*. New York: Psychological Corporation.

Wechsler, D. (1987). *Wechsler Memory Scale—Revised*. New York: Psychological Corporation.

Weinberger, D. R. (1984). CAT scan findings in schizophrenia: Speculation on the meaning of it all. *Journal of Psychiatric Research, 18*, 477–490.

Weinberger, D. R. (1987). Implications of normal brain development for the pathogenesis of schizophrenia. *Archives of General Psychiatry, 44*, 660–669.

Weinberger, D. R. (1988). Schizophrenia and the frontal lobe. *Trends in Neuroscience, 11*, 367–370.

Weinberger, D. R. (1995). The neurodevelopment hypothesis of schizophrenia. In S. R. Hirsch & D. R. Weinberger (Eds.), *Schizophrenia*. Oxford: Blackwell Scientific Publications.

Weinberger, D. R., Berman, K. F., & Daniel, D. G. (1991). Prefrontal cortex dysfunction in schizophrenia. In H. S. Levin, H. M. Eisenberg & A. L. Benton (Eds.), *Frontal lobe function and dysfunction*. (pp. 275–287). New York: Oxford University Press.

*Weinberger, D. R., Berman, K. F., Iadarola, M., Driesen, N., & Zec, R. F. (1988). Prefrontal cortical blood flow and cognitive function in Huntington's disease. *Journal of Neurology, Neurosurgery, and Psychiatry, 51*, 94–104.

Weinberger, D. R., Wagner, R. L., & Wyatt, R. J. (1986), Physiological dysfunction of dorsolateral prefrontal cortex in schizophrenia I. *Archives of General Psychiatry, 43*, 114.

*Weiner, R. U., Opler, L. A., Kay, S. R., Merriam, A. E., & Papouchis, N. (1990). Visual information processing in positive, mixed, and negative schizophrenic syndromes. *Journal of Nervous and Mental Disease, 178*, 616–626.

Weingartner, H. (1986). Automatic and effort demanding cognitive processes in depression. In L. W. Poon (Ed.), *Clinical memory assessment of older adults*. Washington DC: American Psychological Association.

*Weingartner, H., Eckardt, M., Grafman, J., Molchan, S., Purnam, K., Rawlings, R., & Sunderland, T. (1993). The effects of repetition on memory performance in cognitively impaired patients. *Neuropsychology, 7*, 385–395.

Weinshenker, B. G. (1994). Natural history of multiple sclerosis. *Annals of Neurology, 36*, S6-S11.

Weintraub, S., & Caserta, M. (1998). *From neural networks to dementia*. Workshop presented at the annual meeting of the International Neuropsychological Society, Honolulu, Hawaii.

*Weintraub, S., Rubin, N. P., Mesulam, M-M. (1990). Primary progressive aphasia: Longitudinal course, neuropsychological profile, and language features. *Archives of Neurology, 47*, 1329–1335.

*Weiss, K. M., Chapman, H. A., Strauss, M. E., & Gilmore, G. C. (1992). Visual information decoding deficits in schizophrenia. *Psychiatry Research, 44*, 203–216.

*Weiss, K. M., Vortunski, P. B., & Simpson, D. M. (1988). Information overload disrupts digit recall performance in schizophrenics. *Schizophrenia Research, 1*, 299–303.

*Wells, D. S., & Leventhal, D. (1984). Perceptual grouping in schizophrenia: Replication of place and gilmore. *Journal of Abnormal Psychology, 93*, 231–234.

*Welsh, K. A., Butters, N., Hughes, J. P., Mohs, R. C., & Heyman, A. (1992). Detection and staging of dementia in Alzheimer's disease: Use of the neuropsychological measures developed for the consortium to establish a registry for Alzheimer's disease. *Archives of Neurology, 49*, 448–452.

Wernicke, C. (1874). *Des aphasische symptomenkomplex*. Breslau: Cohn and Weigart.

Wheeler, M. A., Stuss, D. T., & Tulving, E. (1995). Frontal lobe damage produces memory impairment. *Journal of the International Neuropsychological Society, 1*, 525–536.

Wheeler, M. A., Stuss, D. T., & Tulving, E. (1997). Toward a theory of episodic memory: The frontal lobes and autonoetic consciousness. *Psychological Bulletin, 121*, 331–354.

White, H. D. (1994). Scientific communication and literature retrieval. In H. Cooper & L. V. Hedges (Eds.), *The handbook of research synthesis*. New York: Russel Sage Foundation.

White, R. F. (1990). Emotional and cognitive correlates of multiple sclerosis. *Journal of Neuropsychiatry and Clinical Neurosciences, 2*, 422–428.

White, R. F., Au, R., Durso, R., & Moss, M. B. (1992). Neuropsychological function in Parkinson's disease. In R. F. White (Ed.), *Clinical syndromes in adult neuropsychology: The practioner's handbook*. UK: Elsevier Science Publishers.

White, R. F., Nyenhus, D. S., & Sax, D. S. (1992). Multiple sclerosis. In R. F. White (Ed.), *Clinical syndromes in adult neuropsychology: The practioner's handbook*. UK: Elsevier Science Publishers.

White, R. F., Vasterling, J. J., Koroshtz, W., & Myers, R. (1992). Neuropsychology of Huntington's disease. In R. F. White (Ed.), *Clinical syndromes in adult neuropsychology: The practioner's handbook*. UK: Elsevier Science Publishers.

*White-Devine, T., Grossman, M., Robinson, K. M., Onishi, K., Biassou, N., & D'Esposito, M. (1996). Verb confrontation naming and word-picture matching in Alzheimer's disease. *Neuropsychology, 10*, 495–503.

*Whitworth, R. H., & Larson, C. M. (1989). Differential diagnosis and staging of Alzheimer's disease with an aphasia battery. *Neuropsychiatry, Neuropsychology, and Behavioral Neurology, 1*, 255–265.

*Wiggs, C. L., Martin, A., & Sunderland, T. (1997). Monitoring frequency of occurrence without awareness: Evidence from patients with Alzheimer's disease. *Journal of Clinical and Experimental Neuropsychology, 19*, 235–244.

*Williams, B. W., Mack, W., Henderson, V. W. (1989). Boston Naming Test in Alzheimer's disease. *Neuropsychologia, 27*, 1073–1079.

Williamson, D. J. G., Scott, J. G., & Adams, R. L. (1996). Traumatic brain injury. In R. L. Adams, O. A. Parsons, J. L. Culbertson, & S. J. Nixon (Eds.), *Neuropsychology for clinical practice: Etiology, assessment, and treatment of common neurological disorders.* (pp. 9–64). Washington, DC: American Psychological Association.

*Williamson, P. C. (1989). Psychological, topographic EEG, and CT scan correlates of frontal lobe function in schizophrenia. *Psychiatry Research, 29*, 137–149.

*Willingham, D. B., Peterson, E. W., Manning, C., & Brashear, H. R. (1997). Patients with Alzheimer's disease who cannot perform some motor skills show normal learning of other motor skills. *Neuropsychology, 11*, 261–271.

Wishart, H., & Sharpe, D. (1997). Neuropsychological aspects of multiple sclerosis: A quantitative review. *Journal of Clinical and Experimental Neuropsychology, 19*, 810–824.

*Wishart, H. A., Struass, E., Hunter, M., & Moll, A. (1995). Interhemispheric transfer in multiple sclerosis. *Journal of Clinical and Experimental Neuropsychology, 17*, 937–940.

Wolf, F. M. (1986). *Meta-analysis: Quantitative methods for research synthesis.* Newbury: Sage.

*Wood, F. B., & Flowers, D. L. (1990). Hypofrontal vs. hypo-sylvian blood flow in schizophrenia. *Schizophrenia Bulletin, 16*, 413–424.

Woodruff, P. W. R., McManus, I. C., & David, A. S. (1995). Meta-analysis of corpus-callosum size in schizophrenia. *Journal of Neurology, Neurosurgery, and Psychiatry, 58*, 457–461.

World Health Organization. (1992). *The ICD–10 classification of mental and behavioural disorders.* Geneva: World Health Organization.

*Xenakis, Blonder, L., Gur, R. E., Gur, R. C., Saykin, A. J., & Hurtig, H. I. (1989). Neuropsychological functioning in hemiparkinsonism. *Brain and Cognition, 9*, 244–257.

*Yamamoto, H., Tanabe, H., Kashiwasi, A., Ikertiri, Y., Fukuyama, H., Okuda, J., Shiraishi, J., & Nishimura, T. (1990). A case of slowly progressive aphasia without generalized dementia in a Japanese patient. *Acta Neurologica Scandinavica, 82*, 102–105.

*Yates, W. R., Swaze II, V. W., & Andreasen, N. C. (1990). Neuropsychological effect of global and focal cerebral atrophy in schizophrenia. *Neuropsychiatry, Neuropsychology, and Behavioral Neurology, 3*, 98–106.

*Young, A. H., Blackwood, D. H. R., Roxborough, H., McQueen, J. K., Martin, M. J., & Kean, D. (1991). A magnetic resonance imaging study of schizophrenia: Brain structure and clinical symptoms. *British Journal of Psychiatry, 158*, 158–164.

Young, D. A., Zakzanis, K. K., Bailey, C., Davila, R., Griese, J., Sartory, G., & Thom, A. (1998). Further parameters of insight and neuropsychological deficit in schizophrenia and other chronic mental disease. *The Journal of Nervous and Mental Disease, 186*, 44–50.

*Yurgelun-Todd, D. A., & Kinney, D. K. (1993). Patterns of neuropsychological deficits that discriminate schizophrenic individuals from siblings and control subjects. *Journal of Neuropsychiatry and Clinical Neurosciences, 5,* 294–300.

Zakzanis, K. K. (1998a). Brain is related to behavior (*p* < .05). *Journal of Clinical and Experimental Neuropsychology, 20,* 419–427.

Zakzanis, K. K. (1998b). Indexing temporal-hippocampal integrity in dementia of the Alzheimer's type. *Archives of Clinical Neuropsychology, 13,* 51.

Zakzanis, K. K. (1998c). Neurocognitive deficit in fronto-temporal dementia. *Neuropsychiatry, Neuropsychology, and Behavioral Neurology, 11,* 127–135.

Zakzanis, K. K. (1998d). Neuropsychological correlates of positive vs. negative schizophrenic symptomatology. *Schizophrenia Research, 29,* 227–233.

Zakzanis, K. K. (1998e). Quantitative evidence for neuroanatomic and neuropsychological markers in dementia of the Alzheimer's type. *Journal of Clinical and Experimental Neuropsychology, 20,* 259–269.

Zakzanis, K. K. (1998f). The reliability of meta-analytic review. *Psychological Reports, 83,* 215–222.

Zakzanis, K. K. (1998g). The subcotical dementia of Huntington's disease. *Journal of Clinical and Experimental Neuropsychology, 20,* 565–578

Zakzanis, K. K. (1999). Distinct neurocognitive profiles in multiple sclerosis subtypes. *Archives of Clinical Neuropsychology,* in press.

Zakzanis, K. K., & Freedman, M. (1999). A neuropsychological comparison of demented and nondemented patients with Parkinson's disease. *Applied Neuropsychology,* in press.

Zakzanis, K. K., & Heinrichs, R. W. (1997). *The frontal-executive hypothesis in schizophrenia: Cognitive and neuroimaging evidence.* Paper presented at the annual meeting of the American Psychological Association, August 17, 1997, Chicago, Illinois.

Zakzanis, K. K., & Heinrichs, R. W. (1999). Schizophrenia and the frontal brain: A quantitative review. *Journal of the International Neuropsychological Society,* in press.

Zakzanis, K. K., Leach, L., & Freedman, M. (1998). Structural and functional meta-analytic evidence for fronto-subcortical system deficit in progressive supranuclear palsy. *Brain and Cognition, 38,* 283–296.

Zakzanis, K. K., Leach, L., & Kaplan, E. (1998). On the nature and pattern of neurocognitive deficit in major depressive disorder. *Neuropsychiatry, Neuropsychology, and Behavioral Neurology, 11,* 111–119.

Zald, D. H., & Kim, S. W. (1996). Anatomy and function of the orbital frontal cortex, II: Function and relevance to obsessive-compulsive diseorder. *The Journal of Neuropsychiatry and Clinical Neurosciences, 8,* 249–261.

Zec, R. F. (1993). Neuropsychological functioning in Alzheimer's disease. In R. W. Parks, R. F. Zec & R. S. Wilson (Eds.), *Neuropsychology of Alzheimer's disease and other dementias.* (pp. 3–80). New York: Oxford University Press.

*Zielinski, C. M., Taylor, M. A., & Jurwin, K. R. (1991). Neuropsychological deficits in obsessive compulsive disorder. *Neuropsychiatry, Neuropsychology, and Behavioral Neurology, 4,* 110–126.

*Zipursky, R. B., Marsh, L., Lim, K. O., DeMent, S., Shear, P. K., Sullivan, E. V., Murphy, G. M., Csernansky, J. G., & Pfefferbaum, A. (1994). Volumetric MRI assessment of temporal lobe structures in schizophrenia. *Biological Psychiatry, 35,* 502–516.

FURTHER READING

Adams, R. D., Victor, M., & Ropper, A. H. (1997). *Prinicples of neurology* (6th ed.). Toronto: McGraw-Hill.

Adams, R. L., Parsons, O. A., Culbertson, J. L., & Nixon, S. J. (1996). *Neuropsychology for clinical practice: Etiology, assessment, and treatment of common neurological disorders*. Washington, DC: American Psychological Association.

Cummings, J. L., & Benson, D. F. (1992). *Dementia: A clinical approach*. Boston: Butterworth-Heinemann.

Derix, M. M. A. (1994). *Neuropsychological differentiation of dementia syndromes*. Lisse: Swets & Zeitlinger.

Feinberg, T. E., & Farah, M. J. (1997). *Behavioral neurology and neuropsychology*. New York: McGraw-Hill.

Grant, I., & Adams, K. M. (1996), *Neuropsychological assessment of neuropsychiatric disorders*. New York: Oxford University Press.

Heilman, K. M., & Valenstein, E. (1993). *Clinical neuropsychology* (3rd ed.). New York: Oxford University Press.

Lezak, M. D. (1995). *Neuropsychological assessment* (3rd ed.). New York: Oxford University Press.

Mitrushina, M. N., Boone, K. B., & D'Elia, L. F. (1999). *Handbook of normative data for neuropsychological assessment*. New York: Oxford University Press.

Parks, R. W., Zec, R. F., & Wilson, R. S. (1993). *Neuropsychology of Alzheimer's disease and other dementias*. New York: Oxford University Press.

Patten, J. (1995). *Neurological differential diagnosis*. London: Springer.

Snowden, J. S., Neary, D., & Mann, D. M. A. (1996). *Fronto-temporal lobar degeneration: Fronto-temporal dementia, progressive aphasia, semantic dementia*. New York: Churchill Livingstone.

Snyder, P. J., & Nussbaum, P. D. (1998). *Clinical neuropsychology: A pocket handbook for assessment*. Washington, DC: American Psychological Association.

Spreen, O., & Strauss, E. (1998). *A compendium of neuropsychological tests* (2nd ed.). New York: Oxford University Press.

Strub, R. L., & Black, F. W. (1993). *The mental status examination in neurology*. Philadelphia: F. A. Davis Company.

Subject Index

Index of Tests

(BSRT = Buschke Selective Reminding Test; BVRT = Benton Visual Retention Test; CVLT = California Verbal Learning Test; DRS = Dementia Rating Scale; RAVLT = Rey Auditory Verbal Learning Test; ROCF = Rey Osterrieth Complex Figure; WAIS-R = Wechsler Adult Intelligence Scale-Revised; WCST = Wisconsin Card Sorting Test; WMS-R = Wechsler Memory Scale Revised)